Fodor's 2010

D0843780

TORONTO

Where to Stay and Eat
for All Budgets

Must-See Sights
and Local Secrets

Ratings You Can Trust

Fodor's Travel Publications   New York, Toronto, London, Sydney, Auckland
www.fodors.com

FODOR'S TORONTO 2010
Editor: Cate Starmer

Editorial Contributors: Shannon Kelly, Sarah Richards, Amy Rosen

Production Editor: Jennifer DePrima
Maps & Illustrations: David Lindroth, Ed Jacobus, *cartographers;* Bob Blake, Rebecca Baer, *map editors;* William Wu, *information graphics*
Design: Fabrizio La Rocca, *creative director;* Guido Caroti, Siobhan O'Hare, *art directors;* Tina Malaney, Chie Ushio, Ann McBride, Jessica Walsh, *designers;* Melanie Marin, *senior picture editor*
Cover Photo: (Queen Street West): OBI/Spectrum Stock
Production Manager: Angela L. McLean

ISBN 978–1–4000–0420–1

ISSN 1044–6133

SPECIAL SALES
This book is available at special discounts for bulk purchases for sales promotions or premiums. Special editions, including personalized covers, excerpts of existing books, and corporate imprints, can be created in large quantities for special needs. For more information, write to Special Markets/Premium Sales, 1745 Broadway, MD 6-2, New York, New York 10019, or e-mail specialmarkets@randomhouse.com.

AN IMPORTANT TIP & AN INVITATION
Although all prices, opening times, and other details in this book are based on information supplied to us at press time, changes occur all the time in the travel world, and Fodor's cannot accept responsibility for facts that become outdated or for inadvertent errors or omissions. So **always confirm information when it matters,** especially if you're making a detour to visit a specific place. Your experiences—positive and negative— matter to us. If we have missed or misstated something, **please write to us.** We follow up on all suggestions. Contact the Toronto editor at editors@fodors.com or c/o Fodor's at 1745 Broadway, New York, NY 10019.

PRINTED IN THE UNITED STATES OF AMERICA

10 9 8 7 6 5 4 3 2 1

Be a Fodor's Correspondent

Your opinion matters. It matters to us. It matters to your fellow Fodor's travelers, too. And we'd like to hear it. In fact, we need to hear it.

When you share your experiences and opinions, you become an active member of the Fodor's community. That means we'll not only use your feedback to make our books better, but we'll publish your names and comments whenever possible. Throughout our guides, look for "Word of Mouth," excerpts of your unvarnished feedback.

Here's how you can help improve Fodor's for all of us.

Tell us when we're right. We rely on local writers to give you an insider's perspective. But our writers and staff editors—who are the best in the business—depend on you. Your positive feedback is a vote to renew our recommendations for the next edition.

Tell us when we're wrong. We're proud that we update most of our guides every year. But we're not perfect. Things change. Hotels cut services. Museums change hours. Charming cafés lose charm. If our writer didn't quite capture the essence of a place, tell us how you'd do it differently. If any of our descriptions are inaccurate or inadequate, we'll incorporate your changes in the next edition and will correct factual errors at fodors.com immediately.

Tell us what to include. You probably have had fantastic travel experiences that aren't yet in Fodor's. Why not share them with a community of like-minded travelers? Maybe you chanced upon a beach or bistro or B&B that you don't want to keep to yourself. Tell us why we should include it. And share your discoveries and experiences with everyone directly at fodors.com. Your input may lead us to add a new listing or highlight a place we cover with a "Highly Recommended" star or with our highest rating, "Fodor's Choice."

Give us your opinion instantly at our feedback center at www.fodors.com/feedback. You may also e-mail editors@fodors.com with the subject line "Toronto Editor." Or send your nominations, comments, and complaints by mail to Toronto Editor, Fodor's, 1745 Broadway, New York, NY 10019.

You and travelers like you are the heart of the Fodor's community. Make our community richer by sharing your experiences. Be a Fodor's correspondent.

Happy traveling!

Tim Jarrell, Publisher

CONTENTS

ABOUT THIS BOOK

Sometimes you find terrific travel experiences and sometimes they just find you. But usually the burden is on you to select the right combination of experiences. That's where our ratings come in.

As travelers we've all discovered a place so wonderful that its worthiness is obvious. And sometimes that place is so experiential that superlatives don't do it justice: you just have to be there to know. These sights, properties, and experiences get our highest rating, **Fodor's Choice**, indicated by orange stars throughout this book.

Black stars highlight sights and properties we deem **Highly Recommended,** places that our writers, editors, and readers praise again and again for consistency and excellence.

By default, there's another category: any place we include in this book is by definition worth your time, unless we say otherwise. And we will.

Disagree with any of our choices? Care to nominate a place or suggest that we rate one more highly? Visit our feedback center at www.fodors.com/feedback.

Restaurant and hotel price categories from ¢ to $$$$ are defined in the opening pages of the Where to Eat and Where to Stay chapters. For attractions, we always give standard adult admission fees; reductions are usually available for children, students, and senior citizens. Want to pay with plastic? **AE, D, DC, MC, V** following restaurant and hotel listings indicate if American Express, Discover, Diners Club, MasterCard, and Visa are accepted.

Unless we state otherwise, restaurants are open for lunch and dinner daily. We mention dress only when there's a specific requirement and reservations only when they're essential or not accepted—it's always best to book ahead.

Hotels have private bath, phone, TV, and air-conditioning and operate on the European Plan (aka EP, meaning without meals), unless we specify that they use the Continental Plan (CP, with a Continental breakfast), Breakfast Plan (BP, with a full breakfast), or Modified American Plan (MAP, with breakfast and dinner) or are all-inclusive (including all meals and most activities). We always list facilities but not whether you'll be charged an extra fee to use them, so when pricing accommodations, find out what's included.

Many Listings
★ Fodor's Choice
★ Highly recommended
⊠ Physical address
✛ Directions or Map coordinates
⌂ Mailing address
☎ Telephone
🖷 Fax
⊕ On the Web
✍ E-mail
🖼 Admission fee
☉ Open/closed times
Ⓜ Metro stations
▤ Credit cards

Hotels & Restaurants
🏨 Hotel
🛏 Number of rooms
♿ Facilities
🍽 Meal plans
✕ Restaurant
🕴 Reservations
🏛 Dress code
🚭 Smoking
🍷 BYOB

Outdoors
⛳ Golf
⛺ Camping

Other
🐾 Family-friendly
⇨ See also
⊠ Branch address
☞ Take note

Experience Toronto

WHAT'S WHERE

1 The Harbourfront, The Financial District, and Old Town. Between the waterfront and Queen Street, the city's main attractions are packed in: the CN Tower, Harbourfront Centre, Hockey Hall of Fame, Ontario Place amusement park, Rogers Centre, St. James Cathedral, and the St. Lawrence food market. Most of the lofty peaks in Toronto's skyline are in this epicenter of Canadian financial power. Stroll through Old Town, including the Historic Distillery District entertainment complex, or hop a ferry heading for the Toronto Islands.

2 Chinatown, Kensington Market, and Queen West. Tourists and locals alike battle for bargains on everything from fresh produce to vintage clothing in some of Toronto's most colorful and animated neighborhoods, centered near the intersection of Dundas and Spadina streets. West of Bathurst as far as Dufferin Street, Queen Street draws cutting-edge artists, designers, and entrepreneurs.

3 Queen's Park, The Annex, and Yorkville. Toronto's political and intellectual sets, as well as its most well-heeled citizens are all found around Queen's Park. Ivy-covered Gothic Revival buildings of the 60,000-student U of T campus are interspersed with bargain-price eateries and pubs. Heading north you'll hit the Annex, the city's academic and artsy haunt, and then the mansion Casa Loma, surrounded by leafy streets and lavish homes; southeast, near Avenue Road, are Yorkville's high-class designer shops, upscale groceries, and European cafés.

4 Dundas Square Area. This area is both the square, which hosts frequent performances in summer, and the surrounding neighborhood of Broadway-style theaters, family-style restaurants, and department stores.

5 Greater Toronto. Attractions such as Canada's Wonderland theme park, Ontario Science Centre, and the Toronto Zoo lure visitors from downtown. Sprinkled around Toronto's major neighborhoods are pockets like funky Cabbagetown on the east side; gritty expat haven Little Portugal on the west side; and quiet High Park, a collection of Tudor brick homes surrounding downtown's largest green space.

M Spadina
M St. George
3
5

Bay
M Bloor–Yange
Bloor St. E.

Spadina

St. George

Sussex Ave.

Brunswick Ave.

Sussex Mews

Spadina Ave.

Major St.

Robert St.

Huron St.

QUEEN'S PARK

Hoskin Ave.

University of Toronto

Willcocks St.

St. George St.

King's

College

Cir.

Queen's Park Cir. W.

Queen's Park

Queen's Park Cir. E.

M Museum

Avenue Rd.

St. Thomas St.

Bay St.

Hayden St.
Charles St. E.

Isabella St.

Gloucester St.

St. Joseph St.

Wellesley St. W.

M Wellesley
Wellesley St. E.

CHURCH-WELLESLEY

Dundonald St.

Yonge St.

Church St.

Breadalbane St.

Maitland Ave.

Ontario Legislative Building

Grosvenor St.

Alexander St.

Grenville St.

Wood St.

M College

College St.

M Queen's Park

Russell St.

Cecil St.

Beverley St.

Henry St.

University Ave.

Elizabeth St.

Bay St.

Carlton St.

Carlton St.

Allan Gardens

Gerrard St. E.

Gerrard St. W.

CHINATOWN

Baldwin St.

D'Arcy St.

McCaul St.

St. Patrick

Chestnut St.

Toronto Coach Terminal

Elm St.

Edward St.

Gould St.

O'Keefe St.

George St.

Pembroke St.

Seaton St.

DUNDAS SQUARE AREA

Dundas St. W.

M Dundas
Dundas St. E.

Dundas St. W.

4

Augusta Ave.

Spadina Ave.

Soho St.

St. Patrick St.

Simcoe St.

Beverley St.

Grange Park

Victoria St.

Sullivan St.

2

Butwer St.

Renfrew Pl.

Pullan Pl.

City Hall

Nathan Phillips Square

James St.

Shuter St.

Church St.

Mutual St.

Jarvis St.

Moss Gardens

QUEEN WEST

Queen St. W.

M Osgoode

Queen

Queen St. E.

Peter St.

John St.

Widmer St.

Duncan St.

Nelson St.

York St.

University Ave.

Bay St.

Richmond St. E.

FINANCIAL DISTRICT

Adelaide St. E.

Pearl St.

King St. W.

King St. E.

Toronto St.

OLD TOWN

Sherbourne St.

Colborne St.

Mercer St.

Wellington St. W.

1

Wellington St. E.

Front St. E.

ENTERTAINMENT DISTRICT

Front St. W.

M Union

Yonge St.

The Esplanade

The Esplanade

llington St. W.

St. W.

Spadina Ave.

Brenner Blvd.

Gardiner Expy.
Lake Shore Blvd. E.

Gardiner Expy.

Harbour St.

Queens Quay E.

HARBOURFRONT

Queens Quay W.

Lake Ontario

TORONTO PLANNER

When to Go

Toronto is most pleasant from late spring through early fall, when there are outdoor concerts, frequent festivals, and open-air dining. On the other hand, some hotels drop their prices up to 50% in the off-season. And fall through spring is prime viewing time for dance, opera, theater, and classical music. The temperature frequently falls below freezing from late November into March when snowstorms can wreak havoc on travel plans. Though Toronto's climate is one of Canada's mildest, thanks to the regulating properties of Lake Ontario, it can still be harsh in winter. Prolonged snowfalls rarely come to the lake's northern shores, and many a December and January snowfall soon melts away. The same weather lures skiing enthusiasts to the resorts north of the city. Downtown, underground shopping concourses of the PATH allow you to avoid the cold in the winter months.

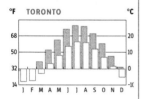

Getting Here

For more detailed information, see Travel Smart.

Most flights arrive and depart from Pearson International Airport (YYZ), about a 30-minute drive northwest of downtown. Cabs from the airport are C$42–C$50 for most downtown locations—it's a flat rate determined by zone. The Toronto Transit Commission (TTC) operates the 192 Airport Rocket, a shuttle to the Kipling subway station; the TTC fare of C$2.75 applies. The Island Airport (YTZ), right downtown at the end of Bathurst Street, is served only by Porter Airlines, which flies to Chicago, Newark, NJ, and several cities in eastern Canada.

Amtrak and VIA Rail trains pull into Union Station at Bay and Front Streets.

Major highways converge here: the QEW from the west (Buffalo, Detroit), the 401 from the east (Montréal, Ottawa), and the 400 from the north (Barrie, Algonquin Park).

Getting Around

Car Travel. While a car is convenient for getting to some attractions in Greater Toronto (such as the zoo, Black Creek Pioneer Village), having wheels downtown isn't necessary and is sometimes a hassle. Street parking can be difficult and parking garage fees can add up. Garages usually charge C$2–C$4 per hour, C$9–C$18 per day, and up to C$25/day during special events.

Taxi Travel. Taxis are easy to hail in front of hotels, performance venues, and museums; in areas with many restaurants and bars; and at Union Station. Or you can call 416/829–4222 for pickup. The meter starts at C$4 and you are charged C25¢ for each additional 0.155 km (roughly 1//10 mi) after the first 0.155 km.

TTC Travel. Most downtown attractions are accessible by subway or streetcar. Buses serve outlying areas. The subway is clean and efficient, with trains arriving every few minutes; streetcars and buses are a bit slower. A single transferable fare is C$2.75; day and week passes are available. Most systems operate from about 6 AM to 1 AM Monday through Saturday, and 9 AM until 1 AM Sunday.

Festivals and Events

For more information, contact **Tourism Toronto** (☎ 800/363–1990 ⊕ www.torontotourism.com).

Jan.–Feb. WinterCity (☎ 416/395–0490 ⊕ www.toronto. ca/special_events) celebrates the season with concerts, theater, ice-skating parties, and Winterlicious, a program offering discount prix-fixe menus at top restaurants.

Apr.–Nov. The **Shaw Festival** (☎ 905/468–2172 or 800/511–7429 ⊕ www.shawfest.com), held in Niagara-on-the-Lake, presents plays by the British curmudgeon George Bernard Shaw and his contemporaries. The **Stratford Shakespeare Festival** (☎ 416/363–4471 or 800/567–1600 ⊕ www.stratfordfestival.ca) is a theater festival featuring the works of William Shakespeare, held in Stratford, 150 km west of Toronto.

May Hot Docs (☎ 416/203–2155 ⊕ www.hotdocs.ca), North America's largest documentary film fest, takes over independent cinemas for two weeks.

June Luminato (☎ 416/368–3100 ⊕ www.luminato.com) is a 10-day, all-purpose arts festival throughout the city. **NorthbyNortheast** (☎ 416/863–6963 ⊕ www.nxne. com) is a five-day music and film festival in mid-June with mostly new pop and rock. **Pride Week** (☎ 416/927–7433 ⊕ www.pridetoronto.com) is 10 days of the city's premier gay and lesbian event; it includes cultural and political programs and a parade. The **Toronto Jazz Festival** (☎ 416/928–2033 ⊕ www.tojazz.com) brings big-name jazz artists to the indoor and outdoor venues for 12 days.

July The **Beaches International Jazz Festival** (☎ 416/698–2152 ⊕ www.beachesjazz.com) is a 10-day, free jazz event in the Beaches neighborhood with a street festival and outdoor concerts. The **Caribana Festival** (☎ 416/466–0321 or 877/672–2742 ⊕ www.caribana.com) is a 10-day cultural showcase with Caribbean music, dance, and arts put on by the West Indian communities.

Aug. The **Canadian National Exhibition** (☎ 416/393–6300 ⊕ www.theex.com), the biggest fair in the country, has rides, entertainment, and more. "The Ex" is held (as it has been since 1879) on the Lake Ontario waterfront.

Sept. Toronto International Film Festival (☎ 416/968–3456 ⊕ www.tiff07.ca) is renowned worldwide and considered more accessible to the general public than Cannes, Sundance, and other major film festivals.

Nov. Royal Agricultural Winter Fair (☎ 416/263–3400 ⊕ www.royalfair.org), held since 1922 at Exhibition Place, is North America's most prestigious agricultural fair.

Savings Tips

Toronto CityPass (⊕ www.citypass.com) includes admission to the CN Tower, Casa Loma, the Royal Ontario Museum, the Ontario Science Center, and the Toronto Zoo for a one-time fee of C$59—a savings of C$52 were you to pay for all attractions individually. The pass is valid for nine days.

Buying a day or weekly pass on the TTC can save you money and make getting around the city easier. A day pass is C$9 and a weekly pass is C$32.25. The day pass is an especially good deal on weekends or holidays, when it's good for two adults and up to four children.

Many of the events listed on the city's Web site (⊕ www.toronto. ca/events) are free.

The Harbourfront Centre (⊕ www. harbourfrontcentre.com) hosts numerous free cultural programs in summer.

Many museums have a free, pay-what-you-can, and/or half-price evening each week. Always free (by donation) are the University of Toronto Art Centre and the Museum of Contemporary Canadian Art.

Safety

Toronto is a fairly safe city compared to most large metropolitan areas in the U.S. However, there is some crime—mainly theft—and it's advisable to take precautions that you would take in any major city.

QUINTESSENTIAL TORONTO

Leafs Nation

Top-notch venues for American favorites such as Blue Jays baseball, Raptors basketball, and Argonauts football generate ample sports fever, but the hearts of die-hard fanatics were stolen long ago by the nation's one true love, ice hockey. Despite the fact that the Toronto Maple Leafs, haven't won the Stanley Cup since 1967, Leafs fans—or "Leafs Nation" as they are known collectively—stand by every year praying for a slot in the playoffs. If the opportunity arises to attend a game (don't bank on it—nearly every game has been sold out for six decades), count yourself luckier than most Torontonians. For hockey fans or anyone wanting an intro to the sport, the Hockey Hall of Fame is a must. And if not, head for a sports bar, grab a brewski, and join locals in heckling the refs on bad calls. When the Leafs score, the mirth is contagious.

International Outlook

With around half the urban population born outside Canada, and even more with foreign roots, Toronto redefines "cosmopolitan." Ethnic enclaves—Little Portugal, Greektown, Corso Italia, and Koreatown—color downtown. It's fun to explore the unique architecture and shopping in each neighborhood, and dining out can be as exotic as you choose. Toronto's multiculturalism is evident in many of its annual festivals: the glittering West Indian Caribana along the waterfront; the Taste of the Danforth, featuring Greek musicians, dances, and plenty of souvlaki; the raucous celebration of Mexican Independence Day in Nathan Phillips Square; and the India Bazaar's annual festival with dancing, chaat (savory snacks), and henna tattooing.

To get a sense of Toronto's culture and indulge in some of its pleasures, start by familiarizing yourself with the rituals of daily life. These are a few highlights—things you can take part in easily.

Coffee and Donuts

Morning rush hour is the best time to observe, but not participate (lines are out the door) in, the ritual of caffeine and sugar intake at Tim Horton's, a coffee chain with a uniquely "Canadian" image—think hockey dads armed with hot coffee for long, chilly morning practices—and affordable prices. In Toronto you'll see hundreds of locals sporting the familiar brown cups, even high-rolling Financial District execs. For your own experience, order a "double-double" (two cream, two sugar) and a box of Timbits (donut holes). But Toronto's caffeine fix extends beyond "Tim's." The city has no shortage of independently owned cafés with stellar espresso and often a fair trade and organic brew, especially along Queen Street (east of Broadview and west of Spadina Avenues) and in the Annex and Little Italy.

Lake Escapes

You don't need a car to escape Toronto's bustle and summer heat and indulge in a calm, cool day by the lake. A rite of passage for each and every Torontonian is a warm-weather trip to the Islands at the base of Toronto's urban sprawl—a 15-minute ferry trip from downtown—whether for a barbecue, a picnic, bike rides along the car-less paths, or the kiddie rides at Centreville amusement park. Or head to the east side of the city for strolls along the boardwalk in the Beach neighborhood. Those with wheels spend weekends on the Niagara Peninsula dallying in antiques shops in charming rustic towns and sampling wines, or head north to relax in the Muskoka Lakes cottage country or hike and camp in Algonquin Provincial Park.

IF YOU LIKE

Wining and Dining

Those in search of haute cuisine are pampered in Toronto, where some of the world's finest chefs vie for the attention of the city's sizable foodie population. Toronto's range of exceptional eateries, from creative Asian fusion to more daring molecular gastronomy, offers wining and dining potential for every possible palate. Aromas of finely crafted sauces and delicately grilled meats emanate from eateries in Yorkville, where valet service and designer handbags are de rigueur; and the strip of bistros in the Entertainment District gets lively with theater-going crowds. Weekdays at lunch, the Financial District's Bay Street is a sea of Armani suits, crisply pressed shirts, and clicking heels heading to power lunches to make deals over steak frites. To conduct your own taste tests, check out some of the following places:

Bymark. An ultramodern and ultracool spot primed for the Financial District set; chef–owner Mark McEwan aims for perfection with classy contemporary fare.

Canoe. Toronto's most famous "splurge" place. Sit back, enjoy the view and let the waiter pair your dish with a recommended local Ontario wine.

Bistro 990. Staff here are sure to be attentive—they're used to serving celebrities and power-wielding bigwigs who fill the tables on weekday afternoons.

Colborne Lane. Star chef Claudio Aprile's venture is *the* place to sample cutting-edge creations that blur the boundary between dinner and science project.

Fressen. Dimly-lit, ultra-trendy vegan nouvelle cuisine with a wine list to rival any steak house.

Hot Hoods

Toronto's coolness doesn't emanate from a downtown core, or even a series of town centers. The action is physically everywhere in the city. Dozens of neighborhoods, each with its own scene and way of life, coexist within the vast metropolitan area. Here are just a few worth investigating:

West Queen West. As Queen Street West (to Bathurst Street or so) becomes more commercial and rents increase, more local artists and designers have set up shop here, but it's also home to a burgeoning night scene and experimental restaurants.

Kensington Market. This well-established bastion of bohemia for hippies of all ages is a grungy and multicultural several-block radius of produce, cheese, by-the-gram spices, fresh empanadas, used clothing, head shops, and funky restaurants and cafés.

The Annex. The pockets of wealth nestled in side streets add diversity to this scruffy strip of Bloor, the favorite haunt of the intellectual set, whether starving student or world-renowned novelist.

The Beach. This bourgeois-bohemian neighborhood is the habitat of young professionals who frequent the yoga studios and sushi restaurants along Queen Street East and walk their pooches daily along Lake Ontario's boardwalk.

Performing Arts

Toronto has one of North America's most thriving theater scenes, apparent in large Broadway-style musicals and various performances by small independent companies. Refurbished iconic theaters such as the Royal Alexandra and Canon theaters host a number of big-ticket shows in elegant surroundings. More modern venues such as the Princess of Wales highlight local and Broadway performances. It takes the amazing talent at the exciting summer festivals of Stratford and Niagara-on-the-Lake to entice Toronto's theatrically inclined to leave the city. The Four Seasons Centre is home to both the National Ballet of Canada and the Canadian Opera Company, which shares the music scene with the Toronto Symphony Orchestra and mainstream concerts at the Sony Centre and Massey Hall. Indie artists are attracted to the bars and grimy music venues on Queen Street West. A few of the many performance venues worth visiting:

Rivoli. In this multifaceted venue, you can dine while admiring local art, catch a musical act, or watch stand-up. Before they were megastars, Beck, Indigo Girls, Iggy Pop, Janeane Garofalo, and Tori Amos all made appearances here.

Elgin and Winter Garden Theatres. These two 1913 Edwardian theaters, stacked on top of each other, provide sumptuous settings for classical music performances, musicals, opera, and Toronto International Film Festival screenings.

The Second City. The comedic troupe here always puts on a great performance. Photo collages on the wall display the club's alumni, including Mike Myers, Dan Aykroyd, and Catherine O'Hara.

Architecture

At one point, Toronto's only celebrated icon was the CN Tower, but architects have been working hard to rejuvenate the cityscape. The Royal Ontario Museum's Michael Lee-Chin Crystal geometrically shaped extension, designed by Daniel Libeskind, was unveiled in 2007, and the Frank Gehry–designed Art Gallery of Ontario followed in 2008. Fine examples of architectural variety exist in the Financial District; single spectacular buildings are scattered throughout the city:

Philosopher's Walk. This scenic path winds through the University of Toronto, from the entrance between the Royal Ontario Museum and the Victorian-era Royal Conservatory of Music, past Trinity College's Gothic chapel and towering spires.

ROMwalks. From May to September, free walks organized by the Royal Ontario Museum tour some of the city's landmark buildings, such as the Church of the Redeemer, the Royal Conservatory of Music, and the Gardiner Museum.

Art Gallery of Ontario. A C$250 million renovation, added thousands of square feet of gallery space in the AGO's Frank Gehry–designed building in 2008. The wooden facades, glass roofs and four-story blue titanium wing are spectacular to admire from the outside or within.

Sharp Centre for Design. Locals are split on the eye-catching black-and-white rectangle and its colorful stilts standing above the Ontario College of Art and Design.

GREAT ITINERARIES

5 DAYS IN TORONTO

To really see Toronto, a stay of at least one week is ideal. However, these itineraries are designed to inspire thematic tours of some of the city's best sights, whether you're in town for one day or five. We've also included a two- to three-day escape to the Niagara region.

One Day: Architecture and Museums

Start at Queen and Bay by pondering Finnish architect Viljo Revell's eye-shaped **City Hall** and then its regal predecessor, **Old City Hall**, across the street. From here, head south through the **Financial District** to admire the historic skyscrapers before swinging west on Front Street to the spectacular **CN Tower**. It's not hard to find—just look up. Walk up to King and catch a streetcar east to the restored Victorian industrial buildings of the **Historic Distillery District**; choose any of the amazing restaurants here for lunch.

Begin the afternoon at the **Royal Ontario Museum**. If the steep entrance fee makes you wince, admire the modern Crystal Gallery from outside before moving on to the **Ceramic Museum**, across the street, or the quirky **Bata Shoe Museum** at St. George Street. Breathtaking views from **Panorama**, on the 51st floor of the Manulife Centre at Bay and Bloor streets, set the scene for a relaxing drink or dinner.

One Day: Shopping Around the World

Before the crowds descend at lunchtime, head for the aesthetically chaotic Spadina Avenue–Dundas Street intersection, the core of **Chinatown**, to browse the stalls overflowing with exotic fruits and vegetables, fragrant herbal tonics, and flashy Chinese baubles. Either pause here for a steaming plate of fried noodles, or try one of the juice bars, vegan restaurants,

or empanada stands in nearby **Kensington Market** (head west on Spadina to Augusta and turn right). After lunch, browse the Eastern European, South American, and Caribbean shops and groceries, modern cafés, and funky clothing boutiques. Take the College streetcar east to Coxwell Avenue (about a 30-minute ride), where the dazzling bejeweled saris and shiny bangles of the **India Bazaar** beckon. A fiery madras curry washed down with a mango lassi (yogurt drink) or Kingfisher beer is the perfect way to end the day.

One Day: With Kids

If the weather is behaving, make an early departure for the **Toronto Zoo**, where more than 700 acres of dense forests and winding creeks are home to more than 5,000 animals and 460 species. Or venture out to the equally enthralling indoor exhibits and demonstrations of the **Ontario Science Centre**. If your kids are sports fans, the **Hockey Hall of Fame**, at Yonge and Front streets, might be just the ticket. The afternoon is best spent exploring the kid-friendly attractions along the shore of Lake Ontario, starting with the either the water park and IMAX theater at **Ontario Place** or a ride up **CN Tower** to test your nerves on the glass floor that "floats" over a 1,122-foot drop and take in a view that extends far enough to let you see the mist from the Falls. Dinner at **Richtree Market** in Brookfield Place is extremely kid-friendly—market-style stalls prepare burritos, pizzas, and crepes.

One Day: Island Life

Start by picking up picnic supplies from **St. Lawrence Market** (closed Sunday and Monday), whose stalls offer a cornucopia of imported delicacies and delicious prepared foods. From here, walk to the **docks** at the foot of Bay Street and Queen's Quay to catch one of the ferries to the **Toronto**

Islands; the view of the city skyline is an added bonus. In summer, kids have the run of **Centre Island. Hanlan's Point** is infamous for its nude bathing; and **Ward's Island** has great sandy beaches and a restaurant, the Rectory Café, with a lakeside patio. One of the allures of Island life is the slow pace, so spend the afternoon just rambling. If you'd like to cover more ground, rent a bicycle at the ferry docks. Winter is not without charms, namely cross-country skiing and snowshoeing. When you're back downtown in the evening, keep the outdoorsy theme with an alfresco dinner in **The Danforth, Little Italy,** or the **Historic Distillery District**—Toronto's pedestrian-friendly entertainment village.

One Day: Neighborhood Watching
Begin the day window-shopping along the rows of restored Victorian residences on **Yorkville Avenue,** or reading at an outdoor café along **Cumberland Street.** In the 1960s, before the country's most exclusive shops settled here, Yorkville was a hippie haven, attracting emerging Canadian musical artists Joni Mitchell and Gordon Lightfoot. The shops spill onto **Bloor Street West,** and the strip between Yonge Street and Avenue Road is sometimes referred to as Toronto's Fifth Avenue. The **Royal Ontario Museum** is worth a peek, even if just from the street, to admire the shiny crystal-inspired modern structure. In stark contrast to Yorkvillian sophistication, the grungy shops along Bloor west of St. George are housed in less lovingly restored turn-of-the-20th-century homes. Rest your legs in either **Future Bakery & Café,** a trendy outpost for comfort food, or the more upscale, Mediterranean spot **Splendido.** In the evening, take in a play, a concert, or a comedy show downtown at **The Second City.**

A Few Days: Niagara Getaway
If you have a few days to spare, start by succumbing to the force and brilliance of **Niagara Falls.** A ride on the **Maid of the Mist** is highly recommended, and in the afternoon—especially if you have kids—you may want to experience **Clifton Hill** in all its tacky, amusement park–like glory. Alternatively, head along the scenic Niagara Parkway to visit the **Botanical Gardens** or **White Water Walk,** more peaceful and natural attractions. Get dressed up for dinner at the Skylon Tower or another restaurant overlooking the falls and tuck in for a night at the slots. Admire the **fireworks** at 10 PM (Friday and Sunday in summer) from either your Falls-view hotel room or **Konica Minolta Tower Centre.** The next day, a good breakfast is essential, perhaps at one of the many options in the Fallsview Casino Resort, to prepare for a day of wine tasting and strolling in bucolic **Niagara-on-the-Lake.** You'll need a car to follow the beautiful Niagara Parkway north to **Queen Street**—for shopping. Nibble and tipple the day away along the **Wine Route,** which follows Regional Road 81 as far west as Grimsby. Dinner at one of the wineries or at one of the excellent hotel restaurants, such as **Zees,** then a night in one of the region's boutique hotels or luxurious bed-and-breakfasts is an indulgent end to a great weekend. If you're here during the **Shaw Festival** (April–December), book a ticket for a play by Shaw or one of his contemporaries.

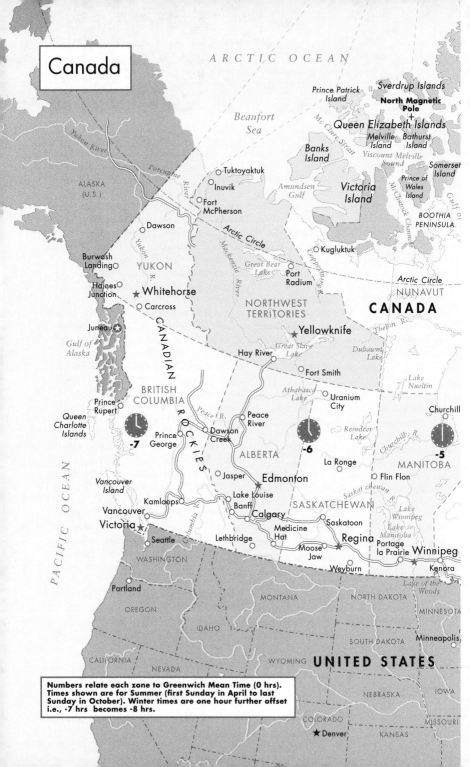

Canada

ARCTIC OCEAN

Prince Patrick Island

Sverdrup Islands

North Magnetic Pole +

Queen Elizabeth Islands

Melville Island

Bathurst Island

Beaufort Sea

McClure Strait

Viscount Melville Sound

Banks Island

Amundsen Gulf

Victoria Island

Prince of Wales Island

Somerset Island

McClintock Channel

Gulf of

BOOTHIA PENINSULA

Yukon River

ALASKA (U.S.)

Porcupine

Porcupine River

Tuktoyaktuk

Inuvik

Fort McPherson

Arctic Circle

Kugluktuk

Dawson

Mackenzie River

Coppermine R.

Arctic Circle

Burwash Landing

YUKON

Yukon R.

Great Bear Lake

Port Radium

NUNAVUT

Haines Junction

Whitehorse

Carcross

NORTHWEST TERRITORIES

Yellowknife

Thelon R.

CANADA

Juneau

Gulf of Alaska

CANADIAN

Hay River

Great Slave Lake

Dubawnt Lake

Lake Nueltin

Fort Smith

Athabasca Lake

Uranium City

Churchill

BRITISH COLUMBIA

Prince Rupert

Queen Charlotte Islands

ROCKIES

Peace R.

Peace River

Reindeer Lake

Churchill R.

MANITOBA

-7

Prince George

Dawson Creek

ALBERTA

-6

La Ronge

-5

Jasper

Edmonton

Flin Flon

PACIFIC OCEAN

Vancouver Island

Kamloops

Lake Louise

Banff

Columbia R.

SASKATCHEWAN

Saskatchewan R.

Lake Winnipeg

Vancouver

Calgary

Saskatoon

Lake Manitoba

Victoria

Medicine Hat

Regina

Portage la Prairie

Winnipeg

Seattle

Lethbridge

Moose Jaw

Kenora

WASHINGTON

Weyburn

Lake of the Woods

Portland

OREGON

MONTANA

NORTH DAKOTA

MINNESOTA

IDAHO

SOUTH DAKOTA

Minneapolis

CALIFORNIA

NEVADA

WYOMING

UNITED STATES

NEBRASKA

IOWA

COLORADO

KANSAS

MISSOURI

★ Denver

Numbers relate each zone to Greenwich Mean Time (0 hrs). Times shown are for Summer (first Sunday in April to last Sunday in October). Winter times are one hour further offset i.e., -7 hrs becomes -8 hrs.

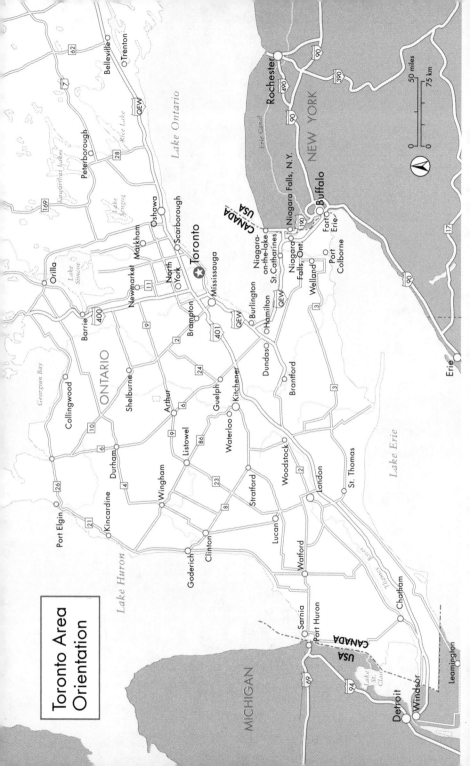

Exploring
Toronto

Updated by
Sarah Richards

"Toronto is like New York, as run by the Swiss," actor Peter Ustinov is rumored to have said. Indeed, this is a big, beautiful, and efficient city, one that has emerged from relative obscurity over the past half century to become the center of culture, commerce, and communications in Canada. With its colorful ethnic mix, rich history, and breathtaking architecture, Toronto is nonstop adventure for the willing tourist, from the top of the CN Tower to as far as the eye can see.

Nearly two-thirds of the 4.5 million residents who now live in the greater Toronto area were born and raised somewhere else. And that somewhere else was often very far away. Nearly 500,000 Italians give Toronto one of the largest Italian communities outside Italy. It is also the home of the largest Chinese community in Canada and the largest Portuguese community in North America. The city hosts close to 150,000 Jewish people, nearly as many Muslims, and tens of thousands of Germans, joined by Greeks, Hungarians, East Indians, West Indians, Vietnamese, Maltese, South Americans, and Ukrainians—more than 80 ethnic groups in all, speaking more than 80 different languages. Toronto is also the home of Canada's largest gay and lesbian community.

Although the assimilation of these various cultures into the overall fabric of the city is ongoing, several ethnic neighborhoods have become attractions on their own for locals and visitors. These include Kensington Market (west of Spadina Avenue between College and Dundas), Chinatown (around the Spadina Avenue and Dundas Street intersection), Greektown (Danforth Avenue between Chester and Jones), Little Italy (College Street between Euclid and Shaw), Little Poland (Roncesvalles Avenue between Queen and Dundas), Portugal Village (Dundas Street West, west of Bathurst), India Bazaar (Gerrard Street between Coxwell and Greenwood), and Koreatown (Bloor Street West between Bathurst and Christie).

What this immigration has meant to Toronto is the rather rapid creation of a vibrant mix of cultures that has echoes of turn-of-the-20th-century New York City—but without the slums, crowding, and tensions. Torontonians embrace, and take pride in, their multicultural character, their tradition of keeping a relatively clean and safe city, and their shared belief in the value of everyone getting along and enjoying the basic rights of good health care, education, and a high standard of living.

Toronto is also a city filled with boutiques, restaurants, and cafés, and there are plenty of shops, both aboveground and on the PATH, Toronto's underground city—an 11-km-long (7-mi) subterranean walkway lined with eateries, shops, banks, and medical offices.

And then there are the oft-overlooked gems of Toronto: the beach-fringed Toronto Islands. These eight tree-lined islands—and more than a dozen smaller islets—that sit in Lake Ontario just off the city's downtown offer a welcome touch of greenery. They've been attracting visitors since 1833, especially during summer, when the more than 550 acres of parkland on the islands are most irresistible. From any of the islands you have spectacular views of Toronto's skyline, especially as the setting sun turns the city's skyscrapers to gold, silver, and bronze.

ORIENTATION AND PLANNING

GETTING ORIENTED

The boundaries of what Torontonians consider downtown, where most of the city sights are located, are subject to debate, but everyone agrees on the southern cutoff—Lake Ontario and the Toronto Islands. The other coordinates of the rectangle that compose the city core are Bathurst Street to the west, Parliament Street to the east, and Eglinton Avenue to the north. Beyond these borders are numerous Greater Toronto sights that make excellent morning, afternoon, or full-day excursions. An ideal way to get a sense of the city's layout is from one of the observation decks at the CN Tower on a clear day; the view is especially lovely at sunset.

Most city streets are organized on a grid system: with some exceptions, street numbers start at zero at the lake and increase as you go north. On the east–west axis, Yonge (pronounced "young") Street, Toronto's main thoroughfare, is the dividing line: you can expect higher numbers the farther away you get from Yonge.

Traffic is dense and parking expensive within the city core. If you have a car with you, leave it at your hotel when exploring the city and use it for excursions to outlying attractions or to towns like Stratford. ■ TIP➔ **In the city, take taxis or use the excellent Toronto transit system (TTC). A single ride costs C$2.75 and one-day passes are C$9.** Just one pass will cover up to two adults and four children on weekends. *For more information on transportation within Toronto, ⇨ see Getting Here and Around in Travel Smart Toronto.*

DISCOUNTS AND DEALS

Culture on the cheap—it can be done. There are several ways to sightsee on a shoestring, starting with the Toronto **CityPass** (⊕ *www.citypass. com*), which saves money and time (you can bypass ticket lines) when visiting the city's top six attractions: the CN Tower, Art Gallery of Ontario, Royal Ontario Museum, Casa Loma, Ontario Science Centre, and Toronto Zoo.

Some museums and art collections are free all the time, including the Gallery of Inuit Art in the TD Centre and the Power Plant gallery. There's also free entry to the Bata Shoe Museum on Thursday after 5 PM, the Gardiner Museum of Ceramic Art after 4 PM on Friday, the Museum of Textiles on Wednesday after 5 PM, and the Art Gallery of Ontario on Wednesday after 6 PM.

There are free festivals year-round in Toronto, but especially in summer. Check local listings and you'll find information on everything from the Toronto Outdoor Arts Exhibition in July to the Greek "Taste of the

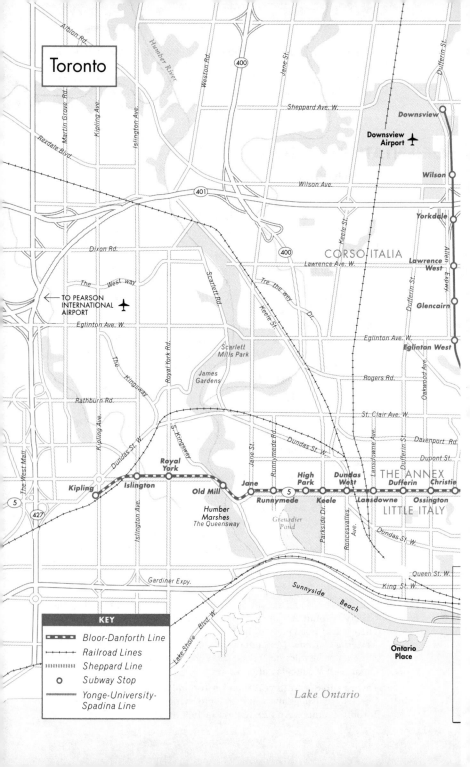

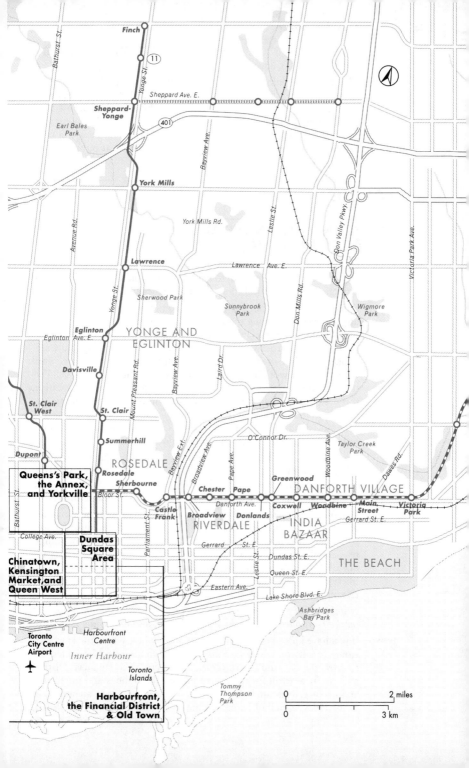

Danforth" and to North America's largest Ukrainian street festival in the Bloor West Village.

The free old standbys of churches, cemeteries, and parks are stellar in Toronto. From the beautiful St. James and St. Michael's cathedrals to the Necropolis cemetery, from the labyrinthian gardens across from the Church of the Holy Trinity to the music gardens by Harbourfront, some of the city's most thought-provoking sights don't cost a cent. Strolling in one of Toronto's many parks or skating at public rinks is always free.

EXPLORING

HARBOURFRONT, THE FINANCIAL DISTRICT, AND OLD TOWN

Packed into this area, which runs from Bay Street east to Parliament Street and from Queen Street south to Lake Ontario, you'll find the city's main attractions and historical roots, and the financial hub of the nation.

Today cranes dot the skyline as condominium buildings seemingly appear overnight along the Harbourfront. Before the drastic decline of trucking due to the 1970s oil crisis reduced the Great Lakes trade, Toronto's waterfront was an important center for shipping and warehousing. The area fell into commercial disuse and was neglected until the city began working to develop the waterfront in the 1980s. This trend toward people-friendly purposes continues today. In fair weather, this area is appealing for strolls, and myriad recreational and amusement options make it ideal for those traveling with children. The nearby Toronto Islands provide a perfect escape from the sometimes stifling heat of downtown during the summer months.

Farther north lies the Financial District with its unique and wonderful architectural variety of skyscrapers. Most of the towers have bank branches, restaurants, and retail outlets on their ground floors and are connected to the PATH, an underground city of shops and tunnels.

East of the Financial District is Old Town, where the city got its municipal start as the village of York in 1793. A pleasing natural disorder now prevails in this neighborhood, which blends old and new buildings, residential and commercial space. At the far east end of Old Town is one of Toronto's hottest entertainment destinations, the Historic Distillery District, in which contemporary galleries, bustling pubs, and chic restaurants fill restored Victorian-era factories.

Numbers in the text and in the margin correspond to points of interest on the Harbourfront, the Financial District, and Old Town map.

TIMING   If you have kids in tow, plan on spending a whole day in the Harbourfront area. If you're going to the Toronto Islands, add 45 minutes just to cross the bay and return on the same ferry. The Financial District makes a nice stroll for its myriad historical buildings and interesting architecture. Museum buffs will want to linger for at least an hour each in the Hockey Hall of Fame and the Design Exchange. In Old Town,

TORONTO DAY TOURS

Tourism Toronto (☎ *416/203–2500 or 800/499–2514* ⊕ *www.seetoron-tonow.com*) can provide further tour information.

BOAT TOURS

If you want to get a glimpse of the skyline, try a boat tour. **Toronto Tours** (☎ *416/869–1372* ⊕ *www.torontotours.com*) runs one-hour tours of the waterfront from mid-April through late October, which cost about C$24. There are many boat-tour companies operating all along the boardwalk of Harbourfront; it's up to you to decide which one best suits your interest and wallet. To further your appreciation for man-made beauty, **Great Lakes Schooner Company** (☎ *416/203–2322* ⊕ *www.tallshipcruisestoronto.com*) lets you see Toronto's skyline from the open deck of the tall ship *Challenge*. Tours are available early June to the end of September and cost about C$22, depending on length.

BUS TOURS

For a look at the city proper, take one of the many available bus tours, both of these take you around the city on a two-hour loop. A ticket good for three days costs about C$35. Part of Toronto Tours, **Toronto City Tours** (☎ *416/869–1372* ⊕ *www.torontotours.com*) offers and two-hour guided tours in 24-passenger buses for C$40. If you want the freedom to get on and off the bus when the whim strikes, take a hop-on, hop-off tour. **Gray Line Sightseeing Bus Tours** (✉ *610 Bay St., north of Dundas St.* ☎ *800/594–3310* ⊕ *www.grayline.ca*) has London-style double-decker buses and turn-of-the-20th-century trolleys.

Toronto Hippo Tours (☎ *877/635–5510 or 416/703–4476* ⊕ *www.torontohippotours.com*) gives an amphibious narrated land-water tour—in what's basically a boat with retractable wheels—that takes in downtown sights then splashes into the lake, floating along the waterfront for C$38.

SPECIAL-INTEREST TOURS
Toronto Field Naturalists (☎ *416/593–2656* ⊕ *www.torontofieldnaturalists.org*) schedules about 150 guided tours during the year, each focusing on some aspect of nature, such as geology or wildflowers, and with starting points accessible by public transit. The **Bruce Trail Association** (☎ *800/665–4453* ⊕ *www.brucetrail.org*) arranges day and overnight hikes around Toronto and its environs.

WALKING TOURS

To give a feel for Toronto's outstanding cultural diversity, **Heritage Toronto** (☎ *416/338–3886* ⊕ *www.heritagetoronto.org*) has free guided walking tours on weekends and occasional holidays from mid-April to early October. They last 1½ to 2 hours and cover one neighborhood or topic, such as the historic theater block. The **Royal Ontario Museum** (☎ *416/586–8097* ⊕ *www.rom.on.ca/programs*) runs 1½- to 2-hour ROMwalk tours on such topics as the city's upper-crust neighborhood, Rosedale. Several free walks are given weekly. **A Taste of the World** (☎ *416/923–6813* ⊕ *www.torontowalksbikes.com*) runs food-, literary-, and ghost-theme tours of various lengths in several neighborhoods. Reservations are essential.

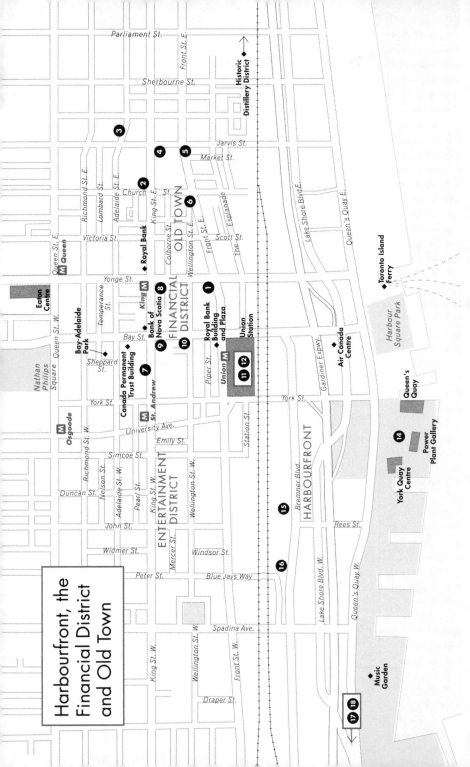

Harbourfront, the Financial District and Old Town

Parliament St.

Front St. E.

Sherbourne St.

Historic
Distillery District ◆

❸

❹ ❺

Richmond St. E.

Lombard St.

Adelaide St. E.

Church St.

❷

Jarvis St.

Market St.

King St. E.

❻

Colborne St.

Wellington St. E.

OLD TOWN

Front St. E.

Scott St.

The Esplanade

Victoria St.

◆ Royal Bank

Queen St. E.

Ⓜ Queen

Eaton
Centre

Yonge St.

King Ⓜ

Bank of
Nova Scotia ❽

FINANCIAL
DISTRICT

❶

Lake Shore Blvd. E.

Queen's Quay E.

Toronto Island
Ferry ◆

Temperance
St.

❾ ❿

Royal Bank
Building
and Plaza ◆

Union
Station

Harbour
Square Park

Queen St. W.

Bay-Adelaide
Park

Bay St.

Canada Permanent
Trust Building ◆

Sheppard
St.

❼

Union Ⓜ

⓫ ⓬

Piper St.

Nathan
Philips
Square

York St.

Ⓜ St. Andrew

Queen St. W.

Gardiner Expwy.

Air Canada
Centre ◆

Queen's
Quay

Ⓜ Osgoode

Richmond St. W.

University Ave.

Emily St.

Station St.

York St.

HARBOURFRONT

Queen's Quay W.

Power
Plant Gallery

⓮

Simcoe St.

York Quay
Centre

Nelson St.

Adelaide St. W.

Pearl St.

ENTERTAINMENT
DISTRICT

Wellington St. W.

Bremner Blvd.

Duncan St.

King St. W.

John St.

Mercer St.

Rees St.

⓯

Windsor St.

Widmer St.

Peter St.

Blue Jays Way

⓰

Lake Shore Blvd. W.

Spadina Ave.

King St. W.

Wellington St. W.

Front St. W.

Queen's Quay W.

Music
Garden ◆

Draper St.

⓱ ⓲

2

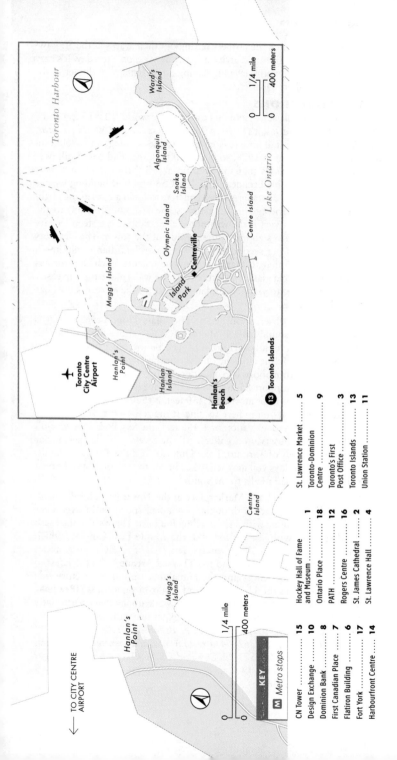

Toronto Harbour

Ward's
Island

Algonquin
Island

Olympic Island

Snake
Island

Mugg's Island

◆ **Centreville**

Island
Park

Lake Ontario

Centre Island

1/4 mile

400 meters

0

0

**Toronto
City Centre
Airport**

Hanlan's
Point

Hanlan
Island

Hanlan's
Beach ◆

13 **Toronto Islands**

← TO CITY CENTRE
AIRPORT

Centre
Island

Mugg's
Island

Hanlan's
Point

1/4 mile

400 meters

0

0

KEY

M *Metro stops*

CN Tower **15**
Design Exchange **10**
Dominion Bank **8**
First Canadian Place **7**
Flatiron Building **6**
Fort York **17**
Harbourfront Centre **14**

Hockey Hall of Fame
and Museum **1**
Ontario Place **18**
PATH **12**
Rogers Centre **16**
St. James Cathedral **2**
St. Lawrence Hall **4**

St. Lawrence Market **5**
Toronto-Dominion
Centre **9**
Toronto's First
Post Office **3**
Toronto Islands **13**
Union Station **11**

if you want to catch the farmers setting out their wares at the St. Lawrence Market, you should arrive as early as 5 AM on Saturday. It's easy to while away an entire evening having a few pints with dinner in the Historic Distillery District.

TOP ATTRACTIONS

⑮ **CN Tower.** The tallest freestanding tower in the world is 1,815 feet and 5

☾ inches high—and yes, it's listed in the *Guinness Book of World Records*.

FodorśChoice The CN Tower is tall for a reason: prior to the opening of this telecom-

★ munications tower in 1976, so many tall buildings had been built over the previous decades that lower radio and TV transmission towers were having trouble broadcasting. The C$63 million building weighs 130,000 tons and contains enough concrete to build a curb along Highway 401 from Toronto to Kingston, some 262 km (162 mi) to the east. It's worth a visit if the weather is clear, despite the steep fee. Six glass-front elevators zoom up the outside of the tower. The elevators travel at 20 feet per second and the ride takes less than a minute—a rate of ascent similar to that of a jet-plane takeoff. Each elevator has one floor-to-ceiling glass wall—three opaque walls make the trip easier on anyone prone to vertigo—and at least one of the elevators now has glass floor panels.

There are four observation decks. The **Glass Floor Level,** which is exactly what it sounds like, is about 1,122 feet above the ground. It's like walking on a cloud. This could well be the most photographed indoor location in the city—lie on the transparent floor and have your picture taken from above like countless before you. Don't worry—the glass floor can support 85,000 pounds. Above is the **Look Out Level,** at 1,136 feet; one floor more, at 1,150 feet, is the excellent **360 Revolving Restaurant.** If you're here to dine at the restaurant, your elevator fee is waived. At an elevation of 1,465 feet, the **Sky Pod** is the world's highest public observation gallery. All the levels provide spectacular panoramic views of Toronto, Lake Ontario, and the Toronto Islands. On really clear days you may see Lake Simcoe to the north and the mist rising from Niagara Falls to the south.

On the ground level, the **Marketplace at the Tower** has 12,500 square feet of shopping space with quality Canadian sports and travel items and souvenirs, along with a shop selling Inuit art. There's also the **Fresh Market Cafe,** with seating for 300; the **Maple Leaf Cinema,** which screens the 20-minute documentary *The Height of Excellence*, about the building of the Tower; and the **Themed Arcade,** with the latest in virtual-game experiences and the Himalamazon motion picture ride based loosely on the Himalayan and Amazon regions. ■**TIP→ Peak visiting hours are 11 to 4; you may wish to work around them, particularly on weekends.** Ticket packages get more expensive with the more attractions included. ⊠ *301 Front St. W, at Bremner Blvd., Harbourfront* ☎ *416/868–6937, 416/362–5411 restaurant* ⊕ *www.cntower.ca* ⬛ *First 2 observation levels C$21.99, Sky Pod C$26.99, combined packages start at C$32.99* ☽ *Oct.–Apr., daily 9 AM–10 PM; June–Sept., daily 9 AM–11 PM* Ⓜ *Union.*

A BRIEF HISTORY OF TORONTO

The city officially became Toronto on March 6, 1834, but its roots are much more ancient than that. In the early 1600s a Frenchman named Etienne Brûlé was sent into the not-yet-Canadian wilderness by the famous explorer Samuel de Champlain to see what he could discover. He discovered plenty: the river and portage routes from the St. Lawrence to Lake Huron, possibly Lakes Superior and Michigan, and eventually Lake Ontario. The native Huron peoples had known this area between the Humber and Don rivers for centuries—and had long called it "Toronto," believed to mean "meeting place." Later, a bustling village called Teiaiagon grew up here, and then it was the site of a French trading post. After the British won the Seven Years' War, the trading post was renamed "York" in 1793. More than 40 years later the city again took the name Toronto. Following an unsuccessful American invasion in 1812, several devastating fires, and a rebellion in 1837, there was a slow but steady increase in the population of white Anglo-Saxon Protestants leading into the 20th century. Since World War II, though, Toronto has attracted residents from all over the world. And unlike the American "melting pot" phenomenon that melds everyone together, Toronto is more of a "tossed salad" of diverse ethnic groups.

2

⑩ **Design Exchange.** A delightful example of streamlined moderne design
★ (a later and more austere version of art deco), this building is clad in polished pink granite and smooth buff limestone, with stainless-steel doors. Between 1937 and 1983 the DX (as it's now known) was the home of the Toronto Stock Exchange. Don't miss the witty stone frieze carved above the doors—a banker in top hat marching behind a laborer and sneaking his hand into the worker's pocket. Only in Canada, where socialism has always been a strong force, would you find such a political statement on the side of a stock exchange.) In the early 1990s the building reopened as a nonprofit center devoted to promoting Canadian design. The permanent collection contains examples of contemporary and older decorative arts, furniture, graphic design, housewares, lighting, and tableware. The old trading floor is now used for rotating exhibits—check their Web site or the local papers for information. ✉ *234 Bay St., at King St., Financial District* ☎ *416/363–6121* ⊕ *www.dx.org* 🎫 *C$5* ⊙ *Weekdays 10–5, weekends noon–5* Ⓜ *King, St. Andrew.*

★ **Historic Distillery District.** Under careful restoration, North America's best-preserved collection of Victorian industrial architecture is in this historic enclave in downtown Toronto. Formerly the Gooderham & Worts Distillery (founded in 1832), the Distillery has been developed as a center for arts, culture, and entertainment. This 13-acre cobblestone site includes 45 19th-century buildings and a pedestrian-only village that houses more than 100 tenants—including galleries, artist studios and workshops, boutiques, retail stores, a brewery, upscale restaurants, bars, cafés, and even a spa. Live music, outdoor exhibitions, fairs, and special events take place year-round, but the summer months are really the best time to visit. Walking tours (C$19) take place every day except Monday at 11:30 AM and 3:30 PM ✉ *55 Mill St., south of Front St. and east of Parliament St., Old Town* ☎ *416/364–1177* ⊕ *www.thedistillerydistrict.com* 🅿 *Parking C$5* ⊙ *Mon.–Wed. 11–7, Thurs. and Fri. 11–9, Sat. 10–9, Sun. 11–6; individual tenant hrs may vary, including restaurants, cafés, and boutiques* Ⓜ *King, then streetcar 504 east.*

❶ **Hockey Hall of Fame and Museum.** Even if you're not a hockey fan, it's
🅲   worth a trip here to see this shrine to Canada's favorite sport. Exhib-
★   its include the original 1893 Stanley Cup, as well as displays of goalie masks, skate and stick collections, great players' jerseys, video displays of big games, and a replica of the Montréal Canadiens' locker room. Grab a stick and test your speed and accuracy in the "shoot out" virtual experience, or strap on a goalie mask and field shots from big-name players like Gretzky and Messier with the "shut out" computer simulation. The details of the beautifully ornate 1885 building, a former Bank of Montréal branch designed by architects Darling & Curry, have been well preserved: note the richly carved Ohio stone and the Hermès figure supporting the chimney near the back of the building. ■TIP➔ **Entrance is through Brookfield Place on the lower level of the east side.** ✉ *30 Yonge St., at Front St., Financial District* ☎ *416/360–7765* ⊕ *www.hhof.com* 🅿 *C$15* ⊙ *Sept.–June, weekdays 10–5, Sat. 9:30–6, Sun. 10:30–5; July and Aug., Mon.–Sat. 9:30–6, Sun. 10–6* Ⓜ *Union.*

▮ QUICK BITES   **Brookfield Place (✉ *181 Bay St., between Front St. W and Wellington St. W, Financial District* Ⓜ *Union*), a modern office and retail complex cleverly designed to incorporate the Bank of Montréal building and other older structures under a glass roof, is not only one of the most impressive architectural spaces in Toronto, the atrium is also a pleasant place to sit and enjoy a cup of coffee.**

❺ **St. Lawrence Market.** Built in 1844 as the first true Toronto city hall, the
Fodor's Choice   building now has an exhibition hall upstairs—the Market Gallery—
★   where the council chambers once stood. It is also a food market, which began growing up around the city hall in the early 1900s. Considered to be one of the world's best food markets, it is renowned for its local and imported foods such as fresh shellfish, sausage varieties, and cheeses. Stop and snack on Canadian bacon, also known as "peameal bacon," at the Market's Carousel Bakery. The plain brick building across Front Street, on the north side, is open on Saturday mornings for the 200-year-old farmers' market; it's a cornucopia of fine produce and homemade jams, relishes, and sauces from farms just north of Toronto. On Sunday the wares of more than 80 antiques dealers are on display in the same building. ✉ *Front and Jarvis Sts., Old Town* ☎ *416/392–7219* ⊕ *www. stlawrencemarket.com* ⊙ *Tues.–Thurs. 8–6, Fri. 8–7, Sat. 5–5; farmers' market Sat. 5–2; antiques market Sun. 5–5* Ⓜ *Union.*

⓭ **Toronto Islands.** These eight narrow, tree-lined islands, plus more than a
🅲   dozen smaller islets, just off the city's downtown in Lake Ontario, pro-
★   vide a welcome touch of greenery. The more than 550 acres of parkland

are hard to resist, especially in the summer, when they're usually a few degrees cooler than the city.

Sandy beaches fringe the Islands; the best are on the southeast tip of Ward's Island, the southernmost edge of Centre Island, and the west side of Hanlan's Island. In 1999 a portion of Hanlan's Beach was officially declared "clothing-optional" by Toronto's City Council. The declaration regarding Ontario's only legal nude beach passed without protest—perhaps a testament to the truly cosmopolitan flavor of the city. The section frequented by gays and lesbians is at the east end; the straight section is more westerly. There are free changing rooms near each beach. Lake Ontario's water is declared unfit for swimming a few days every summer, so call ☎416/392–7161 or check ⊕ www.toronto.ca/beach for water quality reports. Swimming in the lagoons and channels is prohibited. In summer, Centre Island has rowboat and canoe rentals. Pack a cooler with picnic fixings or something to grill on one of the park's barbecue pits. Note that the consumption of alcohol in a public park is illegal in Toronto. There are supervised wading pools, baseball diamonds, volleyball nets, tennis courts, and even a Frisbee course. The winter can be bitterly cold on the islands, but snowshoeing and cross-country skiing with downtown Toronto over your shoulder are appealing to many.

> ### HERE'S WHERE
>
> Although known more these days for nude bathing than baseball trivia, Hanlan's Point was the sight of baseball legend Babe Ruth's first professional home run. He hit it at Hanlan's Point Stadium (demolished in 1937 and located roughly where the airport stands today), when he was a pitcher for the Providence Grays and in town battling the Toronto Maple Leafs in 1914.

All transportation on these interconnected islands comes compliments of your feet: no cars (except for emergency and work vehicles) are permitted. The boardwalk from Centre Island to Ward's Island is 2½ km (1½ mi) long. Centre Island gets so crowded that no bicycles are allowed on its ferry from the mainland during summer weekends. Consider renting a bike for an hour or so once you get there and working your way across the islands. Bike rentals can be found south of the Centre Island ferry docks on the Avenue of the Islands.

There are more than a dozen rides, including a restored 1890s merry-go-round with more than four dozen hand-carved animals, at the children's amusement park **Centreville** (⊠ *Centre Island* ☎ *416/203–0405* ⊕ *www.centreisland.ca* ⊠ *Day Pass C$29.50* ☉ *June weekdays 10:30–5, weekends 10:30–8; May, Sept., weekends 10:30–6; July–Aug., daily 10:30–8*). It's modeled after a late-19th-century village, with shops, a town hall, and a small railroad station. The free Far Enough Farm has all kinds of animals to pet and feed, including piglets, geese, and cows. There's no entrance fee to the modest 14-acre park, although there's a charge for rides. ■ TIP→ **A day pass is worthwhile instead of tickets for more than two rides.** You may want to take one of the equally frequent ferries to Ward's or Hanlan's Island. Both islands have tennis courts and picnic and sunbathing spots. Late May through early September, the ferries run between the docks at the bottom of Bay

Street and the Ward's Island dock between 6:35 AM and 11:45 AM; for Centre and Hanlan's islands, they begin at 8 AM. Ward's Island Ferries run roughly at half-hour intervals most of the working day and at quarter-hour intervals during peak times such as summer evenings. On Canada Day (July 1) the lines are slow-moving. In winter the ferries run only to Ward's Island on a lim-

WORD OF MOUTH

"Seeing Toronto from the water is well worth the trip and walking the island is so peaceful. It is a great park. We made ourselves at home in a marina, had a couple of beers and just watched the boats and Toronto skyline."   —cd

ited schedule. ✉ *Ferries at foot of Bay St. and Queen's Quay, Harbourfront* ☎ *416/392–8186 for island information, 416/392–8193 for ferry information* ⊕ *www.toronto.ca/parks/island/* ⌨ *Ferry C$6.50 roundtrip* Ⓜ *Union, then streetcar 509 or 510.*

❾
★ **Toronto-Dominion Centre.** Mies van der Rohe, a virtuoso of modern architecture, designed this five-building masterwork, though he died before the last building's completion in 1985. As with his acclaimed Seagram Building in New York, Mies stripped the TD Centre's buildings to their skin and bones of bronze-color glass and black-metal I-beams. The tallest building, the Toronto Dominion Bank Tower, is 56 stories high. The only decoration consists of geometric repetition, and the only extravagance is the use of rich materials, such as marble counters and leather-covered furniture. In summer, the plazas and grass are full of office workers eating lunch and listening to one of many free outdoor concerts. Inside the low-rise square banking pavilion at King and Bay streets is a virtually intact Mies interior.

Inside the TD Centre's Waterhouse Tower is the **Gallery of Inuit Art** (✉ *79 Wellington St. WM5K 1A1* ☎ *416/982–8473* ⌨ *Free* ☉ *Daily 8–4* Ⓜ *St. Andrew*). It's one of just a few such galleries in North America. The collection, equal to that of the Smithsonian, focuses on the bank's renowned collection of Inuit art from the vast Arctic region in northern Canada. ✉ *55 King St. W, at Bay St., Financial District* Ⓜ *St. Andrew.*

⓫ **Union Station.** Popular historian Pierre Berton wrote that the planning of Union Station recalled "the love lavished on medieval churches." Indeed, this train depot can be regarded as a cathedral built to serve the god of steam. Designed in 1907, and opened by the Prince of Wales in 1927, it has a 40-foot-high Italian tile ceiling and 22 pillars weighing 70 tons apiece. The vast main hall, with its lengthy concourse and light flooding in from arched windows at each end, was designed to evoke the majesty of the country that spread out by rail from this spot. The names of the towns and cities across Canada that were served by the country's two railway lines, Grand Trunk (incorporated into today's Canadian National) and Canadian Pacific, are inscribed on a frieze that runs along the inside of the hall. Train travel declined and the building came very near to being demolished in the 1970s, but public opposition eventually proved strong enough to save it, and Union Station is now a vital transport hub. Commuter, subway, and long-distance trains stop here. ✉ *65–75 Front St. W, between Bay and York Sts., Financial District* Ⓜ *Union.*

WORTH NOTING

8 Dominion Bank. Frank Darling, the designing architect here, was also responsible for the voluptuous Bank of Montréal branch at Yonge and Front streets. The 1913–14 Dominion Bank is a classic Chicago-style skyscraper that retains its original facade. The upper 46 stories have been turned into 550 luxury rental suites and commercial space. ⊠ *1–5 King St. W, at Yonge St., Financial District* Ⓜ *King.*

QUICK BITES

If you like to sit on a bench and watch the world go by, you won't find a better spot than nearby **King Street West.** Grab a hot dog or a veggie dog, take a seat, and watch theatergoers and maybe even actors walk by. Don't like hot dogs? Don't worry: Italian, Greek, French, and Canadian restaurants and bars can all be found next to the theaters for pre- and postshow bites.

7 First Canadian Place. The 72 stories of this 1970s building are faced with white marble to contrast with the black of the Toronto-Dominion Centre to the south and the nearby silver of I.M. Pei's Bank of Commerce tower. First Canadian Place is also known as the Bank of Montréal tower, but it's best known for being the home of the **Toronto Stock Exchange.** This tower was an early and successful real-estate project of the Reichman brothers, who later came to fiscal grief when their Canary Docks project in London, England, failed to capture the imagination—and rental contracts—of that city's financial community. ⊠ *100–130 King St. W, at Bay St., Financial District* ☎ *416/363–4669* Ⓜ *King.*

6 Flatiron Building. This three-sided building's cousins live in wedge-shape lots all over North America. Toronto's Flatiron, a redbrick building that occupies the triangular block between Wellington, Scott, and Front streets, was erected in 1892 as the head office of the Gooderham and Worts distilling company. On the back of the building, a witty trompe l'oeil mural by Derek Besant is drawn around the windows. The mural depicts even larger windows, which look like the windows on the south side of Front Street. The illusion? It appears that the whole thing has been tacked up on the wall and is peeling off. ⊠ *Front St. between Church and Scott Sts., Old Town* Ⓜ *King.*

17 Fort York. The most historic site in Toronto is a must for anyone interested in the origins of the city. The founding of Toronto occurred in 1793 when the British built Fort York to protect the entrance to the harbor during Anglo-American strife. Twenty years later the fort was the scene of the bloody Battle of York, in which explorer and general Zebulon Pike led U.S. forces against the fort's outnumbered British, Canadian, and First Nations defenders. The Americans won this battle—their first major victory in the War of 1812—and burned down the provincial buildings during a six-day occupation. A year later British forces retaliated when they captured Washington and torched its public buildings, including the Executive Mansion. Exhibits include restored barracks, kitchens, and gunpowder magazines, plus changing museum displays. ⊠ *100 Garrison Rd., between Bathurst St. and Strachan Ave., Harbourfront* ☎ *416/392–6907* ⊕ *www.toronto.ca/culture/fort_york.htm* 🎟 *C$8* ⊙ *May–Aug., daily 10–5; Sept.–Apr., weekdays 10–4, weekends 10–5* Ⓜ *Bathurst, then streetcar 511 south.*

FINANCIAL DISTRICT ARCHITECTURE WALK

From St. Andrew station, walk one short block east along King and past York Street, where you see the 72-storied, white marble **First Canadian Place** complex. This skyscraper has been the tallest office building in Canada since its construction in 1975. It houses the **Toronto Stock Exchange (TSX).** From here, proceed half a block east on Adelaide to Bay to the **Canada Permanent Trust Building,** built during the Roaring Twenties and designed in New York wedding-cake style. Look up at the ornate stone carvings that grace both the lower and top stories, where stylized faces peer down to the street below. A block south on Bay leads to the **Bank of Nova Scotia,** which has sculptural panels inspired by Greek mythology above its large windows. In the lobby, bas-reliefs symbolize four regions of Canada; look up to see a brightly colored gilt-plaster ceiling. Cross King and head east to Yonge, where you'll come across the **Dominion Bank,** a classic Chicago-style skyscraper that retains its original facade. At the northeast corner of the same intersection is the original **Royal Bank** building: note the distinctive cornice, the overhanging roof, the sculpted ox skulls above the ground-floor windows, and the classically detailed leaves at the top of the Corinthian columns. Now walk back west along King Street to Bay Street, and go a block south, past the **Design Exchange,** the wonderful art deco building that housed the old Toronto Stock Exchange. Continue south on Bay Street for less than a block to reach the modern **Royal Bank Building and Plaza—** impossible to miss for its glittering exterior coated with 2,500 ounces of gold. The surface creates gorgeous reflections of sky, clouds, and other buildings and is especially dramatic in full-force sunset; this is the jewel in the crown of the Toronto skyline.

⑭ **Harbourfront Centre.** Stretching from just west of York Street to Spadina Avenue, this culture-and-recreation center is a match for San Francisco's Pier 39 and Baltimore's Inner Harbor. The original Harbourfront opened in 1974, rejuvenating more than a mile of city. Today Harbourfront Centre, a streamlined version of the original concept, draws more than 3 million visitors to the 10-acre site each year. **Queen's Quay Terminal** (⊠ *207 Queen's Quay W* ☎ *416/203–0510* ⊕ *queensquay.sites.toronto.com*) at Harbourfront Centre is a former Terminal Warehouse building, where goods shipped to Toronto were stored before being delivered to shops in the city. In 1983 it was transformed into a magnificent, eight-story building with specialty shops, eateries, the 450-seat Premiere Dance Theatre—and harbor views. Exhibits of contemporary painting, sculpture, architecture, video, photography, and design are mounted at the **Power Plant** (⊠ *231 Queen's Quay W* ☎ *416/973–4949* ⊕ *www.thepowerplant.org* 🎟 *C$5* ⊙ *Tues. and Thurs.–Sun. noon–6, Wed. noon–8; tours Sun. at 2*). It can be spotted by its tall red smokestack. It was built in 1927 as a power station for the Terminal Warehouse's ice-making plant. Wednesday from 5 PM to 8 PM admission is free. Developed by renowned cellist Yo-Yo Ma and garden designer Julie Moir Messervy, the **Music Garden** on the south side of Queen's Quay was planned for Boston, but when that venue fell through, Toronto was the pair's next choice. The garden is Yo-Yo Ma's interpretation of J.S. Bach's *Cello Suite No. 1* (which consists of six movements—Prelude, Allemande, Courante, Sarabande, Minuet, and Gigue). Each movement is reflected in the park's elaborate design: undulating riverscape, a forest grove of wandering trails, a swirling path through a wildflower meadow, a conifer grove, a formal flower parterre, and giant grass steps. **York Quay Centre** (☒ *235 Queen's Quay W* ☎ *416/973–4000, 416/973–4866 rink info, 416/973–4963 craft studio*) hosts concerts, theater, readings, and even skilled artisans. The Craft Studio, for example, has professional craftspeople working in ceramics, glass, metal, and textiles from February to December (Tuesday through Sunday), in full view of the public. A shallow pond outside is used for canoe lessons in warmer months and as the largest artificial ice-skating rink in North America in more wintry times. At the nearby Nautical Centre, many private firms rent boats and give lessons in sailing and canoeing. Among the seasonal events in Harbourfront Centre are the Ice Canoe Race in late January, Winterfest in February, a jazz festival in June, Canada Day celebrations and the Parade of Lights in July, the Authors' Festival and Harvest Festival in October, and the Swedish Christmas Fair in November. ☒ *410 Queen's Quay W, Harbourfront* ☎ *416/973–4000 event hotline, 416/973–4600 offices* ⊕ *www.harbourfrontcentre.com* Ⓜ *Union, then streetcar 509 or 510 west.*

QUICK BITES There are plenty of places inside **Queen's Quay** for a quick sandwich, freshly squeezed juice, or ice-cream concoction. You can also check out one of the food trucks outside, selling french fries, with the peel still on, and salt and vinegar, if you like.

⑱ Ontario Place. The waterfront entertainment complex stretches along three man-made islands and includes Soak City, downtown Toronto's only water park; pedal boats at Bob's Boat Yard; Wilderness Adventure Ride; and Mars Simulator Ride. The **Cinesphere,** an enclosed dome with a six-story movie screen, uses the world's first IMAX projection system, a Canadian invention. The 16,000-seat outdoor **Molson Amphitheatre** stages performances by singers and rock groups throughout summer, and the **Atlantis Pavilions** is a 32,000-square-foot entertainment and dining facility. Live children's entertainment on two stages is included in the admission price to the park. *The Big Comfy Couch, Toopy and Binoo,* and other children's favorites are featured. ■TIP➔The Play All Day Pass allows unlimited use of most rides and attractions, including daytime Cinesphere IMAX and large-format films. Weekends in September bring several annual events to this venue: the Great White North Dragon Boat Challenge, the Toronto In-Water Boat Show, and the Fall Fishing Festival and Kids' Fishing Derby. ☒ *955 Lake Shore Blvd. W, across from Exhibition Place, Harbourfront* ☎ *866/663–4386 recording* ⊕ *www.ontarioplace.com* ☒ *Grounds C$17.75, pass C$33.50* ☉ *May, mid-Sept.–late Sept., weekends 10–6; June, weekdays 10–6, weekends 10–8; July–early Sept., daily 10–8* Ⓜ *Union, then streetcar 509 southwest.*

⑫ PATH. This subterranean universe emerged in the mid-1960s partly to replace the retail services in small buildings that were demolished to make way for the latest round of skyscrapers, and partly to protect office workers from the harsh winter weather. As each major building went up, its developers agreed to build and connect their underground shopping areas with others and with the subway system. You can walk from beneath Union Station to the Fairmont Royal York hotel, the Toronto-Dominion Centre, First Canadian Place, the Sheraton Centre, the Bay, Eaton Centre, and City Hall without ever seeing the light of day, encountering everything from art exhibitions to buskers (the best are the winners of citywide auditions, who are licensed to perform throughout the subway system) and walkways, fountains, and trees. There are underground passageways in other parts of the city—one beneath Bloor Street and another under College Street (both run from Yonge to Bay Street)—but this is the city's most extended subterranean network.

⑯ Rogers Centre. One of Toronto's most famous landmarks, the Rogers Centre is home to baseball's Blue Jays, and was the world's first stadium with a fully retractable roof. Rogers Communications, the owner of the Blue Jays, bought the stadium, formerly known as the SkyDome, in February 2005 for a mere C$25 million. A new playing surface and a state-of-the-art integrated scoring and display system were added that includes one main screen to replace the existing one, and two color screens display the action on either side of the outfield wall. One way to see the huge 52,000-seat stadium is to buy tickets for a Blue Jays or Argos game or one of the many other events that take place here. You might watch a cricket match, Wrestlemania, a monster-truck race, a family ice show, or a rock concert—even the large-scale opera *Aïda* has been performed here. You can also take a one-hour guided walking tour. Depending on several factors, you may find yourself in the middle of the field, in a press box, in the dressing rooms, or, if a roof tour is available, 36 stories above home plate on a catwalk. ⊠ *1 Blue Jays Way, tour entrance at Front and John Sts., between Gates 1 and 2, Harbourfront* ☎ *416/341–2770 for tours, 416/341–3663 for events and shows, 416/341–1234 or 888/654–6529 for Blue Jays information* ⊕ *www.rogerscentre.com* 🎫 *Tour C$13.75* ⊘ *Tours daily; times vary based on scheduled events* Ⓜ *Union.*

❷ St. James Cathedral. Even if bank towers dwarf it now, this Anglican church with noble Gothic spires has the tallest steeple in Canada. Its illuminated spire clock once guided ships into the harbor. This is the fourth St. James Cathedral on this site; the third burned down in the Great Fire of 1849. As part of the church's bicentennial in 1997, a new peal of bells was installed. Stand near the church most Sundays after the 9 AM service ends (about 10:10 AM) and be rewarded with a glorious concert of ringing bells. ⊠ *65 Church St., at King St., Old Town* ☎ *416/364–7865* ⊕ *www.stjamescathedral.on.ca* Ⓜ *King.*

❹ St. Lawrence Hall. Erected on the site of the area's first town hall, the St. Lawrence Hall, built in 1850–51, demonstrates Renaissance Revival architecture at its finest. Erected for musical performances and balls, it is here that Jenny Lind sang, where antislavery demonstrations were held, and where P.T. Barnum first presented the midget Tom Thumb. Take time to admire the exterior of this architectural gem, now used for everything from concerts to wedding receptions and graduation parties. ✉ *157 King St. E, Old Town* ☎ *416/392–7130* Ⓜ *Union.*

❸ **Toronto's First Post Office.** Dating from 1833, this working post office ⏱ continues to use quill pens, ink pots, and sealing wax. Exhibits include reproductions of letters from the 1820s and 1830s. Distinctive cancellation stamps are used on all outgoing cards and letters. ✉ *260 Adelaide St. E, Old Town* ☎ *416/865–1833* ⊕ *www.townofyork.com* ✉ *Free* ⊘ *Weekdays 9–4, weekends 10–4* Ⓜ *King.*

CHINATOWN, KENSINGTON MARKET, AND QUEEN WEST

The areas along Dundas and Queen streets typify Toronto's ethnic makeup and vibrant youthfulness. To many locals, the Dundas and Spadina intersection means Chinatown and Kensington Market, while Queen West, which was the home of '90s comedy troupe Kids in the Hall and pop-rockers Barenaked Ladies, has always been a haven for shoppers and trendsetters. On the western fringe, the rejuvenated West Queen West neighborhood is quickly becoming Toronto's newest hot spot.

Numbers in the margin correspond to points of interest on the Chinatown, Kensington Market, and Queen West map.

TIMING   In Queen West, the Campbell House merits at least a half hour; the Art Gallery an hour or more. Chinatown is at its busiest (and most fun) on Sunday, but be prepared for very crowded sidewalks and much jostling. Kensington is great any time, although it can feel a bit sketchy at night, and it gets mobbed on weekend afternoons. Just strolling around any of these neighborhoods can gobble up an entire afternoon.

TOP ATTRACTIONS

❷ **Art Gallery of Ontario.** From extremely modest beginnings in 1900, the AGO is now in the big leagues in terms of its exhibitions of landscape paintings throughout the 19th and 20th centuries. In November 2008, a transformed AGO opened to the public with a major expansion designed by world-renowned architect and Toronto native son Frank Gehry. The AGO is now hard to miss, its monumental glass and titanium facade hovering over the main building is a stunning beauty.

Fodor'sChoice ★

The Canadian Wing includes major works by such northern lights as Emily Carr, Cornelius Krieghoff, David Milne, and Homer Watson, plus the Thomson Collection with pieces by Paul Kane, Tom Thomson, and Lawren Harris. The AGO also has a growing collection of

SIGHTS AND SMELLS

From either College or Queen's Park station, take the streetcar west to **Augusta**. Meander south, taking in the scents of earthy vegetable stalls and mouthwatering burrito dives. At Baldwin, head east a block to the core of **Kensington Market**, where Victorian-era storefronts are flanked by vintage clothing racks. Taking a left at Dundas leads you to the chaotic Spadina–Dundas intersection, the center of Toronto's main **Chinatown**. Wander north along Spadina for deals on kitschy Chinese trinkets, or follow Dundas east for the heady odors of medicinal herbs.

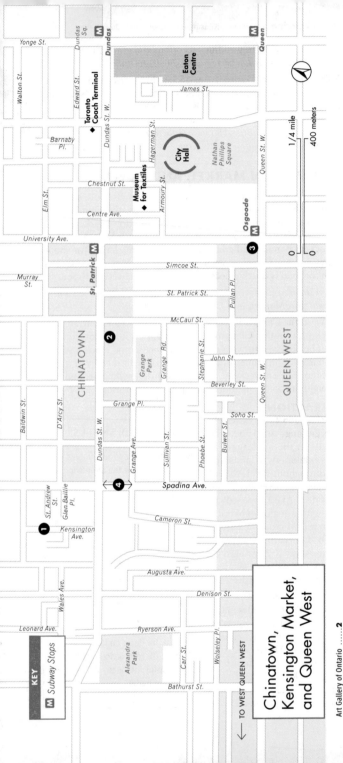

Chinatown,
Kensington Market,
and Queen West

KEY
M Subway Stops

TO WEST QUEEN WEST

CHINATOWN

QUEEN WEST

City Hall

Nathan Phillips Square

Eaton Centre

Toronto Coach Terminal

◆ Museum for Textiles

Grange Park

Alexandra Park

1/4 mile
400 meters

M Subway stops — St. Patrick, Osgoode, Dundas, Queen

Yonge St.
Walton St.
Dundas Sq.
Dundas
Edward St.
Barnaby Pl.
Elm St.
Chestnut St.
Centre Ave.
University Ave.
Murray St.
Dundas St. W.
Hagerman St.
Armoury St.
James St.
Queen St. W.
Simcoe St.
St. Patrick St.
McCaul St.
Grange Rd.
Stephanie St.
John St.
Beverley St.
Soho St.
Bulwer St.
Phoebe St.
Sullivan St.
Grange Ave.
Grange Pl.
Pullan Pl.
Queen St. W.
Baldwin St.
D'Arcy St.
St. Andrew St.
Glen Baillie Pl.
Kensington Ave.
Cameron St.
Augusta Ave.
Denison St.
Wales Ave.
Leonard Ave.
Ryerson Ave.
Carr St.
Wolseley Pl.
Bathurst St.
Spadina Ave.

works by such world-famous artists as Rembrandt, Hals, Van Dyck, Hogarth, Reynolds, Chardin, Renoir, de Kooning, Rothko, Oldenburg, Picasso, Rodin, Degas, Matisse, and many others. A rediscovered early-17th-century piece by Flemish painter Peter Paul Rubens, *Massacre of the Innocents*, was unveiled in 2008. On Sunday, the Anne Tannenbaum Gallery School explores painting, printmaking, and sculpting in Toronto's most spectacular studio space. Visitors of all ages enjoy climbing in and around Henry Moore's large *Two Forms* sculpture, which is just outside the AGO, on McCaul Street. ✉ *317 Dundas St. W, at McCaul St., Chinatown* ☎ *416/979–6648* ⊕ *www.ago.net* ✉ *C$18; free on Wed. after 6* PM ⊙ *Tues., Thurs.–Sun. 10–5:30, Wed. 10–8:30* Ⓜ *St. Patrick.*

Chinatown. Compact and condensed, Toronto's Chinatown—which is actually the main or original Chinatown in the city, as five other areas with large Chinese commercial districts have sprung up elsewhere in metropolitan Toronto—covers much of the area of Spadina Avenue from Queen Street to College Street, running along Dundas Street nearly as far east as Bay Street. The population is more than 100,000, which is especially impressive when you consider that just over a century ago there was only a single Chinese resident, Sam Ching, who ran a hand laundry on Adelaide Street.

Especially jumbled at its epicenter, the Spadina-Dundas intersection, Chinatown's rickety storefronts selling (real and fake) jade trees, lovely sake sets, Chinese herbs, and fresh fish are packed every day of the week. On Sunday, Chinese music blasts from storefronts, cash registers ring, and bakeries, markets, herbalists, and restaurants do their best business of the week. ✉ *Spadina Ave., at Dundas St. W, Chinatown* ⊕ *www.chinatownbia. com* Ⓜ *St. Patrick, then streetcar 505 west.*

QUICK BITES

Queen Street West is lined with cafés and restaurants. Consider the **Queen Mother Café** (✉ **208 Queen St. W, at St. Patrick St., Queen West** ☎ **416/598–4719** Ⓜ **Osgoode**), a neighborhood institution popular with art students and broadcast-media types. Serving Lao-Thai and Italian cuisine, the "Queen Mum" is open until 1 AM (Sunday until 11 PM) for wholesome meals and fabulous desserts at reasonable prices.

❶ **Kensington Market.** This raucous, European-style marketplace titillates all the senses. On any given day you can find Russian rye breads, barrels of dill pickles, fresh fish on ice, mountains of cheese, and bushels of ripe fruit. Kensington's collection of vintage-clothing stores is the best in the city.

Kensington Market sprang up in the early 1900s, when Russian, Polish, and Jewish inhabitants set up stalls in front of their houses. Since then the market—named after the area's major street—has become a sort of United Nations of stores. Unlike the members of the UN, however, these vendors get along well with one another. Jewish and Eastern European shops sit side by side with Portuguese, Caribbean, and East Indian ones, as well as with a sprinkling of Vietnamese and Chinese establishments. ■ TIP➔ Saturday is the best day to visit, preferably by public transit; parking is difficult. Note that many stores are closed on Sunday. ✉ *Bordered by College St. on the north, Spadina Ave. on the east, Dundas St. on*

NEIGHBORHOOD WATCH: W. QUEEN WEST

Grunge meets chic along Queen Street west of Bathurst, confusingly called "West Queen West" by locals. While it's still possible to find a run-down hardware store shouldering a high-end martini bar, more of the latter are making their debuts these days. Almost completely devoid of the familiar chains that plague older sister Queen West, this more westerly 'hood is instead filling with vegan spa resorts, trendy ethnic restaurants, and European kitchenware shops; much farther west, a bustling art scene is blossoming.

Although fairly new, the neighborhood already has some landmarks. The Drake Hotel and the Gladstone, both hip boutique hotels, enjoy much success both for their creative, eclectic decor and for their happening night scene. Businesses like these could be responsible for revolutionizing the once shabby district, or at least helping to enhance the über-cool image it wears nowadays.

Boundaries: From Bathurst westward along Queen Street West.

Getting Here: Take the subway to Queen or Osgoode TTC stop, then the streetcar 501 west.

the south, and Bellevue Ave. on the west, Kensington Market ⊙ *Daily dawn–dusk* Ⓜ *St. Patrick, then streetcar west.*

QUICK BITES   In a neighborhood where the bohemian vegetarian lifestyle is the norm, **King's Café** (✉ *192 Augusta Ave., Kensington Market* ☎ *416/591–1340* Ⓜ *St. Patrick, then streetcar 505 west*) has become a mainstay with locals and others seeking healthy grub with an Asian accent. Artsy types, chatty students, and young professionals flock to this serene and airy interior with wide front windows overlooking bustling Augusta Avenue. Specialties include enoki mushrooms in seaweed and spinach, and King's Special Vegetable Soup— a hearty broth with homemade veggie nuggets, taro, and fried tofu.

WORTH NOTING

❸ **Campbell House.** The stately Georgian mansion of Sir William Campbell, the sixth chief justice of Upper Canada, is now one of Toronto's best house museums. Built in 1822 in another part of town, the Campbell House was moved to this site in 1972. It has been tastefully restored with elegant early-19th-century furniture. Costumed guides detail the social life of the upper class. Note the model of the town of York as it was in the 1820s, and the original kitchen. ✉ *160 Queen St. W, Queen West* ☎ *416/597–0227* ⊕ *www.campbellhousemuseum.ca* ✉ *C$6* ⊙ *Oct.–mid-May, Tues–Fri., 9:30–4:30; mid-May–Sept., Tues–Fri., 9:30–4:30, weekends noon–4* Ⓜ *Osgoode.*

❹ **Spadina Avenue.** Spadina (pronounced "Spa-*dye*-nah"), running from the lakeshore north to College Street, has never been chic. For decades it has housed a collection of inexpensive stores, factories that sell wholesale if you have connections, ethnic food stores, and eateries, including some first-class, if modest-looking, Chinese restaurants. Each new wave of immigrants—Jewish, Chinese, Portuguese, East and West Indian, South

American—has added its own flavor to the mix, but Spadina-Kensington's basic bill of fare is still bargains galore. Here you can find discounts of up to half the prices of Yorkville stores, yards of remnants piled high in bins, designer clothes minus the labels, and the occasional rock-and-roll nightspot and interesting greasy spoon. A streetcar line runs down the wide avenue to Front Street.

> **WORD OF MOUTH**
>
> "When we reached Spadina and the uniquely Toronto sight of the red streetcars criss-crossing in all directions adjacent the hustle and bustle of Chinatown that my friend said, 'Now this area I like! I feel like I'm somewhere that says "Toronto" now!'" —Daniel_Williams

The history behind Spadina Avenue's width—it is 132 feet wide, double the width of almost every other old street in town—goes back to 1802, when a 27-year-old Irish physician named William Warren Baldwin came to muddy York. He married a rich young woman, built a pleasant home where Casa Loma and Spadina House now sit, and decided to cut a giant swath through the forest from Bloor Street down to Queen Street so they could look down, literally and socially, on Lake Ontario. Alas, their view disappeared in 1874, when a thankless granddaughter sold the land at the crescent just above College Street for the site of Knox College. The college vacated the building several decades later and moved to the University of Toronto campus. Now covered with vines, the Victorian building still sits in the crescent, a number of the chestnut trees planted by Dr. Baldwin remaining on the west side. Little else remains of Dr. Baldwin's Spadina, except for a handful of Victorian mansions.

OFF THE BEATEN PATH

The Beach. Queen Street West represents the city's mainstream trends, but the Beach neighborhood, 15 minutes east of the Queen subway stop, via streetcar 501 on Queen Street, is old-school bohemian. This area of pricey real estate is bordered by Neville Park Road to the east and Woodbine Avenue to the west, although the border is being pushed farther west every year by the addition of huge high-income housing developments. The main strip, Queen Street East has a funky flair *and* a small-town feel, and it's easy to spend an afternoon strolling the delightful yet crowded (in summer) boardwalk along the shore of Lake Ontario. Musicians often perform at the several public parks fronting the boardwalk, where you're also likely to see artists selling their wares. You could also do some leisurely window-shopping on Queen Street East, which is lined with antiques stores and specialty boutiques and shops. An annual international jazz

> **"THE BEACH" OR "BEACHES"**
>
> This neighborhood's official name has been a source of controversy since the 1980s. It boils down to whether you view the four separate beaches—Woodbine, Balmy, Kew, and Scarboro—as one collective entity or in the plural. When the area decided to welcome tourists with fancy, emblematic street signs, the long-running, deep-seated debate surfaced. "The Beach" folks won, but not before the dispute was settled fairly with a democratic vote in spring 2006.

festival in July attracts more than 400 musicians and thousands of listeners to this laid-back community.

One of the more unusual neighborhood stores is the **Three Dog Bakery** (⊠ 2014 Queen St. E, The Beach ☎ 416/693–3364), a bakery for dogs. For something to drink in the Beach, you can stop at one of several Irish pubs, such as **Murphy's Law** (⊠ 1702 Queen St. E, The Beach ☎ 416/690–5516). **Licks** (⊠ 1962 Queen St. E, The Beach ☎ 416/362–5425) is a neighborhood restaurant for great burgers and ice cream.

QUEEN'S PARK, THE ANNEX, AND YORKVILLE

Bounded by College Street to the south, Bay Street to the east, Dupont Street to the north, and Bathurst Avenue to the west, this area brings together Toronto's upper crust, Ontario's provincial politicians, and Canada's intellectual set.

The large, oval Queen's Park circles the Ontario Provincial Legislature and is straddled by the sprawling, 160-acre downtown campus of the University of Toronto. Wandering this neighborhood will take you past century-old colleges, Gothic cathedrals, and plenty of quiet benches overlooking leafy courtyards and student-filled parks.

The University of Toronto's campus overflows westward into the Annex, where students and scholarly types while away the hours after class. This frantic section of Bloor Street West abounds with ethnic restaurants and plenty of student-friendly cafés and bars, plus two of the cities must-see attractions: the Bata Shoe Museum and Casa Loma.

At the eastern end of the Annex, near St. George Street, Bloor Street West morphs into Yorkville, an affluent neighborhood characterized by the domineering Royal Ontario Museum at its northern tip. Big-name boutiques and elegant cafés are tucked into the small Victorian houses that line the small, tidy back streets to the north—Yorkville Avenue and Cumberland Street.

Numbers in the margin correspond to points of interest on the Queen's Park, the Annex, and Yorkville map.

TIMING   The Queen's Park, Annex, and Yorkville area is a nice place to take a stroll any time of year because many of the attractions bring you indoors. A visit to the legislature and one or two of the museums or libraries would make a nice half-day (or more) program; allot at least one hour each for the Royal Ontario and Gardiner museums. Give yourself at least a few hours for a full tour of Casa Loma and about an hour for Bata Shoe Museum.

TOP ATTRACTIONS

❶ **Bata Shoe Museum.** Created by Sonja Bata, wife of the founder of the Bata
★ Shoe Company, the permanent collection contains 10,000 varieties of foot coverings and, through the changing fashions, highlights the craft and sociology of making shoes. Some items date back more than 4,000 years. Pressurized sky-diving boots, iron-spiked shoes used for crushing chestnuts, and smugglers' clogs are among the items on display. Elton John's boots have proved wildly popular, but Marilyn Monroe's red leather pumps give them a run for the money. Ongoing exhibits such as

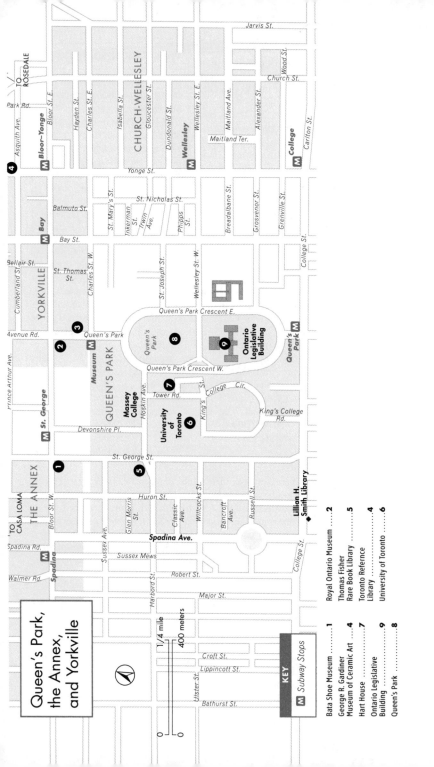

Queen's Park, the Annex, and Yorkville

THE ANNEX

YORKVILLE

CHURCH-WELLESLEY

QUEEN'S PARK

University of Toronto

Massey College

Queen's Park

Ontario Legislative Building

King's College Rd.

TO ROSEDALE

TO CASA LOMA

Jarvis St.
Wood St.
Church St.
Park Rd.
Bloor St. E.
Hayden St.
Charles St. E.
Isabella St.
Gloucester St.
Dundonald St.
Wellesley St. E.
Maitland Ave.
Alexander St.
Maitland Ter.
Breadalbane St.
Grosvenor St.
Grenville St.
Carlton St.
College St.
Yonge St.
Balmuto St.
St. Mary's St.
St. Nicholas St.
Inkerman St.
Irwin Ave.
Phipps St.
Bellair St.
Cumberland St.
St. Thomas St.
Charles St. W.
St. Joseph St.
Wellesley St. W.
Avenue Rd.
Queen's Park
Queen's Park Crescent E.
Queen's Park Crescent W.
Prince Arthur Ave.
Hoskin Ave.
Tower Rd.
College Cir.
King's College Rd.
Devonshire Pl.
St. George St.
Huron St.
Glen Morris St.
Classic Ave.
Willcocks St.
Bancroft Ave.
Russell St.
Bloor St. W.
Spadina Rd.
Walmer Rd.
Sussex Ave.
Sussex Mews
Harbord St.
Robert St.
Major St.
Croft St.
Lippincott St.
Ulster St.
Bathurst St.
Spadina Ave.
College St.

Asquith Ave.

Lillian H. Smith Library

M Bloor-Yonge
M Bay
M Museum
M St. George
M Spadina
M College
M Wellesley
M Queen's Park

1/4 mile
400 meters
0

KEY

M Subway Stops

Bata Shoe Museum 1
George R. Gardiner
Museum of Ceramic Art ...4
Hart House 7
Ontario Legislative
Building 9
Queen's Park 8

Royal Ontario Museum 2
Thomas Fisher
Rare Book Library 5
Toronto Refernce
Library 4
University of Toronto 6

"Chronicles of the Riches" featured the bear-fur shoes of Japanese *samurai* and Napoléon's black silk socks. Admission is free every Thursday from 5 to 8 PM. ✉ *327 Bloor St. W, at St. George St., The Annex* ☎ *416/979–7799* ⊕ *www.batashoemuseum.ca* ✆ *C$12* ⊗ *Tues., Wed., Fri., and Sat. 10–5, Thurs. 10–8, Sun. noon–5* Ⓜ *St. George.*

🕐 **Casa Loma.** A European-style castle, Casa Loma was commissioned by Sir Henry Pellatt, a soldier and financier. This grand display of extravagance has 98 rooms, two

towers, creepy passageways, and lots of secret panels. The home's architect, E.J. Lennox, also designed Toronto's Old City Hall and the King Edward Hotel. Pellatt spent more than C$3 million to construct his dream (that's in 1913 dollars), only to lose it to the tax man just over a decade later. Some impressive details are the giant pipe organ; the reproduction of Windsor Castle's Peacock Alley; the majestic, 60-foot-high ceiling of the Great Hall; the mahogany-and-marble stable, reached by a long, underground passage; and the extensive, 5-acre estate gardens (open May–October). The rooms are copies of those in English, Spanish, Scottish, and Austrian castles. This has been the location for many a horror movie and period drama—and for an episode of the BBC's *Antiques Roadshow*. Self-guided audio tours are available in eight languages for C$2. The admission price includes a docudrama about Pellatt's life. ■TIP➡ **A tour of Casa Loma is a good 1½-km (1-mi) walk, so wear sensible shoes.** ✉ *1 Austin Terr., The Annex* ☎ *416/923–1171* ⊕ *www.casaloma.org* ✆ *C$17* ⊗ *Daily 9:30–5, last admission at 4* Ⓜ *Dupont.*

❼ **Hart House.** A neo-Gothic student center built in 1911–19, Hart House represents the single largest gift to the University of Toronto. Vincent Massey, a student here at the turn of the 20th century, regretted the absence of a meeting place and gym for students and convinced his father to build one. It was named for Vincent's grandfather, Hart, the founder of Massey-Ferguson, once the world's leading supplier of farm equipment. Originally restricted to male students, Hart House has been open to women since 1972.

Keep your eyes peeled for artwork scattered throughout the building, including evocative pieces by the Group of Seven landscape painters, and a revolving collection of famed Canadians like Emily Carr. The **Justina Barnicke Gallery** (☎ *416/978–8398* ⊗ *Mon.–Wed. 11–5, Thurs. and Fri. 11–7, weekends 1–5*) comprises two rooms of mixed-media art showcasing homegrown talent. The stained-glass windows and vaulted ceiling in the Great Hall of Hart House are impressive, but so is chef Suzanne Baby's cuisine at the resident **Gallery Grill** (☎ *416/978–2445* ⊗ *Sept.–June, weekdays 11:30–2:30, Sun. 11–2*). Try one of the grilled fish dishes, a juicy steak, or a creative vegetarian torte while enjoying the elegant surroundings. ✉ *U of T, 7 Hart House Circle, Queen's Park* ☏ *416/978–2452* ⊕ *www.harthouse.utoronto.ca* Ⓜ *Museum.*

❷ **Royal Ontario Museum.** Since its inception in 1912, the ROM, Canada's largest museum, has amassed more than 6 million items. What makes the ROM unique is that science, art, and archaeology exhibits are

> **WORD OF MOUTH**
>
> "For another take on the 'village in the city', try The Annex. Walk straight along Bloor from St. George and Bloor along as far as Bathurst. Then meander the side streets to your heart's content to see some marvelous old mansions." —LJ

all appealingly presented in one gigantic complex. A C$200 million refurbishment project, envisioned by world-renowned architect Daniel Libeskind (the designer of the Jewish Museum in Berlin) added 40,000 square feet and the ultramodern **Michael Lee-Chin Crystal** gallery in 2009—a series of interlocking prismatic cubes spilling out onto Bloor Street.

Highlights include the Learning Centre—a state-of-the-art educational facility for the 220,000 schoolchildren expected annually—and the **Crystal Court,** a four-storied atrium slashed on all sides by sliver-thin windows through which shards of light pour into the open space. A look through the windows reveals parts of the treasures inside, such as the frightful creatures from the **Age of Dinosaurs** exhibit standing guard. The **Institute for Contemporary Culture** hangs 110 feet over Bloor Street from its fourth floor perch. The Crystal Five Bistro or "C5" for short on the fifth floor feels a bit like the Ten-Forward lounge on Star Trek's Enterprise, and after sampling a selection of perfectly presented tapas and the region's finest wines, you may wonder if they're hiding a food "replicator" in the kitchen.

The **Herman Herzog Levy Gallery** exhibits a stunning range of large and colorful textiles, paintings, and prints from the museum's acclaimed Asian collection; the **Chinese Sculpture Gallery** in the Matthews Family Court displays 25 stone Buddhist sculptures dating from the 2nd through 16th centuries; and the **Gallery of Korean Art** is North America's largest permanent gallery devoted to Korean art and culture. The **Patricia Harris Gallery of Textiles and Costume** houses a selection of Chinese imperial court garments, early Canadian quilts, and a survey of European fashions from the 18th century to present. ■TIP→ **Admission is free after 4:30 on Wednesday and reduced to C$11 on Friday after 4:30.** ✉ *100 Queen's Park, Yorkville* ☏ *416/586–5549* ⊕ *www.rom.on.ca* ✆ *C$22* ☉ *Mon.–Thurs. and weekends 10–5:30, Fri. 10–9:30* Ⓜ *Museum.*

The Annex. Born in 1887, when the burgeoning town of Toronto engulfed the area between Bathurst Street and Avenue Road north from Bloor Street to the Canadian Pacific Railway tracks at what is now Dupont Street, the countrified Annex soon became an enclave for the well-to-do; today it attracts an intellectual set. Timothy Eaton of department-store fame built a handsome structure at 182 Lowther Avenue (since demolished). The prominent Gooderham family, owners of a distillery, erected a lovely red castle at the corner of St. George Street and Bloor Street, now the home of the exclusive York Club.

As Queen Victoria gave way to King Edward, the old money gave way to the new money and ethnic groups came and went. Upon the arrival of developers—many Edwardian mansions were demolished to make room for bland 1960s-era apartment buildings.

Still, the Annex, with its hundreds of attractive old homes, can be cited as a prime example of Toronto's success in preserving lovely, safe streets within the downtown area. Examples of late-19th-century architecture can be spotted on Admiral Road, Lowther Avenue, and Bloor Street, west of Spadina Avenue. Round turrets, pyramid-shape roofs, and conical (some even comical) spires are among the pleasures shared by some 20,000 Torontonians who live in this vibrant community, including professors, students, writers, lawyers, and other professional and artsy types. Bloor Street between Spadina and Palmerston keeps them fed and entertained with its bohemian collection of used-record stores, whole-foods shops and juice bars, and restaurants from elegant Italian to hearty Polish and aromatic Indian. ⊠ *From Bathurst St. to Huron St. along Bloor St. W, The Annex* Ⓜ *St. George, Spadina.*

❻ **University of Toronto.** Almost a city unto itself, U of T has a staff and student population of around 60,000. The institution dates to 1827, when King George IV signed a charter for a "King's College in the Town of York, Capital of Upper Canada." The Church of England had control then, but by 1850 the college was proclaimed nondenominational, renamed the University of Toronto, and put under the control of the province. Then, in a spirit of Christian competition, the Anglicans started Trinity College, the Methodists began Victoria, and the Roman Catholics begat St. Michael's; by the time the Presbyterians founded Knox College, the whole thing was a bit out of hand. Now the 10 schools and faculties are united, and they welcome anyone who can meet the admission standards and afford the tuition, which, thanks to government funding, is reasonable. The architecture is interesting, if uneven, as one might expect on a campus that's been built in bits and pieces over 150 years. From June to August there are historical campus walks in addition to general, daily tours. Walking tours leave from the Nona Macdonald Visitors Centre. ⊠ *Visitors Centre, 25 King's College Circle, Queen's Park* ☎ *416/978–5000* ⊕ *www.utoronto.ca* ▨ *Tours free* ☉ *Walking tours weekdays at 11 and 2, weekends at 11; historical tours June–Aug., weekdays 10:30, 1, and 2:30* Ⓜ *St. George, Queen's Park.*

Yorkville. Toronto's equivalent to Rodeo Drive or Madison Avenue is packed with restaurants, galleries, specialty shops, and high-price stores stocked with designer clothes, furs, and jewels. It's also the neighborhood where much of the excitement takes place in September during the annual Toronto International Film Festival. This is said by many to be the world's largest and most people-friendly film festival, where the public actually gets to see premieres and hidden gems and attend industry seminars. Klieg lights shine over skyscrapers, bistros serve alcohol until 2 AM, cafés teem with the well-heeled, and everyone practices air kisses. Yorkville is also home to a unique park on Cumberland Street, designed as a series of gardens along old property lines and reflecting both the history of the Village of Yorkville and the diversity of the Canadian landscape. *From Avenue Rd. to Yonge St., north of and including Bloor St. W* Ⓜ *Bay.*

WORTH NOTING

❹ **George R. Gardiner Museum of Ceramic Art.** This collection of rare ceramics includes 17th-century English delftware and 18th-century yellow European porcelain; its pre-Columbian collection dates to Olmec and Maya times. Other galleries feature Japanese *Kakiemon*-style pottery and Chinese white-and-blue porcelain. Free guided tours take place at 2 on Tuesday, Thursday, and Sunday. ■ TIP→ **Admission is free on Friday after 4.** ✉ *111 Queen's Park Crescent, Yorkville* ☎ *416/586–8080* ⊕ *www.gardinermuseum.on.ca* 🎟 *C$12* ☉ *Mon.–Thurs. 10–6, Fri. 10–9, weekends 10–5* Ⓜ *Museum.*

> ## A STROLL THROUGH PARADISE
>
> The posh residential neighborhood north of Yorkville has charming curving roads (it's one of the few neighborhoods to have escaped the city's grid pattern), many small parks, and a jumble of oversized late-19th-century and early-20th-century houses in Edwardian, Victorian, Georgian, and Tudor styles. In the 1920s, Sheriff William Jarvis and his wife, Mary, settled here on a 200-acre estate. The neighborhood is still the home of old and new wealth and many who wield power. It makes a pleasant escape from the congestion downtown. Bounded by Yonge Street, Don Valley Parkway., St. Clair Avenue, and Rosedale Ravine.

❾ **Ontario Legislative Building.** Like City Hall, the home to the provincial parliament was the product of an international contest among architects, in this case won by a young Briton residing in Buffalo, New York. The 1893 Romanesque Revival building, made of pink Ontario sandstone, has a wealth of exterior detail; inside, the huge, lovely halls echo half a millennium of English architecture. The long hallways are hung with hundreds of oils by Canadian artists, most of which capture scenes of the province's natural beauty. Take one of the frequent tours to see the chamber where the 130 MPPs (members of Provincial Parliament) meet. The two heritage rooms—one each for the parliamentary histories of Britain and Ontario—are filled with old newspapers, periodicals, and pictures. The many statues dotting the lawn in front of the building, facing College Street, include one of Queen Victoria and one of Canada's first prime minister, Sir John A. Macdonald. The lawn is also the site of Canada Day celebrations and the occasional political protest. These buildings are often referred to simply as Queen's Park, after the park surrounding them. ✉ *1 Queen's Park, Queen's Park* ☎ *416/325–7500* 🎟 *Free* ☉ *Guided tour mid-May–mid-Sept., daily 9–4; mid-Sept.–mid-May, weekdays 10–4* Ⓜ *Queen's Park.*

❽ **Queen's Park.** Many visitors consider this to be the intellectual hub of Toronto. Surrounding the large oval-shape patch of land are medical facilities to the south, the University of Toronto to the west and east, and the Royal Ontario Museum to the north. To most locals, Queen's

NEIGHBORHOOD WATCH: LITTLE ITALY

Once a quiet strip of College Street with just a few unfrequented clothing shops and the odd, obstinate pizzeria, Little Italy has become one of the hippest haunts in Toronto. This is the southern edge of the city's Italian community, and though not much remains of this heritage—most Italians now live in the suburbs and throughout the city—the flavor lingers on many a table and a few food markets.

Whether you're in the mood for old-world Italian fare, old school (think checkered table cloths), or polished martini bars, Little Italy won't disappoint. Pasta and pizza are not the only things on the menus here—new ethnic restaurants open monthly, and every corner holds fashionable cafés and diners to match.

Surprisingly, this edge of downtown has a nightlife that rivals the clubs and bars of the Entertainment District (around Adelaide Street West). Bars and coffeehouses are packed into the night, and summer months bring out booming cruise-mobiles, patio revelers, and plenty of pedestrian animation.

Boundaries: College Street, west of Bathurst Street, between Euclid Avenue and Shaw Street.

Getting Here: From Queen's Park subway station, take streetcar 506 west.

Park is chiefly synonymous with politics, as the Ontario Legislative Building sits in its center. ⊠ *Queen's Park Circle between College St. and Bloor St. W, Queen's Park* Ⓜ *Museum.*

❺ **Thomas Fisher Rare Book Library.** Early writing artifacts such as a Babylonian cuneiform tablet, a 2,000-year-old Egyptian papyrus, and books dating to the beginning of European printing in the 15th century are shown here in rotating exhibits, which change three times annually. Subjects of these shows might include Shakespeare, Galileo, Italian opera, or contemporary typesetting. ⊠ *U of T, 120 St. George St., Queen's Park* ☎ *416/978–5285* 🖷 *416/978–1667* ⊕ *www.library.utoronto.ca/fisher* 🖾 *Free* ☉ *Weekdays 9–4:45* Ⓜ *St. George.*

❹ **Toronto Reference Library.** Designed by one of Canada's most admired architects, Raymond Moriyama, who also created the Ontario Science Centre, this five-story library is arranged around a large atrium, affording a wonderful sense of open space. There is a small waterfall in the foyer, and glass-enclosed elevators glide swiftly and silently up and down. One-third of the more than 4 million items—spread across 45 km (28 mi) of shelves—are open to the public. Audio carrels are available for listening to your choice among the nearly 30,000 music and spoken-word recordings. The largest Performing Arts Centre in a public library in Canada is on the fifth floor, as is the **Arthur Conan Doyle Room** (☉ *Tues., Thurs., and Sat. 2–4, and by appointment*), which is of special interest to Baker Street regulars. It houses the world's finest public collection of Holmesiana, including records, films, photos, books, manuscripts, letters, and even cartoon books starring Sherlock Hemlock of *Sesame Street.* ⊠ *789 Yonge St., Yorkville* ☎ *416/395–5577* ⊕ *www.*

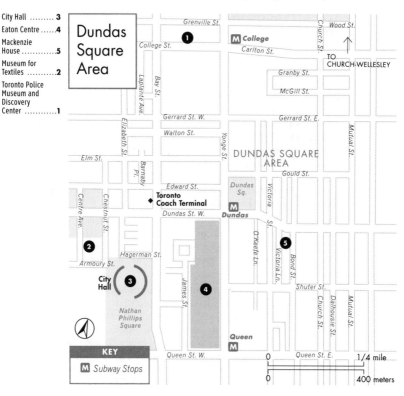

torontopubliclibrary.ca ☉ *Mon.–Thurs. 9:30–8:30, Fri. 9:30–5:30, Sat.
9–5, Sun. 1:30–5 (Sept.–June only)* Ⓜ *Bloor-Yonge.*

DUNDAS SQUARE AREA

Yonge Street is the central vein of Toronto, starting at Lake Ontario
and slicing the city in half as it travels through Dundas Square, and
then northbound to the suburbs. Tourists gather below the bright billboards and flashy lights in Dundas Square, especially in the summertime, when the large public area comes alive with outdoor festivals
and entertainment. The few sights in this neighborhood, namely the
Eaton Centre and Nathan Phillips Square, get a lot of attention from
both locals and visitors.

*Numbers in the margin correspond to points of interest on the Dundas
Square Area map.*

TIMING   Depending on your patience and the contents of your wallet, you could
spend anywhere from one to 10 hours in the colossal Eaton Centre,
literally shopping until you drop. The MacKenzie House, Museum for
Textiles, and Toronto Police Museum merit an hour each; and you could
easily while away an afternoon people-watching in Dundas Square or
Nathan Phillips Square.

TOP ATTRACTIONS

❸ City Hall. Toronto's modern city hall was the outgrowth of a 1958 international competition to which some 520 architects from 42 countries submitted designs. The winning presentation by Finnish architect Viljo Revell was controversial—two curved towers of differing height. But there is a logic to it all—an aerial view of City Hall shows a circular council chamber sitting like an eye between the two tower "eyelids" containing offices of 44 municipal wards, with 44 city councillors. A remarkable mural within the main entrance, *Metropolis*, was constructed by sculptor David Partridge from 100,000 common nails. Revell died before his masterwork was opened in 1965, but within months City Hall became a symbol of a thriving metropolis, with a silhouette as recognizable in its own way as the Eiffel Tower. The positive influence that the development of this building has had on Toronto's civic life is detailed in Robert Fulford's book *Accidental City.*

Annual events at City Hall include the Spring Flower Show in late March; the Toronto Outdoor Art Exhibition in early July; and the yearly Cavalcade of Lights from late November through Christmas, when more than 100,000 sparkling lights are illuminated across both new and old city halls.

In front of City Hall, 9-acre **Nathan Phillips Square** (named after the mayor who initiated the City Hall project) has become a gathering place, whether for royal visits, protest rallies, picnic lunches, or concerts. The reflecting pool is a delight in summer, and even more so in winter, when office workers skate at lunchtime. The park also holds a Peace Garden for quiet meditation and Henry Moore's striking bronze sculpture *The Archer.* ⊠ *100 Queen St. W, at Bay St., Dundas Square Area* ☎ *416/338–0338, 416/338–0889 TDD* ⊕ *www.toronto.ca* ⊙ *Weekdays 8:30–4:30* Ⓜ *Queen.*

Dundas Square. A public square surrounded by oversize billboards and explosive light displays, Toronto's answer to New York's Times Square is well on its way to becoming one of the fastest-growing tourist destinations in the city. Visitors and locals converge on the tables and chairs that are scattered across the square when the weather is fine; while kids (and the young at heart) frolic in one of the 20 water fountains that shoot out of the cement floor like miniature geysers. From May to October, there's something happening every weekend—it could be an artisan market, an open-air film viewing, a summertime festival, or a live musical performance. ⊠ *Yonge St., at Dundas St., Dundas Square Area* ⊕ *www.ydsquare.ca* Ⓜ *Dundas.*

❹ Eaton Centre. The 3-million-square-foot Eaton Centre shopping mall has been both praised and vilified since it was built in the 1970s, but it remains incredibly popular. From the graceful glass roof, arching 127 feet above the lowest of the mall levels, to Michael Snow's exquisite flock of fiberglass Canada geese floating poetically in open space, there is plenty to appreciate.

Such a wide selection of shops and eateries can be confusing, so here's a simple guide: Galleria Level 1 contains two food courts; popularly priced fashions; photo, electronics, and music stores; and much "convenience" merchandise. Level 2 is directed to the middle-income shopper; Level 3, suitably, has the highest fashion and prices. In the late 1990s a branch of eatons (formerly Eaton's) opened here, though most of the chain's stores across Canada had already closed. The Centre now retains the famous family's name, but the biggest tenants are Sears and H&M. The southern end of Level 3 has a skywalk that connects the Centre to the seven floors of the Bay (formerly Simpsons) department store, across Queen Street.

> **WORD OF MOUTH**
>
> "I wandered back along the Dundas/Yonge intersection and watched the locals ready themselves for a Friday night. The giant electronic billboards and endless traffic queues reminded me of London's Piccadilly Circus. There was a frenetic energy about the place"   —SandyBlandy

Safe parking garages with spaces for some 1,800 cars are sprinkled around Eaton Centre. The building extends along the west side of Yonge Street all the way from Queen Street up to Dundas Street (with subway stops at each end). ✉ *220 Yonge St., Dundas Square Area* ☎ *416/598–8560* ⊕ *www.torontoeatoncentre.com* ☉ *Weekdays 10–9, Sat. 9:30–7, Sun. noon–6* Ⓜ *Dundas, Queen.*

❺ Mackenzie House. Once home to journalist William Lyon Mackenzie, who was born in Scotland at the end of the 18th century and emigrated to Canada in 1820, this National Historic Site is now a museum and library. Mackenzie started a newspaper that so enraged the powers that be (a clique known as "the Family Compact") that they dumped all his type into Lake Ontario. An undeterred Mackenzie stayed on to be elected the first mayor of Toronto in 1834 and is said even to have designed the coat of arms of his new city; his grandson, William Lyon Mackenzie King, became the longest-serving prime minister in Canadian history.

Mackenzie served only one year as mayor. Upset with the government big shots in 1837, he gathered some 700 supporters and marched down Yonge Street to try to overthrow the government. His minions were roundly defeated, and Mackenzie fled to the United States with a price on his head. When the Canadian government granted him amnesty years later, he was promptly elected to the legislative assembly and began to publish another newspaper. By this time, though, he was so down on his luck that some friends bought his family this house. Mackenzie enjoyed the place for only a few years before his death in 1861. Among the period furnishings and equipment preserved here is the fiery Scot's printing press. ✉ *82 Bond St., at Dundas St. W, Dundas Square Area* ☎ *416/392–6915* ▧ *C$6* ☉ *Jan.–Apr., weekends noon–5; May–Labor Day, Tues.–Sun. noon–5; Sept.–Dec., Tues.–Fri. noon–4, weekends noon–5* Ⓜ *Dundas.*

QUICK BITES

The Café at the Church of the Holy Trinity (✉ *10 Trinity Sq., facing Bay St., Dundas Square Area* ☎ *416/598–4521* Ⓜ *Dundas*) is a charming eatery serving sandwiches, soups, pastries, and tea. It's open weekdays 9 to 5. The church itself is fully operational and available for quiet contemplation in the midst of one of downtown Toronto's busiest sections.

WORTH NOTING

2 Museum for Textiles. Ten galleries showcase cultural displays—men's costumes from northern Nigeria, for example—as well as the latest in contemporary design. Rugs, cloth, and tapestries from around the world are exhibited. Wednesday evenings (after 5) admission is pay what you can. ⊠ *55 Centre Ave., at Dundas St. W Dundas Square Area* ☎ *416/599–5321* ⊕ *www.textilemuseum.ca* 🖃 *C$12* ⊙ *Thurs.–Tues. 11–5, Wed. 11–8* Ⓜ *St. Patrick.*

1 Toronto Police Museum and Discovery ℭ Centre. Highlights are a replica of a 19th-century police station, a collection of firearms, and exhibits about infamous crimes. Interactive displays include law-and-order quizzes and the opportunity to study your own fingerprints. Kids have fun with the 1914 paddy wagon, car-crash videos, and, especially, a Harley Davidson they can jump on. They also enjoy climbing in and out of a car sliced in half and hearing a dispatcher squawk at them. Tours are self-guided only. ⊠ *40 College St. at Bay St., Dundas Square Area* ☎ *416/808–7020* ⊕ *www.torontopolice.on.ca/museum* 🖃 *Donations accepted* ⊙ *Weekdays 8:30–4* Ⓜ *College.*

> **DID YOU KNOW?**
>
> Toronto's Yonge Street, which divides the city neatly into east and west, was once named the longest street in the world—at 1,900 km (1,180 mi)—by the *Guinness Book of World Records.* Though many Torontonians still believe that to be true, it was only the case when Yonge was part of Highway 11, which runs all the way from Barrie, ON, to the Minnesota–North Dakota border. Today's Yonge Street is still long at 56 km (34 mi), but has lost its longest road title to the Pan-American Highway.

OFF THE BEATEN PATH

Cabbagetown. Mockingly named by outsiders for the cabbages that grew on tiny lawns and were cooked in nearly every house, the term is used with a combination of inverse pride and almost wistful irony today. Although there are few tourist attractions per se here, it's fun to stroll around and enjoy the architectural diversity of this funky residential area. The enclave extends roughly from Parliament Street on the west—about 1½ km (1 mi) due east of Yonge Street—to the Don River on the east, and from Bloor Street on the north to Queen Street East on the south.

The St. James Cemetery at the northeast corner of Parliament and Wellesley streets contains interesting burial monuments, including the small yellow-brick Gothic **Chapel of St. James-the-Less** with a handsome spire rising from the church nave. Built between 1859 and 1860, it is still considered one of the most beautiful church buildings in the country. Riverdale Park, which once hosted the city's main zoo, is now home to **Riverdale Farm**, a free farm museum that is a special treat for children, who may enjoy brushing the horses or attempting to milk the goats. Demonstrations of crafts such as quilting and spinning are offered daily. Permanent residents include Clydesdale horses, cows, sheep, goats, pigs, donkeys, ducks, geese, chickens, and a small assortment of other domestic animals. The park adjacent to the farm has a wading pool. Also nearby is **Necropolis Cemetery**, the resting place of many of Toronto's pioneers—including Toronto's first mayor, William

Lyon Mackenzie. The 1872 chapel, gate, and gatehouse of the nonsectarian burial ground constitute one of the most attractive groupings of small Victorian buildings in Toronto.

GREATER TORONTO

Explore beyond the downtown areas to find the ethnic enclaves, parks, museums, and attractions that make Toronto interesting. High Park is the city's main green space and has Shakespeare productions in summer. Edwards Gardens, in North York, is the city's botanical gardens. The McMichael Canadian Art Collection, north of the city, is an exceptional gallery not to be missed for its Group of Seven pieces. Black Creek Pioneer Village, a living-history museum, and Canada's Wonderland, an enormous theme park, are extremely kid-friendly.

Numbers in the margin correspond to points of interest on the Greater Toronto map.

TIMING You can explore each Greater Toronto sight independently or combine a couple of sights in one trip. You can reach High Park and Black Creek Pioneer Village via public transportation, but a car is necessary for visiting the Kortright Centre and is helpful for getting to other sights. A special GO Transit bus serves Canada's Wonderland in summer.

TOP ATTRACTIONS

Canada's Wonderland. Yogi Bear, Fred Flintstone, and Scooby Doo are part of Canada's first theme park, filled with more than 200 games, rides, restaurants, and shops. Favorite attractions include Kidzville, home of the Rugrats and the Top Gun looping inverted jet coaster. In Nickelodeon Central, three rides star Nickelodeon characters Jimmy Neutron, Dora the Explorer, and Arnold from *Hey Arnold!* The Whitewater Bay wave pool, the Black Hole waterslide, and a children's interactive water-play area are all a part of Splash Works, the 20-acre on-site water park. Look for the strolling *Star Trek* characters, the Studio Store, miniature golf, and batting cages as well. Other entertainment includes concerts, musicals, sea-lion shows, and cliff divers. Check newspapers, chain stores, and hotels for discount coupons. ■ TIP→ **The park is about 30 minutes north of downtown Toronto by car or via the "Wonderland Express" GO Bus from the Yorkdale and York Mills subway stations.** ✉ *9580 Jane St., Vaughan* ☎ *905/832–7000 or 905/832–8131 Kingswood Theatre tickets* ⊕ *www.canadaswonderland.com* 🎟 *C$46.69* ☉ *Late May–June, weekdays 10–6, Sat. 10–10, Sun. 10–8; late June–Aug., daily 10–10; Sept., weekends 10–8; Oct., weekends 10–5.*

McMichael Canadian Art Collection. On 100 acres of lovely woodland in Kleinburg, 30 km (19 mi) northwest of downtown, the McMichael is the only major gallery in the country with the mandate to collect Canadian art exclusively. The museum holds impressive works by Tom Thomson, Emily Carr, and the Group of Seven landscape painters, as well as their early-20th-century contemporaries. These artists were inspired by the wilderness and sought to capture it in bold, original styles. First Nations art and prints, drawings, and sculpture by Inuit artists are well represented. Strategically placed windows help you appreciate the scenery as

Greater Toronto

KEY

▬ ▬ ▬ *Bloor-Danforth Line*

○ *Subway Stop*

┼┼┼ *Railroad Lines*

▪▪▪▪ *Sheppard Line*

▬▬ *Yonge-University-Spadina Line*

0 — 2 miles

0 — 3 km

you view art that took its inspiration from the vast outdoors. Inside, wood walls and a fireplace set a country mood. ✉ *10365 Islington Ave., west of Hwy. 400 and north of Major Mackenzie Dr., Kleinburg* ☎ *888/213–1121 or 905/893–1121* ⊕ *www.mcmichael.com* 💲 *C$15, parking C$5* ⊙ *Daily 10–4.*

❼ Ontario Science Centre. ⟳ ★ It has been called a museum of the 21st century, but it's much more than that. Where else can you stand at the

COMING WITH YOUR OWN MENAGERIE?

If you're visiting the zoo with kids, you may want to visit the Discovery Zone (open June through August), where they can discover backyard bug, butterfly, and pond displays, dive into Slash Island water play area, and dig for fossils in the Kidszoo. Rides cost extra.

edge of a black hole, work hand-in-clamp with a robot, or land on the moon? Even the building itself is extraordinary: three linked pavilions float gracefully down the side of a ravine and overflow with exhibits that make space, technology, and communications fascinating. A dozen theaters show films that bring the natural world to life. Demonstrations of glassblowing, papermaking, lasers, electricity, and more take place daily; check the schedule when you arrive. The museum has a cafeteria, a restaurant, and a gift store with a cornucopia of books and scientific doodads. The 25,000 square-foot Weston Family Innovation Centre, rife with hands-on activities, is all about experience and problem-solving. Make a music sound track, take a lie-detector test, and measure fluctuations in your own body chemistry as you flirt with a virtual celebrity. ✉ *770 Don Mills Rd., at Eglinton Ave., North York* ☎ *416/696–1000* ⊕ *www.ontariosciencecentre.ca* 💲 *C$18, parking C$8* ⊙ *Daily 10–5* Ⓜ *Eglinton, then No. 34 Eglinton East bus to Don Mills Rd. stop; then walk ½ block south.*

❻ Toronto Zoo. ⟳ ★ With its varied terrain, from river valley to dense forest, the Rouge Valley was an inspired choice of site for this 710-acre zoo in which mammals, birds, reptiles, and fish are grouped according to their natural habitats. Enclosed, climate-controlled pavilions have botanical exhibits, such as the Africa pavilion's giant baobab tree. Look over an Events Guide, distributed at the main entrance, to help plan your day; activities might include chats with animal keepers and animal and bird demonstrations. An "Around the World Tour" takes approximately three hours and includes the Africa, Americas, Australasia, Indo-Malayan, and the "Canadian Domain" pavilions. From June through early September, the Zoomobile can take you through the outdoor exhibit area.

The African Savanna is the country's finest walking safari, a dynamic reproduction that brings rare and beautiful animals and distinctive geological landscapes to the city's doorstep. You can also dine in the Savanna's Safari Lodge and camp overnight in the Serengeti Bush Camp (reservations required). The zoo is a 30-minute drive east from downtown; parking is free from November through March. ✉ *Meadowvale Rd., Exit 389 off Hwy. 401, Scarborough* ☎ *416/392–5900, 416/392–9106, 416/392–5947 for camping reservations* ⊕ *www.torontozoo.com* 💲 *C$21, parking C$8* ⊙ *Mid-Mar.–late May and early Sept.–mid-Oct.,* *daily 9–6; late May–early Sept., daily 9–7:30; Oct.–mid-Mar., daily 9:30–4:30* Ⓜ *Kennedy, then bus 86A or Don Mills, then bus 85.*

WORTH NOTING

❺ **Black Creek Pioneer Village.** Less than a half-hour drive from downtown
Ⓒ is a rural, mid-19th-century living-history-museum village that makes you feel as though you've gone through a time warp. Black Creek Pioneer Village is a collection of 40 buildings from the 19th- and early-20th centuries, including a town hall, a weaver's shop, a printing shop, a blacksmith's shop, and a school complete with a dunce cap. The mill dates from the 1840s and has a 4-ton wooden waterwheel that grinds up to a hundred barrels of flour a day (bags are available for purchase).

As men and women in period costumes go about the daily routine of mid-19th-century Ontario life, they explain what they're doing and answer questions. Free wagon rides, farm animals, a hands-on discovery center, and a decent restaurant contribute to a satisfying outing. In winter you can also skate, toboggan, or hop on a sleigh ride. ✉ *1000 Murray Ross Pkwy., near the intersection of Jane St. and Steeles Ave., North York* ☎ *416/736–1733* ⊕ *www.blackcreek.ca* 🎫 *C$15, parking C$6* ⊙ *May and June, weekdays 9:30–4, weekends 11–5; July and Aug., weekdays 10–5, weekends 11–5; Sept.–Dec., weekdays 9:30–4, weekends 11–4:30* Ⓜ *Finch, then bus 60 west or Jane, then bus 35.*

❽ **Edwards Gardens.** The beautiful 35-acre gardens (once owned by
Ⓒ industrialist Rupert Edwards) flow into one of the city's most visited
★ ravines. Paths wind along colorful floral displays and exquisite rock gardens. Refreshments and picnic facilities are available, but no pets are allowed. There's also a signposted "teaching garden." For a great ravine walk, start at the gardens' entrance and head south through Wilket Creek Park and the winding Don River valley. Pass beneath the Don Valley Parkway and continue along Massey Creek. After hours of walking (or biking or jogging) through almost uninterrupted park, you reach the southern tip of Taylor Creek Park on Victoria Park Avenue, just north of the Danforth. From here you can catch a subway back to your hotel. ✉ *777 Lawrence Ave. E, entrance at southwest corner of Leslie St. and Lawrence Ave. E, North York* ☎ *416/392–8188* ⊕ *www. toronto.ca/parks/parks_gardens/edwardsgdns.htm* ⊙ *Daily dawn–dusk* Ⓜ *Eglinton, then bus 54 or 54A.*

❸ **High Park.** One of North America's loveliest parks, High Park (at one
Ⓒ time the privately owned countryside "farm" of John George Howard,
★ Toronto's first city architect) is especially worth visiting in summer, when the many special events include professionally staged Shakespeare productions. Hundreds of Torontonians and guests arrive at dinnertime and picnic on blankets before the show. Admission is by donation. **Grenadier Pond** in the southwest corner of High Park is named after the British soldiers who, it is said, crashed through the soft ice while rushing to defend the town against invading American forces in 1813. In summer there are concerts on Sunday afternoons, and there is skating in winter. At the south end of High Park, near Colborne Lodge, is the **High Park Zoo** (☎ *416/392–8186* ⊙ *Daily 7*

NEIGHBORHOOD WATCH: THE DANFORTH

This area along Danforth Avenue has a dynamic ethnic mix, although it's primarily a Greek community. Once English-settled (although it was named after Asa Danforth, an American contractor who cut a road into the area in 1799), the neighborhood is now Italian, Greek, East Indian, Latin American, and, increasingly, Chinese. But a large percentage of the 120,000 Greek Canadians in metropolitan Toronto live here, and the area is still referred to as "Greektown." Late-night taverns, all-night fruit markets, and some of the best ethnic restaurants in Toronto abound. ■ **TIP→ Summer is the best season to visit, since most eateries have patios, most of which are open and busy until the wee hours of morning.**

Every August the local festival, **Taste of the Danforth** (☎ 416/469–5634 ⊕ www.tasteofthedanforth.com), pays tribute to this little nook of foodie paradise. More than a million visitors flock to the festival to sample the fare—mainly dolmades, souvlaki, and other Greek specialties—for C$1 to C$5 per taste. The festival motto—"Don't eat for a week before coming"—is helpful advice.

Boundaries: The Danforth is bounded by Broadview Avenue to the west and Donlands Avenue to the east.

Getting Here: Take the subway to the Broadview (west end of the neighborhood), Chester or Pape (heart of the neighborhood), or Donlands (eastern end) TTC stop.

AM–*dusk*). It's more modest than the Toronto Zoo, but a lot closer to downtown and free. Even young children won't tire walking among the deer, Barbary sheep, peacocks, rabbits, and buffalo. **Colborne Lodge** (☎ 416/392–6916 ⊠ C$4, holidays C$5.50 ⊙ Jan.–Apr., Fri.–Sun. noon–4; May–Aug., Tues.–Sun. noon–5; Sept., weekends noon–5; Oct.–Dec., Tues.–Sun. noon–4) was built more than 150 years ago by John George Howard on a hill overlooking Lake Ontario. This Regency-style "cottage" contains its original fireplace, bake oven, and kitchen, as well as many of Howard's own drawings and paintings. Other highlights of the 398-acre park are a large swimming pool, tennis courts, fitness trails, and hillside gardens with roses and sculpted hedges. There's limited parking along Bloor Street north of the park, and along the side streets on the eastern side. ⊠ *Bordered by Bloor St. W, Gardiner Expressway, Parkside Dr., and Ellis Park Rd. Main entrance off Bloor St. W at High Park Ave., Greater Toronto* ☎ 416/392–1111, 416/392–1748 walking tours Ⓜ High Park.

❶ **Kortright Centre for Conservation.** Only 15 minutes north of the city, this delightful conservation center has three aquariums and more than 16 km (10 mi) of hiking trails through forest, meadow, river, and marshland. In winter some of the trails are reserved for cross-country skiing (C$12 to use the trail, equipment rentals available). In the magnificent woods there have been sightings otf foxes, coyotes, rabbits, deer, wild turkeys, pheasants, chickadees, finches, and blue jays. Seasonal events include a dogsled race, a spring maple-syrup festival, and a Christmas crafts fair. To get here, drive 3 km (2 mi) north along Highway 400,

NEIGHBORHOOD WATCH: INDIA BAZAAR

"Little India" and "Indian Village" all refer to Gerrard India Bazaar, the largest collection of South Asian restaurants, sari stores, and Bollywood movie-rental shops in North America. Follow your nose through the dozens of sweets shops, food stalls, and aromatic curry restaurants, and allow your eyes to be dazzled by storefront displays of gold jewelry, Hindu deities, and swaths of sensuous fabrics dripping with glittering sequins.

Mornings are generally quiet. Afternoons see a trickle of visitors, but the area really comes alive in the evening when hungry bellies stroll the sidewalks in search of a fiery madras, creamy korma, or hearty masala curry. Many of the restaurants offer buffet lunches and dinners with prices hovering around C$10 per person, which draw in huge crowds on the weekends. Sunday afternoons set the familiar scene of Indian families crowding the sidewalks, enjoying corn on the cob and *paan*—an Indian stall food of spices, fruits, and sometimes sugar wrapped in leaves of the betel pepper—window-shopping their way up and down Gerrard Street.

Boundaries: This little piece of Bombay is crammed into the strip of Gerrard Street between Coxwell and Greenwood avenues.

Getting Here: Use the College streetcar east to get here from downtown.

exit west at Major Mackenzie Drive, and continue south 1 km (½ mi) on Pine Valley Drive to the gate. ⊠ *9550 Pine Valley Dr., Woodbridge* ☎ *905/832–2289* ⊕ *www.kortright.org* ✉ *C$6* ☉ *Daily 10–4.*

Where to Eat

Updated by
Amy Rosen

Immigration flourishes in Toronto, and even if you've come from a far-flung corner of the world, you can often find home cooking here. The abundant fresh produce of Ontario province, once filtered through French, British, and Italian cooking techniques, now stars in dishes ranging from the sweet and pungent flavors of the Middle East to the soulful dishes of Latin America. In one short block of Baldwin Street at Kensington Market, there are 23 eateries—a de facto United Nations of gastronomy, if you will.

The Toronto restaurant scene is in a state of perpetual motion. New restaurants open and close at breakneck speed to meet the demands of a savvy dining public. Even haute-cuisine establishments, which had all but faded into Toronto's gastronomic history, are experiencing a renaissance, joining the ever-swelling ranks of bistros, trattorias, tapas bars, noodle bars, wine bars, and smart cafés. Red meat has made a comeback, but along with steak houses have come more vegetarian-friendly restaurants. With a perfect storm of locally grown talent and ingredients coming together with traditional techniques and modern bravado, the dining-out scene is more exciting than it's ever been. In fact, a popular TV show, *Opening Soon,* visits new restaurants in the days and weeks before opening, finishing with their premieres.

Brilliant young chefs such as Tom Thai (of Foxley bistro) and Claudio Aprile (of Colborne Lane) stay ahead of the public's evolving tastes by drawing from a number of Asian and Latin cuisines and spiffing them up with classical French and new-wave Spanish preparations. Rather than following tradition, today's chefs are creating their own trends and signature dishes. Tasting menus running from 5 to 12 courses with wine pairings tempt epicurean diners, while the value-conscious will be happy to learn they can still get a great meal in Chinatown for under C$5. And the public speaks out about the results, loudly: everyone who sits in a restaurant is a critic, and word of mouth has closed unsuccessful eateries faster than you can say "mushy pasta and patronizing service." Though utterly fresh fish and seafood were once difficult to come by, you can now feast on fish that were swimming in the Azores hours earlier. But the latest trend is thinking global while eating local, and many of Toronto's best chefs take pains to note the local provinance of just about everything on their menus—from the feta on your salad to those wild Ontario blueberries in your finishing slice of pie.

Recommending restaurants in an up-and-coming foodie destination is a difficult task, especially in a city that's evolving as quickly as Toronto. There's not enough space to mention many worthy kitchens in the suburbs and outlying areas. Whichever restaurant you choose, globalization has created a clientele with a sophisticated palate and a demand for high-quality international cuisines. Some of the newer restaurants are all pop and no sizzle, yet most carry with them great expectations, so they don't last long if they fail to serve up truly tasty goods. And by and large, the city delivers.

WHAT IT COSTS IN CANADIAN DOLLARS					
	¢	$	$$	$$$	$$$$
AT DINNER	under C$8	C$8–C$12	C$13–C$20	C$21–C$30	over $30

Prices are per person for a main course at dinner.

Use the coordinate (✢ 2:B) at the end of each listing to locate a site on the corresponding map.

HARBOURFRONT, THE FINANCIAL DISTRICT, AND OLD TOWN

It skirts a serene Lake Ontario, yet is the engine that drives the city. The area is one of historic marvels like St. Lawrence Market, tourist hot spots ranging from the Hockey Hall of Fame to the Princess of Wales theater, and a lovely waterfront for biking or a stroll. Yet it's also home to a jumble of glassy 50-story skyscrapers and the business types that fill them. Little wonder, then from steak houses to take-out sushi, you'll find it here.

THE FINANCIAL DISTRICT

$–$$

AMERICAN

✕ **Beer Bistro.** A renowned beer writer–taster and a creative chef have teamed up in a happy/hoppy partnership where beer is king. Each menu item uses beer as an ingredient: the chef panfries catfish and pairs it with black-eyed peas and orzo cooked with pilsner; a chunky beef stew is slowly braised in La Maudite to melting tenderness. Start with a flight of beer in 3-ounce tasting glasses, to be drunk in order from mild to bold. The comfortable, modern interior includes a huge angled mirror on the wall above the kitchen, which allows a peek into the heart of the restaurant. The patio is a joy in summer. ✉ *18 King St. E, Financial District* ☎ *416/861–9872* ⊕ *ww.beerbistro.com* ▤ *AE, DC, MC, V* ☉ *Closed Sun.* Ⓜ *King* ✢ *6:F*

$$$$

MODERN
CANADIAN

✕ **Bymark.** Wood, glass, and water create drama in a space anchored by a 5,000-bottle wine "cellar" inside a two-story glass column. The menu offers delectability and perfection: poached sea scallops with seared foie gras, crème fraîche, and sake beurre blanc; an 8-ounce burger with molten brie de Meaux and grilled porcini. The bar one floor up oozes extreme comfort and has a good view of architect Mies van der Rohe's TD Centre Plaza. The service matches the food, and in summer, patio tippling and dining are dreamy. ✉ *66 Wellington St. W, concourse level, Financial District* ☎ *416/777–1144* ⊕ *ww.bymark.ca* ⚐ *Reservations essential* ▤ *AE, DC, MC, V* ☉ *Closed Sun.* Ⓜ *St. Andrew* ✢ *6:F*

$$$–$$$$

MODERN
CANADIAN

Fodor's Choice
★

✕ **Canoe.** Look through huge windows on the 54th floor of the Toronto Dominion Bank Tower and enjoy the breathtaking view of the Toronto Islands and the lake while you dine. Classics include foie gras and truffles. A seven-course tasting menu takes you from coast to coast with dishes like roast hind of Yukon caribou with zucchini corn-bread cobbler and

TORONTO DINING PLANNER

DRESS

Dress in Toronto restaurants is casual but neat. In the fashionable spots downtown, especially Yorkville, Queen Street, and Little Italy, diners always look pulled together in trendy and classic attire. In the more elegant and expensive restaurants, men are likely to feel more comfortable wearing a jacket. Aggressive air-conditioning in summer makes many women bring a light sweater or shawl with them. We mention dress only when men are required to wear a jacket or a jacket and tie.

RESERVATIONS

Reservations are always a good idea; we mention them only when they're essential or not accepted. Book as far ahead as you can. (Large parties should always call to check the reservations policy.)

SMOKING

Toronto restaurants prohibit smoking. Some let diners get away with smoking in outdoor dining areas.

MEALTIMES

Lunch typically starts at 11:30 or noon and dinner service begins

around 5:30 or 6. Many restaurants close between lunch and dinner (roughly the hours of 2:30 to 5:30). On weekdays, kitchens usually close around 10:30 PM. Chinatown, Yorkville, and Danforth have a few late-night spots. There are few all-night restaurants in the city. Unless otherwise noted, the restaurants listed in this guide are open daily for lunch and dinner. *In Chapter 2: Exploring, look for "Quick Bites" places—perfect for a snack while sightseeing.*

PAYING

Credit cards are widely accepted in Toronto restaurants though some may accept only MasterCard and Visa.

DISCOUNTS

For six weeks during January and February, more than 100 of the city's best restaurants offer the Winterlicious Program, where a fixed-price, three-course lunch is C$15 to C$20, and dinner is C$20 to C$30, along with their regular menu.

partridge-berry juice. Desserts, such as fireweed honey-butter tart with roasted plum sauce and cream, are quite serious. ■TIP➜**The restaurant and lounge Canoe is a great place to sample Niagara wines.** ⊠ *Toronto-Dominion Centre, 66 Wellington St. W, 54th fl., Financial District* ☎*416/364–0054* ⊕ *www.oliverbonacini.com* ⌔ *Reservations essential* ⊟*AE, DC, MC, V* ⊙ *Closed weekends* Ⓜ *King* ✚ *6:F.*

$$$–$$$$ ✕**Far Niente.** It's the updated face of fine dining, relaxed and approach-
MODERN able with energy and warmth. This more than 10-year-old stalwart
CANADIAN stays current with oversized hanging lamp shades, flattering lighting, banquettes, and a color scheme that's all black and camel—very New York. As for the food, chef Gordon Mackie has focused on fancified comfort classics that are stealing Bay Street hearts, like lobster potpie, homey fondue hit with truffle, and a snappy horizontal salad of Niagara prosciutto, arugula, and oven-dried tomatoes on a dense Parmesan foam. There are gourmet s'mores for dessert. ⊠ *187 Bay St., Financial*

BEST BETS FOR TORONTO DINING

Where can I find the best food the city has to offer? Fodor's writers and editors have selected their favorite restaurants by price, cuisine, and experience in the lists below. In the first column, the Fodor's Choice properties represent the "best of the best" across price categories. You can also search by area for excellent eats—just peruse our complete reviews on the following pages.

Fodor's Choice ★

C5, $$$$, p. 79
Canoe, $$$-$$$$, p. 63
Foxley, $$-$$$, p. 77
Jamie Kennedy Wine Bar, $-$$, p. 68

By Price

¢

Future Bakery & Café, p. 78
Swatow, p. 76

$

7 West Cafe, p. 79
Crepes a GoGo, p. 81
Duff's Famous Wings, p. 89
Richtree Market Restaurant, p. 66
Spring Rolls, p. 85

$$

Beer Bistro, p. 63
Jamie Kennedy Wine Bar, p. 68
Live Organic Food Bar, p. 78
Peter's Chung King, p. 74
PJ O'Brien, p. 68
Takesushi, p. 66
Terroni, p. 69

$$$

Allen's, p. 85
Foxley, p. 77
Pastis Express, p. 91

$$$$

C5, p. 79
Canoe, p. 63
Colborne Lane, p. 67
Lucien, p. 68
One, p. 81

By Cuisine

CHINESE

Lai Wah Heen, $$$-$$$$, p. 74
Peter's Chung King, $-$$, p. 74
Spadina Garden, $-$$, p. 74
Spring Rolls, $-$$, p. 85

FRENCH

Bistro 990, $$$, p. 84
The Fifth, $$$$, p. 76
La Palette, $$-$$$, p. 76
Truffles, $$$$, p. 83

ITALIAN

Filippo's Gourmet Pizza, $$, p. 89
Mistura, $$$-$$$$, p. 90
Sotto Sotto, $$$-$$$$, p. 83
Terroni, $-$$, p. 69
Zucca, $$-$$$, p. 91

MODERN CANADIAN

Bymark, $$$$, p. 63
Canoe, $$$$, p. 63
Far Niente, $$$-$$$$, p. 64
The Gardiner Café, $$$, p. 81

By Experience

BUSINESS DINING

Bymark, $$$$, p. 63
Canoe, $$$$, p. 63
Reds Bistro & Bar, $$$-$$$$, p. 66
Starfish, $$$, p. 66
Vertical, $$$$, p. 67

CELEB-SPOTTING

Bistro 990, $$$, p. 84
One, $$-$$$, p. 81
Sotto Sotto, $$$-$$$$, p. 83
Studio Café, $$$-$$$$, p. 83

CHILD-FRIENDLY

Duff's Famous Wings, $-$$, p. 89
Il Fornello, $$-$$$, p. 72
Spadina Garden, $-$$, p. 74
Terroni, $$, p. 69

MOST ROMANTIC

C5, $$$$, p. 79
The Fifth, $$$$, p. 76
La Palette, $$-$$$, p. 76
Truffles, $$$$, p. 83

District ☎ 416/214–9922 ⊕ *www.farnienterestaurant.com* ⧂ *Reservations essential* 🍽 *AE, DC, MC, V* ⊗ *No lunch Sat., closed Sun.* Ⓜ *King* ✛ *6:F.*

$$$–$$$$ ✕ **Reds Bistro & Bar.** A clubby and
AMERICAN vibrant decor emphasizes natural materials as a backdrop for Chef Michael Steh's updated classics. Still catering to the office-tower set, the bustling ground-floor bar is the place to sample international picks from the broad wine list (60 by the glass) and updated bar snacks like ginger-and-scallion-stuffed chicken wings. Visit the upstairs dining room for starters like tender octopus salad, and Hokkaido seared scallops in a truffly cauliflower soup, or entrées like Ontario heirloom beets with smoked whitefish and dill crème fraîche and fried chicken with sweet corn and potato hash. ⊠ *77 Adelaide St. W, Financial District* ☎ *416/862–7337* ⊕ *www.redsbistro.com* 🍽 *AE, DC, MC, V* ⊗ *Closed Sun. No lunch Sat.* Ⓜ *King* ✛ *6:E.*

$–$$ ✕ **Richtree Market Restaurants.** Herbs grow in pots, fresh fruits and veg-
AMERICAN etables are piled high, an enormous snowbank holds bright-eyed fish,
☯ and fresh pasta spews from pasta makers, ready to be cooked to order in this European-style market. At this self-service restaurant the best bet is the rosti: buttery traditional Swiss-style Yukon gold potatoes grated and fried into a crisp pancake. A side of house-cured salmon and a rich dollop of sour cream is a must. A rotisserie roasts lacquer-crisp game birds and European sausages. Bread and croissants are baked before your eyes, and pizza is prepared to order. This high-concept, low-price dining adventure is open daily 7:30 AM–2 AM. Smaller versions are all over town; see all their locations online. ⊠ *Brookfield Place, 42 Yonge St., Financial District* ☎ *416/366–8986* ⊕ *www.richtree.ca* 🍽 *AE, DC, MC, V* Ⓜ *King* ✛ *6:F.*

$$$ ✕ **Starfish.** In his smart, naturally comfortable restaurant, Patrick
SEAFOOD McMurray—who won the 48th World Oyster Opening Championship in Galway, Ireland, by shucking 30 oysters in under four minutes—is a walking encyclopedia of oyster lore. He gives you a still-quivering pink scallop, an Emerald Cove, a Belon, or a Malpeque and informs you of the qualities of each. His oven-roasted black cod, East Coast lobsters, crisp salads, and homemade desserts will make you fall for Starfish hook, line, and sinker. ⊠ *100 Adelaide St. E, Financial District* ☎ *416/366–7827* *www.starfishoysterbed.com* ⧂ *Reservations essential* 🍽 *AE, DC, MC, V* ⊗ *Closed Sun. No lunch Sat.* Ⓜ *King* ✛ *6:G.*

$$–$$$ ✕ **Takesushi.** Dramatic black and deep-blue decor centered by a grove of
JAPANESE bamboo is an introduction to a food experience that focuses on presentation, with both a sushi bar and table service. Master chefs thrill customers with an array of spectaculars: jumbo shrimp wrapped with cucumber and tied with basil, king crab barbecued in the shell, sliced duck breast with

miso paste, and salmon fashioned into a blossom—just to start. Choose from a vast selection of sake and sake cocktails. ⊠ *22 Front St. W, Financial District* ☎ *416/862–1891* ⊕ *www.takesushi.ca* ⌂ *Reservations essential* ▭ *AE, DC, MC, V* ⊘ *Closed Sun. No lunch Sat.* Ⓜ *King* ✥ *6:G.*

$$$–$$$$
MEDITERRANEAN

✕ **Vertical.** Tawfik Shehata is part of a new breed of young Canadian chefs who are changing the culinary scene for the better. The slick, soaring room is tucked away off First Canadian Place's food court; the chef's menu is a winning combo of Mediterranean (mostly Italian, really) engaged but not quite married to Moroccan. Lamb rack meets almond tahini, and skate wing mingles with blood-orange *marmellata* (marmalade). Signature wine-braised octopus is charred then tossed with olives, capers, and other goodies, while Parmesan *gnudi* (similar to gnocchi) is sure to become your new best friend. ⊠ *First Canadian Place, 100 King St. W, Financial District* ☎ *416/214–2252* ⊕ *www.verticalrestaurant.ca* ▭ *AE, DC, MC, V* ⊘ *Closed weekends* Ⓜ *King* ✥ *6:E.*

HARBOURFRONT

$$$–$$$$
STEAK

✕ **Harbour Sixty Steakhouse.** When you are eating the finest foodstuffs, an opulent setting is the only way to go, and you won't be disappointed as you walk up stone steps to the grand neoclassical entrance of the restored Harbour Commission building. A baroque-inspired foyer leads to a gold-toned granite bar. Beyond the bar is an open kitchen, with a cooler stocked with steaks, ruby-red tuna steaks, lobsters on ice, oysters, and bright Atlantic salmon. Slow-roasted prime rib is delicious; fresh fish are grilled to your taste. Sit in comfortable high-backed armchairs or spacious, curved booths. ⊠ *60 Harbour St., Harbourfront* ☎ *416/777–2111* ⊕ *www.harboursixty.com* ▭ *AE, DC, MC, V* ⊘ *No lunch weekends* Ⓜ *Union* ✥ *6:F.*

OLD TOWN

$$$–$$$$
MODERN
CANADIAN

✕ **Colborne Lane.** Claudio Aprile, heir apparent to the Canadian molecular gastronomy throne, eschews loyalty to any single trend or cuisine in his fun and funky domain, housed in a modern room with consciously rough edges. Choose four or five delicious and complex dishes (from a list of two dozen on the à la carte menu) that sound like mains but are appetizer size, like a bowl of lobster bisque, lobster wonton, and coconut tofu, infused with lime leaves and chili. Lamb rib eye is crusted in pumpernickel and dried olives with a spiced eggplant sidekick; tuna sashimi is accompanied by an intriguing frozen soy-sauce powder. Dessert may be a composed chocolate fondue with chocolate sponge and freeze-dried cherries already swimming in the luscious mix. A 15- to 20-course set menu is served only at an enclosed, semiprivate table in the kitchen. ⊠ *45 Colborne La., Old Town* ☎ *416/368–9009* ⊕ *www.colbornelane.com* ▭ *AE, DC, MC, V* ⊘ *Closed Sun. and Mon. No lunch* Ⓜ *King* ✥ *6:F.*

$$
IRISH

✕ **Irish Embassy Pub & Grill.** Even if you don't work in finance and aren't wearing a blue suit, you can still enjoy the vaguely private-club feel of this après-work watering hole. The soaring ceilings and columns and dark wood all make for a very handsome room. And there's the Guinness. Since it's an Irish pub, do stick to the approachable lineup of imported beers, such as Smithwick's, Harp, Kilkenny. As for the pub food, both the mini Irish cocktail sausages with brown sauce and the bowl of fries with curry sauce quickly morph from vaguely disturbing to disturbingly delicious. ⊠ *49 Yonge St., Old Town* ☏ *416/866–8282* ⊕ *ww.irish embassypub.com* ☰ *AE, MC, V* ☺ *Closed Sun.* Ⓜ *King* ✛ *6:F.*

$–$$
MODERN
CANADIAN
Fodor'sChoice
★

✕ **Jamie Kennedy Wine Bar.** This sleek, spare wine bar and dining room is amazingly popular, due in part to the charm of owner-chef Kennedy and key staff. If Canada has a celebrity chef, he's it. Kennedy has been at the forefront of the Canadian food movement for more than 20 years. And those tall, dark, and lanky good looks mean he's as easy on the eyes as his food is on the belly. The wine bar has dining counters, a few tables, and a wall of the chef's own preserves in gleaming glass jars. Sit on comfy bar stools and watch as Kennedy sautés, grills, seasons, and cooks. From the daily-changing list of 21 items, favorites are an oval scoop of pâté with the chef's own pickled veggies, and tempting artisanal cheeses. Sommeliers offer tasting glasses from a spectacular list to match each dish. There is usually a wait for seating. Reservations are available only for lunch. ⊠ *9 Church St., Old Town* ☏ *416/362–1957* ⊕ *ww.jamiekennedy.ca* ⚓ *Reservations essential* ☰ *AE, DC, MC, V* Ⓜ *Union* ✛ *6:G.*

$$$–$$$$
MODERN
CANADIAN

✕ **Kultura.** They call it "social dining," which is fitting since chef and co-owner Roger Mooking's Kultura, as well as Nyood, his similarly stylish Queen West outpost, have become celebrity central during September's International Film Festival. At street level, people sip from a diverse wine card, including 11 types of bubbly, at communal tables with low-slung club chairs. On the menu are small plates for sharing, called "trans-ethnic dishes," like Jamaican chicken risotto and toasted lobster ravioli with lobster saffron bisque. Brunch, also made for sharing, is offered in the renovated 1820s heritage building: eggs Florentine on rounds of puff pastry, and fingers of French toast with caramel brittle, a *brunois* (small dice) of candied apple, and spiked whipped cream. ⊠ *169 King St. E, Old Town* ☏ *416/363–9000* ⊕ *www.kulturarestaurant.com* ☰ *AE, DC, MC, V* Ⓜ *King* ✛ *6:G.*

$$$–$$$$
MODERN
CANADIAN

✕ **Lucien.** If Anne Rice opened a Parisian bistro, it would look like this—backlit filigree, red ceiling, sparkly chandeliers, and a touch of mystery wrapped around those heavy curtains. The menu is not what you would expect from a traditional bistro either. A busy room that seats 50—while you wait have a nibble of house-made organic charcuterie at the bar: A snappy composed plate includes various cured offerings—mortadella, venison sausage, a curl of snowy *lardo* (cured pork fat)—plus seasonal pickles and preserves. Foie gras ravioli oozes under fork and knife like molten foie should, the plate scattered with bits and bobs of heirloom beets, wee tart balls of green apple, and a white chocolate foam. Fun takes on old standards include "fried" organic hen, deconstructed (breast is cooked *sous vide*; skin crisped), while house-made "the good humor" ice-cream bars illustrate chef's fun side. Because at its heart, Lucien is fun stuff for grown-ups. ⊠ *36 Wellington St. E, Old Town* ☏ *416/504–9990* ⊕ *lucienrestaurant.com* ☰ *AE, DC, MC, V* ☺ *Closed Sun. No lunch* Ⓜ *King* ✛ *6:G.*

$$
IRISH

✕ **PJ O'Brien.** A meal of Irish Kilkenny Ale–battered fish-and-chips, Irish stew, or corned beef and cabbage ends with bread pudding steeped in whiskey and custard, just like Gran made. Close your eyes and think of Dublin. The dining room has polished-wood floors, furniture, and moldings, a collection of antique musical instruments, a brigade of lively servers, and an engaging kitchen. The bar upstairs is even cozier than the one on the main floor. ⊠ *39 Colborne St., Old Town* ☎ *416/815–7562* ⊕ *www.pjobrien.com* ⊟ *AE, MC, V* ⊙ *Closed Sun.* Ⓜ *King* ⚬ *6:G.*

$$$–$$$$ ✕ **Romagna Mia Osteria Pizzeria.** Traditional Emilia-Romagna regional
ITALIAN cooking and congenial service fly under the flag of the familiar and promising red-checkered tablecloth. Sautéed duck breast atop crispy polenta with vegetables in a luscious San Giovese wine reduction is truly a treat, as are the homemade pastas. For theatrics, order risotto; rice imported from Vercelli is finished table-side in a hollowed wheel of Parmigiano-Reggiano. It's authentic and wonderful. ⊠ *106 Front St. E, Old Town* ☎ *416/363–8370* ⊕ *www.romagna-mia.com* ⊟ *AE, DC, MC, V* ⊙ *Closed Sun.* Ⓜ *King* ⚬ *6:G.*

$$ ✕ **Terroni.** This cool pizza joint, whose open shelving is lined with Italian
ITALIAN provisions, has a menu to suit one and all. Funghi Assoluti—baked oyster
⚘ mushrooms with parmigiano on a bed of arugula, dressed to kill in balsamic vinaigrette—is a must. The thin-crust pies, bubbled and blistered, are the best in town, and generous panini are also buono. Daily specials are hit and miss, but desserts (like a flourless wedge of Nutella chocolate cake) are almost universally delicious. Two other locations include 720 Queen St. West (hipsters), and 1 Balmoral Avenue at Yonge (wealthy Rosedalers). ⊠ *57 Adelaide St. E, Financial District* ☎ *416/203–3093* ⊕ *www.terroni.ca* ⊟ *AE, DC, MC, V* Ⓜ *Queen* ⚬ *6:G.*

$$–$$$ ✕ **Toshi Sushi.** This simple yet well-kept room is where Toshi caters to
JAPANESE lovers of both raw and cooked Japanese food. The daily lunch special is an implausibly good deal (C$9.50) for warming miso or a bento box loaded with al dente green beans in luscious sesame-mirin sauce, crunchy shrimp and veg tempura, ginger-tinged green salad, proper sticky rice topped with chicken teriyaki, and happy orange wedges to finish. Don't bypass the stellar sushi lineup, including Westernized riffs like torched foie gras or buttered bread-crumb oysters, and chef specials such as tuna carpaccio and crispy flounder. ■ TIP→ **Call ahead for the** *omakase* **(chef's choice) menu and join the in-the-know Japanese businesspeople at the eight-seat bar at the back.** ⊠ *565 King St. W, Old Town* ☎ *416/260–8588* ⊕ *www.toshisushi.ca* ⊟ *AE, DC, MC, V* ⊙ *Closed Sun.* Ⓜ *King* ⚬ *6:G.*

ENTERTAINMENT DISTRICT

$$$ ✕ **Crush Wine Bar.** Polished hardwood floors in the old building give it a
MODERN fresh veneer, and an open kitchen lets you see the corps of chefs at work
CANADIAN at this gastro-pub. The gastro-pub menu is a dreamscape of the chefs' expertise and locally sourced ingredients. Try the Crush Burger with Lincolnshire poacher and Niagara double-smoked bacon, oven-dried tomato and Woolwich goat cheese tart, or grilled Dorset mackerel with marinated green and white asparagus. A sommelier does wine pairings by the glass with panache, suggesting just the right tipple for duck ravioli with roasted garlic or bison rib eye with red-wine reduction. ⊠ *455*

KEY

- ■ Restaurants
- Ⓜ Subway Stops
- ⟷ following dining reviews indicates a map-grid coordinate

A

Lennox St.

Harbord St.

LITTLE ITALY

Ulster St.

Clinton St.
Manning Ave.
Euclid Ave.

College St.

Mansfield Ave.

Palmerston Blvd.

Markham St.

Bellwoods Pl.

Claremont St.

Robinson St.

← ■ Black Hoof

← ■ Foxley

← ■ Oyster Boy

Mitchell Ave.

Tecumseth St.

← ■ Young Thailand

0 ___ 1/4 mile
0 ___ 400 meters

B

■ Live Organic Food Bar

Albany Ave.
Howland Ave.

Bloor St. W.

■ Southern Accent

■ Future Bakery & Café

Borden St.

Sussex Ave.

Brunswick Ave.

Croft St.
Lippincott St.

Bathurst St.

La Palette ■

Oxford St.

Nassau St.

Bellevue Ave.
Augusta Ave.

Alexandra Park

Carr St.

Wolseley St.

Denison St.

Fressen ■

Bathurst St.

Richmond St. W.

Portland St.

Adelaide St. W.

Toshi Sushi ■

Lee's ■   ■ Madeline's

TO HARBOURFRONT
↓

C

THE ANNEX

Spadina Ave.
Madison Ave.

SPADINA Ⓜ

Sussex Ave.

■ Loire   Messis ■

Spadina Ave.
Major St.
Robert St.

Willcocks St.

Russell St.

Peter's Chung King ■

CHINATOWN

Baldwin St.

Swatow ■

Dundas St. W.

Augusta Ave.

Spadina Ave.

QUEEN WEST

Bulwer St.

Queen St. W.

Peter St.

Spice Route ■

King St. W.

Rodney's Oyster House ■   ■ Crush Wine Bar

ENTERTAINMENT DISTRICT

D

Lowther Ave.

■ Studio Café
■ Truffles

ST. GEORGE Ⓜ

Hoskin Ave.

UNIVERSITY OF TORONTO

King's College Cir.

Huron St.
St. George St.

Huron St.
Beverley St.
Henry St.

Cecil St.

Wah Sing Seafood Restaurant ■
■ Matahari Grill

D'Arcy St.

Grange Park

Sullivan St.

Beverley St.
Soho St.

Renfrew Pl.

The Fifth ■

Nelson St.

Widmer St.
John St.
Duncan St.
McCaul St.

Mercer St.

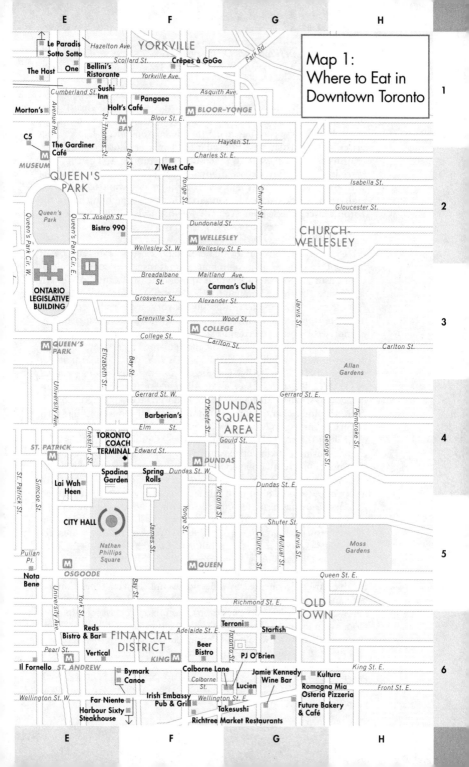

Map 1:
Where to Eat in
Downtown Toronto

King St. W, Entertainment District ☎ *416/977–1234* ⊕ *www.crush-winebar.com* ♨ *Reservations essential* 🖃 *AE, DC, MC, V* ⊗ *Closed Sun.* Ⓜ *St. Andrew* ✛ *6:C.*

$$-$$$ ✕ **Il Fornello.** Pizza aficionados especially love the 10-inch thin-crust
ITALIAN pie, baked in a wood-burning oven, at this warm and cheerful yet
☾ modern chain. Orchestrate your own medley from 50 to 60 toppings. Since 2005, a new chef has made the kitchen upscale, while keeping prices low. Try pasta with braised leg of lamb, or risotto cooked with veal shank and topped with pine nuts and lemon zest. The *zuppa de pesce* is a larger-than-expected bowl of tomato-basil broth brimming with poached fish and shellfish. You might not want to share the molten chocolate cake or lemon tart. There are nine branches in the Toronto area; check their Web site for locations. ⊠ *214 King St. W, Entertainment District* ☎ *416/977–2855* ⊕ *www.ilfornello.com* Ⓜ *St. Andrew* ✛ *6:E.*

$$-$$$ ✕ **Lee's.** Everyone looks beautiful here, on pink pedestals in the glow of
ASIAN fuchsia Lucite tables, in a room hung with transparent copper screens. Chef Susur Lee's creations, which mix Southeast Asian and Western sensibilities, are served on handmade plates from mainland China and Hong Kong. Small, perfect dishes like savory duck confit with oven-dried pineapple, spiced chestnuts, and goat cheese; silken squash soup glamorized with ginger, cucumber, and honey; and caramelized black cod with Cantonese preserves, hit the spot for lunch, a pre- or post-theater meal, or a full-scale dinner. ⊠ *603 King St. W, Entertainment District* ☎ *416/504–7867* ⊕ *www.susur.com* ♨ *Reservations essential* 🖃 *AE, MC, V* ⊗ *Closed Sun.* Ⓜ *St. Andrew* ✛ *6:B.*

$$$-$$$$ ✕ **Madeline's.** When Chef Susur Lee announced he was shuttering Susur,
ASIAN Toronto's food cognoscenti went into unofficial mourning. But then he turned Susur into Madeline's (named after his mother), and all was right with the world. Lee's longtime sous, Dominic Amaral, is now chef de cuisine, cooking up executive chef Lee's Asian-inspired family-style plates in a room done up in every wallpaper pattern and brocade known to man. As for the dishes, there are several dozen, running from a copper pot simply filled with sautéed Chanterelle mushrooms sauced in Marsala cream to roasted duck breast with a honey and chili orange glaze to crispy lobster with toasty butter, chili lime, and lemon balm in pert lettuce wrap cups. ⊠ *601 King St. W., Entertainment District* ☎ *416/603–2205* ⊕ *www.susur.com/madelines* 🖃 *AE, MC, V* ⊗ *Open for dinner. Closed Sun.* Ⓜ *St. Andrew* ✛ *B:6.*

$$-$$$ ✕ **Rodney's Oyster House.** This playful basement raw bar is a hotbed of
SEAFOOD bivalve variety frequented by dine-alones and showbiz types. Among the options are soft-shell steamers, quahogs, and "Oyster Slapjack Chowder," plus salty Aspy Bays from Cape Breton or perfect Malpeques from owner Rodney Clark's own oyster beds in Prince Edward Island. A zap of Rodney's own line of condiments or a splash of vodka and freshly grated horseradish are certain eye-openers. ■**TIP**➜ **Shared meals and half orders are okay. Be sure to ask about the daily "white-plate" specials.** ⊠ *469 King St. W, Entertainment District* ☎ *416/363–8105* ⊕ *www.rodneysoysterhouse.com* 🖃 *AE, DC, MC, V* ⊗ *Closed Sun.* Ⓜ *St. Andrew* ✛ *6:C.*

CLOSE UP

Local Chains Worth a Taste

For those times when all you want is a quick bite, consider these local chains where you're assured of fresh, tasty food and good value.

Harvey's: Harvey's says they make a hamburger a beautiful thing, and we agree—whether it's a beef, salmon, or veggie burger. The made-to-order toppings will please even the most discerning kids. The fries are a hit, too. ⊕ www.harveys.ca

Freshii: A healthier choice (formerly named Lettuce Eatery) where baseball-capped salad artists get through the lunch rush like a championship team. All steely white and blond wood, designer greens and custom-made sandwiches clearly appeal to the masses. The Cobb is a standout. ⊕ www.freshii.com

Lick's: Great Homeburgers, turkey burgers, plus the best veggie burger you'll ever taste. Onion rings, fresh fries, extra-thick milk shakes, and frozen yogurt keep them coming back for more. ⊕ www.lickshomeburgers.com

Milestones: Duck into the cool comfort of this very happening spot for Cajun popcorn shrimp or stone-oven pizza. Spit-roasted half chicken with curly fries and gloriously spicy cornbread muffins may be the kitchen's best. ⊕ www.milestonesrestaurant.com

Spring Rolls: For Asian favorites on the fly: appealing soups and spiced salads, savory noodle dishes—and spring rolls—all satiate lunchtime hunger pangs. ⊕ www.springrolls.ca

Second Cup: You'll find coffees plain and fancy, as well as flavored hot chocolates, a variety of teas, Italian soft drinks, and nibbles that include muffins, bagels, and raspberry–white chocolate scones. ⊕ www.secondcup.com

Swiss Chalet Rotisserie and Grill: Children are welcome at this Canadian institution known for its rotisserie chicken and barbecued ribs, in portions that suit every family member. ■TIP➔ **Ask for extra sauce for your french fries.** ⊕ www.swisschalet.ca

Tim Horton's: They never close, and coffee is freshly made every 20 minutes. Check out the irresistible variety of fresh donuts, muffins, bagels, and soup-and-sandwich combos. ⊕ www.timhortons.com

---

$$$ ✕**Spice Route.** This massive, sunken-style space decorated with offbeat
ASIAN Zen furnishings, such as a 16-foot rotating vertical waterfall, screen-printed images, and statues of Buddha scattered throughout, is the place to go for both the hip and not-so-hip. Entrées, including the mussels steamed in red Thai curry and Kaffir lime, and Indian spiced roast chicken, are meant to be shared. End your meal with the banana tempura and apple-mango dragon roll or try one of their tasty beverages such as a lychee martini, or one of their hot and cold spiked teas. The DJ's nightly music can get loud, so request a table in a corner if possible. ⊠ *499 King St. W., Entertainment District* ☎ *416/849–1808* ⊕ *www.spiceroute.ca* ⊗ *No lunch Sat. and Sun.* ▤ *AE, MC, V* Ⓜ *St. Andrew* ✛ *6:C.*

CHINATOWN, KENSINGTON MARKET, AND QUEEN WEST

Queen West keeps moving farther west, so much so that now there's an area known as Queen West West, or West Queen West, depending on whom you talk to. Either way, it's a boisterous 'hood of cafés, organic food shops, galleries, funky clothing stores, and lots of good restaurants at manageable price points. The Entertainment District is experiencing changes of its own, and the ongoing condo boom along this downtown strip means an ongoing restaurant boom, which is good news for the area's young bucks with money to burn. Still, it's nice to know that some areas in this cosmopolitan city stay the same, as is the case with Chinatown, one of the largest in North America, where you can enjoy the same hot-and-sour soup you had as a child. So too, the multicultural, earthy vibe of Kensington Market, the most laid-back area in town and a virtual spice rack of dining possibilities, from tacos to empanadas.

CHINATOWN

$$$–$$$$
CHINESE
Fodor's Choice
★

✕ **Lai Wah Heen.** In an elegant room with a sculpted ceiling, etched-glass turntables, and silver serving dishes, the service is formal; here mahogany-color Peking duck is wheeled in on a trolley and presented with panache. Excellent choices from the 100-dish inventory include wok-fried shredded beef and vegetables in a crisp potato nest. At lunch, dim sum is divine: baked meat–filled morsels and translucent dumplings burst with juicy fillings of shark's fin sprinkled with bright red lobster roe, and shrimp dumplings with green tops reminiscent of baby bok choy. Sister restaurant **Lai Toh Heen**, which opened in the Yonge and Eglinton neighborhood in 2008 (⌧ *692 Mt. Pleasant Rd.* ☎ *416/489–8922* ⊕ *www.laitohheen.com*), also steals hearts with dishes like fragrant seafood consommé served within a cooked papaya and tea-smoked duck breast over seaweed salad. ⌧ *Metropolitan Hotel, 108 Chestnut St., 2nd fl., Chinatown* ☎ *416/977–9899* ⊕ *www.metropolitan* ⌕ *Reservations essential* ▤ *AE, DC, MC, V* Ⓜ *St. Patrick* ✛ *4:E.*

$–$$
CHINESE
☾

✕ **Peter's Chung King.** The room may be weathered and austere (the color palate runs from gray to beige), but you're here for a classic, family-style Chinese dining experience in one of North America's largest and most authentic Chinatowns. Here, it's all about that tiny Szechuan pepper. Try hot-and-sour soup, guilty-pleasure fried spring rolls, House Special Noodle (thick lo mein with all the fixins), garlicky Asian eggplant, and most importantly, their signature crunchy shredded ginger beef that's at once sweet, spicy, and meaty. ⌧ *281 College St., Chinatown* ☎ *416/928–2936* ▤ *AE, DC, MC, V* Ⓜ *Spadina* ✛ *3:C.*

$–$$
CHINESE
☾

✕ **Spadina Garden.** The Chen family has owned Spadina Garden for more than a decade, and the restaurant's dishes are Toronto classics. This is largely the cuisine of inland northwest China, so there is no tank of finny creatures to peruse. Start with barbecued honey-garlic spareribs or spring rolls before moving on to serious entrées. Orange beef is a dark and deliciously saucy dish seasoned with dried orange peel and hot red peppers; sliced beef is served with black mushrooms and oyster sauce. The room itself is calm, with standard black lacquer, high-back chairs and red paper lanterns. ⌧ *114 Dundas St. W, Chinatown* ☎ *416/977–3413 or 416/977–3414* ⊕ *www.spadinagarden.com* ▤ *AE, MC, V* Ⓜ *St. Patrick or Dundas* ✛ *4:F.*

CLOSE UP

Vegetarian Restaurants

The days when a vegetarian had few menu options other than a limp iceberg salad are past. Today meatless options in Toronto abound, and vegetarian restaurants are increasingly creative and delicious.

In Kensington Market, **Kings Café** (⊠ *192 Augusta Ave.* ☎ *416/591–1340* ⊕ *www.kingscafe.com* ⊟ *No credit cards*) is spacious and airy. This large Chinese vegetarian- and health-oriented center of calm in the bustling market offers vegan delights like mushroom, cabbage, and ginger dumplings, and eggplant and broccoli stir-fry. Hot ginger tea is a must.

Another herbivore option is **Full Moon Vegetarian** (⊠ *638 Dundas St. W, Chinatown* ☎ *416/213–1210* ⊕ *www.vegfoodbank.ca* ☉ *Closed Wed.*), offering delicious faux meaty dishes such as lemon chicken and stir-fried beef made with bean curd.

At **Urban Herbivore** (⊠ *64 Oxford St., Kensington Market* ☎ *416/927–1231* ⊕ *www.fressenrestaurant.com*), in an old house with an exposed-brick open kitchen, sit on stools at high tables and try rustic daily soups or design your own salads and sandwiches on house-made flax bread.

If you want to try something completely different, check out "live food" at **Live Organic Food Bar** (⊠ *264 Dupont St., at Spadina Ave., The Annex* ☎ *416/515–2002* ☉ *Closed Sun. and Mon.* ⊟ *No credit cards*). The unique vegetarian dishes are completely raw and free of dairy, wheat, and preservatives. Try the lasagna of zucchini layered with cashew ricotta; the buckwheat pizza with guacamole, tomatoes, and olives; and the butterscotch hemp mousse. ■TIP→ **This tiny spot seats only four, so do reserve.**

If you visit the India Bazaar area, dine on authentic south India dosas at **Udupi Palace** (⊠ *1460 Gerrard St. E* ☎ *416/405–8138* ⊕ *www.udupipalace.ca*). Paper-thin, and crisp and soft at the same time, they are stuffed with potato, onions, mustard seeds, and lentils. The mild spicing will appeal to all ages. Soups are loaded with veggies and sing of coconut and coriander. It's gently priced, with complete dinners C$12 per person.

Queen Street West has always been ahead of the curve, and there have been vegetarian restaurants there for years. These days, the best is **Fressen** (⊠ *478 Queen St. W* ☎ *416/504–5127* ⊕ *www.fressenrestaurant.com, see full review*), where diners can remain true to their vegan souls. Tofu with an exotic turn and exceptionally tasty pasta dishes appeal even to carnivores.

The hearty Asian and Middle Eastern fare and great selection of energy elixirs and smart drinks at **Fresh by Juice for Life** (⊠ *521 Bloor St. W, The Annex* ☎ *416/531–2635* ☎ *416/599–4442* ⊕ *www.freshrestaurants.ca*) will make your day.

3

KENSINGTON MARKET

$$–$$$ ✕ **La Palette.** This Kensington-area bright spot has staked its claim as one
FRENCH of Toronto's truly authentic bistros for many reasons, but one in particular: though it's not actually written on the menu, they serve horse tenderloin by request. This unassuming boîte, all dark-red with vinyl chairs
and checkered tablecloths, has all of 30 seats, with French doors leading
to a few more on the very appealing patio out front. Favorite dishes
include luscious Camembert fritters, garlicky escargots, good steak frites,
rack of lamb, and many quaffable wines, including a long list of European choices. A three-course prix-fixe (C$30) is also available. Great for
brunch, too. ✉ *256 Augusta Ave., Kensington Market* ☎ *416/929–4900*
⊕ *www.lapalette.ca* ▤ *AE, DC, MC, V* Ⓜ *College* ✛ *3:C.*

$$ ✕ **Matahari Grill.** It's hard to pass up any of the dishes here, so you might
MALAYSIAN use size as a decision-making tool. If you have a taste for adventure,
order the chef's daily creation: the Southeast Asian dim sum platter for
two from the section marked SMALL. Then traverse to LARGE for steamed
arctic char on Shanghai rice cakes with garlic black-bean sauce, or
rack of lamb with an Asian touch. The seafood curry grill is scallops,
prawns, calamari, tomatoes, and okra served in a tantalizing coconut-
curry broth. In summer there is a tiny outdoor patio, but most people
prefer the sophisticated green-and-black decor inside. ✉ *39 Baldwin
St., Kensington Market* ☎ *416/596–2832* ⊕ *www.mataharigrill.com*
⚑ *Reservations essential* ▤ *AE, DC, MC, V* ⊘ *Closed Mon. No lunch
weekends* Ⓜ *St. Patrick* ✛ *4:D.*

$–$$ ✕ **Swatow.** This is all a city can ask of its Chinatown—soulful, cheerful,
CHINESE and uttery delicious. In bright and clean surrounds, communal diners
enjoy heaping bowls of congee and customized noodle soups, including
the best shrimp dumpling bowl in town. Rice dishes are also a cheap
and filling specialty, the best of which, Fuk-kin, tosses fried rice together
with shrimp, crab, scallops, chicken, and egg. ✉ *309 Spadina Ave.,
Kensington Market* ☎ *416/977–0601* ▤ *MC, V* Ⓜ *Dundas* ✛ *4:C.*

$–$$ ✕ **Wah Sing Seafood Restaurant.** Just one of a jumble of Asian eateries
CHINESE clustered on a tiny Kensington Market street, this meticulously clean
and spacious restaurant has two-for-one lobsters (in season, which
is almost always). They're scrumptious and tender, with black-bean
sauce or ginger and green onion. You can also choose giant shrimps
Szechuan-style or one of the lively queen crabs from the tank. Chicken
and vegetarian dishes for landlubbers are good, too. ✉ *47 Baldwin St.,
Kensington Market* ☎ *416/599–8822* ▤ *MC, V* Ⓜ *College* ✛ *4:D.*

QUEEN WEST

$$$$ ✕ **The Fifth.** Enter through the Easy Social Club, a main-floor dance club,
FRENCH and take a freight elevator to the Fifth, a semiprivate dining club and
loft space with the right balance of formality and flirtation. The mood
is industrial-strength romantic. In winter, sit on a sofa in front of a huge
fireplace; in summer, dine on a gazebo terrace. Entrées include steak,
black cod, roasted chicken, and rack of lamb. You could also make a
meal of a selection of intriguing sides such as mahogany and basmati
rice with caramelized onions. ✉ *225 Richmond St. W, Queen West*
☎ *416/979–3005* ⊕ *www.thefifthgrill.com* ⚑ *Reservations essential*
▤ *AE, DC, MC, V* ⊘ *Closed Sun.–Wed. No lunch* Ⓜ *Osgoode* ✛ *5:D.*

$$-$$$

ASIAN

Fodor'sChoice

★

✕**Foxley.** Like the appealingly bare-bones aesthetic of the space (exposed brick, hardwoods, candlelight), this creative bistro offers unadorned dishes that are jammed with flavor. After traveling for a year, chef–owner Tom Thai returned to Toronto with newfound inspiration from places like Asia, Latin America, and the Mediterranean. There are daily ceviches like Spanish bonito with pomegranate and crispy capers, as well as a couple dozen other tapas-style offerings, including spicy blue crab and avocado salad, lamb and duck prosciutto dumplings, and grilled side ribs with sticky shallot glaze. All can be paired with an impressive list of sparkling, sake and soju, whites and reds, running from dry Hungarian Tokaji to a bold Barolo—most modestly priced. ■TIP➔Note that the foodies have found it and the restaurant doesn't take reservations. Plan accordingly. ✉ *207 Ossington St., Queen West* ☎ *416/534-8520* ⊕ *www.foxleybistro.com* ⚇ *Reservations not accepted* ▭ *MC, V* ⊙ *No lunch* ✛ *5:A.*

$$

VEGETARIAN

✕**Fressen.** A feast of herbivorous cuisine jumps off the meat- and dairy-free menu here (some dishes contain eggs). Vegetable soups are silken and perfumed with coconut milk and ginger; pasta dishes are plump with mushrooms and vegetables. Desserts like the chocolate terrine amaze. Sip a groove juice (made from cucumber, celery, kale, and other greens) while you wait for your main course. It's all served in a room decorated with natural materials: ceiling pipes are covered by woven twigs, and piles of rocks and herb-filled jars enhance the environment. ✉ *478 Queen St. W, Queen West* ☎ *416/504–5127* ⊕ *www.fressenrestaurant.com* ▭ *MC, V* ⊙ *No lunch weekdays* Ⓜ *Osgoode* ✛ *5:C.*

$$$-$$$$

MODERN
CANADIAN

✕ **Nota Bene.** From Chef David Lee and partners, the team behind high-end stalwart Splendido has moved on to create this more affordable option—if the pedigree doesn't get you, the crispy duck salad will. A stone's throw away from the Four Seasons Opera House, this elegantly spaced room is all Brazilian cherry wood, chartreuse leather banquettes and flashes of contemporary art. Here, the chef turns out finely wrought French-Latin-Asian-inspired dishes with seasonal Canadian ingredients. Try sumac-dusted crispy duck tossed with green papaya slaw and cashews or dive into the private stock of naturally raised 60-day dry-aged steaks served with Café de Paris butter. ✉ *180 Queen St. W, Queen West* ☎ *416/977–6400* ⊕ *www.notabenerestaurant.com* ⚇ *Reservations recommeded* ▭ *AE, DC, MC, V* ⊙ *Closed Sun. No lunch Sat.* Ⓜ *Osgoode* ✛ *E:5.*

$$-$$$

SEAFOOD

✕**Oyster Boy.** Whether you get them baked (in one of 12 different ways), fried, or raw, the oyster is the thing here, and at this casual neighborhood spot it seems you can't have too much of good thing. A chalkboard spells out what's fresh and available, along with sizing and price per bivalve. There's a pleasing array of house condiments with which to slurp your choices. Other treats include salt-cod fish cakes, seared fish of the day, and excellent onion rings. A nice selection of complementary wines and beers, as well as coolly friendly servers, makes for a fun night out. ✉ *872 Queen St. W, Queen West* ☎ *416/534–3432* ⊕ *www.oysterboy.ca* ▭ *AE, DC, MC, V* ⊙ *No lunch* Ⓜ *Queen* ✛ *5:A.*

QUEEN'S PARK, THE ANNEX, AND YORKVILLE

The Annex caters to a winning mix of students, professors, historic homes and treed spaces, a kind of bookish coffee clatch amid the hubbub of the city. Come here for everything from authentic fish-and-chips to a thriving new restaurant row along Harbord Street. Little Italy, meanwhile, is an enduring hot spot for people-watching from a sunny patio while consuming everything from pizza and vino to gelato in the area that while almost fully gentrified, still maintains its neighborly charms.

THE ANNEX

¢
CAFÉ

✕ **Future Bakery & Café.** This European-style bakery also serves old European recipes like beef borscht, buckwheat cabbage rolls, and potato-cheese pierogies slathered with thick sour cream. This place is beloved by the pastry-and-coffee crowd, health-conscious foodies looking for fruit salad with homemade yogurt and honey, students wanting generous portions, and people-watchers from 7 AM to 2 AM. A St. Lawrence Market branch (95 Front Street E) sells just bread and pastries and closes early in the evening. ⊠ *483 Bloor St. W, The Annex* ☎ *416/922–5875* ⌫ *Reservations not accepted* ▭ *MC, V* Ⓜ *Bathurst* ⊕ *www.futurebakery.com* ▭ *MC, V* Ⓜ *King* ✛ *1:B, 6:G.*

$$
FRENCH

✕ **Le Paradis.** This is the kind of comfortable neighborhood place you'd look for in Paris: checkerboard floors, sunny walls hung with black-and-white photographs, and waiters rushing around in white aprons. University types, writers, and actors from the area come to this authentic French bistro-on-a-budget for the ambience and gently priced wine list. Steak frites, crisp herb-roasted chicken, and exotic *tajine de volaille* (a Moroccan stew of chicken, prunes, olives, and a shopping list of seasonings) get the creative juices flowing. ⊠ *166 Bedford Rd., The Annex* ☎ *416/921–0995* ⊕ *www.leparadis.com* ▭ *AE, DC, MC, V* Ⓜ *Dupont* ✛ *E:1.*

$–$$
VEGETARIAN

✕ **Live Organic Food Bar.** Sunny decor will charm you while the imagination of the enthusiastic owners will amaze you in this raw-food spot. Almond-herb spread atop a buckwheat crusty biscuit and olive-cashew mix between paper-thin turnip wraps are tasty. The stove is used ever so slightly for "roasting" root vegetables served over mixed greens with balsamic drizzle, and for warm tomato soup. A long list of seriously fresh-squeezed juices is served. Be aware: service is casual. ⊠ *264 Dupont St., The Annex* ☎ *416/515–2002* ⊕ *www.livefoodbar.com* ▭ *DC, MC, V* ⊗ *Closed Mon. No dinner Sun.* Ⓜ *Spadina* ✛ *B:1.*

$$$
FRENCH

✕ **Loire.** A close-to-perfect neighborhood bistro, named for the place where the French owners grew up and formed their palates. Now it's where locals enjoy lightly finessed dishes of oysters with horseradish and lemon mignonette, PEI mussels cooked in local Steam Whistle beer with crispy onions, Angus beef burgers, tagliatelle tossed with chicken thighs and king oyster mushrooms, Ontario rainbow trout, and wonderful wines, many from the Loire Valley. Finishing cheese plates feature Quebec and French selections. The spare room is warm with soft lighting; the service is impeccable (it's usually the owner–sommelier dancing about the narrow space), and one can't help but be instantly enchanted. ⊠ *119 Harbord St., The Annex* ☎ *416/850–8330* ⊕ *www. loirerestaurant.ca* ⊟ *AE, MC, V* ⊗ *Closed Sun. and Mon. No lunch Sat.* Ⓜ *Spadina* ✛ *C:2.*

3

$$–$$$
MODERN
CANADIAN

✕**Messis.** A skillful chef-owner presents fresh, pretty dishes. Herb-marinated veal loin and a rack of New Zealand lamb with Southern Comfort–rosemary glaze exemplify the inspired comfort food. Enjoy grilled free-range cornish hen with Pommery mustard glaze and a sauté of red potatoes, mushrooms, and sun-dried tomatoes. Messis is a favorite for small celebrations because of lovely desserts like a phyllo package of wild blueberries and white chocolate. The summer patio twinkles with lights at night. ⊠ *97 Harbord St., The Annex* ☎ *416/920–2186* ⊟ *AE, DC, MC, V* ⊕ *www.messis.ca* ⊗ *No lunch Sat.–Mon.* Ⓜ *Spadina* ✛ *2:C.*

$$–$$$
SOUTHERN

✕**Southern Accent.** This funky Cajun and Creole restaurant sits on a street lined with antiques shops, bookstores, and galleries. Perch at the bar, order a martini and hush puppies, and chat with the resident psychic. Whimsical knickknacks adorn every inch of the place. Dining rooms on two floors offer a market-driven menu. Some constants are bayou chicken (Southern fried, with dark and spicy sauce); cracker catfish (a fillet coated with spiced crackers) served with lime tartar sauce; and shrimp *étouffée* with caramelized vegetables. ⊠ *595 Markham St., The Annex* ☎ *416/536–3211* ⊕ *www.southernaccent.com* ⊟ *AE, DC, MC, V* ⊗ *Closed Mon. No lunch* Ⓜ *Bathurst* ✛ *1:B.*

QUEEN'S PARK

$–$$
AMERICAN

✕**7 West Cafe.** It's surprising how many people hunger for pasta primavera or a bagel melt at 3 AM. Luckily, such cravings can be indulged at this 24-hour haven for the hip and hungry. Everything is homemade and comes with a green salad. Soups like Moroccan lentil and vegetarian chili are delicious. The dinner-size sandwiches (grilled honey-and-herb chicken breast, for example) are huge. All three floors here are chic and trendy, but people don't come after midnight for the decor. ⊠ *7 Charles St. W, Queen's Park* ☎ *416/928–9041* ⊕ *www.7westcafe.com* ⊟ *AE, MC, V* Ⓜ *Bloor-Yonge* ✛ *2:F.*

$$$$
MODERN
CANADIAN
Fodor's Choice
★

✕**C5.** You can't miss the angular, Daniel Libeskind–designed "Crystal" addition to the Royal Ontario Museum as it juts and jabs over Bloor Street, and you shouldn't miss dining at C5, the starkly designed, unapologetically modernist restaurant on the addition's fifth floor. Its regionally focused cuisine is suitably arrayed in five courses, including one of the city's best cheese plates. The menu relies heavily on dishes built in layers, like succulent lobster tail nestled between tender brioche and a crusted poached egg or moist black cod set atop lentil salad and under lobster hollandaise. Visitors also enjoy panoramic city views, while savvy locals know to arrive early for a drink in the stylish lounge. ∎TIP➙ Time your

CLOSE UP

Alfresco Dining

From the first sign of warm weather until September's cool evenings, Torontonians hit the deck, the patio, the courtyard, and the rooftop terrace.

In summer, Yorkville bursts into bloom. **Summer's Ice Cream** (⊠ *101 Yorkville Ave., Yorkville* ☎ *416/944–2637* ⊕ *summersicecream.com*) is the spot for grabbing homemade ice cream in just-made waffle cones, then strolling in Yorkville Park. **MBCo** (⊠ *100 Bloor St. W, Yorkville* ☎ *416/961–6226* ⊕ *www.mbco.com*) offers glorious sandwiches, wraps, pizza, and soups to eat on the patio or in the park. Enjoy lunch or sip a cosmo and watch the sunset at the **Roof Lounge** (⊠ *Park Hyatt Hotel, 4 Avenue Rd.* ☎ *416/924–5471* ⊕ *park-toronto.hyatt.com*). A light-wrapped tree glimmers in the garden at **Michelle's Bistro** (⊠ *162 Cumberland St., Yorkville* ☎ *416/944–1504*). **Hemingway's** (⊠ *142 Cumberland St., Yorkville* ☎ *416/968–2828* ⊕ *www.hemingways.to*) attracts throngs to the flower-filled roof garden. The patio at **Amber** (⊠ *119 Yorkville Ave., Yorkville* ☎ *416/926–9037* ⊕ *www.amberinyorkville.com*) rocks with cool, late-night people. The **Prego della Piazza** (⊠ *150 Bloor St. W, Yorkville* ☎ *416/920–9900* ⊕ *www.pregodellapiazza.com*) patio, flanked by the Church of the Redeemer, is a favorite.

Kensington Market is home to melting-pot cuisine. **Supermarket** (⊠ *265 Augusta Ave., Kensington Market* ☎ *416/840–0501* ⊕ *www.supermarkettoronto.com*) has a boisterous patio and tasty *izakaya* (Japanese pub food). Savor oversized empanadas on the tented patio of **Jumbo Empanadas** (⊠ *245 Augusta Ave., Kensington Market* ☎ *416/977–0056* ⊕ *www.jumboempanadas.com*).

Torito (⊠ *276 Augusta Ave., Kensington Market* ☎ *647/436–5874*) has excellent ceviche and sangria.

When they're rolling up the sidewalks elsewhere, the Greek area of the Danforth is just getting lively. The sidewalk patio at **Christina's** (⊠ *513 Danforth Ave., Danforth* ☎ *416/465–1751* ⊕ *www.christinas.ca*) is a good place to check out the Greek scene. A popular place to sit at outdoor tables and sip ouzo is **Myth** (⊠ *417 Danforth Ave., Danforth* ☎ *416/461–8383* ⊕ *www.myth.to*).

The Italians practically invented the art of sipping espresso outdoors and watching the world go by. Window-walls open to the street so the patio combines with the front of the restaurant at **Giovanna** (⊠ *637 College Ave., Little Italy* ☎ *416/538–2098*). **Trattoria Giancarlo** (⊠ *41 Clinton St., Little Italy* ☎ *416/533–9619* ⊕ *www.giancarlotrattoria.com*) has tasty grilled meats you can savor at outdoor picnic tables.

The Entertainment District—Queen Street between University Avenue and Bathurst Street—is filled with dining adventures. The **Rivoli** (⊠ *322 Queen St. W, Queen West* ☎ *416/596–1908* ⊕ *www.rivoli.ca*) is a hot outdoor spot. The garden at the **Queen Mother Café** (⊠ *208 Queen St. W, Queen West* ☎ *416/598–4719* ⊕ *www.queenmothercafe.com*) is a cool place for East–West dishes. The **Black Bull Tavern** (⊠ *298 Queen St. W, Queen West* ☎ *416/593–2766* ⊕ *www.blackball.ca*) is still the largest and most affordable. Way west, the **Drake Hotel** (⊠ *1150 Queen St. W, Queen West* ☎ *416/531–5042* ⊕ *www.thedrakehotel.ca*) has an interesting rooftop patio with pretty clientele.

reservation for sunset. ⊠ *100 Queen's Park, 5th fl., enter from Bloor St., Queen's Park* ☎ *416/586–7928 www.c5restaurant.ca* ⌖ *Reservations essential* ☰ *AE, MC, V* ☺ *No dinner Sun.–Wed.* Ⓜ *Museum* ⚓ *2:E.*

$$$
MODERN
CANADIAN

✕ **The Gardiner Café.** Jamie Kennedy is still at the helm here even if his name is no longer at the top. All limestone, slate, blond oak, and glass, the airy room is a fitting accompaniment to a new focus on sandwiches and salads. A lunch crowd that has always enjoyed Jamie Kennedy's seasonal starters at his wine bar will appreciate offerings like a smooth Ontario sweet corn bisque with a plump, seared scallop. Count on excellent signature frites with lemon mayo, fabulous cheese plates and charcuterie, a great burger, salade niçoise, and innovative Sri Lankan Hoppers complemented by a dazzling array of house-made condiments: lime pickle, coconut-based *pol sambol*, ghee-fried shallots, green-mango chutney, and more. Wines are matched with each dish, including many from Ontario's Niagara region—home, too, to the berries in the pleasingly retro strawberry shortcake. ⊠ *111 Queen's Park, Queen's Park* ☎ *416/362–1957* ⊕ *www.jkkitchens.com* ☰ *AE, MC, V* ☺ *Open for lunch 7 days, dinners on Fri.* Ⓜ *Museum* ⚓ *2:E.*

$$–$$$
MODERN
CANADIAN

✕ **One.** Mark McEwan's One is the restaurant at the hot Hazelton Hotel—Yabu Puschelberg–designed and as modern and elegant (rich woods, smoked glass, cowhide, and onyx) as his other two high-end contemporary restaurants, Bymark and North 44. The number-one celeb spot during the Toronto International Film Festival, it's the place to be seen in Yorkville. McEwan's ingredient-driven cuisine runs from a first course of ruby tuna sashimi with yuzu (fragrant citrus) and chili to the deeply satisfying "ultimate street burger." Many dishes like the USDA Prime strip arrive perfectly cooked but simply prepared and are meant to be accompanied by generous family-style sides, such as frites with citrus aioli and tender heirloom carrots. The all-Canadian cheese lineup is an especially proud menu moment. The chef ages his own beef, and many agree his steaks are the best in the city. ⊠ *The Hazelton Hotel Toronto, 118 Yorkville Ave., Queen's Park* ☎ *416/963–6300* ⊕ *www. onehazelton.com* ☰ *AE, MC, V* Ⓜ *Bay* ⚓ *1:E.*

YORKVILLE

$$–$$$
ITALIAN

✕ **Bellini's Ristorante.** Never wavering from its focus on elegance, good taste, classic food, and professional service, Bellini's has stood the test of time. How can one choose from dishes such as veal *agnolotti* with grilled oyster mushrooms; roasted pistachio-crusted sea bass; the siren call of Provimi veal osso buco with saffron risotto and lemon-thyme jus; or lobster risotto with honey mushrooms, mascarpone cheese, and chervil? This is a romantic haven and a quiet oasis for visiting celebs. ⊠ *101 Yorkville Ave. W, Yorkville* ☎ *416/929–9111* ⊕ *www.bellinis-ristorante.com* ☰ *AE, DC, MC, V* ☺ *No lunch* Ⓜ *Bay* ⚓ *1:I.*

$
FRENCH
☺

✕ **Crêpes à GoGo.** In this casual bistro, proprietress Veronique and crew turn out simple sandwiches and buckwheat crepes, also known as galettes, from a semisweet crepe mixture grilled on a dry skillet, using a technique that has been passed down for generations. Signature items include the Flo—a crisped crepe folded around the sharpness of red onion, the fatty nuttiness of Swiss, an herbaceous hit of parsley, and a bit of tangy sour cream. Big Ben is made with mozzarella cheese and raspberry jam; La Véronique, with Brie, strawberries, baby spinach, and maple syrup. Apple cider, a traditional Breton beverage of apple juice fermented in the bottle just like Champagne, is also served. Crepes are presented in the distinctive square Bretonne-style fold, whereupon Veronique tears down the paper bag's edges, looks every patron in the eye, and says, "Bon appétit." ⊠ *18 Yorkville Ave., Yorkville* ☎ *416/ 922–6765* ⊕ *www.crepesagogo.com* ⊟ *AE, DC, MC, V* Ⓜ *Bay* ✛ *1:F.*

$$–$$$ ✕**Holt's Café in Holt Renfrew.** Terrazzo floors, white walls, red-leather seat-
CAFÉ   ing, and a bank of windows overlooking Bloor Street make this café a fashionable break from shopping the high-end department store. Enjoy a midday cocktail or a delicious *tartine* (ritzy open-faced sandwich) like seared ahi tuna spiced up with wasabi mayo or smoked salmon, poached eggs, and sautéed wild mushrooms. All are prepared on the famous Poilâne bread (thick-crusted whole wheat sourdough) imported from Paris three times a week. ⊠ *50 Bloor St. W, Yorkville* ☎ *416/922–2333* ⊕ *www.holtrenfrew.com* ⊟ *AE, DC, MC, V* Ⓜ *Bay* ✛ *1:F.*

$–$$ ✕**The Host.** Dine in the garden room among flowering plants or in the
INDIAN   handsome main room at this well-established Indian spot. Waiters rush around carrying baskets of hot *naan* (a gorgeous, puffy flat bread) from the oven. Tandoori *machi*, whole fish baked in a tandoor oven and served on a sizzling plate with onion and coriander, is an excellent dish. Tender sliced lamb is enfolded in a curry of cashew nuts and whole car- damom. End your meal with such exotic Indian desserts as *golabjabun*, little round cakes soaking in rosewater-scent honey. ⊠ *14 Prince Arthur Ave., Yorkville* ☎ *416/962–4678* ⊕ *www.welcometohost.com* ⤲ *Reser- vations essential* ⊟ *AE, MC, V* ☯ *Closed Mon.* Ⓜ *Bay* ✛ *1:G.*

$$$–$$$$ ✕**Morton's.** Just when you thought this top-notch international chain
STEAK   couldn't possibly get better, they added glorious additional steak varia- tions to their repertoire, including steak au poivre, with yummy pep- percorn-cognac sauce; filet Oskar, topped with crab, asparagus, and béarnaise; and filet Diane, with sautéed mushrooms in a rich mustard sauce. Or you can still dine on a New York strip or a 48-ounce porter- house. All beef is shipped chilled, not frozen, from one Chicago supplier. The interior has a handsome, wood-panel clubbiness. ⊠ *4 Avenue Rd., Yorkville* ☎ *416/925–0648* ⊕ *www. mortons.com* ⊟ *AE, D, MC, V* Ⓜ *Bay* ✛ *1:E.*

$$$–$$$$ ✕**Pangaea.** In this tranquil room
CANADIAN   with an aura of restrained sophisti- cation, unprocessed, seasonal ingre- dients and the freshest produce are always used. Soups such as lobster bisque with fiddlehead greens are unique; salads are creative construc- tions of organic greens. Soy-honey- glazed quail comes with tempura onion rings; veal, Australian lamb, and caribou are served with truffle- whipped potatoes. Vegetarians can

---

WORD OF MOUTH

"Pangaea came highly recom- mended and did not disappoint... I think it definitely fits the bill for a special evening destina- tion. We were there just for lunch and shared three appetiz- ers: lobster bisque, foie gras, and lamb sausage. All were excellent. The atmosphere was modern and yet not cold, and the service was perfect."   —Maggie

find bliss in this caring kitchen, too. Seasonal sweets are created by Joanne Yolles, the preeminent pastry chef in the city. ⊠ *1221 Bay St., Yorkville* ☎ *416/920–2323* ⊕ *www.pangaearestaurant.com* ⊟ *AE, DC, MC, V* Ⓜ *Bay* ⊹ *1:F.*

$$$–$$$$
ITALIAN

✕ **Sotto Sotto.** A coal cellar in a turn-of-the-20th-century home was dug out, its stone walls and floor polished, and a restaurant created in what has become a dining oasis for locals and international jet-setters alike. The menu of more than 20 pasta dishes gives a tantalizing tug at the taste buds. Gnocchi is made daily. The *orecchiette* ("ear-shape" disks of pasta), with a toss of prosciutto, mushrooms, black olives, and fresh tomatoes, is a symphony of textures. Cornish hen is marinated, pressed, and grilled to a juicy brown, and the swordfish and fresh fish of the day are beautifully done on the grill. ⊠ *116-A Avenue Rd., Yorkville* ☎ *416/962–0011* ⊕ *www.sottosotto.ca* ⊟ *AE, DC, MC, V* ⊗ *No lunch* Ⓜ *Bay* ⊹ *1:E.*

$$$–$$$$
CAFÉ

✕ **Studio Café.** At this well-lighted, comfortable café—a combination hotel coffee shop, restaurant, and contemporary glass-and-art gallery—you can have a full Japanese or Canadian breakfast. Trendsetting dishes include a complex Asian stir-fry; chicken curry with all the chutneys, pickles, and sauces; and risotto with sautéed leeks and tomatoes. Still, sandwiches such as smoked turkey clubhouse with cranberry sauce, and one of the city's best beef burgers—with roasted onions, mushrooms, and aged cheddar—are what draw the foodies. ⊠ *Four Seasons Toronto hotel, 21 Avenue Rd., Yorkville* ☎ *416/964–0411* ⊕ *www.fourseasons. com* ⊟ *AE, DC, MC, V* Ⓜ *Bay* ⊹ *1:E.*

$$–$$$
JAPANESE

✕ **Sushi Inn.** Conveniently located in Yorkville, Sushi Inn lets you a breather from high-end shopping for dependable appetizers and fresh *maki* (sushi rolls). Crisp *gyoza* (dumplings), miso-marinated cod, seaweed salad, and ethereal tempura are a good way to start. Follow up with a filling bento box or signature maki rolls including the Sushi Inn—eel, avocado, salmon skin, *tobiko* (flying fish roe)—or Dragon B—California roll with shrimp tempura topped with gossamer salmon slices. The service is workmanlike, and dillydallying at your table is not encouraged. ⊠ *120 Cumberland St., Yorkville* ☎ *416/923–9992* ⊕ *www.sushiinn.net* ⊟ *AE, DC, MC, V* Ⓜ *Bay* ⊹ *1:E.*

$$$$
FRENCH

✕ **Truffles.** Sophisticated yet warm, this special-occasion eatery serves contemporary cuisine grounded in authentic French flavors. Appetizers include thyme-roasted sweetbreads with lentil ragout, foie-gras *torchon* (poached in cheesecloth), and the signature spaghettini with Perigord Black Gold truffle foam. Entrées such as pepper-seared loin of venison and truffled honey squab breast are pleasures for the palate. Superb wine matchings and an enviable cheese list make for a languid evening. ⊠ *Four Seasons Toronto hotel, 21 Avenue Rd., Yorkville* ☎ *416/928–7331* ⊕ *www.fourseasons.com* ⌂ *Reservations essential* ⊟ *AE, D, DC, MC, V* ⊗ *Closed Sun. and Mon. No lunch* Ⓜ *Bay* ⊹ *1:C.*

CHURCH-WELLESLEY AND DUNDAS SQUARE AREA

Yorkville is a chichi outpost of designer shops, a museum row, and magical green and treed areas around Queen's Park, perfect for wandering or relaxing with a cappuccino on a sidewalk café. Especially in the electrifying gay village that is Church and Wellesley. Wherever you choose to eat, make sure you look fabulous!

CHURCH-WELLESLEY

$$$–$$$$
FRENCH

✕**Bistro 990.** A superior kitchen is seamlessly paired with bistro informality. Start your experience with traditional pâté de maison, partnered with quince marmalade, wine preserves, and plenty of homemade croutons. Oven-roasted halibut with salsa and feta cheese is a treat, and a roasted half chicken with herb garlic au jus crackles with crispness and Provençal flavor. Ask about the wild-game dish of the day. Faux stone walls stenciled with Cocteau-esque designs, sturdily upholstered chairs, and a tiled floor make the dining area sophisticated but comfortable. ⊠ *990 Bay St., Church–Wellesley* ☎ *416/921–9990* ⊕ *www.bistro990. ca* ⌚ *Reservations essential* ☰ *AE, DC, MC, V* ⊙ *No lunch weekends* Ⓜ *Bloor-Yonge, Wellesley* ✛ *2:F.*

$$$$
STEAK

✕**Carman's Club.** Arthur Carman opened this steak house in 1959, and nothing has changed except the prices. In a room that's outdated but wears its age with pride, with his collection of pewter, copper, porcelain, and paintings, he still offers prime steaks with the nine items that make up the package: garlic toast, baked potato with all the trimmings, cottage cheese, olives, peppers, *tzatziki* (yogurt and cucumber dip), baklava, and coffee or tea. The kitchen has a way with lobster,

> ### WORD OF MOUTH
>
> "Everything at Carman's is top notch. I have gone there every year for 4 years and the service and food have been impeccable every time. The ambiance and wine selection is also most excellent. The chateaubriand is the best and anyone can smell garlic the minute they walk in the door."
> —Dana

Dover sole, and garlic shrimp, too. Meander along the hallway and view the photos of stars from the '50s up to now. They all loved the steak. And come on—how many places still serve a chateaubriand meal for two? ⊠ *26 Alexander St., Church–Wellesley* ☎ *416/924–8697* ⊕ *carmen. sites.toronto.com* ⌚ *Reservations essential* ☰ *AE, MC, V* ⊙ *Closed Sun. No lunch* Ⓜ *College* ✛ *3:F.*

DUNDAS SQUARE AREA

$$$$
STEAK

✕**Barberian's.** A Toronto landmark where wheeling, dealing, and lots of eating have gone on since 1959, Barberian's is also romantic: Elizabeth Taylor and Richard Burton got engaged here (for the first time). The menu is full of steak-house classics, like starters of tomato and onion salad and jumbo shrimp cocktail. Mains are all about the meat, be it a perfectly timed porterhouse, New York strip loin, or rib steak. Fresh fish of the day and lemony grilled free-range capon also hold their charms. One of the oldest steak houses in the city, Barberian's has an excellent selection of Bordeaux. ⊠ *7 Elm St., Dundas Square Area*

☎ *416/597–0335* ⊕ *barberians.com* ⟐ *Reservations essential* ▭ *AE,*
MC, V ☉ *Closed Sun.* Ⓜ *Dundas* ✛ *4:F.*

$–$$ ✕ **Spring Rolls.** Torontonians embrace pan-Asian spring rolls as if they'd
ASIAN   cut their teeth on these appetizers. You too can choose from the enormous
hot or cold selection at this chain, where the food far outshines the generic,
modern decor. A Thai red curry (with jasmine rice, chilies, and herb-
touched coconut milk) will leave you breathless. There are also locations
at 85 Front Street in Old Town and 40 Dundas Street West in Chinatown.
✉ *693 Yonge St., Queen's Park* ☎ *416/972-7655* ⊕ *www.springrolls.ca*
Ⓜ *Bloor-Yonge* ✛ *4:F* ▭ *AE, MC, V* ⟐ *Reservations essential.*

GREATER TORONTO

Pockets of good restaurants are to be found across Greater Toronto,
including great neighborhood haunts in Cabbagetown and the Yonge
and Eglinton area (nicknamed "Young and Eligible" for its lively single young professionals). While the Danforth is also known as Greektown—the street signs are even translated into Greek, things have been
changing on this restaurant-heavy strip. The area has always been alive
with the buzz of people, chic meze spots, family-style souvlaki empori-
ums and lots of places for drinks and gelato. But now there's everything
from sushi to bakeshops, upscale Canadian, and old-school burgers.
The annual Taste of Danforth Festival celebrates the mouthwatering
diversity of the city as it welcomes millions to the strip each August.

*Use the coordinate (✛ 2:B) at the end of each listing to locate a site on
the corresponding map.*

DANFORTH

$$–$$$ ✕ **Allen's.** Slide into a well-worn
AMERICAN   wood booth or sit at a red-and-
white-checker-clothed table at this
vintage New York saloon, a solid
bastion of Irish Americana complete with oak bar, pressed-tin ceiling, and short-order counter. There
are many draft and bottled beers,
a vast wine and whiskey selection,
and what is possibly the best beef
burger in town. The braised lamb

> **TASTE OF THE
> DANFORTH FESTIVAL**
>
> The annual **Taste of the Danforth
> Festival** (⊕ *www.tasteofthedan-
> forth.com*) celebrates the mouth-
> watering diversity of the city as
> it welcomes millions to the strip
> each August.

shank with mashed potatoes and the liver and onions get raves. Servers may recommend the chocolate bread pudding with caramel sauce,
bourbon, and pecans; trust them. ✉ *143 Danforth Ave., Danforth*
☎ *416/463–3086* ⊕ *allens.to* ⟐ *Reservations essential* ▭ *AE, DC, MC,*
V Ⓜ *Broadview* ✛ *5:C.*

$$–$$$ ✕ **Christina's.** Who doesn't have a foodie love affair with Greek dips?
GREEK   Here they're served individually or as a large platter combination,
☾   *pikilia mezedakia,* which comes with warm pitas. A bottle of Greek
wine and specials like *saganaki,* an iron plate of Kefalograviera cheese
flamed in brandy, and you may shout *"Opa"* with the waiters. Order
a fish or meat mixed grill and the tray of food almost covers the table.

This cheery place, with the colors of the Aegean Sea and sun on the walls, has live music and uninhibited Greek dancing—by patrons and staff alike—on weekends. ✉ *492 Danforth Ave., Danforth* ☎ *416/463–4418* ⊕ *www.christinas.ca* ⊟ *AE, DC, MC, V* Ⓜ *Chester* ✛ *4:D.*

$$$–$$$$
MODERN
CANADIAN

✕ **Globe Bistro.** This Danforth strip choice has offered a welcome change to mezes and souvlaki since 2007. Here, it's all about locally produced ingredients used at the peak of their seasons. Carmelized pork belly meets seared scallops, roasted caribou leg marries goat cheese soufflé; black pepper ricotta gnocci in a mushroomy broth has become an instant classic. ✉ *124 Danforth Ave., Danforth* ☎ *416/466–2000* ⊕ *www.globebistro.com* ⊟ *AE, DC, MC, V* ⊘ *No lunch on Sat.* Ⓜ *Chester* ✛ *4:C.*

$$$
FRENCH

✕ **Provence Delices.** This French-style villa is an almost 30-year-old Cabbagetown landmark with a potbellied stove and a delightful summer patio. The eight-item sampling menu satisfies the curious with a tartare of scallops; a *tartine* (open-face sandwich) with cured salmon, goat cheese, and garlic mayo; a chicken roulade with orange sauce; and other small dishes. If classic Provençal fish soup appeals, this is the place to try it. Duck confit with olive sauce is crisp and juicy at the same time. Authentic patisserie, including tarte tatin, with caramelized apples and a buttery crust, makes a fine ending. ✉ *12 Amelia St., Greater Toronto* ☎ *416/924–9901* ⊕ *www.provencerestaurant.com* ⊟ *AE, MC, V* Ⓜ *Sherbourne, College* ✛ *5:C.*

LITTLE ITALY

$$–$$$
ITALIAN

✕ **Bar Italia.** A fixture in Little Italy, this is where the city's glitterati can be found getting their fix of the classics: well-prepared pasta, risotto, fish of the day, and a traditional favorite of sautéed mushroom salad with arugula and Parmesan. In the summer, sip a glass of wine on the patio and dig into a specialty, the Cubano sandwich of roasted pork, avocado, *pancetta* (thick, hand-cut bacon), and garlicky mayo on a huge Italian bun. Close your eyes and pretend you're in southern Italy; you'll still hear Italian spoken at many tables. ✉ *582 College St., Little Italy* ☎ *416/535–3621* ⊕ *www.bar-italia.ca* ⊟ *AE, DC, MC, V* Ⓜ *Bathurst, Queen's Park* ✛ *5:A.*

$$$
MODERN
CANADIAN

✕ **The Black Hoof.** A typical evening spent in this tiny new hot spot that opened in late 2008 features exotic meats and loving attention from the two owners: one as manager and the other as chef. House made charcuterie plates including bites of rabbit *rillettes* terrine, venison *bresaola* and duck prosciutto by chef Grant van Gameren, plus some octopus salad and roasted bone marrow. And the house specialty: tapas-sized horse tartare. A first for many in Toronto—and not available in the U.S. The tartare is delicious: a somehow clean, lean meat, not gamey at all, like the purest, lightest beef. ✉ *928 Dundas Street W, Little*

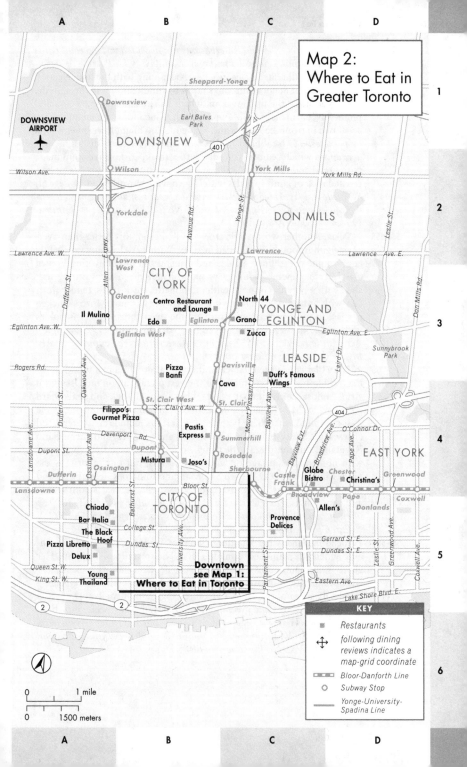

Map 2:
Where to Eat in
Greater Toronto

1

DOWNSVIEW
AIRPORT

Downsview

Sheppard-Yonge

Earl Bales
Park

DOWNSVIEW

401

Wilson Ave.

Wilson

York Mills

York Mills Rd.

2

Yorkdale

Yonge St.

DON MILLS

Lawrence Ave. W.

Avenue Rd.

Lawrence

Lawrence   Ave. E.

Leslie St.

Don Mills Rd.

Lawrence
West

Allen Expwy.

CITY OF
YORK

Glencairn

Centro Restaurant
and Lounge

North 44

YONGE AND
EGLINTON

3

Il Mulino

Edo

Eglinton

Grano

Eglinton Ave. E.

Sunnybrook
Park

Eglinton Ave. W.

Eglinton West

Zucca

Laird Dr.

LEASIDE

Rogers Rd.

Dufferin St.

Oakwood Ave.

Pizza
Banfi

Davisville

Cava

Duff's Famous
Wings

Mount Pleasant Rd.

Bayview Ave.

St. Clair West

St. Claire Ave. W.

St. Clair

404

4

Filippo's
Gourmet Pizza

Davenport   Rd.

Dupont

Pastis
Express

Summerhill

Bayview Ext.

Broadview Ave.

O'Connor Dr.

EAST YORK

Dupont St.

Mistura

Joso's

Rosedale

Sherbourne

Castle
Frank

Globe
Bistro

Chester

Christina's

Pape Ave.

Greenwood

Lansdowne Ave.

Ossington Ave.

Ossington

Dufferin

Bloor St.

CITY OF
TORONTO

Broadview

Pape

Allen's

Donlands

Greenwood Ave.

Coxwell

Lansdowne

Bathurst St.

University Ave.

Castle Frank

5

Chiado

Bar Italia

The Black
Hoof

College St.

Provence
Delices

Pizza Libretto

Delux

Dundas St.

Gerrard St. E.

Leslie St.

Coxwell Ave.

Dundas St. E.

Queen St. W.

Young
Thailand

King St. W.

Downtown
see Map 1:
Where to Eat in Toronto

Parliament St.

Eastern Ave.

Lake Shore Blvd. E.

2

2

KEY

Restaurants

⊕ following dining
reviews indicates a
map-grid coordinate

Bloor-Danforth Line

○ Subway Stop

Yonge-University-
Spadina Line

6

0   1 mile

0   1500 meters

Italy ☎ *416/551–8854* ⏴ *Reservations not accepted* ⊟ *No credit cards* ⊘ *Open for dinner only, Thursday to Monday.* Ⓜ *St. Patrick* ✛ *A:5.*

$$$–$$$$
PORTUGUESE

✕**Chiado.** It's all relaxed elegance here, beginning with the fine selection of appetizers at Senhor Antonio's tapas bar and continuing through the French doors to the dining room, which has polished wood floors and plum-velvet armchairs. The exquisite fish, which form the menu's basis, are flown in from the Azores and Madeira. You might have bluefin tuna or *peixe espada* (scabbard fish). Traditional Portuguese dishes include *açorda,* in which seafood is folded into a thick, custardlike soup made with bread and eggs. There's much for meat eaters, too—for example, a roasted rack of lamb sparkles with Douro wine sauce. ⊠ *864 College St. W, Little Italy* ☎ *416/538–1910* ⊕ *www.chiadorestaurant.com* ⏴ *Reservations essential* ⊟ *AE, DC, MC, V* ⊘ *No lunch weekends* Ⓜ *Bathurst, Queen's Park* ✛ *A:5.*

$$–$$$
FRENCH

✕ **Delux.** Another worthwhile stop on Ossington, this better-than-average neighborhood bistro opened in 2008. With its welcoming yet slightly edgy room, streamlined service and a menu full of comforting French classics, this newbie is full every night. There are oysters on the half shell with a playful Granny Smith mignonette, steak-frites, tender short ribs with horseradish crème, while chef-owner Corinna Mozo's chicken is roast to juicy perfection. Hot-from-the-oven chocolate chip cookies with a milk kicker keeps the kids coming back for more. ⊠ *92 Ossington Ave., Little Italy* ☎ *416/537–0134* ⏴ *Reservations recommeded* ⊟ *AE, MC, V* ⊘ *Open for dinner only.* Ⓜ *St. Patrick* ✛ *A:5.*

$$
ITALIAN

✕ **Pizza Libretto.** Authentic Neapolitan pizzas are fired in a wood-burning oven imported from Italy to the newest pizza joint on the Ossington strip. Amidst the communal wood tables, exposed brick and chalkboard paint, owner Max Rimaldi adheres to the rules of classic pizza set by the Associazione Verace Pizza Napoletana. Starters include charcuterie and cheeses like house-made duck prosciutto and four year-old Parmegiano Reggiano, but the pizza's the thing—crunchy, blistered crusts topped with homemade sausage or wild mushrooms, but our favorite is the pizza Margherita D.O.P. with San Marzano tomatoes, fresh basil, and local (nearby Ingersoll) Fiore di Latte Mozzarella. Service is both speedy and charming. ⊠ *221 Ossington Ave., Little Italy* ☎ *416/532–8000* ⊕ *www.pizzerialibretto.com* ⏴ *Reservations not accepted* ⊟ *AE, MC, V* ⊘ *Open for dinner only.* Ⓜ *St. Patrick* ✛ *A:5.*

$$–$$$
THAI

✕**Young Thailand.** Chef Wandee Young set Toronto's taste buds a-wagging when she launched Canada's first Thai restaurant in 1980. Her gently spiced authentic staples are just as delicious now. Chicken satay with peanut sauce, Thai-spiced calamari with sweet chili, and refreshing salad rolls are a nice start. Move on to zingy lemon chicken soup, and more shared mains like green mango salad, red-curry beef, spicy basil chicken, and Thai-style eggplant. It's pretty hard to order wrong here. ⊠ *936 King St. W, Little Italy* ☎ *416/366–8424* ⊕ *www.youngthailand. com* ⊟ *MC, V* ⊘ *No lunch weekends* Ⓜ *Dundas* ✛ *A:5.*

YONGE AND EGLINTON

$$$–$$$$
SPANISH

✗ **Cava.** After spending 11 years creating 12-course, high-concept "adventure menus," chef Chris McDonald traded his restaurant Avalon for this tapas place. A *salumi* (cured meat) bar serving house-cured meats is rounded out by a menu with a couple of dozen small plates like chickpeas with beef tripe and cumin-spiked squab. The drinks list offers Spanish sparkling wines and lots of sherries. Desserts are the evening's biggest treat, especially spiced-plum *clafoutis* with pistachio ice cream. ✉ *1560 Yonge St., Yonge and Eglinton* ☎ *416/979–9918* ⊕ *www.cavarestaurant.ca* ⌲ *Reservations essential* ═ *AE, DC, MC, V* ◔ *No lunch.* Ⓜ *St. Clair* ✛ *4:C.*

3

$$$–$$$$
ECLECTIC

✗ **Centro Restaurant and Lounge.** Showpiece chandeliers and 28-foot ceilings with pillars draped in cream suede to complement brown-suede chairs make for a drop-dead gorgeous, 138-seater attitude. The New American cuisine encompasses Italian, French, Asian—but not on one plate. Try pastas such as gnocchi with asparagus pesto or seafood cannelloni in cognac-tomato cream sauce. Mains are a global trip: tandoori-spiced pork tenderloin, organic honey-ginger salmon, or pan-roasted veal steak with marsala sauce. Desserts and cheeses are divine. ∎**TIP**➜ **A downstairs lounge has buzz, its own small, less-expensive menu ($$), and live music weekends.** ✉ *2472 Yonge St., at Eglinton Ave., Yonge and Eglinton* ☎ *416/483–2211* ⊕ *www.centro.ca* ⌲ *Reservations essential* ═ *AE, DC, MC, V* ◔ *Closed Sun. No lunch* Ⓜ *Eglinton* ✛ *3:C.*

$–$$
AMERICAN
☺

✗ **Duff's Famous Wings.** Plump with meat and crisp-skinned, wings and drumettes are served with pristine celery sticks and creamy dill or blue-cheese dressings. Ordering a pitcher of beer is the right thing to do. If you go with the hot wings (as opposed to other flavors like honey garlic), which you should, Duff's wing sauces are measured in Scoville heat units (SHU), the standard for measuring the heat of a pepper: 0 plain, 800 mild, 10,000 medium (their most popular), 500,000 death, and 850,000 Armageddon. If you take the kids, they can have burgers, hot dogs, or intriguing deep-fried mac-and-cheese nuggets. ✉ *1604 Bayview Ave., Yonge and Eglinton* ☎ *416/544–0100* ⊕ *www.duffsfamouswings. ca* ═ *AE, MC, V* Ⓜ *Eglinton* ✛ *3:C.*

$$–$$$
JAPANESE

✗ **Edo.** Aficionados of Japanese food may have to stop themselves from ordering everything on the menu at this chain. Even the uninitiated are mesmerized by the intriguing dishes, including plates of *yaki kinoko* (grilled mushrooms) or thickly sliced eggplant, baked to a silken texture, that's both sweet and sour. If soft-shell crab is on the menu, it's a worthy choice. The chef is an artist with sushi and sashimi, but if you can't decide, the set menus give you balanced and exciting Japanese meals. ✉ *484 Eglinton Ave. W, Yonge and Eglinton* ☎ *416/481–1370* ⊕ *www.edosushi.com* ◔ *No lunch* ⌲ *Reservations essential* ═ *AE, DC, MC, V* Ⓜ *Eglinton* ✛ *3:B.*

$$
ITALIAN

✗ **Filippo's Gourmet Pizza.** LIFE IS LIKE A PIZZA—THE MORE YOU PUT IN, THE RICHER IT GETS is written on a slate map of Italy that hangs on the wall of this charming spot. A big wooden display table inside beckons with antipasti—polenta and olives, potato and fried onion, crisp green beans, and grilled peppers and eggplant. Bruschetta is piled high with chopped tomato and fresh basil. The enthusiasm of owner

Filippo DiNatale is transferred to all his dishes—rigatoni with fennel, capers, and anchovies; rich and creamy risottos; and wonderful pizzas handmade to order. ⊠ *744 St. Clair Ave. W, Yonge and Eglinton* ☎ *416/658–0568* ⊟ *AE, MC, V* Ⓜ *St. Clair West* ⊹ *4:B.*

$$–$$$
ITALIAN
Ⓒ

✕ **Grano.** What started as a bakery and take-out antipasto bar has grown into a cheerful collage of the Martella family's Italy. Come for animated talk, good food, and great bread in lively rooms with faux-ancient plaster walls, wooden tables, and bright chairs. Choose, if you can, from 40 delectable vegetarian dishes and numerous meat and fish antipasti. Lucia's homemade gnocchi and ravioli are divine, as is the white-chocolate-and-raspberry pie. A seat under the tree on the rear patio is the next best thing to being in Italy. ⊠ *2035 Yonge St., between Eglinton and Davisville Aves., Yonge and Eglinton* ☎ *416/440–1986* ⊕ *www.grano.ca* ⊟ *AE, DC, MC, V* ⊘ *Closed Sun.* Ⓜ *Eglinton* ⊹ *3:C.*

WORD OF MOUTH

"Roberto always seems to be a presence at Grano and he has made a fixture on this part of Yonge St. The food remains consistently imaginative (walnut gnocchi and a trio of finely seasoned and grilled baby sardines). The atmosphere is always lively. Whether you are coming from the city suburbs or San Diego or San Juan, you end the evening feeling like you have come to a part of your own neighbourhood." —LJ

$$$–$$$$
ITALIAN

✕ **Il Mulino.** A ceiling arched like the ancient wine cellars of Italy, a cool gray-and-white color scheme, sculpted leather chairs, and subdued lighting induce comfort, while the food and the carefully chosen wine list inspire joy. Begin with elegant octopus carpaccio or wild-mushroom *agnolotti* (crescent-shape stuffed pasta) with veal juice and walnut sauce; then graduate to a whole baby black bass, cleanly filleted in the kitchen. Carnivores love the handsome breaded veal chop. End the evening with the chocolate volcano—warm chocolate cake with decadent molten interior. ⊠ *1060 Eglinton Ave. W, Yonge and Eglinton* ☎ *416/780–1173* ⊕ *www.ilmulinorestaurant.com* ⊟ *AE, DC, MC, V* ⊘ *Closed Sun. June–Aug. No lunch Tues.* Ⓜ *Eglinton West* ⊹ *3:A.*

$$$–$$$$
SEAFOOD

✕ **Joso's.** This two-story seafood institution is decorated with intriguing wall hangings, sensuous paintings of nudes and the sea, and signed celebrity photos. The kitchen prepares dishes from the Dalmatian side of the Adriatic Sea, and members of the international artistic community who frequent the place adore the unusual and healthful array of seafood and fish. The black risotto with squid is a must. A dish of grilled prawns, their charred tails pointing skyward, is often carried aloft by speed-walking servers. ⊠ *202 Davenport Rd., Yonge and Eglinton* ☎ *416/925–1903* ⊕ *www.josos.com* ⊛ *Reservations essential* ⊟ *AE, DC, MC, V* ⊘ *Closed Sun. No lunch Sat.* Ⓜ *Dupont* ⊹ *4:B.*

$$$–$$$$
ITALIAN

✕ **Mistura.** Mistura's combination of comfort and casual luxury and its innovative menu make for an ongoing buzz. Choose from one of more than a dozen delectable starters, like savory Maryland crab cakes with lemon aioli on chopped salad or grilled calamari. Duck two ways—crispy confit and roasted breast with port-infused dried cherries—is a specialty. Balsamic-glazed lamb ribs are always a hit, as are homemade pastas like veal ravioli. Daily whole fish is a carefully thought-out triumph. Vegetarians are given their due with dishes like red-beet risotto. **Sopra** ($$–$$$), a second-floor Italian lounge and jazz bar, offers bite-size delights. Conceived as a million-dollar playroom for grown-ups, it's all zebrawood and onyx, tapas and tipples, complete with an $80,000 Steinway. ☒ *265 Davenport Rd., ½ block west of Avenue Rd., Yonge and Eglinton* ☎ *416/515–0009* ⊕ *www.mistura.ca* ▭ *AE, DC, MC, V* ✆ *Closed Sun. No lunch* Ⓜ *Dupont* ✛ *4:B.*

$$$$ ✕ **North 44.** The lighting here creates a refined, sophisticated environ-
MODERN ment, and appetizers match: Parma ham with mascarpone-stuffed figs,
CANADIAN frisée salad, and a lobster taco with crisp beet wrapper, jicama salad, and scallion awaken your taste buds. Just try to choose from chef-owner Marc McEwen's creative and exciting main courses, including whole roasted Dover sole in brown butter and a crisp shoestring basket, and braised lamb shank with fried onion–potato mousse. There are more than 50 wines sold by the glass, enough to complement any dish. ☒ *2537 Yonge St., 4½ blocks north of Eglinton Ave., Yonge and Eglinton* ☎ *416/487–4897* ⊕ *www.north44restaurant.com* ▭ *AE, MC, V* ✆ *Closed Sun. No lunch* Ⓜ *Eglinton* ✛ *3:C.*

$$–$$$ ✕ **Pastis Express.** Menu items are etched into the frosted-glass windows,
FRENCH and plastered walls are the color of the morning sun in Provence. The food is good, but this place could run on the Gallic charm of owner George Gurnon alone. Expect pure bistro fare here, like homemade ravioli with snails and garlic herb butter, and fish-and-chips. Thick saffron-flavored fish soup, plump with fish and crustaceans, comes with three tidy add-ons: rouille, croutons, and grated cheese. A tasting plate of three French mini-desserts satisfies. ☒ *1158 Yonge St., at Summerhill, Yonge and Eglinton* ☎ *416/928–2212* ▭ *AE, DC, MC, V* ✆ *Closed Sun. and Mon. No lunch* Ⓜ *Summerhill* ✛ *4:B.*

$–$$ ✕ **Pizza Banfi.** No matter what day or time, there's usually a lineup here
ITALIAN for two reasons: one, they don't take reservations, and two, the food's
🕓 really good. Thin-crust pizzas are tossed in full view, then baked with aplomb, especially the popular pesto, chicken, and roasted red pepper combo. Pastas, generously portioned, are just as good, and their stellar Caesar salad tops just about every table. ☒ *333B Lonsdale Rd., Forest Hills* ☎ *416/322–5231* ♙ *Reservations not accepted* ▭ *AE, DC, MC, V* ✆ *Closed Sun.* Ⓜ *Eglinton Avenue West* ✛ *3:B.*

$$–$$$ ✕ **Zucca.** Chef-owner Andrew Milne-Allan delivers the purest made-
ITALIAN from-scratch Italian food in a modern, sleek, and friendly room. All the pasta is handmade and hand-rolled. Options include semolina pasta with mushrooms and radicchio, chestnut-flour fettuccine with wild boar, and squid-ink pasta with seafood. Meat lovers are also well cared for with veal cutlet coated with pine nuts and walnuts and Cornish hen pressed and roasted on the grill. ☒ *2150 Yonge St., Yonge and Eglinton* ☎ *416/488–5774* ⊕ *www.zuccatrattoria.com* ♙ *Reservations essential* ▭ *AE, DC, MC, V* Ⓜ *Eglinton* ✛ *3:C.*

Where to Stay

"Toronto's a good hotel city, sort of like New York. . . . Hotels are clustered around City Hall, in the Entertainment District, and in the Yorkville area along Bloor Street, near Yonge and over to near Spadina. There's lots to be said for each area."

—BAK

Updated by
Sarah Richards

Given that more than 100 languages and dialects are spoken in the Greater Toronto area, it's not surprising that much of the downtown hotel market is international-business-traveler savvy. Wi-Fi connections are standard at most high-end properties, and business services abound. But these same core hotels are close to tourist attractions — Harbourfront and the Toronto Islands, the cavernous Rogers Centre, the Air Canada Centre, the Four Seasons Centre for the Performing Arts, and the Royal Ontario Museum.

Not wanting to miss out on potential customers, hotels like the Delta Chelsea have instituted perks for the younger set, such as complimentary milk and cookies, kid-size bathrobes, and children's day camp. Another key trend in Toronto's downtown lodgings is the emergence of small, upscale boutique hotels, such as the Hotel Le Germain, the Pantages and Cosmopolitan hotels, and the swank SoHo Metropolitan. There are also a growing number of bed-and-breakfasts and hostels.

City-center accommodations are usually within a few minutes' walk of Yonge Street and the glittering lights of the Entertainment District, the soaring office towers of the Financial District, the shops of the Dundas Square Area, and the bars and art galleries of Queen West. Within a 15-minute drive west of downtown are the forested High Park and the meandering Humber River, an area where there are few major hotels but an ample array of B&Bs and the lovely Old Mill Inn. The growing West Queen West area has some unique places to stay, such as the restored Gladstone and Drake hotels, as well as funky restaurants and galleries. Lester B. Pearson International Airport is 29 km (18 mi) northwest of downtown; airport hotels are airport hotels, but staying in this area also means quick connections to cities beyond, such as Niagara Falls.

Downtown lodgings are for people who want to be in the heart of the action and nightlife, and who don't mind relying on public transit or walking. For an Eastern European feel, others may prefer to stay in the High Park/Old Mill area of Greater Toronto, as many immigrants from Ukraine, Latvia, Poland, and other countries tended to settle here. The northern edge of the city, known as York Mills or North York, contains a sizable Jewish population, whereas the northwest areas are populated with Italian, African, and Caribbean newcomers. In the eastern regions of this sprawling metropolis, Greek, Asian, Indian, and Pakistani people are to be found. But downtown remains a true mosaic of Toronto life, with a sometimes-astonishing number of nationalities represented.

WHAT IT COSTS IN CANADIAN DOLLARS				
	¢	$	$$	$$$	$$$$
For two people	under C$75	C$75–C$125	C$126–C$175	C$176–C$250	over C$250

Prices are for two people in a standard double room in high season, excluding 13% hotel tax.

HARBOURFRONT, THE FINANCIAL DISTRICT, AND OLD TOWN

Use the coordinate (✛ 2:B) at the end of each listing to locate a site on the corresponding map.

Situating yourself here is a good idea for exploring the greatest concentration of Toronto's must-see attractions, such as St. Lawrence Market, the Historic Distillery District, the Rogers Centre, Ontario Place, and the CN Tower. You'll find that while boisterous during the day, these areas really quiet down after the sun sets.

FINANCIAL DISTRICT

$$ 🏨 **Cambridge Suites.** This self-dubbed boutique hotel has just 12 suites per floor and focuses on high-quality service: rooms are cleaned twice daily, there's same-day dry cleaning and laundry, free access to a downtown fitness club, and complimentary airline boarding pass kiosk in the lobby. The inexpensive suites, which come equipped with full kitchens, spacious living rooms, dining rooms, and one or two bedrooms, are decorated in muted earthy tones. At Portico, the hotel's restaurant, chef Ano Choi churns out creative pastas and innovative salads against a chic backdrop of contemporary furniture, gleaming hardwood, and quirky art work. **Pros:** central location; extras like free shoe shines; in-and-out parking privileges. **Cons:** some services are expensive, like parking and Internet (in lower-priced rooms). ⊠ *15 Richmond St. E, at Victoria St., Financial District* 🕾 *416/368-1990* ⊕ *www.cambridgesuitestoronto.com* ✒ *229 suites* ⅄ *In-room: safe (some), kitchen, refrigerator, Wi-Fi. In-hotel: restaurant, gym, laundry facilities, laundry service, Internet, Wi-Fi, parking (paid), no-smoking rooms.* ▤ *AE, DC, MC, V* Ⓜ *Queen* ✛ *5:F.*

$$$$ 🏨 **Cosmopolitan Toronto Hotel.** Tucked away on a side street in the heart of Toronto, this überboutique hotel opened in 2005. Here an Eastern aesthetic and spirituality are seamlessly blended with typical Western hotel amenities. Each suite contains floor-to-ceiling windows, flat-screen LCD TVs, a gleaming kitchen, comfy living room, a washer and dryer, and a bubbling gemstone fountain (which can be turned off anytime). Ask for an 03 suite between floors 17 and 23 for the best view of Lake Ontario, or blow your budget and rent the split-level penthouse for C$2,500. The on-site Shizen ("nature" in Japanese) Spa 3500 contains a 12-person hot tub. Eight Wine Bar, the hotel restaurant, in tones of bright reds and deep browns, offers contemporary dishes by well-established chef Derek Kennedy that emphasize local and organic produce. The Cosmo, as locals call the hotel, is poised to be the *in* place to be for the more modern, downtown crowds. **Pros:** private and quiet; hipness factor; great breakfast

BEST BETS FOR TORONTO LODGING

Fodor's offers a selective listing of quality lodging experiences at every price range, from the city's best budget motel to its most sophisticated luxury hotels. Here, we've compiled our top recommendations by price and experience. The very best properties—those that provide a particularly remarkable experience in their price range—are designated in the listings with a Fodor's Choice logo.

Fodor'sChoice★

The Hazelton Hotel, p. 108

Neill-Wycik Summer Hotel, p. 112

SoHo Metropolitan Hotel, p. 106

Windsor Arms, p. 110

By Price

¢

Global Village Backpackers, p. 104

Neill-Wycik Summer Hotel, p. 112

$

Massey College Student Residence, p. 107

Ryerson University Residences, p. 112

Suite Dreams, p. 107

$$

By the Park B&B, p. 116

Howard Johnson Toronto, p. 109

The Suites at One King West, p. 99

$$$

Delta Chelsea Hotel, p. 111

Gladstone Hotel, p. 115

Hotel Le Germain, p. 104

$$$$

Cosmopolitan Toronto Hotel, p. 95

The Fairmont Royal York, p. 99

The Hazelton Hotel, p. 108

SoHo Metropolitan Hotel, p. 106

Windsor Arms, p. 110

By Experience

BEST FOR ROMANCE

Cosmopolitan Toronto Hotel, p. 95

The Hazelton Hotel, p. 108

Hotel Le Germain, p.104

Park Hyatt Toronto, p. 109

SoHo Metropolitan Hotel, p. 106

BEST FOR BUSINESS

Fairmont Royal York Hotel, p. 99

InterContinental Toronto Centre, p. 105

Westin Harbour Castle, p. 102

BEST VIEWS

Four Seasons Toronto, p. 108

Radisson Plaza Hotel Admiral, p. 102

Sheraton Centre, p. 106

The Suites at One King West, p. 99

The Westin Harbour Castle, p. 102

BEST CELEBRITY RETREAT

Four Seasons Toronto, p. 108

The Hazelton Hotel, p. 108

Park Hyatt Toronto, p. 109

SoHo Metropolitan Hotel, p. 106

Sutton Place, p. 108

BEST INTERIOR DESIGN

Drake Hotel, p. 115

Gladstone Hotel, p. 115

Hazelton Hotel, p. 108

Hotel Le Germain, p. 104

WHERE SHOULD I STAY?

	NEIGHBORHOOD VIBE	PROS	CONS
Harbourfront, The Financial District, and Old Town	This tourist hub includes Toronto's first buildings in Old Town, the towering skyscrapers of the Financial District, and the many activities of Harbourfront.	Good eats in the St. Lawrence Market and Historic Distillery District, close to Island escapes in Lake Ontario, and surrounded by the city's top attractions.	Quiet at night and a bit removed from the action of Toronto's more lively neighborhoods. Rooms are often smaller and more expensive than in other areas.
The Entertainment District	Toronto's highest concentration of nightclubs and the city's thriving theater district.	Hotels here cater to more adventurous pleasure-seekers. Plenty of restaurants serve pre- and post-theater dinners and lots of late-night conveniences.	When the clubs let out at around 3 AM, it can get extremely noisy and rowdy on the streets.
Queen's Park, The Annex, and Yorkville	Abundant ethnic restaurants and secondhand bookstores line Bloor Street West. Further south is the airy Queen's Park; while to the east, upscale shops fill sophisticated Yorkville.	Beautifully restored Victorian houses make for unique B&B accommodations. Alternatively, splash out in one of the big, luxurious hotels in Yorkville.	High prices in Yorkville could clean out your wallet, and the area's central artery, Bloor Street West, attracts many panhandlers.
Church-Wellesley and Dundas Square Area	Dundas Square, Toronto's hottest new events center, faces the mammoth Eaton Centre shopping mall. Farther northeast is Canada's largest gay community, Church-Wellesley.	These areas have a festival-like atmosphere and patios teem at sunset.	Things can get slightly sketchy late at night, and there aren't many of recommended restaurants in the immediate vicinity.
Queen West	Funky boutiques, cutting-edge design shops, and experimental restaurants and hotels.	This area sets the trends in Toronto, the restaurants and bars attract diverse clientele, and the Queen Street streetcar is frequent and runs 24 hours.	The western end of the neighborhood feels shady after dark, and there aren't many parking options.
Greater Toronto	Most hotels in the northeast end of the city surround the city's great green expanse, High Park, and this area feels like a pleasant resort town with interesting shops and restaurants.	Safe, quiet, and relatively inexpensive area of Toronto, set against the 400-acre High Park.	Unlike central Toronto, the vibe here is more small-town. It can take up to a half hour to get to Toronto's attractions by subway or car.

4

TORONTO LODGING PLANNER

The lodgings we list are the cream of the crop in each price category. Properties are assigned price categories based on the price of a standard double room during Toronto's busy summer season. We always list the facilities that are available, such as in-house spas or gym access, but we don't specify whether they cost extra. When pricing accommodations, always ask what's included and what costs extra.

SERVICES

Unless otherwise noted in individual descriptions, all the hotels listed have private baths, central heating, air-conditioning, and private phones. Almost all hotels have Wi-Fi and phones with voice mail. Most large hotels have video or high-speed checkout capability, and many can arrange babysitting. Web TV, in-room video games, DVD players, as well as CD players are also provided in many hotels.

Bringing a car to Toronto can be a headache unless your hotel provides free parking. Garages cost around C$20 per day, and streetside parking is not available in most neighborhoods, but many city-owned parking lots have favorable rates on weekends and holidays.

Assume that hotels operate on the European Plan (EP, no meals) unless we specify that they use the Breakfast Plan (BP, with full breakfast), Continental Plan (CP, Continental breakfast), Full American Plan (FAP, all meals), Modified American Plan (MAP, breakfast and dinner) or are all-inclusive (AI, all meals and most activities).

RESERVATIONS

Hotel reservations are a necessity—rooms fill up quickly, so book as far in advance as possible. Summer is the busiest time, and if you plan on visiting during the Pride Festival (late June), Caribana Festival (late July), or during the Toronto International Film Festival (September), note that hordes of visitors will be joining you in a search for a room, especially anywhere in the downtown core. At these times it doesn't hurt to look farther afield, but look for places along the subway lines to the north, west, or east, unless you have a car.

Be aware that the city is a popular destination for leisure travelers, and it also draws many conventions. These conventions book huge blocks of hotel rooms, particularly April through November. (This can mean annoying lobby bustle, but it also tends to ensure that properties in this competitive city have plenty of amenities and high levels of service.) If conventioneers bother you, ask the hotel you're interested in whether any large gatherings will coincide with your stay.

WHAT IT COSTS

Although paying with U.S. dollars no longer gives you the advantage it has in the past, there are other ways to save money during a visit. Many hotels that cater to business travelers cut rates for weekends and these hotels typically have special packages for couples and families, too. Toronto hotels typically slash rates a full 50% in January and February. Smaller hotels and apartment-style accommodation downtown are also moderately priced (and therefore popular in summer).

buffet. **Cons:** side street dark at night; trendiness may get stale; no handy newsstand or kiosk. ⊠ *8 Colborne St., at Yonge St., Financial District* ☎ *416/945–5455 or 800/958–3488* ⊕ *www.cosmotoronto.com* ⤳ *95 suites, 2 penthouse suites* ♿ *In-room: kitchen, DVD, Wi-Fi. In-hotel: restaurant, bar, gym, spa, concierge, parking (paid), no-smoking rooms* ⊟ *AE, D, DC, MC, V* Ⓜ *King* ✛ *6:F.*

WORD OF MOUTH
"If price is not a factor, I would pick the Royal York. As others have said, it's a grand old hotel. It's also very convenient to the Rogers Centre and the rest of downtown Toronto." —laverendrye

$$$$ ⬚ **The Fairmont Royal York.** Like a proud grandmother, the Royal York stands serenely on Front Street in downtown Toronto, surrounded by gleaming skyscrapers and the nearby CN Tower. Once the tallest building in the British Commonwealth, it has watched Toronto become one of the world's great cities since it opened its doors in 1929. It remains one of the biggest hotels in the city, and a favorite of royalty—the real thing and that of Hollywood. The hotel has been restored and renovated, and guest rooms are decorated in muted dark tones with some period furnishings. In 2001, the excellent lobby restaurant, Epic, opened. In keeping with the times, it uses organically grown and locally sourced food products wherever possible, including some from its own rooftop garden. **Pros:** grand royal experience; excellent health club; environmentally conscious; large Canadian wine list. **Cons:** big hotel with small rooms; certain food outlets may close during slow weeks; charge for in-room Internet access. ⊠ *100 Front St. W, at York St., Financial District* ☎ *416/368–2511 or 800/441–1414* ⊕ *www.fairmont.com/royalyork* ⤳ *1,304 rooms, 61 suites* ♿ *In-room: Wi-Fi. In-hotel: 5 restaurants, room service, bars, pool, gym, laundry service, concierge, executive floor, public Wi-Fi, parking (paid), no-smoking rooms* ⊟ *AE, D, DC, MC, V* Ⓜ *Union* ✛ *6:E.*

$$ ⬚ **Hotel Victoria.** A local landmark built in 1909, the Vic is Toronto's second-oldest hotel, with a long-standing reputation for service excellence. Architectural traces of the early 20th century are evident in the columned and marbled lobby, stately crown moldings, and floor-to-ceiling windows. Rooms are rather diminutive but clean and comfortable. Wingback chairs and quilted bedcovers are nice touches. **Pros:** gym privileges at nearby health club; complimentary newspapers. **Cons:** inconvenient, off-site parking; second-floor rooms noisy from street; slow elevator. ⊠ *56 Yonge St., at Wellington St., Financial District* ☎ *416/363–1666 or 800/363–8228* ⊕ *www.hotelvictoria-toronto.com* ⤳ *56 rooms* ♿ *In-room: refrigerator (some), Wi-Fi. In-hotel: restaurant, laundry services, parking (paid), no-smoking rooms* ⊟ *AE, DC, MC, V* Ⓜ *King* ✛ *6:F.*

$$ ⬚ **The Suites at One King West.** This 51-story hotel made up entirely of suites rises atop the old Dominion Bank of Canada (circa 1912) in the city's downtown business and shopping core. It is the tallest residential building in Canada and each of the suites includes a washer-dryer unit and equipped kitchen (service for two). High-value packages are available for those staying more longer term, and the nightly rates are low considering the excellent location at the busy intersection of King and

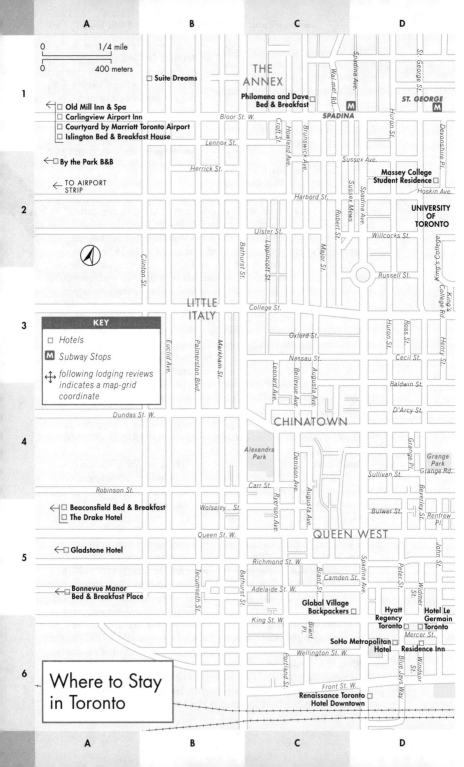

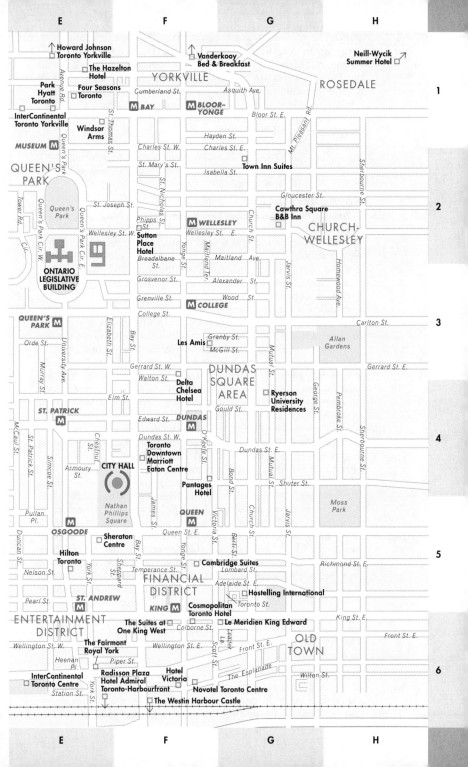

Yonge streets. A small fitness center, valet parking, a 24-hour concierge, a connection to the PATH, and a complimentary limousine service within the downtown area are bonuses. Many rooms face the atrium, but for a little more you can request a suite facing south on an upper floor for a magnificent view of the lake and Toronto Islands. **Pros:** great views from upper floors; self-catering facility; central locale. **Cons:** slightly inexperienced front desk staff; slow elevators. ⊠ *1 King St. W, at Yonge St., Financial District* ☎ *416/548–8100 or 866/470–5464* ⊕ *www.onek-ingwest.com* ⇗ *570 condominiums* ♿ *In-room: safe, kitchen, DVD, Ethernet. In-hotel: restaurant, gym, parking (paid), no-smoking rooms* ☰ *AE, DC, MC, V* Ⓜ *King* ✛ *6:F.*

HARBOURFRONT

$$$ ⌖ **Radisson Plaza Hotel Admiral Toronto–Harbourfront.** You can't get much closer to Toronto's waterfront, and unobstructed Lake Ontario and verdant Toronto Islands vistas come standard. This small hotel has an appropriately maritime design, with deep-blue accents; plush seating trimmed in rich, full-grain woods; and the requisite brass embellishments. The full bank of windows at Commodore's Restaurant provides a spectacular panorama of the lake. The seafood specialties are some of the finest in the city: lobster and sweet-corn bisque, grilled Atlantic salmon, and pasta with scallops in dill cream sauce are delicious. **Pros:** good value for its location; easy access to Toronto Islands ferries and convention center; now entirely smoke-free; free Wi-Fi. **Cons:** quiet and seems out of the way in winter and spring. ⊠ *249 Queen's Quay W, at York St., Harbourfront* ☎ *416/203–3333 or 888/201–1718* ⊕ *www. radisson.com* ⇗ *157 rooms* ♿ *In room: Wi-Fi. In-hotel: 2 restaurants, bar, room service, pool, gym, laundry service, parking (paid), no-smoking rooms* ☰ *AE, D, DC, MC, V* Ⓜ *Union* ✛ *6:E.*

$$$ ⌖ **The Westin Harbour Castle.** On a clear day you can see the skyline of Rochester, New York, across the sparkling blue Lake Ontario from most rooms at this elegant, high-end hotel. Guest office rooms contain a printer and scanner; six guest rooms have wheelchair access; and one is fully handicapped accessible. The property is completely no-smoking. The decor is all modern luxury with marble bathrooms and Heavenly Beds in every room; many have 32-inch flat-screen TVs. Each room has an electric coffeemaker with coffee and tea. Take the glass elevator to Toulà, the hotel's Italian restaurant. An enclosed walkway links the hotel to the Westin Harbour Castle Conference Centre. **Pros:** very comfortable beds; bustling lobby. **Cons:** not right downtown; hotel can feel overwhelmingly large and very spread out. ⊠ *1 Harbour Sq., at Bay St., Harbourfront* ☎ *416/869–1600* ⊕ *www.westin.com/harbourcastle* ⇗ *977 rooms* ♿ *In-room: Wi-Fi. In-hotel: 2 restaurants, room service, bars, tennis court, pool, gym, laundry service, concierge, public Internet, parking (paid), no-smoking rooms* ☰ *AE, D, DC, MC, V* ⧌ *EP* Ⓜ *Union* ✛ *6:F.*

OLD TOWN

¢ ⌖ **Hostelling International.** Central and no-frills, this hostel is open to adventurers of all ages. Private and 4- to 10-bed dormitory rooms are available. Smaller dorms have en suite bathrooms, and large dorms share common baths on the same floor. Amenities include a shared kitchenette, a television lounge, a rooftop deck, Wi-Fi, lockers, linen rental, and discounts on attractions and restaurants. You don't have to be a member of Hostelling International to stay here, but nonmembers pay a small extra fee. **Pros:** convenient location; international feel; roof deck popular in summer. **Cons:** neighborhood a bit sketchy at night; cramped when busy. ✉ *76 Church St., at Adelaide St. E, Old Town* ☏ *416/971–4440 or 877/848–8737* ⊕ *www.toronto-youth-hostel.com* ↦ *35 rooms, 154 beds* ♿ *In-room: no phone, no TV. In-hotel: laundry facilities, Internet terminal, Wi-Fi, no-smoking rooms* ▭ *MC, V* Ⓜ *Union* ♦ *5:G.*

$$$ ⛨ **Le Meridien King Edward.** Now being managed by Starwood Hotels and Resorts, Toronto's "King Eddy" Hotel continues to be a landmark property for special occasions and a nod to the more genteel grand hotels of the past. Victoria's Restaurant has moved to a more prominent location off the main lobby, but the opulent room decor is gone, although the oil paintings that grace the walls do add an elegant touch. The lobby's Consort Bar overlooking bustling King Street East, once home to a grand piano, now offers four flat-screen TVs instead: a sad reminder of the present, even if classic jazz plays from the sound system. Junior suites are comfortably large and may offer access to the Royal Club on the 11th floor where a well-presented continental breakfast and complimentary Ontario wines and cheeses are served. **Pros:** great location; historical; friendly service. **Cons:** no mirror above sink in some rooms; high daily Internet fee; brass elevator doors heavily scratched. ✉ *37 King St. E, east of Yonge St., Old Town* ☏ *416/863–9700 or 800/543–4300* ⊕ *www.lemeridien.com* ↦ *292 rooms, 29 suites* ♿ *In-room: Internet. In-hotel: restaurant, bar, room service, gym, spa, laundry service, concierge, executive floor, public Internet, parking (paid), no-smoking rooms* ▭ *AE, DC, MC, V* Ⓜ *King* ♦ *6:G.*

$$ ⛨ **Novotel Toronto Centre.** A good-value, few-frills, modern hotel, the Novotel is in the heart of the animated, bar-lined Esplanade area, near the St. Lawrence Market, the Air Canada Centre, Union Station, and the Entertainment District. The fitness facilities are especially extensive for the price. Local calls are free and all rooms have coffeemakers. The restaurant, Café Nicole, serves a heaping plate of scrumptious steak frites. **Pros:** excellent location; good value; laptop-size in-room safes. **Cons:** small in-hotel parking spaces; spotty housekeeping; noisy neighborhood. ✉ *45 The Esplanade, at Church St., Old Town* ☏ *416/367–8900 or 800/668–6835* ⊕ *www.novotel.com* ↦ *262 rooms* ♿ *In-room: Wi-Fi. In-hotel: restaurant, bar, room service, pool, gym, laundry service, parking (paid), no-smoking rooms* ▭ *AE, DC, MC, V* Ⓜ *Union* ♦ *6:F.*

THE ENTERTAINMENT DISTRICT

It's hard to imagine the quiet, empty-looking warehouses in the Entertainment District spontaneously exploding with activity, but when the sun goes down it's party central in this neighborhood. The bustle and excitement generated by Toronto's clubbers, theatergoers, and night owls keep the action alive until 3 AM most nights.

¢ ⊡ **Global Village Backpackers.** Formerly known as the Spadina Hotel, this centrally located hostel is filled with international students roaming the world. It's friendly, with a lounge, patio, and bar on premises. Clean linen and towels are supplied at check-in, and the welcoming staff know the city very well. The airport express shuttle drops you two blocks from the hostel. Dorms start at $27 per person and the rooms sleep 6, 10, or 14, but most are quads, sleeping 4, with shared bathrooms. There are six private rooms with double beds in each. There are a long list of freebies here, including Wi-Fi and a daily pancake breakfast. **Pros:** spirited atmosphere with live music in the bar; fun extras. **Cons:** some groups may be noisy; on western edge of Entertainment District; must have valid hostelling or student ID card for low rates. ⊠ *460 King St. W, at Spadina Ave., Entertainment District* ☎ *416/703–8540* ⊕ *www. globalbackpackers.com* ⇆ *30 rooms with 190 beds* ⟳ *In-hotel: bar, laundry facilities, Internet terminal, Wi-Fi* ⊟ *MC, V* Ⓜ *St. Andrew or Union, then streetcar 504 or 508 west* ✛ *5:D.*

$$$ ⊡ **Hotel Le Germain Toronto.** The Germain Group is known for beautiful, chic, upscale boutique hotels, and the Toronto model is no exception. A retro, redbrick exterior—accented by a soaring glass-and-stainless-steel frontage—works well with the historic architecture of the surrounding theater district. The dazzling lobby contains a library, a cappuccino bar, and a double-side, open-hearth fireplace. Sleek furnishings fill ultramodern rooms, which have plasma-screen televisions. Suites have separate bedrooms and living rooms, wet bars, fireplaces, and private terraces that afford superb views of the skyline. The restaurant, Chez Victor, serves first-class French-inspired cuisine. **Pros:** complimentary breakfast; attentive staff; on a quiet street in a bustling neighborhood. **Cons:** spotty temperature controls; some guest rooms could use a coat of paint. ⊠ *30 Mercer St., at John St., Entertainment District* ☎ *416/345–9500 or 866/345–9501* ⊕ *www.germaintoronto.com* ⇆ *118 rooms, 4 suites* ⟳ *In-room: Wi-Fi. In-hotel: restaurant, gym, laundry service, parking (paid), some pets allowed (fee), no-smoking rooms* ⊟ *AE, DC, MC, V* ⭘❘ *CP* Ⓜ *St. Andrew* ✛ *6:D.*

$$$ ⊡ **Hyatt Regency Toronto.** Request views of Lake Ontario, the downtown skyline, or the Rogers Centre at this brand new luxury hotel smack in the middle of the pulsating Entertainment District. Guest rooms don't disappoint with 42-in flat-screen TVs, iPod docks, and spa-inspired toiletries. The eclectic menu in the King Street Social Restaurant is divided into "East" and "West"; a few hits include spicy "Phuket Chicken," Ontario lamb loin, and risotto with goat cheese and red wine. An outdoor swimming pool provides nice views from its 17th-floor perch, and the 24-hour fitness center is open to all guests.**Pros:** closest large hotel to King Street West theaters; dozens of excellent restaurants and cinemas nearby. **Cons:** in-hotel restaurant is pricey; guest rooms on lower floors facing King Street may be especially noisy. ⊠ *370 King St. W, Entertainment District* ☎ *416/343–1234, 800/633–7313 in U.S.* ⊕ *www.torontoregency.hyatt.com* ⇆ *394 rooms, 32 suites* ⟳ *In-room: Wi-Fi, refrigerator. In-hotel: restaurant, room service, pool, gym, laundry service, Internet terminal, parking (paid), no-smoking rooms* ⊟ *AE, D, DC, MC, V* Ⓜ *St. Andrew* ✛ *6:D.*

$$$$ ⛨ **InterContinental Toronto Centre.** Attached to the Metro Toronto Convention Centre, this large but unassuming hotel is a good bet for visiting businesspeople, but the leisure traveler will also find some deals on weekends or during slower periods. It's less than a five-minute walk to the stellar live theater and restaurants on King Street West. The hotel has an excellent day spa (allegedly the haunt of Catherine Zeta-Jones when she's in town), a very good restaurant, Azure, and a quiet elegance—even when full. Former Prime Minister of Canada Jean Chretien favored this hotel for its efficient security measures and businesslike but less-than-ostentatious atmosphere. **Pros:** nontypical convention hotel; bright and airy lobby restaurant; haberdashery in lobby. **Cons:** no shopping nearby; neighborhood streets quiet at night. ⊠ *225 Front St. W, west of University Ave., Entertainment District* ☎ *416/597–1400 or 800/422–7969* ⊕ *www.torontocentre.intercontinental.com* ➾ *440 rooms, 136 suites* ⚭ *In-room: dial-up, Wi-Fi. In-hotel: restaurant, bar, room service, pool, gym, spa, laundry service, concierge, parking (paid), no-smoking rooms* ▭ *AE, DC, MC, V* Ⓜ *Union* ✛ *6:E.*

$$$ ⛨ **Renaissance Toronto Hotel Downtown.** Where else can you watch a baseball game, pop-star concert, or monster-truck rally from the comfort of your room? This is the world's only hotel completely integrated into a massive sports and entertainment dome. All the guest rooms are large, but the most popular are the 70 rooms overlooking the stadium, along with six bi-level field-view suites. The price of these rooms may vary with the event. The hotel is completely no-smoking. **Pros:** likable staff; free lobby Internet; guest rooms best place to watch Blue Jays baseball games. **Cons:** very long hallways; little natural light in guest rooms overlooking field; gym needs a makeover. ⊠ *1 Blue Jays Way, at Front St. W, Entertainment District* ☎ *416/341–7100 or 800/237–1512* ⊕ *www.renaissancehotels.com* ➾ *313 rooms, 35 suites* ⚭ *In-room: Wi-Fi. In-hotel: restaurant, bar, room service, gym, laundry service, executive floor, Internet terminal, parking (paid), no-smoking rooms* ▭ *AE, DC, MC, V* Ⓜ *Union* ✛ *6:D.*

$$ ⛨ **Residence Inn.** A big hit with families and long-term visitors to Toronto, the very modern suites (built in 2007) at the Residence Inn come with full kitchens, spacious living and dining rooms, and very comfortable bedrooms. Still not convinced? The location says it all: just steps from the CN Tower, Rogers Centre, Air Canada Centre, and a short walk from the Queen West boutiques and Entertainment District clubs. Be sure to check if there are any special packages before reserving; you may get a gas card, tickets to the Royal Ontario Museum, or dinner at a medieval restaurant thrown in with the price of a room. A hot buffet breakfast and evening wine reception are free for all guests. **Pros:** close to Toronto's major attractions; room layout is great for families; good for the budget-conscious; no minimum stay. **Cons:** valet parking only; street is very quiet at night; breakfast buffet gets very crowded during peak season. ⊠ *255 Wellington St. W, at Windsor St., Entertainment District* ☎ *416/581–1800* ⊕ *www.marriott.com* ➾ *256 suites* ⚭ *In-room: safe (some), kitchen, refrigerator, Wi-Fi. In-hotel: pool, gym, laundry facilities, laundry services, Internet, Wi-Fi, parking (paid), some pets allowed, no smoking rooms* ▭ *AE, DC, MC, V.* Ⓜ *Union* ✛ *6:D.*

$$$$ ⛶ **Sheraton Centre.** Views from this hotel in the city center are marvelous—to the south are the CN Tower and the Rogers Centre; to the north, both new and old city halls. Guest rooms and suites have pillow-top mattresses, crisp bed linens, and cozy duvets. Perhaps owing to its great size, there are plenty of places to escape: a garden with waterfalls, a 24-hour fitness center, and Toronto's largest year-round indoor-outdoor pool. Club Level rooms have bathrobes and provide access to the complimentary Continental breakfast and cocktail hour at the 43rd-floor Club Level Lounge. STEAK, a moderately priced steak house, is attached and there are lunch options at the attached Bistro on Two and Traders restaurants. **Pros:** underground access to shopping in PATH network; pool open until late evening; walk to Four Seasons Centre for Performing Arts. **Cons:** slightly sterile; service spotty in lobby bar; hotel is overwhelmingly massive. ✉ *123 Queen St. W, at Bay St., Entertainment District* ☎ *416/361–1000 or 800/325–3535* ⊕ *www.starwoodhotels.com* 🛏 *1,302 rooms, 75 suites* ♿ *In-room: Wi-Fi. In-hotel: 3 restaurants, bar, room service, pool, gym, spa, laundry service, executive floor, Internet terminal, parking (paid), no-smoking rooms* ▭ *AE, DC, MC, V* Ⓜ *Osgoode* ✛ *5:E.*

$$$$
Fodor's Choice
★

⛶ **SoHo Metropolitan Hotel.** Ultraluxury is the only standard at the SoHo Met: Frette linens, European down duvets, walk-in closets, marble bathrooms with heated floors, and upmarket bath products. The "sleep concierge" offers amenities such as tea and biscotti, bubble baths, and aromatherapy eye pillows. Glamour begins in the cosmopolitan open-concept lobby, where a stunning blown-glass installation by world-renowned Dale Chihuly dazzles guests and passersby. The hotel has the finest amenities, including a state-of-the-art fitness center, lap pool, full-service day spa, and Clefs d'Or concierge services. Spaciousness and floor-to-ceiling windows create the feeling of luxury, without pretension, throughout. The two-level penthouse suite, one of the finest in the city, has attracted stars like Madonna. Senses Restaurant is known for its unique menu of East meets West, wine cellar, and service. **Pros:** no detail left to chance including heated bathroom floors and electric do-not-disturb signs and curtains; stylish but not showy. **Cons:** lap pool only 3 feet deep; toiletries not restocked daily; located slightly away from main streets. ✉ *318 Wellington St. W, east of Spadina Ave., Entertainment District* ☎ *416/599–8800 or 800/668–6600* ⊕ *www.soho.metropolitan.com* 🛏 *72 rooms, 19 suites* ♿ *In-room: Wi-Fi. In-hotel: restaurant, bar, room service, pool, gym, spa, laundry service, concierge, Internet terminal, parking (paid), no-smoking rooms* ▭ *AE, DC, MC, V* Ⓜ *St. Andrew* ✛ *6:D.*

QUEEN'S PARK, THE ANNEX, AND YORKVILLE

Thanks to its neighbor, the University of Toronto, the Queen's Park area has numerous budget options and dormitory lodgings. The Annex may bustle along Bloor Street West, but the long residential streets running north hide quiet B&Bs that lend a small-town feel to the middle of the city. Yorkville, in keeping with its lofty image as Toronto's most upscale neighborhood, boasts a handful of glamorous, ultradecadent hotels.

THE ANNEX

$ 🖭 **Philomena and Dave Bed & Breakfast.**

Relax, lemonade in hand, on the third-floor balcony overlooking a small woods after a hard day power-shopping along Bloor Street West, the Annex's main thoroughfare, or in fashionable Yorkville. Whatever you do, this cheerful, three-story, 1910 B&B is a welcoming spot to

WORD OF MOUTH

"One of the most comfortable college/university residences is Massey College. And they have great food. Plus a serene inner courtyard with a goldfish-filled pond."   —CanadaKate

return to. Many original fixtures remain, including oak doors and trim and large stained-glass bay windows. Two of the rooms have broadloom carpets and the third has original hardwood. Furnishings are eclectic: traditional, solid-wood dressers meet sleek, modern, Scandinavian-style closets. The family cat roams the premises. English, German, and Italian are spoken here. **Pros:** friendly, ethnic neighborhood; hospitable hosts; kitchenette for light snacks. **Cons:** very limited space; shared bath; transit or long walk to downtown. ✉ *31 Dalton Rd., at Bloor St. W, The Annex* ☎ *416/962–2786* ⊕ *www.bbcanada.com/2072.html* 🛏 *3 rooms without bath* ⚐ *In-room: no a/c (some), no phone. In-hotel: no elevator, Internet terminal, parking (no fee), no-smoking rooms* ⊟ *No credit cards* ❣ *BP* Ⓜ *Spadina* ✠ *1:C.*

$ 🖭 **Suite Dreams.** This elegant B&B in the heart of the Annex comprised of three lovely suites is just a stone's throw away from Christie subway station. The owner, Mr. Tan, is friendly, easy-going and very knowledge-able about Toronto, and his breakfasts are delicious. Simple, modern furniture is balanced with colorful textiles. Two of the three rooms offer ensuite bathrooms; one room has shared facilities but boasts a private entrance to the leafy backyard. Long-distance phone calls within North America are free, as is Wi-Fi. **Pros:** close to subway; helpful host; immaculately clean rooms. **Cons:** limited space; repeat customers means reservations are hard to secure. ✉ *390 Clinton St., at Bloor St. W, The Annex* ☎ *416/898–8461* ⊕ *www.suitedreamstoronto.com* 🛏 *3 rooms, 2 with bath* ⚐ *In-room: no phone, Wi-Fi. In-hotel: Wi-Fi, parking (free), some pets allowed, no-smoking rooms.* ⊟ *AE, DC, MC, V.* ❣ *BP* Ⓜ *Christie* ✠ *1:B.*

QUEEN'S PARK

$ 🖭 **Massey College Student Residence.** You can crash at the modern student residence at the University of Toronto between early May and mid-August. Rates vary with length of stay (daily, weekly, and monthly), by the month (May through July are higher than August), and by type of room. Single and double junior suites have shared bathrooms, and single and double senior suites have private bathrooms. Rooms are spartan, but linens, towels, and housekeeping services are provided. Breakfast is included; cafeteria-style lunch and dinner cost C$8 and C$14.80 respectively. Massey is a stone's throw from the Royal Ontario Museum and other major attractions. **Pros:** vegetarian fare available; room fans upon request; Common Room has daily newspapers and air-conditioning. **Cons:** no frills; no Internet; no fitness facility. ✉ *4 Devonshire Pl., south of Bloor St. W, Queen's Park* ☎ *416/946–7843* ⊕ *www.utoronto.ca/*

massey/summer.html ↩ *40 rooms, 5 with bath* ☖ *In-room: no a/c, no phone, no TV. In-hotel: restaurant, laundry facilities, parking (paid), no-smoking rooms* ▤ *MC, V* ☉ *Closed Sept.–Apr.* Ⓜ *St. George* ⊕ *2:D.*

$$$ 🔲 **Sutton Place Hotel.** Visiting film and stage stars still stay here because of the commitment to service and privacy. Tapestries, swaths of floral arrangements, antiques, and plush chairs fill the public areas. Guest rooms, in tan and navy tones, have a French provincial style with cut-crystal bedside lamps and some antiques. A chiropractic sleep system guarantees that you awaken refreshed. Luxury suites come with full kitchens and whirlpool baths. It's near the Church-Wellesley neighborhood, the Royal Ontario Museum, trendy Yorkville shops, the Eaton Centre, and an array of excellent ethnic restaurants. Accents, the main-floor restaurant, is popular for a snack and a glass of wine, or something as elaborate as poached lobster with scallops, shrimp, and baby vegetables. You can also venture across the street to the popular restaurant, Bistro 990. **Pros:** quiet location; helpful concierges; valet parking. **Cons:** some rooms have dated furnishings; limited room-service menu; slightly faded glamour. ✉ *955 Bay St., at Wellesley St. W, Queen's Park* ☎ *416/924–9221 or 866/389–8866* ⊕ *www.suttonplace.com* ↩ *230 rooms, 64 suites* ☖ *In-room: Wi-Fi. In-hotel: restaurant, bar, room service, pool, gym, concierge, laundry service, parking (paid), no-smoking rooms* ▤ *AE, DC, MC, V* Ⓜ *Wellesley* ⊕ *2:F.*

YORKVILLE

$$$$ 🔲 **Four Seasons Toronto.** Some of Toronto's most luxurious guest rooms are here, in fashionable Yorkville. Amenities include antique-style writing desks, comfortable robes, and oversize towels. Many of the corner rooms have furnished balconies; ask for upper rooms to get views facing downtown and the lake. The Studio Café serves modern American dishes and is one of the best places for business breakfasts and lunches in town, the more formal Truffles restaurant has contemporary French cuisine with an acclaimed wine list, and the Lobby Bar has a popular afternoon tea. If people-watching is your goal, check out the Avenue Bar, which overlooks busy Yorkville Avenue. **Pros:** movie-star hangout; desirable neighborhood; acclaimed cuisine. **Cons:** movie-star prices; not as lavish as other Four Seasons; a trifle pretentious. ✉ *21 Avenue Rd., at Bloor St. W, Yorkville* ☎ *416/964–0411 or 800/819–8053* ⊕ *www.fourseasons. com* ↩ *230 rooms, 150 suites* ☖ *In-room: Wi-Fi. In-hotel: 2 restaurants, bars, room service, pool, gym, laundry service, concierge, parking (paid), no-smoking rooms* ▤ *AE, D, DC, MC, V* Ⓜ *Bay* ⊕ *1:E.*

$$$$ 🔲 **The Hazelton Hotel.** The much-anticipated Hazelton opened its doors
Fodor's Choice   just prior to the 2007 Toronto International Film Festival—an astute
★   marketing move, as Hollywood converged on both the city and the hotel. You'll get the same celebrity treatment as you step into the discreet check-in reception area and are personally ushered through the dim, plush hallways. Stunning guest rooms feature sumptuous furnishings, 9-foot ceilings, floor-to-ceiling windows, individual doorbells, and electronic housekeeping controls, and are set apart from the main hallways to ensure absolute silence. No expense was spared in bathrooms either: with their fog-free LCD televisions built into the mirror, three distinct showerheads, plunge tubs, heated floors, and enough marble to please a monarch.

You'll feel intimately acquainted with the jovial bustle of Yorkville life as you open your (soundproof) French doors or step out onto your balcony. In-room dining is 24 hours, and the menu changes frequently at the hands of celebrity chef Mark McEwan, who runs the hugely popular lobby restaurant One (⇨ *see full review in Where to Eat)*. **Pros:**

Toronto's hottest address; well-equipped techno gym; private spa; great in-room amenities. **Cons:** Toronto's hottest address (good luck getting a room). ⊠ *118 Yorkville Ave., at Avenue Rd., Yorkville* ☎ *416/963–6300 or 866/473–6301* ⊕ *www.thehazeltonhotel.com* ⮎ *62 rooms, 15 suites* ⚥ *In-room: safe, refrigerator, DVD, Wi-Fi. In-hotel: restaurant, room service, pool, gym, spa, laundry service, concierge, parking (paid), no-smoking rooms* ⊟ *AE, D, DC, MC, V* Ⓜ *Bay* ⊹ *1:E.*

4

$$ 🛏 **Howard Johnson Toronto Yorkville.** The rooms are standard fare and the amenities are frugal, but the location is a big asset. The stylish boutiques, antiques shops, and posh eateries of trendy Yorkville are just around the corner, and steps from the lobby door are key public-transit-intersection points. Kids under 12 stay free in their parents' rooms. Ask about discounts for senior citizens and auto-club members. **Pros:** complimentary continental breakfast; discount parking voucher on request; best value in pricey neighborhood. **Cons:** staff could use some polishing; breakfast not fancy; interiors show some wear and tear. ⊠ *89 Avenue Rd., north of Bloor St. W, Yorkville* ☎ *416/964–1220 or 800/446–4656* ⊕ *www.hojoyorkville.com* ⮎ *69 rooms* ⚥ *In-room: Wi-Fi. In-hotel: laundry service, parking (paid), no-smoking rooms* ⊟ *AE, DC, MC, V* ⦿ *CP* Ⓜ *Bay* ⊹ *1:E.*

$$$$ 🛏 **InterContinental Toronto Yorkville.** This handsome and intimate member of a respected international hotel chain is a two-minute walk from the Yorkville shopping area and directly across from the Royal Ontario Museum's stunning Crystal cube. Service is top-notch. Art-deco touches enhance the public areas and the spacious guest rooms. Signatures Restaurant is elegant and comfortably classic, and its patio, SkyLounge, offers breezy alfresco dining in season. Relax in the clublike opulence of the Proof Bar: it's perfect for snacks, tea, or a cocktail with one of 50 brands of vodka. **Pros:** close to the Royal Ontario and Gardiner museums; knowledgeable concierges; ultracool lobby bar. **Cons:** ongoing construction in neighborhood; some front-desk staff inexperienced. ⊠ *220 Bloor St. W, west of Avenue Rd., Yorkville* ☎ *416/960–5200 or 800/267–0010* ⊕ *www.toronto.intercontinental.com* ⮎ *185 rooms, 23 suites* ⚥ *In-room: Wi-Fi. In-hotel: restaurant, bar, room service, pool, gym, laundry service, concierge, public Internet, parking (paid), no-smoking rooms* ⊟ *AE, DC, MC, V* Ⓜ *Museum* ⊹ *1:E.*

$$$$ 🛏 **Park Hyatt Toronto.** The experience here is *très* New York Park Avenue. Elegant guest rooms are a generous 300 to 400 square feet, with wide windows overlooking Queen's Park and Lake Ontario. Two-level loft suites have designer kitchenettes, and the 2,500-square-foot Algonquin

Suite affords three different skyline views. The Stillwater Spa is one of the city's finest. Check the gift boutique for fine toiletries, soaps, and skin-care items. The Roof Lounge has been a haven for literati for decades, and a retro lunch or drink is not to be missed. The Mezzanine Lounge offers complimentary antipasto 5 PM to 7 PM nightly, and the Annona Dining Room is held in high regard. The steak house Morton's is attached. **Pros:** large marble baths; fast room service; impeccably appointed. **Cons:** inexpensive breakfasts unavailable; locker rooms for paying spa guests only. ⊠ *4 Avenue Rd., at Bloor St. W, Yorkville* ☎ *416/925–1234 or 800/778–7477* ⊕ *www.parktoronto.hyatt.com* ⮑ *301 rooms, 45 suites* ⟐ *In-room: Wi-Fi. In-hotel: 2 restaurants, bar, room service, gym, spa, laundry service, concierge, executive floor, public Internet, parking (paid), no-smoking rooms* ▭ *AE, D, DC, MC, V* Ⓜ *Museum* ⟐ *1:E.*

$$$$
Fodor's Choice
★

🛈 **Windsor Arms.** Service is the motto here, with a staff-to-guest ratio of 1:6 and 24-hour butler service. Lavish suites have handmade furnishings, luxurious bedcover fabrics, state-of-the-art DVD and CD sound systems, and whirlpool tubs. You can dine in the beautifully appointed Courtyard Café, have tea in the cozy Tea Room, or relax and hide away in the Club 22 bar. The on-site spa is a heavenly retreat, with a peaceful, elegant 24-hour swimming pool and state-of-the-art gym. The building's graceful neo-Gothic facade has been painstakingly restored, contributing to the hotel's genteel refinement. **Pros:** high repeat business due to privacy and personal service; ultracomfortable beds; complimentary Continental breakfast. **Cons:** some fourth-floor rooms noisy due to downstairs functions; no newsstand or gift shop. ⊠ *18 St. Thomas St., at Bloor St. W, Yorkville* ☎ *416/971–9666 or 877/999–2767* ⊕ *www.windsorarmshotel. com* ⮑ *2 rooms, 26 suites* ⟐ *In-room: Ethernet. In-hotel: restaurant, bar, room service, pool, gym, spa, laundry service, public Internet, no-smoking rooms* ▭ *AE, DC, MC, V* ⦿I *CP* Ⓜ *Bay* ⟐ *1:E.*

CHURCH-WELLESLEY AND DUNDAS SQUARE AREA

Once a run-down strip of downtown, this area near the tourist-centric Eaton Centre and bright lights of Dundas Square has undergone a renaissance in recent years. Hotels in this neighborhood are centrally located, making perfect bases for exploring the city.

CHURCH-WELLESLEY

$$$
🛈 **Cawthra Square B&B Inn.** Once the residence of a sergeant in the York Militia, Cawthra Square is now a restored 4,400-square-foot gay-friendly inn. Antiques, including a queen-size mahogany canopy bed, furnish Victoria's Room. Mary's Room has a mahogany four-poster bed and private terrace. Ric's luxury suite occupies an entire floor, with two bedrooms, a whirlpool bath, and a terrace. The large country kitchen has tin ceilings and access to an adorable garden with a gurgling pond and flowering plants. Continental breakfast includes a cornucopia of fresh baked goods, as does afternoon tea. Two other homes, at 512 and 514 Jarvis Street, just moments away, provide additional accommodation. **Pros:** personalized service; safe neighborhood; spotless. **Cons:** no on-site fitness facilities; may be difficult to reserve room in mid-summer.

✉ *10 Cawthra Sq., east of Yonge St., Church–Wellesley* ☎ *416/966–3074 or 800/259–5474* ⊕ *www.cawthrasquare.com* 🛏 *6 rooms, 4 with bath* ⚷ *In-room: Wi-Fi. In-hotel: no elevator, laundry service, public Internet, parking (paid), some pets allowed, no-smoking rooms* 🖃 *AE, D, MC, V* ⧄ *CP* Ⓜ *Wellesley* ✛ *1:F.*

$$ 🛏 **Town Inn Suites.** Long a favorite of airline and film crews and visitors to the city for Toronto's annual Pride Week and the International Film Festival, the all-suites Town Inn is more popular than ever. Floors 19 and 20 are considered the Executive Floors, with smart chocolate-brown leather furniture, flat-screen TVs, free Wi-Fi, king beds with duvets, and a business center. As the building was designed originally as an apartment complex, there are kitchens in every suite and ample underground parking. About 40 suites are considered luxury suites with more space and more amenities. The on-site restaurant, O Noir, is Canada's first to offer dining in the dark, and an entire staff that is blind. **Pros:** location; self-catering; outdoor patio. **Cons:** no full-length mirrors in some suites; harsh lighting in some bathrooms; no boxes for recyclables. ✉ *620 Church St., south of Bloor St. E, Church–Wellesley* ☎ *416/964–3311* ⊕ *www.towninn.com* 🛏 *200 rooms* ⚷ *In-room: kitchen, Wi-Fi. In-hotel: restaurant, bar, room service, pool, gym, concierge, laundry service, parking (paid), no-smoking rooms* 🖃 *AE, DC, MC, V* Ⓜ *Wellesley* ✛ *2:G.*

DUNDAS SQUARE AREA

$$$ 🛏 **Delta Chelsea Hotel.** Canada's largest hotel has long been popular with families and tour groups, so be prepared for a flurry of activity here. The Family Fun Zone has a children's creative center, the Starcade Games Room, a family pool, and the four-story "Corkscrew"—downtown Toronto's only heated indoor waterslide. Camp Chelsea entertains kids while parents step out (daily from late June to early September, Friday night and Saturday the rest of the year). The Delta Chelsea has standard kitchenettes and deluxe guest rooms, as well as one- and two-bedroom suites. **Pros:** all-inclusive cruise-ship-like atmosphere; excellent service; adults-only floors. **Cons:** many children in public areas; busy and noisy lobby at times; unmemorable guest rooms. ✉ *33 Gerrard St., at Yonge St., Dundas Square Area* ☎ *416/595–1975 or 800/243–5732* ⊕ *www.delta-chelsea.com* 🛏 *1,590 rooms, 46 suites* ⚷ *In-room: Wi-Fi. In-hotel: 3 restaurants, bar, room service, pools, gym, children's programs (ages 3–12), laundry facilities, laundry service, executive floor, public Wi-Fi, parking (paid), no-smoking rooms* 🖃 *AE, D, DC, MC, V* Ⓜ *College* ✛ *3:F.*

$ 🛏 **Les Amis.** The charming Parisian host Paul-Antoine fills this Victorian-era house with beautiful photos of his travels through South America and Africa, and the tantalizing aromas of his legendary fruit crepes and Belgian-style waffles. If you feel like lingering after the filling breakfast, guests have access to a small kitchen on the third floor, where unlimited coffee, tea, and tisane are available any time of the day. Rooms are cozy with wood accents, colorful textiles, and lots of plants. Despite its proximity to busy Yonge Street and the bustling Dundas Square Area, Les Amis is tucked away on a quiet residential street with very little traffic. What really sets it apart from the other B&Bs in Toronto is the 100% vegetarian breakfasts with plenty of creative vegan options. **Pros:**

central location; quiet neighbor-hood; vegetarian breakfasts. **Cons:** smallish rooms; shared bathrooms. ✉ *31 Granby St., at Yonge St., Dundas Square Area* ☎ *416/928–1348* ⊕ *www.bbtoronto.com* ⇛ *3 rooms without bath* ♿ *In-room: Wi-Fi. In-hotel: Wi-Fi, no-smoking rooms.* ☐ *AE, MC, V.* ☉ *BP* Ⓜ *College* ✢ *3:F.*

¢   🏨 **Neill-Wycik Summer Hotel.** From

Fodor's Choice ★ early May through late August, 15 of the 22 floors in this Ryerson University residence become value nonstudent lodging. There are four apartment-style units on each floor; within each unit—equipped with linens, towels, and pillows—are either four or five bedrooms and two bathrooms. Each unit has a common area, a television lounge, and a kitchen (bring your own dishes and utensils). The roof deck has grills for guest use and a great view of the city. The fifth floor has a terrace. A free Continental breakfast is included with room rates. **Pros:** sauna; rooftop sundeck; barbeques; coin-operated lockers. **Cons:** no-frills decor; may be noisy; housekeeping may be slack. ✉ *96 Gerrard St. E, at Church St., Dundas Square Area* ☎ *416/977–2320 or 800/268–4358* ⊕ *www. neill-wycik.com* ⇛ *300 rooms without bath* ♿ *In-room: no a/c (some), kitchen, no TV. In-hotel: restaurant, laundry facilities, parking (paid)* ☐ *MC, V* ☉ *CP* ☽ *Closed Sept.–Apr.* Ⓜ *Dundas* ✢ *1:H.*

$$$ 🏨 **Pantages Hotel.** The contemporary design has clean lines, gleaming hardwood flooring, and brushed-steel accents. All rooms are equipped with down duvets and pillows, LCD flat-screen televisions, and Wi-Fi. Many rooms have sofa beds, closeted washer–dryer units, and galley kitchens. As befits a hotel named after the legendary Pantages Theatre (now the Canon Theatre), there is a sense of drama in the lobby, with both hotel guests and condominium residents coming and going, although room views are unspectacular. The yoga and meditation-oriented Osho Channel is complimentary, and yoga mats are supplied in the guest rooms. A full-size gym and a full-service spa are selling points. Romantic packages, starting at $300 per couple, include chocolate-dipped strawberries, champagne, breakfast in bed, and rose petals leading to the bed in the deluxe guest rooms; couples spa packages are additional options. The in-house chef prepares breakfasts, room service, and the Martini Bar menu. **Pros:** quiet but very central location for shopping; excellent spa; great for long stays. **Cons:** lobby can be noisy; darkish hallways. ✉ *200 Victoria St., at Shuter St., Dundas Square Area* ☎ *416/362–1777 or 866/852–1777* ⊕ *www.pantageshotel.com* ⇛ *111 suites* ♿ *In-room: kitchen (some), Wi-Fi. In-hotel: restaurant, room service, bar, gym, spa, concierge, laundry facilities, parking (paid), no-smoking rooms* ☐ *AE, DC, MC, V* ☉ *CP* Ⓜ *Queen* ✢ *4:F.*

$ 🏨 **Ryerson University Residences.** These large student residences, on the nonsmoking Ryerson campus, consist of two adjacent buildings with dormitory-style guest rooms available to nonstudents during the summer months (early May to late August). In Pitman Hall, bathroom and kitchen facilities are shared, and Continental breakfast is included with the cost of each single-occupancy room. Larger single or double bedrooms in the International Centre have en suite baths and cable television but no breakfast. The central location and inexpensive prices make these rooms a hard deal to beat. **Pros:** free local calls; 24-hour security; air-conditioning. **Cons:** few amenities; noisy at times; charge for Internet after first night. ⊠ *160 (Pitman) and 133 (International Centre) Mutual St., north of Dundas St. E, Dundas Square Area* ☎ *416/979–5296, 888/592–8882 in Canada only* ⊕ *www.ryerson.ca/conference* ⊃ *Pitman Hall, 555 rooms without bath; International Living Learning Centre, 252 rooms* ♿ *In-room: no TV (some). In-hotel: restaurant, kitchen (some), laundry facilities, Internet terminal, parking (paid), no-smoking rooms* ⊟ *AE, MC, V* ☯ *Closed Sept.–Apr.* Ⓜ *Dundas* ✛ *4:G.*

$$$ 🖼 **Toronto Downtown Marriott Eaton Centre.** Do you shop in your sleep? Guest rooms at the Marriott's flagship hotel in Canada are connected to Eaton Centre through an aboveground walkway. They're also larger than most in town. An indoor rooftop swimming pool provides a fabulous view of the city. For a similarly stunning vista of Toronto, head for the on-site restaurant, Trios Bistro, which features enormous picture windows. Wi-Fi is available in all public areas, and rooms have 32-inch flat-screen TVs. **Pros:** knowledgeable employees; good value; large guest rooms. **Cons:** may be noisy; parking area can be full; air-conditioning sometimes unreliable. ⊠ *525 Bay St., at Dundas St. W, Dundas Square Area* ☎ *416/597–9200 or 800/905–0667* ⊕ *www.marriotteatoncentre. com* ⊃ *435 rooms, 24 suites* ♿ *In-room: Wi-Fi. In-hotel: 3 restaurants, bar, room service, pool, gym, laundry service, public Wi-Fi, parking (paid), no-smoking rooms* ⊟ *AE, DC, MC, V* Ⓜ *Dundas* ✛ *4:F.*

QUEEN WEST

While some of the large chains, like Hilton, have branches near this very trendy strip of Queen Street West, most of the hotels in this area are beyond Bathurst Street in West Queen West. In this up-and-coming neighborhood, experimental, cutting-edge hotels featuring local art, music, and food thrive.

$$ 🖼 **Beaconsfield Bed & Breakfast.** An artist-and-actress couple owns this architecturally distinct 1882 Victorian B&B in the hip Queen West area. Latin American artifacts and paintings, acquired during the hosts' travels, decorate the colorful, one-bedroom San Miguel Suite. Hand-painted scenic murals cover the walls and ceilings of the panoramic, two-bedroom Ontario Suite. Both have direct access to an outdoor deck overlooking the backyard garden. The third room is smaller and a bit spartan. Breakfasts might include homegrown raspberries from the hosts' yard. Note that this B&B is open in the late spring and summer only, and there's a two-night minimum stay. Eclectic stores, art galleries, and ethnic restaurants are within a few minutes' walk, and there's 24-hour streetcar service nearby. **Pros:** owners extremely hospitable; original artwork very popular with guests; high repeat clientele. **Cons:** no Internet access; long walk or transit to downtown core; open only seasonally. ⊠ *38 Beaconsfield Ave., at Queen St. W, Queen West* ☎ *416/535–3338* ⊕ *www.uniquehomes.ca* ⊃ *3 rooms, 2*

4

Toronto Lodging Alternatives and Resources

APARTMENT RENTALS

If you want a home base that's roomy enough for a family and comes with cooking facilities, consider a furnished rental. Home-exchange directories sometimes list rentals as well as exchanges.

International Agents Hideaways International (☎ 603/430–4433 or 800/843–4433 ⊕ www.hideaways. com); annual membership is US$195.

Local Agents Apartments International Inc. (☎ 416/410–2400 or 888/410–2400 ⊕ www.apts-intl.com) provides upper-end furnished apartments for executives visiting for a month or more.

BED-AND-BREAKFASTS

More than a dozen private homes, all in and around downtown, are affiliated with **Toronto Bed & Breakfast** (☎ 705/738–9449 or 877/922–6522 ⊕ www.torontobandb.com). This free registry has charming lakeside retreats to downtown Victorian gems. Most of these B&Bs fall into the less-expensive price categories. **The Downtown Toronto Association**

of Bed & Breakfast Guest Houses (☎ 416/410–3938 ⊕ www.bnbinfo. com) represents privately owned B&Bs.

HOSTELS

In some 4,500 locations in more than 70 countries, Hostelling International (HI), the umbrella group for a number of national youth-hostel associations, has single-sex, dorm-style beds and, at many hostels, rooms for couples and family accommodations. Toronto's hostels have private rooms for couples and families, as well as dormitory-style rooms. Membership in any HI national hostel association, open to travelers of all ages, allows you to stay in HI-affiliated hostels at member rates; one-year membership is about $28 for adults (C$35 for a two-year minimum membership in Canada); hostels charge about $10 to $30 per night.

Organizations Hostelling International—USA (✉ 8401 Colesville Rd. Ste. 600, Silver Spring, MD ☎ 301/495–1240 ⊕ www.hiusa. org). **Hostelling International—Canada** (✉ 205 Catherine St. Suite 400, Ottawa, ON ☎ 613/237–7884 or 800/663–5777 ⊕ www.hihostels.ca).

with bath ⚹ In-room: no phone, no TV. In-hotel: no elevator, parking (no fee), no-smoking rooms ⊘ Closed Sept.–Apr. ▭ No credit cards ❑ CP Ⓜ Osgoode, then 501 streetcar west ✛ 5:A.

$ 🏨 **Bonnevue Manor Bed & Breakfast Place.** True craftsmen created this 5,000-square-foot house, and it shows in every enchanting nook and cranny, in the high plastered ceilings, and in the richly aged hardwood floors. Rooms at this gay-friendly inn are airy and open, with bathrooms delightfully accented by sleek pedestal sinks. A kind of nostalgic funkiness blends 19th-century antiques and a wood-burning fireplace with modern pieces. Breakfasts brim with home-baked goods, hot cereals, and omelets. It's within walking distance of High Park, Toronto's largest green space, and the white sands of Sunnyside Beach; a 10-minute drive takes you downtown. **Pros:** safe and comfortable neighborhood; excellent breakfasts. **Cons:** two-night minimum stay; old heating system may have problems; no Internet. ✉ 33 Beaty Ave., south of Queen St. W,

Queen West ☎ *416/536–1455* ⊕ *www.bonnevuemanor.com* ↪ *4 rooms* ♨ *In-room: no phone, no TV. In-hotel: restaurant, no elevator, parking (no fee), no-smoking rooms* ⊟ *AE, MC, V* ⦿ *BP* Ⓜ *Osgoode, then streetcar 501 west* ⧉ *5:A.*

$$$ ⟨⟩ **The Drake Hotel.** Once a notorious flophouse, this 19th-century building is now an off-the-wall boutique hotel. Hanging near the lobby's 110-year-old terrazzo staircase is a Rorschach ink-blot mural that spans the lounge and dining room. Vintage 1950s leather couches, slightly tattered ottomans, art curios, and digital-art projections grace the lobby, while flat-screen TVs, hardwood floors, and transparent shower stalls decorate the guest rooms, which are on the smallish side (150 to 250 square feet). One interesting feature is that sex toys are for sale from room service. DJs rock and roll in the lounge, the underground bar, and on the rooftop patio nightly, and there are regular art shows and installations by local artists. The on-site Yoga Den has drop-in classes. **Pros:** attracts Toronto's hippest crowds; food consistently good; forward-thinking. **Cons:** slightly seedy neighborhood; can be noisy at night; not great for children. ⊠ *1150 Queen St. W, at Beaconsfield Ave., Queen West* ☎ *416/531–5042 or 866/372–5386* ⊕ *www.thedrakehotel.ca* ↪ *19 rooms, 1 suite* ♨ *In-room: safe, DVD (some), Wi-Fi. In-hotel: restaurant, bars, laundry service, public Internet, no-smoking rooms* ⊟ *AE, MC, V* Ⓜ *Osgoode, then streetcar 501 west* ⧉ *5:A.*

> ### WORD OF MOUTH
>
> "We have been to Toronto quite a few times now and go back BECAUSE of the Drake! Summer is the best because of the [rooftop patio] and the food is amazing. The place is for the new generation of traveler that pays more attention to boutique hotels and less to room service. The rooms are small with great use of space and the neighborhood is what I wish we had in Chicago. It is not for everyone. If the Ritz is what you want you are barking up the wrong tree. A very hip artist-friendly place that we will continue to recommend and frequent!"   —R Hudon

$$$ ⟨⟩ **Gladstone Hotel.** The Canadian newspaper *The Globe and Mail,* called the Gladstone the "anti-chain-hotel Toronto experience" in 2006, and that's an apt description. A run-down, inner-city property was transformed into a community event space, with artist-designed guest rooms and an emphasis on everything that is one-of-a-kind—even the soaps are handmade and locally produced. The hand-operated 1904 elevator is one of three still working in Toronto. In the Racine Room, maroon-velvet furnishings complement a stack of several vintage steamer trunks—which hide the room's TV and DVD player. Room 304 pays homage to '50s kitsch with a faux-fur wall hanging and a chenille bedspread; the two-story Tower suite, ready for Rapunzel, contains not only a wraparound view of the city but also a bedroom in the tower of the hotel. Some rooms have bidets. **Pros:** every guest room is designed differently; friendly, bohemian place; truly a unique property and experience. **Cons:** downtrodden neighborhood; long walk or transit to downtown core. ⊠ *1214 Queen St. W., at Gladstone Ave., Queen West* ☎ *416/531–4635* ⊕ *www.gladstonehotel.com* ↪ *34 rooms, 3 suites* ♨ *In-room: kitchen*

(some), DVD, Wi-Fi. In-hotel: restaurant, bars, Wi-Fi, no-smoking rooms ⊟ *AE, MC, V* Ⓜ *Osgoode, then streetcar west* ✛ *5:A.*

$$$ ⊡ **Hilton Toronto.** Golds and browns grace the lobby; guest rooms have wood floors, subtle earth tones, and modern furniture. The indoor-outdoor pool is surrounded in towering skyscrapers, which lends a certain eeriness. The executive-floor lounge has a full-time concierge and complimentary breakfast and cocktails. The hotel's decor honors Canada's unique history with the Hudson's Bay Company suite, the glamorous Margery Steele suite, the rugged Heritage suite, and the Panorama suite, a one-bedroom hospitality suite with small kitchen for on-site catering. The Tundra restaurant in the hotel's lobby has stellar Canadian cuisine. Proximity to the entertainment and financial districts makes the Hilton Toronto a convenient base, and it's across the street from the Four Seasons Centre for the Performing Arts. **Pros:** on-site steak house very popular; safe and walkable neighborhood; cozy. **Cons:** rooms generally on the small side; service can lag at times. ⊠ *145 Richmond St. W, at University Ave., Queen West* ☎ *416/869–3456 or 800/267–2281* ⊕ *www.hilton.com* ↽ *601 rooms, 47 suites* ♿ *In-room: Wi-Fi. In-hotel: 3 restaurants, bars, room service, pool, gym, laundry service, Internet terminal, parking (paid), no-smoking rooms* ⊟ *AE, DC, MC, V* Ⓜ *Osgoode* ✛ *5:C.*

GREATER TORONTO

It's no surprise that most of the hotels in Greater Toronto gather around the West End's most prized jewel, the verdant High Park.

$$ ⊡ **By the Park B&B.** By the Park B&B is a real find in the West End, a very desirable Toronto neighborhood. It is located just a few minutes' walk from the Keele subway stop and the vast green space of High Park. The two buildings (a B&B and an apartment-style accommodation in a separate house) are the brainchildren of a married couple who happen to be alumni of the Ontario College of Art and Design, and their attention to detail is evident. The guest rooms are tastefully decorated with Ziggy's impressionistic paintings and Margo's design sense. The Loft on the third floor is most impressive with conservatory-style openness complete with skylights, tropical plants, and a whirlpool tub. Across the street is 89 Indian Grove, and these guest rooms can be rented separately or together as family suites, as there are kitchen facilities available. Breakfasts are delicious and vegetarian, which guests can enjoy in a tiered garden in the backyard of Room 92. Allergy sufferers beware: two cats live at the B&B. **Pros:** free parking; friendly owners; lower rates for long-term stays and cash payments (Canadian dollars only). **Cons:** laundromat a five-minute walk away; subway or bus ride away from downtown. ⊠ *92 & 89 Indian Grove., at Bloor St. W, Greater Toronto* ☎ *416/761–9778, 416/520–6102* ⊕ *www.bythepark.ca* ↽ *4 rooms* ♿ *In-room: Wi-Fi. In-hotel: no elevator, Wi-Fi, parking (no fee), no-smoking rooms* ⊟ *AE, MC, V* ⍝⊙⍝ *BP* Ⓜ *Keele* ✛ *2:A.*

$ ⊡ **Islington Bed & Breakfast House.** Host Joey Lopes takes guests on a leisurely walking tour of the surrounding Humber River valley, describing its history and abundance of flora and birdlife. Islington sits about

20 minutes' ride from downtown. Most guest-room furnishings are mix-and-match, with solid wood pieces; one room showcases art-deco furniture. Hanging paintings and tapestries reflect the local landscape. English, French, and Portuguese are spoken here. **Pros:** suburban living for those who prefer it; clean, quiet neighborhood. **Cons:** kitschy decor; a little far from city. ⊠ *1411 Islington Ave., Greater Toronto* ☎ *416/236–2707* ⊕ *www.islingtonhouse.com* ⟿ *4 rooms, 1 with bath* ⬧ *In-room: no phone, Wi-Fi. In-hotel: no elevator, laundry facilities, parking (no fee), no-smoking rooms* ⊟ *No credit cards* ⎥◯⎢ *BP* Ⓜ *Islington* ⟊ *1:A.*

$$$ ⛶ **The Old Mill Inn & Spa.** Tucked into the Humber River valley, the Old Mill is the only country inn within the city limits of Toronto. Manicured English gardens and a three-arched stone bridge flank the Tudor-style building, constructed in 1914. Burnished mahogany and cherrywood tables, chairs, and beds (some four-poster) grace each guest room. Gas fireplaces and large whirlpool tubs invite romance, and each room has a view of the wooded banks of the Humber River valley. Exposed stone walls and a 50-foot-high solid fir cathedral ceiling define the manor-house restaurant. There's dinner and dancing six nights a week, luncheon buffets, and afternoon tea. It's 15 minutes from downtown and about 25 minutes from the airport. **Pros:** whirlpool tubs; subway and bus stop very close by; live jazz music (Friday). **Cons:** residential neighborhood is sometimes too quiet; no shopping nearby; can be very busy with weddings. ⊠ *21 Old Mill Rd., at Bloor St. W, Greater Toronto* ☎ *416/236–2641 or 866/653–6455* ⊕ *www.oldmilltoronto.com* ⟿ *44 rooms, 13 suites* ⬧ *In-room: Ethernet, Wi-Fi (some). In-hotel: 2 restaurants, bar, room service, gym, spa, laundry service, concierge, Internet terminal, parking (no fee), no-smoking rooms* ⊟ *AE, DC, MC, V* Ⓜ *Old Mill* ⟊ *1:A.*

$ ⛶ **Vanderkooy Bed & Breakfast.** Built in 1910, this immaculate and cozy home has retained many of its original decorative touches, including excellent examples of Edwardian stained-glass windows, antiques, and a collection of original watercolors. Two pet cats wander the premises. A full breakfast—such as Canadian bacon, eggs, preserves, and heavenly French toast from a family recipe—is served on an antique oak table surrounded by fragrant plants and overlooking a colorful garden. Start your morning with a jog through one of the city's quietest neighborhoods, or take a nature hike through Balfour Park, an almost untouched tract of ravine forest, both close at hand. **Pros:** steps to Summerhill subway station; upscale residential neighborhood; accommodating owner. **Cons:** no Internet; limited guest rooms; not for business travelers. ⊠ *53 Walker Ave., at Yonge St., Greater Toronto* ☎ *416/925–8765* ⊕ *www.bbcanada.com/1107.html* ⟿ *3 rooms, 1 with bath* ⬧ *In-room: no phone, no TV. In-hotel: no elevator, parking (no fee), no-smoking rooms* ⊟ *No credit cards* ⎥◯⎢ *BP* Ⓜ *Summerhill* ⟊ *1:F.*

THE AIRPORT STRIP

If you have an early morning departure or late night arrival from Pearson International Airport, staying near the airport might be the best option considering the drive from downtown Toronto can take up to two hours when traffic is at its worst.

$ ⊡ **Carlingview Airport Inn.** There are only three floors to this modest place, but what it lacks in size it makes up for in friendly service. Ergonomic chairs, big desks, complimentary Wi-Fi, and early morning breakfast (from 3 AM) make this unpretentious inn a favorite of savvy business travelers. **Pros:** free parking for up to eight days; free access to pool and fitness center at next door hotel; 24-hour airport shuttle. **Cons:** no-frills amenities; musty smell in hallways. ⊠ *221 Carlingview Dr., off Dixon Rd., Airport Strip* ☎ *416/675–3303 or 877/675–3303* ⊕ *www.carlingview.ca* ⇗ *112 rooms* ⚐ *In-room: Wi-Fi. In-hotel: restaurant, pool, gym, Wi-Fi, laundry service, airport shuttle, parking (no fee), some pets allowed, no-smoking rooms* ▭ *AE, DC, MC, V* ⎮◎⎮ *CP* ⊹ *1:A.*

$$ ⊡ **Courtyard by Marriott Toronto Airport.** Room design caters to business travelers with large, well-lighted desks and ergonomic chairs for added comfort during those long conference calls. The Courtyard Café serves a standard hot-breakfast buffet, with cook-to-order options. A large-screen plasma TV dominates the lounge, where there are plenty of overstuffed sofas on which to unwind and the 24-hour Market store in the lobby provides entertainment for those suffering from jet lag. The big plus here is convenience; you're near the major crossroads of highways 401 and 427, and a 20-minute drive from downtown. **Pros:** 24-hour free airport shuttle bus; complimentary Internet in guest rooms; free parking for up to eight days. **Cons:** front-desk staff may be abrupt. ⊠ *231 Carlingview Dr., Airport Strip* ☎ *416/675–0411 or 866/675–0411* ⊕ *www.marriottcourtyardtorontoairport.com* ⇗ *168 rooms, 1 suite* ⚐ *In-room: Wi-Fi. In-hotel: restaurant, bar, pool, gym, laundry service, Internet terminal, airport shuttle, parking, no-smoking rooms* ▭ *AE, DC, MC, V* ⎮◎⎮ *CP* ⊹ *1:A.*

$$ ⊡ **The Westin Bristol Place Toronto Airport.** This has long been considered one of the ritziest of the airport-strip hotels. It's 100% no-smoking, and bedrooms have plasma TVs and mahogany armoires. A small waterfall cascades in the lobby. For an airport property, it's fairly quiet—rooms that face east are the quietest of all. **Pros:** safety bars in bathrooms; good restaurant fare; pool has solarium. **Cons:** free Internet only in business center; 14 mi from downtown core; older property. ⊠ *950 Dixon Rd., Airport Strip* ☎ *416/675–9444 or 877/999–3223* ⊕ *www.starwoodhotels.com* ⇗ *287 rooms, 5 suites* ⚐ *In-room: safe, Wi-Fi (some). In-hotel: 2 restaurants, room service, bar, pool, gym, executive floor, Internet terminal, airport shuttle, parking (paid), some pets allowed, no-smoking rooms* ▭ *AE, D, DC, MC, V* ⊹ *1:A.*

Nightlife and the Arts

WORD OF MOUTH

"We had purchased [tickets] for a new show that had just started playing at Second City . . . I loved how the cast was able to keep the production so current given the time frame they have to come up with new material. I guess that's what makes improv so great."

—genkav

"When you get here, pick up a copy of NOW, an entertainment newspaper that's free at just about every corner. It comes out on Thursdays or check it out at www.nowtoronto.com. There's a discount ticket booth at Dundas Square."

—goddesstogo

Updated by
Shannon Kelly

Toronto's status as one of the most multicultural cities in the world makes its arts and nightlife scene a diverse and exciting one. As the city continues to grow, new venues emerge and existing ones are refurbished. Ambitious programs from many of the city's new performance ensembles present a rich variety of entertainment for all tastes and budgets. Toronto is Canada's center for performing arts, including the Canadian Opera Company, the National Ballet of Canada, and the Broadway-caliber theater. The exodus of young Canadian performers to the city also fuels many independent theaters, dance companies, and music venues and performances.

Toronto's glamorous nightlife is maintained thanks in part to the string of celebs and other film- and television-industry types who paint the town red while on location here. Toronto's "every-city" quality attracts the location scouts, but it's the Torontonians' reputation for being courteous and leaving the stars alone that brings them back again and again. This means it's not uncommon to brush elbows with celebrities while enjoying a night out on the town.

On any night in Toronto, you can find entertainment in indie-rock mash-ups, obscure rock operas, live bluegrass, and experimental music. Toronto is known for its many nightclubs—be prepared for long lines on weekends. More popular bars and lounges start buzzing around 11 PM and close at 3 AM. But there are also loads of underground parties and several clubs known for their all-night scene, finishing up on weekends at 7 AM. For those who want to have a good time but be home before their carriages turn back into pumpkins, there are plenty of überchic lounges and funky Latino clubs.

THE ARTS

Toronto is the capital of the performing arts in English-speaking Canada, but it hasn't always been. Before 1950, Toronto had no opera company, no ballet, and very little theater worthy of the title "professional." Then came the Massey Report on the Arts, one of those government-sponsored studies that usually help put sensitive subjects on the back burner for several more years. In this case, however, the heavens broke loose—money began to come from a variety of government grants; the Canada Council, the Canadian Opera Company, CBC television, and the National Ballet of Canada were born; and a number of small theaters began to pop up, culminating in an artistic explosion throughout the 1970s in every aspect of the arts. Massive immigration from England and Eastern and Central Europe; a growing sense of independence from the mother country; a recognition that if Canada did not develop its own arts, the Americans would do it for them; and, in general, a growing civic and cultural maturity, added fuel to the fire.

Today Toronto is, after New York and London, the largest center for English-speaking theater in the world. The city's smaller theaters have long been filled with interesting productions of the finest in classic and contemporary Canadian, English, American, and French drama. Since the 1960s the Sony (formerly the Hummingbird) and Royal Alexandra theaters have provided a mix

ARTS AND CULTURE: READ ALL ABOUT IT

The best places for information on the city's cultural events are the free weekly newspapers *NOW* (⊕ www.nowtoronto.com) and *Eye Weekly* (⊕ www.eyeweekly.com). Also worth checking are the "What's On" section of the *Toronto Star* (⊕ www.thestar.com) on Thursday, the Saturday *Globe and Mail* and *National Post*, and the monthly magazine *Toronto Life* (⊕ www.torontolife.com). Whole *Note* is a monthly publication, free on newsstands, dedicated to Toronto's classical music, jazz, opera, and new and world music.

of local and Broadway productions. Restored historic theaters like the Elgin–Winter Garden complex and the Canon Theatre, plus more modern venues, like the Toronto Centre for the Arts and the Princess of Wales, explain why it can truly be called "Broadway North."

Because of the many movies shot here, Toronto, North America's third-largest film production center after L.A. and New York, garnered the nickname "Hollywood North," though that moniker is also used for Vancouver, which is the second-largest TV production center in the world and is beginning to rival Toronto in film production. The availability of excellent crews, pre- and post-production facilities, the variety of locations (Toronto has posed as everything from Paris to Vietnam), and the city's continued investment in the industry—including a C$700 million studio, Filmport, to be completed on the Harbourfront in 2010—keep cameras rolling in Toronto. Next time you watch a film, see if you can spot Toronto. For information about productions in town during your visit, phone the **Toronto Film and Television Office** (☎ 416/338–3456 ⊕ www.toronto.ca/tfto).

TICKETS

Full-price theater tickets run from as low as C$20 to more than C$200. Tickets for major pop concerts are usually C$50 to C$125. On certain slow nights and on Sunday many theaters have pay-what-you-can entry; phone the venue and ask.

Tickets for almost any event in the city can be obtained through **Ticketmaster** (☎ 416/870–8000 ⊕ www.ticketmaster.ca). Another popular ticket seller is **StubHub** (☎ 866/788–2482 ⊕ www.stubhub.com).

CANADA'S NATIVE STARS

Few know that "America's sweetheart" of early Hollywood, Mary Pickford, hailed from Toronto. And in fact, many famous Hollywood or TV actors, Grammy-winning musicians, and other industry types who have made it big in the U.S. are Canadian. To name a few:

Musicians and songwriters: Leonard Cohen, Paul Anka, Diana Krall, Michael Bublé, the Cowboy Junkies, the Guess Who, Glenn Gould, Corey Hart, k.d. Lang, Sarah McLachlan, Joni Mitchell, Anne Murray, Rage Against the Machine, Shania Twain, Neil Young.

Actors: Michael J. Fox, Raymond Burr (aka "Perry Mason"), Rachel McAdams, Kim Cattral, Ryan Gosling, Margot Kidder, Sandra Oh, Jason Priestly, William Shatner, Catherine O'Hara.

Directors: James Cameron, David Cronenberg, Jason Reitman, Norman Jewison.

DISCOUNTS AND DEALS

To get half-price tickets—mainly for theater but also some dance, music, and comedy—on the day of a performance, visit the **T.O. Tix booth** (⊠ *Yonge and Dundas Sts., Yonge-Dundas Square* ☎ *800/541–0499 or 416/536–6468* ⊕ *www.totix.ca* Ⓜ *Dundas*), open in good weather Tuesday through Saturday noon to 6:30 PM. Tickets for Sunday performances are sold on Saturday. In summer the wait can be 45 minutes or more. ■ **TIP→** **If you arrive at around 11:15 you stand the best chance of getting the show you want.** All sales are final, credit cards are accepted (Visa and MasterCard), and a small service charge is added to the price of each ticket.

The Toronto Symphony Orchestra's **tsoundcheck program** (☎ *416/598–3375* ⊕ *www.tsoundcheck.com*) makes $12 tickets available for those ages 15–29. You must apply for a membership card in advance and pick it up at Roy Thomsom Hall before the performance. **Opera for a New Age** (☎ *416/363–6671* ⊕ *www.coc.ca*) sells $20 Canadian Opera Company tickets to those under 30. They can be purchased online or in person at the Four Seasons Centre.

The Canadian Opera Company's **Free Concert Series** (☎ *416/363–6671* ⊕ *www.coc.ca*) takes place September through June with jazz, classical, world, and dance performances every Tuesday and Thursday at noon, and on some Wednesday evenings, in the Four Seasons Centre's Richard Bradshaw Amphitheatre.

CLASSICAL MUSIC AND OPERA

CLASSICAL MUSIC

★ **Glenn Gould Studio.** A variety of classical-, folk-, and jazz, pop, world-music companies perform at this 341-seat space named for the famed Canadian (and Torontonian) pianist. Studio recordings are done here as well, a testament to its excellent acoustics. Gould would have expected nothing less. ⊠ *250 Front St. W, Entertainment District* ☎ *416/205–5000* ⊕ *glenngouldstudio.cbc.com* Ⓜ *Union, St. Andrews.*

The MacMillan Theatre. Performances by professors and grad and undergrad students of the University of Toronto Faculty of Music and visiting artists, ranging from symphony to jazz to full-scale operas, take place in this 815-seat auditorium September through May. ☒ *University of Toronto Faculty of Music, Edward Johnson Bldg., 80 Queen's Park Crescent, Queen's Park* ☎ *416/978–3744* ⊕ *www.music.utoronto.ca* Ⓜ *Museum.*

Tafelmusik. Internationally renowned as one of the world's finest period ensembles, Tafelmusik presents baroque music on original instruments in a historic church. ☒ *Trinity–St. Paul's Centre, 427 Bloor St. W, The Annex* ☎ *416/964–6337* ⊕ *www.tafelmusik.org* Ⓜ *Spadina.*

The Toronto Mendelssohn Choir. This group of 150 vocalists, which often performs with the Toronto Symphony, was begun in 1894 and has since been applauded worldwide. The *Messiah* is performed annually by the choir at Christmastime. ☒ *Roy Thomson Hall, 60 Simcoe St., Entertainment District* ☎ *416/598–0422* ⊕ *www.tmchoir.org* Ⓜ *St. Andrew.*

Toronto Symphony Orchestra. Since 1922 this orchestra has achieved world acclaim with music directors such as Seiji Ozawa, Sir Thomas Beecham, and Sir Andrew Davis. When Canadian-born Peter Oundjian took over as musical director in 2003. Guest performers have included pianist Lang Lang and violinist Joshua Bell. The TSO presents about three concerts weekly at Roy Thomson Hall from September through May when it is not on tour. ☒ *Roy Thomson Hall, 60 Simcoe St., Entertainment District* ☎ *416/598–3375* ⊕ *www.tso.ca* Ⓜ *St. Andrew.*

Walter Hall. This is the place to see avant-garde artists and up-and-coming stars. The intimate venue is suited to jazz groups, baroque ensembles, and student recitals. Because it's run by the music faculty of the University of Toronto, serious and experimental jazz bands and baroque chamber orchestras are often presented during the academic year at little or no cost. The acoustics at this small theater are good, as are all sight lines. ☒ *University of Toronto Faculty of Music, Edward Johnson Bldg., 80 Queen's Park Crescent, Queen's Park* ☎ *416/978–3744* ⊕ *www.music.utoronto.ca* Ⓜ *Museum.*

CONTEMPORARY AND EXPERIMENTAL MUSIC

★ **The Music Gallery.** Toronto's go-to spot for experimental music, the self-titled "centre for Creative Music" presents an eclectic selection of avant-garde and experimental music, from world and classical to jazz and avant-pop in a relaxed setting. Seeing a show in the dramatic main venue, **St. George the Martyr Church** (☒ *197 John St., 1 block north of Queen St., Queen West* Ⓜ *Osgoode*), is recommended, though there are several other venues. ☎ *416/204–1080* ⊕ *www.musicgallery.org.*

OPERA

Canadian Opera Company. Founded in 1950, the COC has grown to be the largest producer of opera in Canada. From the most popular operas, such as *Carmen* and *Otello,* to more modern or rarer works, such as *The Cunning Little Vixen* and *Hansel and Gretel,* the COC has proven trustworthy and often daring. Versions of Verdi's *La Traviata* and Wagner's *The Flying Dutchman* were considered radical by many. The COC often hosts world-renowned performers, and it pioneered the use of scrolling supertitles, which allow the audience to follow the libretto in English in a capsulized translation that appears above the performers. Tickets sell out quickly. The magnificent Four Seasons Centre opera house opened its doors in 2006. Tours ($7) of the facility are given most Saturdays at noon; check the Web site for details. ⊠ *Four Seasons Centre, 145 Queen St. W, at University Ave., Queen West M5H 4G1* ☎ *416/363–8231* ⊕ *www.coc.ca* Ⓜ *Osgoode.*

Opera Atelier. Since its opening in 1985, Opera Atelier has been dedicated to staging 17th- and 18th-century baroque operas "authentically," meaning as they were in that era, with extravagant sets and costumes and original instruments. Performances are at the Elgin Theatre. ☎ *416/703–3767* ⊕ *www.operaatelier.com.*

ARENAS AND CONCERT HALLS

It's not uncommon for a concert hall to present modern dance one week, a rock- or classical-music concert another week, and a theatrical performance the next. Arenas double as sports stadiums and venues for the biggest names in music and the occasional monster truck rally or other spectacle.

The Air Canada Centre. This arena has hosted *Walking With Dinosaurs,* a theatrical show starring animatronic *life-size* dinosaurs, which gives you an idea of its scope. Most arena shows are held here rather than at the larger Rogers Centre due to superior acoustics. Past performances at the 15,000-capacity arena have included Alicia Keyes, Tom Petty, the American Idols Tour, and Cirque du Soleil. ⊠ *40 Bay St., at Gardiner Expressway, Harbourfront* ☎ *416/815–5500* ⊕ *www.theaircanada-centre.com* Ⓜ *Union.*

★ **Elgin–Winter Garden Theatre Centre.** This jewel in the crown of the Toronto arts scene is composed of two former vaudeville halls, built in 1913, one on top of the other. It is the last operating double-decker theater complex in the world and a Canadian National Historic Site. From 1913 to 1928, the theaters hosted silent-film and vaudeville legends like George Burns, Gracie Allen, and Edgar Bergen with Charlie McCarthy. In 1928 the upstairs Winter Garden closed (it remained closed for 60 years), and the Elgin became a cinema. A C$29 million restoration in the 1980s restored the Elgin's dramatic gold-leaf-and-cherub-adorned interior and the Winter Garden's *A Midsummer Night's Dream*–inspired decor, complete with a ceiling hung with beech branches. These stages have since hosted Broadway-caliber musicals such as *Avenue Q,* comedy performances, jazz concerts, operas, Toronto International Film Festival screenings, and much more. The Elgin, downstairs, has about 1,500 seats and is more suited to musicals; the 1,000-seat Winter Garden, upstairs, is comparatively intimate. Both have excellent sight lines. Guided tours for C$10 are given Thursday at 5 PM and Saturday at 11 AM. ⊠ *189 Yonge St., ½ block north of Queen St. E, Yonge-Dundas Square* ☎ *416/872–5555 tickets, 416/314–2871 tours* ⊕ *www.heritagetrust.on.ca* Ⓜ *Queen.*

Fodor's Choice
★ **Massey Hall.** It's always been cramped, but Massey Hall's near-perfect acoustics and its handsome, U-shape tiers have made it a great place to enjoy music since 1894, when it opened with a performance of Handel's *Messiah.* The nearly 2,800 seats are not terribly comfortable, and a small

number are blocked by pillars that hold up the structure, but Massey Hall remains a venerable place to catch the greats of the music world, such as Emmylou Harris, Iggy and the Stooges, and Gilberto Gil. Comedians and dance troupes are also standard fare. ⊠ *178 Victoria St., at Shuter St., Yonge-Dundas Square* ☎ *416/872–4255* ⊕ *www. masseyhall.com* Ⓜ *Queen.*

Rogers Centre. Toronto's largest performance venue, with seating for up to 55,000, is the spot for the biggest shows in town. The former SkyDome has hosted the Rolling Stones, U2, and Cher, though the acoustically superior Air Canada Centre is the more widely used arena venue. ⊠ *1 Blue Jays Way, at Spadina Ave., Harbourfront* ☎ *416/341–3663* ⊕ *www.rogerscentre.com* Ⓜ *Union.*

> **HARBOURFRONT CENTRE: ALL-PURPOSE ARTS**
>
> When looking for cultural events in Toronto, always check the schedule at the Harbourfront Centre (*235 Queen's Quay W, at Lower Simcoe St., Harbourfront* ☎ *416/973–4000* ⊕ *www. harbourfrontcentre.com* Ⓜ *Union*). A cultural playground, it has an art gallery (the Power Plant), two dance spaces, a music garden (co-designed by Yo Yo Ma), and chockablock festivals and cultural events, some especially for kids and many of them free.

★ **Roy Thomson Hall.** The most important concert hall in Toronto opened in 1982. It was named for the billionaire newspaper magnate known as Lord Thomson of Fleet, after his family donated C$4.5 million in his memory. In 2002 a major face-lift improved the hall's acoustics as well as its aesthetics, with blond-wood flooring and pale decorative accents. It is the home of the Toronto Symphony Orchestra and the Toronto Mendelssohn Choir, and also hosts visiting orchestras and popular entertainers. Tours for C$7 highlight the acoustic and architectural features of the striking round structure. ⊠ *60 Simcoe St., Entertainment District* ☎ *416/872–4255 tickets, 416/593–4822 Ext. 363 tours* ⊕ *www.roythomson.com* Ⓜ *St. Andrew.*

Sony Centre for the Performing Arts. When this theater opened in 1960 as the O'Keefe Centre, it showcased the world premiere of *Camelot,* starring Julie Andrews, Richard Burton, and Robert Goulet. Renamed the Hummingbird Centre in 1996 after major renovations, the venue became the Sony Centre under new ownership in 2006. It hosts visiting comedians, rock stars, pre-Broadway shows, and post-Broadway tours. Past performances include Leonard Cohen, David Copperfield, *Swan Lake* on Ice, and *Rent.* Almost anything but the most lavish opera or musical can be accommodated in the cavernous 3,223-seat hall. The acoustics, however, can be subpar from certain seats. ⊠ *1 Front St. E, at Yonge St. Old Town* ☎ *416/872–2262* ⊕ *www.sonycentre.ca* Ⓜ *Union, King.*

St. Lawrence Centre for the Arts. This center has been presenting theater, music, dance, opera, film, and forums on public issues since 1970 and completed a C$4.5 million renovation in 2007. The two main halls are the luxuriously appointed **Bluma Appel Theatre** and the **Jane Mallett Theatre,** both venues for recitals and performances by companies like the Canadian Stage Company, the Toronto Operetta, and Music Toronto (chamber music). ⊠ *27 Front St. E, 1 block east of Yonge St., Old Town* ☎ *416/366–7723* ⊕ *www.stlc.com* Ⓜ *King, Union.*

Toronto Centre for the Arts. Large-scale musicals are performed in the 1,800-seat Main Stage at this arts center, making it one of the city's major theater venues. Past shows have included *Show Boat* and *My Fair Lady*; the current show is *Jersey Boys*. The 200-seat Studio Theatre and 1,032-seat George Weston Recital Hall host smaller plays and classical- and world-music concerts, such as the Bach Children's Chorus and the Toronto Philharmonia. ⊠ *5040 Yonge St., north of Sheppard Ave. E, Greater Toronto* ☎ *416/733–9388, 416/870–8000 tickets* ⊕ *www. tocentre.com* Ⓜ *North York Centre.*

DANCE

Toronto's rich dance scene includes pretty *Swan Lake* interpretations and edgy, emotionally charged modern-dance performances.

National Ballet of Canada. Canada's homegrown and internationally recognized classical-ballet company was founded in 1951 by Celia Franca, an English dancer from the Sadler's Wells tradition, and is supported by infusions of dancers trained at its own school. The season runs from November through June. *Sleeping Beauty, Swan Lake, Onegin*, and the Christmastime *Nutcracker* are included in the permanent repertory. Karen Kain, former National Ballet prima ballerina, became the artistic director in 2005. ■TIP➔ Discounted tickets for students and seniors are available at the box office on performance day. ⊠ *Four Seasons Centre for the Performing Arts, 145 Queen St. W, Queen West* ☎ *416/345–9595, 866/345–9595 outside Toronto* ⊕ *www.national.ballet.ca* Ⓜ *Osgoode.*

Harbourfront Centre. Two venues for dance are here. The **Fleck Dance Theatre** was built specifically for modern dance in 1983. The proscenium stage hosts some of the best local and Canadian modern and contemporary companies in addition to some international acts. The **Enwave Theatre** welcomes these same types of dance performances as well as plays and concerts. It has excellent acoustics. Both theaters are small (425 and 450 seats) so you're never far from the stage, and sight lines are great from every seat. ⊠ *Harbourfront Centre, 207 Queen's Quay W, at Lower Simcoe St., Harbourfront* ☎ *416/973–4000* ⊕ *www. harbourfrontcentre.com* Ⓜ *Union.*

★ **Toronto Dance Theatre.** With roots in the Martha Graham tradition, this theater is the oldest contemporary dance company in the city. Since its beginnings in the 1960s it has created more than 100 works, over a third of which use original scores by Canadian composers. Three or four pieces are performed each year in their home theater in Cabbagetown, and one major production is performed at the Harbourfront Centre's Fleck Dance Theatre. The company tours Canada and has played major festivals in Europe and the United States. ⊠ *80 Winchester St., 1 block east of Parliament St., Cabbagetown* ☎ *416/967–1365* ⊕ *www.tdt.org* Ⓜ *Castle Frank.*

FILM

Toronto has a devoted film audience. The result is a feast of riches—commercial first- and second-run showings, independent films and documentaries, cult classics, myriad festivals, and lecture series for every taste. For movie times, contact the theaters directly, or check Cinema-Clock (⊕ *www.cinemaclock.com)* or the free weekly city papers *NOW* (⊕ *www.nowtoronto.com*) or *Eye Weekly* (⊕ *www.eyeweekly.com*).

FIRST-RUN AND MAINSTREAM MOVIES

Polson Pier Drive-in Theatre. For an old-fashioned treat, park your car at this downtown drive-in (still known as the Docks Drive-in), open from May to early September (weather permitting) for a double feature. First-run flicks are shown on Friday, Saturday, and Sunday evenings, starting at approximately 9 PM. Purchase tickets on-site (C$13 adults); on Sunday, admission is $20 per carload. ⊠ *176 Cherry St., just east of Parliament St., Harbourfront* ☎ *416/465–4653* ⊕ *www.polsonpier.com.*

Scotiabank Theatre (The Paramount). In the heart of the Entertainment District, this megaplex with 14 screens, including an IMAX theater (C$15), shows all the latest blockbusters, usually along with a couple of foreign or independent films. ⊠ *259 Richmond St. W, at John St., Entertainment District* ☎ *416/368–5600* ⊕ *www.cineplex.com* Ⓜ *Osgoode.*

The Varsity and Varsity V.I.P. The 12 screens here show new releases. ■ TIP➔ The smaller, licensed V.I.P. screening rooms (ages 19 and up) have seat-side waitstaff ready to take your concession-stand orders. VIP tickets are C$16.50. ⊠ *Manulife Centre, 3rd fl., 55 Bloor St. W, at Bay St., Yorkville* ☎ *416/961–6303* ⊕ *www.cineplex.com* Ⓜ *Bay.*

INDEPENDENT, FOREIGN, AND REVIVAL FILMS

Bloor Cinema. Classic, cult, independent, and second-run movies are the Bloor's bread and butter. Tickets are C$8, and the first ticket includes a six-month membership that reduces the price of subsequent shows to C$5. Festival screenings and some special presentations are pricier. ⊠ *506 Bloor St. W, at Bathurst St., The Annex* ☎ *416/516–2330* ⊕ *www.bloorcinema.com* Ⓜ *Bathurst.*

The Cinesphere. This theater offers 70mm IMAX films—usually educational in nature—and popular films that benefit from the large format and 24-track sound. This was the world's first permanent IMAX theater. When the Ontario Place park is open (May–September), admission is included in the Play All Day pass; most movies are C$7.50. ⊠ *Ontario Place, 955 Lake Shore Blvd. W, Harbourfront* ☎ *416/314–9900* ⊕ *www.ontarioplace.com* Ⓜ *511 Bathurst streetcar.*

Carlton Cinemas. Head to this nine-screen theater for rarely screened

REEL RESEARCH

The **Film Reference Library** (⊠ *2 Carlton St., mezzanine, at Yonge St., Dundas Square* ☎ *416/967–1517* ⊕ *www.filmreferencelibrary. ca* Ⓜ *College*) is the largest collection of English-language Canadian film material in the world. You can read scripts and watch films in viewing stations. Admission is C$7. The library is open Tuesday, Thursday, and Friday 11–4.

international films as well as some mainstream movies. Admission is C$10.50. ✉ *20 Carlton St., just east of Yonge St., Dundas Square* ☎ *416/598–2309 www.cineplex.com* Ⓜ *College.*

Cinematheque Ontario. A division of the Toronto International Film Festival Group, Cinematheque Ontario screens director retrospectives, actor tributes, national cinema spotlights, and exclusive limited runs in the Art Gallery of Ontario's Jackman Hall. Tickets are about C$10–C$12, plus tax. ✉ *317 Dundas St. W, entrance on McCaul St. just south of Dundas, Chinatown* ☎ *416/968–3456* ⊕ *www.cinemathequeontario.ca* Ⓜ *St. Patrick.*

Cumberland 4. An excellent selection of international and nonmainstream new films is shown at this beloved four-screen cinema. Admission is C$12.95. ✉ *159 Cumberland St., just east of Avenue Rd., Yorkville* ☎ *416/964–9359* Ⓜ *Bay.*

Harbourfront Centre. Documentaries, frequently accompanying summer festivals, cultural events, and retrospectives, are presented ad hoc throughout the year. ✉ *235 Queen's Quay W, at Lower Simcoe St., Harbourfront* ☎ *416/973–4000* ⊕ *www.harbourfrontcentre.com* Ⓜ *Union.*

The Revue. This beloved neighborhood movie house is operated by the nonprofit Revue Film Society. On screen are documentaries, classics (cult and non-), foreign films, some first-run movies, and the occasional oddity like *Giant Killer Shark: The Musical.* Admission (C$12.50) includes a six-month membership that lowers ticket prices to C$6.50. ✉ *400 Roncesvalles Ave., at Howard Park Ave., West Toronto* ☎ *416/531–9959* ⊕ *revuecinema.ca* Ⓜ *Dundas West.*

The Royal. This 1939 single-screen shows second-run movies, documentaries, and indie films. Sound and projection facilities were revamped in 2006. ✉ *608 College St., at Clinton St., Little Italy* ☎ *416/534–5252 www.theroyal.to* Ⓜ *506 College streetcar.*

FILM FESTIVALS AND EVENTS

⇨ *See Toronto Film Festivals box.*

Fodor's Choice ★ **Toronto International Film Festival.** Downtown is dominated by this festival each September. The 10-day event attracts Hollywood's brightest stars to view the latest works of both great international directors and lesser-known independent-film directors from around the world; a selection of Canadian films is always highlighted. You can get

> **WORD OF MOUTH**
>
> "I live in Toronto and have been to the [film] festival numerous times over the years. It's really an amazing event that's totally accessible to the public, unlike Cannes."
> —bittersweet

tickets in advance through an online lottery process that starts in July. Single tickets to available films can be purchased online as well. Many films sell out early for this hugely popular film festival—the largest of its kind in the world—and attending films with big names attached to them usually requires enduring long lines. However, last-minute tickets to something are usually available, and even sold-out shows have a rush line. Arrive at least two hours in advance for rush tickets to popular movies. Screenings are at theaters throughout the city. ☎ 416/968–3456 ⊕ *www.tiffg.ca.*

THEATER

Toronto has the third-largest theater scene in the world, following London and New York. Here you can see Broadway shows as well as a range of smaller Canadian and international productions from reproduced "straight" plays to experimental performances.

For reviews, news, and schedules, check ⊕ *www.stage-door.com* (a wealth of information—this is where industry types browse); *The Globe and Mail* "Arts" section *(⊕ www.theglobeandmail.com/arts)*; and the regulars: *NOW, Eye Weekly,* and *Toronto Life,* all online as well.

COMMERCIAL THEATERS
For more large-theater venues, ⇨ *see Concert Halls.*

Canon Theatre. This 1920 vaudeville theater is one of the most architecturally and acoustically exciting live theaters in Toronto. In 1988–89 then-owner Cineplex Odeon refurbished the magnificent 2,300-seat theater in preparation for the Canadian debut of *The Phantom of the Opera,* Canada's longest-running stage musical, which closed in 1999. Today the theater hosts big-budget musicals, such as *Spamalot* and *The Color Purple,* almost exclusively. The theater itself is one of the most beautiful in the world. Designed by world-renowned theater architect Thomas Lamb, it has Doric, Ionic, and Corinthian columns, a grand staircase, gold-leaf detailing, crystal chandeliers. The orchestra level is wheelchair-accessible. ✉ *244 Victoria St., 1 block south of Dundas St. E, Dundas Square* ☎ *416/872–1212 or 800/461–3333* ⊕ *www.mirvish. com* Ⓜ *Dundas, Queen.*

Princess of Wales. State-of-the-art facilities and wonderful murals by American artist Frank Stella grace this 2,000-seat theater, built by father-and-son producer team Ed and David Mirvish in the early 1990s to accommodate the technically demanding musical *Miss Saigon.* All levels are wheelchair-accessible. Big-budget musicals like *The Lion King* and plays such as *Nicholas Nickleby* are showcased. ✉ *300 King St. W, at John St., Entertainment District* ☎ *416/872–1212 or 800/461–3333* ⊕ *www.mirvish.com* Ⓜ *St. Andrew.*

Royal Alexandra. Since 1907 the "Royal Alex" has been the place to be seen in Toronto. The 1,500 plush red seats, gold brocade, and baroque swirls and flourishes make theatergoing a refined experience. Programs are a mix of blockbuster musicals and dramatic productions, some touring before or after Broadway appearances. The theater is wheelchair-accessible on the first floor only. Second-balcony seats are harder than those in the first balcony. *Dirty Dancing* closed in 2009, and at this writing *Love Never Dies* by Andrew Lloyd Weber is slated for 2010. ✉ *260 King St. W, Entertainment District* ☎ *416/872–3333 or 800/461–3333* ⊕ *www.mirvish.com* Ⓜ *St. Andrew.*

TORONTO FILM FESTIVALS

Toronto is a film city and from April through November it seems that every week brings a different festival. Films are shown at various independent theaters around the city.

MARCH
Cinéfranco (⊕ *www.cinefranco.com*) shows French-language films, many of them French-Canadian, with English subtitles.

APRIL
Reelworld (⊕ *www.reelworld.ca*) focuses on emerging filmmakers and diversity. **Sprockets: the Toronto International Film Festival for Children** (⊕ *sprockets.ca*) features new and classic films aimed at the 4- to 14-year-old crowd. **Hot Docs** (⊕ *www.hotdocs.ca*) is the largest documentary film festival in North America.

The Toronto Jewish Film Festival (⊕ *www.tjff.com*) is nine days of new and classic films by Jewish filmmakers and/or with Jewish themes.

MAY
InsideOut (⊕ *www.insideout.on.ca*) is the city's gay and lesbian film festival. **Toronto Hispano-American Film Festival** (⊕ *www.thaff.com*) shows films from Spain, Latin America, and Canada.

JUNE
Luminato (⊕ *www.luminato.com*) is one of the city's largest arts festivals. The free, documentary films are supplements to the festival's art, theater, dance, and music performances.

Toronto Italian Film Festival (⊕ *www.italianfilmfest.com*) features Italian and Italian-theme films. **NXNE**

(North by Northeast ⊕ *www.nxne.com*), the spinoff music festival from the much larger SXSW (South by Southwest) festival in Austin, also includes showings of music-related films. **Worldwide Short Film Festival** (⊕ *www.worldwideshortfilmfest.com*) is five days of shorts from around the world.

AUGUST
Toronto After Dark (⊕ *www.torontoafterdark.com*) is a festival of horror, sci-fi, and thrillers.

SEPTEMBER
Toronto International Film Festival ⇨ *See full listing.*

OCTOBER
Toronto International Latin Film Festival (⊕ *www.tilff.com*) shows international films in Portuguese, Spanish, French, and Italian, subtitled in English. **ImagineNATIVE** (⊕ *www.imaginenative.org*) is a festival of features, shorts, and animations by indigenous—primarily Canadian and American—filmmakers and producers. **Planet In Focus** (⊕ *www.planetinfocus.org*) showcases films on earth-related topics.

NOVEMBER
Toronto Reel Asian International Film Festival (⊕ *www.reelasian.com*) focuses on films by and about Asians, from Canada to the Far East.

SMALL THEATERS AND COMPANIES

Buddies in Bad Times. Local, nationally, and internationally reknowned thespians and playwrights present edgy, alternative performances in the country's largest gay-centered multitheater complex. Actor Daniel MacIvor has performed here. Many shows are pay what you can. ⊠ *12 Alexander St., just east of Yonge St., Church–Wellesley* ☎ *416/975– 8555* ⊕ *www.artsexy.ca* Ⓜ *Wellesley.*

The Canadian Stage Company. Mounting Broadway, West End, and Canadian plays are at the heart of this company's mission, but "CanStage" is known also for its excellent Dream in High Park Shakespeare productions. ⇨ *See Summer Shakespeare box.* Big, mainstream productions are in the **Bluma Appel Theatre** (27 Front St. E) at the St. Lawrence Centre for the Arts, and edgier and new works are at the **Berkeley Street Theatre** (26 Berkeley St., at Front St. E). ☎ *416/368–3110 or 877/399–2651* ⊕ *www.canstage.com.*

Factory Theatre. This is the country's largest producer of exclusively Canadian plays. Many of the company's shows have gone on to tour the country and have won prestigious awards. ⊠ *125 Bathurst St., at Adelaide St., Entertainment District* ☎ *416/504–9971* ⊕ *www.factory-theatre.ca* Ⓜ *511 Bathurst streetcar to Adelaide St.*

Hart House Theatre. The main theater space of the U of T since 1919, Hart House mounts four emerging-artist and student productions per season (September–April). At least one musical and one Shakespeare are always part of the program. ⊠ *7 Hart House Circle, off Wellesley St. university entrance, Queen's Park* ☎ *416/978–8849* ⊕ *www.harthousetheatre.ca* Ⓜ *Museum, Queen's Park.*

Théâtre Français de Toronto. High-quality French-language drama—with English supertitles—is performed at this theater, whose French and French-Canadian repertoire ranges from classical to contemporary. One kid-centered play and two teen shows are part of the eight-play season. ⊠ *Berkeley Street Theatre, 26 Berkeley St., 2nd fl., at Front St. E, Old Town* ☎ *416/534–6604 or 800/819–4981* ⊕ *www.theatrefrancais.com* Ⓜ *King.*

Lorraine Kimsa Theatre for Young People. Productions like *Cranked*, in which a freestyle MC raps about overcoming his drug addiction, and *Hana's Suitcase*, the story of a young girl orphaned in the Holocaust, do not condescend or compromise on dramatic integrity and are thus as

SUMMER SHAKESPEARE

Every summer the Canadian Stage Company presents **Dream in High Park** (⊠ *High Park, main entrance off Bloor St. W, at High Park Ave.* ☎ *416/367–1652* ⊕ *www.canstage.com* Ⓜ *High Park*), quality productions of Shakespeare in the park's outdoor amphitheater. The productions are usually knockouts and run from July to late August; they're under the stars, so call ahead if it's drizzling. Performances are pay what you can, with a suggested $20 donation. Performances are Tuesday through Sunday at 8 PM; the box office opens at 6 PM. Tickets are on a first-come, first-served basis.

entertaining for adults as for kids. ✉ *165 Front St. E, between Jarvis and Sherbourne Sts., Old Town* ☎ *416/862–2222* ⊕ *www.lktyp.ca* Ⓜ *King.*

★ **Soulpepper Theatre Company.** Established in 1997 by 12 of Canada's leading theater actors and directors, this classical repertory theater company produces classic plays—*Uncle Vanya, The Odd Couple*, and *A Raisin in the Sun* are past shows—year-round. It has been growing steadily in size and popularity, and in 2006 moved into the Young Centre for the Performing Arts in the historic Distillery District. ✉ *55 Mill St., Bldg. 49, Distillery District, Old Town* ☎ *416/866–8666* ⊕ *www.soulpepper. ca* Ⓜ *504 King streetcar to Parliament St.*

★ **Tarragon Theatre.** The natural habitat for indigenous Canadian theater is in this old warehouse and railroad district. The main stage is 205 seats and stages plays by new and established Canadian playwrights. Maverick companies often rent the smaller of the Tarragon's theaters (100 seats) for interesting experimental works. ✉ *30 Bridgman Ave., 1 block north of Dupont St., just north of the Annex* ☎ *416/531–1827* ⊕ *www.tarragontheatre.com* Ⓜ *Dupont.*

Theatre Passe Muraille. Toronto's oldest alternative theater company, established in 1968, has long been the home of fine Canadian collaborative theater and has launched the careers of many Canadian actors and playwrights. ✉ *16 Ryerson Ave., near Queen and Bathurst Sts., Queen West* ☎ *416/504–7529* ⊕ *www.passemuraille.on.ca* Ⓜ *Osgoode.*

NIGHTLIFE

Toronto has all kinds of music and dance clubs, as well as lots of places to lounge. Many have the life span of a butterfly, so call before you set out to make sure they're still open and offering the kind of evening you're searching for. Downtown, Adelaide Street West from University Avenue to Peter Street, has spawned numerous clubs of the loud house and techno variety. Many places there don't charge a cover, and those that do rarely ask more than C$10.

The stretch of College Street between Bathurst and Ossington streets, known as Little Italy, is crammed with martini bars glowing with soft candlelight, and the party often spills out onto the streets. In the Beach, home of the Beaches International Jazz Festival, bars and clubs cater to casual, sporty types who stroll up after playing beach volleyball. The bars on Queen West are some of the hippest in the city, especially with the advent of the Drake and Gladstone. Gay nightlife centers around Church and Wellesley streets northeast of the downtown core.

BARS, PUBS, AND LOUNGES

Have a good time in Toronto, but be aware of the strict drinking-and-driving laws. Police regularly stop cars to check drivers' sobriety with a breath-analysis. If you have a blood-alcohol level higher than 0.08%, it's the judge or jail, no matter where you're from. Under the city's liquor laws, last call in bars is 2 AM; closing time is 3 AM. The minimum drinking age is 19.

Smoking is illegal in bars, pool halls, and casinos. Some venues have patios and separate rooms approved for smoking by the city government.

Some of these hot spots, like the Beaver, Canoe, and the Mill Street Brew Pub, double as restaurants. Kitchens close between 10:30 and midnight. Many bars, like the Drake, are also music venues that either have a separate space (with cover only for that space) or charge a cover for the bar on performance nights.

OLD TOWN, THE HARBOURFRONT, AND THE ENTERTAINMENT DISTRICT

Fodor'sChoice **Canoe.** On the 54th floor of the Toronto Dominion Bank tower, Canoe
★ is known for its panoramic view of the lake, stellar food (most of the huge room is a restaurant), and possibly the city's best Niagara Valley wine selection. Beyond Canadian wines, there's an extensive selection of international bottles, in addition to cocktails and beer. You can spend as much as C$2,500 on a bottle of wine, but plenty are in the C$40–C$60 range; wines by the glass start at around C$10. The appetizer menu includes bar bites such as octopus and fiddlehead salad and red-chili calamari. This spot is popular with brokers and financial wizards from the neighboring towers, who suit the swank surroundings. ■TIP➔ Go just before sunset to get the most of the view. ✉ 66 *Wellington St. W, between York and Bay Sts., Financial District* ☎ 416/364–0054 ⊕ *www. oliverbonacini.com* Ⓜ *King, Union.*

C Lounge. The spa theme of this ultrachic lounge hits you in the form of fruity aromatherapy the moment you walk through the door. In fact, there is a working salon up front, with makeup and hair touch-ups and massages. Loud party music plays indoors, but out back, soft ambient music allows quiet conversation around the shallow-water pool surrounded by beach chairs, coconut palms, and lantern-lit cabinas with couches. ✉ *456 Wellington St. W, just west of Spadina, Entertainment District* ☎ 416/260–9393 ⊕ *www.libertygroup.com* Ⓜ *St. Andrew.*

Bier Markt. With more than 100 beers from 24 countries, this place has a corner on the international beer market. It's cavernous inside and also has sidewalk tables. Lunch and dinner are served. The lines are ridiculous on weekends—do as the locals do and go mid-week instead. ✉ *58 The Esplanade, just west of Church St., Old Town* ☎ 416/862–7575 ⊕ *www.thebiermarkt.com* Ⓜ *Union.* ✉ *600 King St. W, at Bathurst, Entertainment District* ☎ 416/862–1175 Ⓜ *504 King streetcar to Portland St.*

Foundation Room. Descend into this just-below-street-level Middle Eastern–inspired, incense-infused lounge with mirrored and exposed-brick walls, Moroccan lanterns, and banquettes with red-velvet pillows. Enjoy quality mixed drinks, wine, or specialty martinis (lychee, sidecar) to a soundtrack of mellow house, tribal, R&B, and world music. If you're in the mood for a beer, move on—there are only six bottles and no draught. ✉ *19 Church St., at Front St. E, Old Town* ☎ 416/364–8368 or 416/825–6262 ⊕ *www.foundationroom.ca* Ⓜ *King, Union.*

★ **Mill Street Brew Pub.** There may not be a better place in the city for a brewery and pub than in the brick-laned pedestrian-only Distillery District. Sixteen house-brewed beers are on tap, and five are also sold bottled at

CLOSE UP

Beer: The National Drink

The brewing industry has been part of Ontario's heritage since 1840, when Thomas Carling opened his Brewing & Malting Company to supply the British army and the early pioneers. By the 1870s brewing had become a modern industry and maltsters were important businessmen. During the mid-1800s to mid-1900s, there were more than 300 breweries across the province. Prohibition and the Temperance League in 1916 closed most of the small, family-run operations, but even when Prohibition was repealed, the era of the small brewery was over. Restrictive distribution laws, the Depression, and organized, big breweries that delivered good, well-advertised product soon led to consolidation.

The past few decades have seen a resurgence of small, craft breweries. From its beginnings as a licensed brewpub, **Granite Brewery** (⊠ 245 Eglinton Ave. E, Yonge and Eglinton ☎ 416/322–0723) has become a licensed brewery and sells its products off-site. Recommended are the India Pale Ale and the cask-conditioned Best Bitter. **Mill Street Brewery** (⊠ 55 Mill St., Distillery District ☎ 416/681–0338) makes Ontario's only certified organic

lager, and a seasonal Helles Bock. It is open for sampling daily, with free tours at 3 PM. A restaurant-pub is on site. The **Steam Whistle Brewery** (⊠ The Roundhouse, 255 Bremner Blvd., near Rogers Centre, Old Town ☎ 416/362–2337) brews an authentically crafted pilsner and offers tours of its historic premises.

Aficionados say **Smokeless Joe** (⊠ 125 John St., Entertainment District ☎ 416/728–4503) has the best beer selection in Canada, averaging 200 to 300 choices. **C'est What?** (⊠ 67 Front St. E, Downtown ☎ 416/867–9499) has a vast selection of brews. The **Rebel House** (⊠ 1068 Yonge St., Yonge and Eglinton ☎ 416/927–0704) focuses on local beers and has outstanding pub food. **Bier Markt** (see full review, ⊠ 58 The Esplanade, Downtown ☎ 416/862–7575) has an awe-inspiring keg room and a loyal after-five clientele. **Bar Volo** (⊠ 587 Yonge St., Church–Wellesley, ☎ 416/928–0008 ⊕ www.barvolo. com), a classy brick-walled, wood-beamed tavern with a patio, has more than 30 beers from around the world on tap, plus many more by the bottle.

the on-site store (and in Toronto-area shops): an organic lager, coffee porter (smells like coffee, tastes like porter), Tankhouse pale ale, Belgian Wit (wheat), and blonde Stock Ale. The pub serves the expected fare (burgers, nachos) plus beer bread and beer-steamed mussels. Alfresco tables are prime real estate in warm weather. ⊠ 55 Mill St., Distillery District, Old Town ☎ 416/681–6338 ⊕ www.millstreetbrewpub.ca Ⓜ 504 King streetcar to Parliament St.

Pravda Vodka Bar. A deliberate air of faded elegance, like a communist-era club gone a bit rough around the edges, permeates Pravda. Huge paintings of Mao adorn the brick walls, and crystal chandeliers run the length of the two-story room with exposed ductwork. Weekday drink specials draw a healthy after-work clientele to lounge on well-worn leather sofas, around low wooden tables, or in a red-velvet-curtained bordellolike VIP area upstairs. The selection is true to the era, with many Ukranian and Polish vodkas, straightforward martinis, Czech and Russian beers, and accompaniments such as caviar, smoked fish, and pierogies. ⊠ *44 Wellington St. E, between Church at Yonge Sts., Old Town* ☎ *416/863–5244* ⊕ *www.pravdavodkabar.com* Ⓜ *King.*

Wayne Gretzky's. The pregame Blue Jays and Maple Leafs fans and the post-theater crowd from Second City comedy club across the street flock to this sports bar and family-style restaurant. When he's in town, the eponymous hockey icon and part-owner can often be seen in the crowd. On the rooftop patio (open from May through September), considered one of the best in town, a faux waterfall babbles, a faux fire rages, white Christmas lights twinkle, and partygoers order wings and buckets of Coronas and make themselves heard over the blasting music. ⊠ *99 Blue Jays Way, at Mercer St., Entertainment District* ☎ *416/979–7825* ⊕ *www.gretzky.com/restaurant/* Ⓜ *St. Andrew, Union.*

> **A PRE- OR POST-SHOW TIPPLE**
>
> The strip of lounges and restaurants (and a gelato shop) on Wellington Street East, just west of Church Street, are all ideal stop-ins before or after theater, symphony, or opera performances downtown. They all have a slight air of sophistication and since you're already dressed for the occasion, why not?

YORKVILLE, THE ANNEX, AND LITTLE ITALY

The trendy bars of Yorkville tend to draw a well-heeled clientele for some excellent drinks, food, and views. The Annex, along Bloor between Spadina and Bathurst, attracts university students and young professionals to its mix of true-blue pubs and well-loved lounges. Little Italy, along College Street from Spadina to Ossington, is prime for bar-hopping and juxtaposes student-friendly holes in the wall with martini bars and upscale restaurant bars.

Avenue. The Four Seasons Toronto hotel's classy lounge combines New York–style sophistication: dark wood, neutral colors, sofas around low glass-topped tables, rows of tinted glass bottles behind the 20-foot onyx bar. Drinks include custom-made martinis, such as the Luxury Martini, with truffle-infused vodka, elderflower cordial, and fresh lemon ($18). The drinks and food—which is heavy on sushi—are pricey in this buzzy space, but what can you expect from one of the most posh hotels in the country? The attentive service can feel somewhat precious. ⊠ *21 Avenue Rd., at Cumberland St., Yorkville* ☎ *416/928–7332* Ⓜ *Bay.*

★ **Hemingways.** One of the most crowded pubs in Toronto, and one of the few that isn't overtaken by rowdy sports fans or students, Hemingway's is a homey bastion in a sea of Yorkville swank. The three-story complex, with indoor and outdoor spaces—front and back—is a mishmash of booths, tables, several bars, mirrors, artsy posters, and books. It has a full pub menu, and free appetizers are doled out every night at 6. About three-quarters of the middle- to upper-class professionals who frequent this place are regulars. ⊠ *142 Cumberland St., just east of Avenue Rd., Yorkville* ☎ *416/968–2828* Ⓜ *Bay.*

Madison Avenue Pub. On the edge of the U of T campus, and often filled to the gills with college students from fall to spring, the boisterous "Maddy" takes up three Victorian houses, with six levels and 23 rooms of food and drink. It typifies an English pub, with lots of brass, exposed brick, and dart boards. A piano bar, pool tables, and plasma-screen TVs are also part of the scene. The five patios (some heated) are lively in summer, when squeezing your way to one of the 12 bars can become blood sport. ⊠ *14–18 Madison Ave., just north of Bloor St. W, The Annex* ☎ *416/927–1722* ⊕ *www.madisonavenuepub.com* Ⓜ *Spadina.*

Panorama Lounge. Black-leather furniture, glamorous chandeliers, and floor-to-ceiling windows combine for a hip, comfortable night out. ∎ **TIP**➜ **The 51st-floor patio is the highest in Toronto and is a great perch for enjoying the nightscape.** The southern-facing patio has a view of Downtown, the CN Tower, and the lake. It is an ideal spot for celebrity sightings, and there is an excellent selection of cocktails, martinis, and light meals—and a decadent chocolate fondue. A C$5 cover charge applies Friday and Saturday nights. ⊠ *Manulife Centre, 51st fl., 55 Bloor St. W, at Bay St., Yorkville* ☎ *416/967–0000* ⊕ *www.eatertainment.com/restaurants/panorama* Ⓜ *Bay.*

Proof, the Vodka Bar. Green suede sofas and armchairs cluster in conversation areas in this large, contemporary space with floor-to-ceiling windows fronting Bloor Street. Vodka is sold by the shot or in sugary cocktails and martinis. Bottle service is available, as are snacks (ceviche, spring rolls) and a handful of entrées. On Saturday, DJs spin soul and old-school funk. Weeknights are quiet; the large enclosed patio out back is warmed by heat lamps. ⊠ *InterContinental Hotel, 220 Bloor St. W, between Bedford and Avenue Rds., Yorkville* ☎ *416/324–6645* Ⓜ *St. George, Bay.*

Fodor'sChoice
★
The Roof Lounge. Such Canadian literary luminaries as Margaret Atwood and Mordecai Richler used the 18th-floor Roof Lounge as a setting in their writings. It's a quiet, classy, and tiny bar with dark wood and leather accents, lined with windows and pictures of Canadian writers. Martinis and cosmopolitans are the bar's specialties, though the menu also includes a nice selection of single malts and tequilas, and a Cuban cigar menu with seven south-of-the-border stogies ranging in price from C$8 to C$250. (Smoke is allowed on the patio.) Tapas and light meals are available as well. In summer an adjoining patio affords lovely views of the downtown skyline and lake. The bar is cozily petite and does not accept reservations, so arrive in the late afternoon on weekends to avoid a wait. This place is chic and refined without stuffiness or pretension. ⊠ *Park Hyatt Hotel, top fl., 4 Avenue Rd., Yorkville* ☎ *416/925–1234* Ⓜ *Bay.*

Souz Dal. The type of place where you'd expect to find a scholarly chap hunched over a book of Beaudelaire by candlelight, Souz Dal is sophisticated but low-key, with decor inspired by the onion-dome cupolas in the Russian city of Souzdal (Suzdal). The music is smooth (think bossa nova) as are martinis such as the caramilk (vanilla vodka, caramel liquer, crème de cacao). It has a small back patio. There are specials every night, such as $5 mojitos on Monday. ⊠ *636 College St.,* *between Grace and Clinton Sts., Little Italy* ☎ *416/537–1883* Ⓜ *506 College streetcar.*

Victory Cafe. In a brick Victorian on a side street, the Victory feels sufficiently removed from the bustle of Bloor. It's a neighborhood favorite for its solid pub food, microbrewed beers, cozy fireplace in winter, and sidewalk patio in summer. Events featuring local musicians and artists are common. The vibe is always low-key and local. ✉ *581 Markham St., 1 block south of Bloor St. W, The Annex* ☎ *416/516–5787* Ⓜ *Bathurst.*

QUEEN WEST

Beaver Cafe. Upwardly mobile arty professionals down pints, cappuccinos, and burgers at this low-key, alt-classy café/bar in the trendy Parkdale neighborhood. Chic hanging light fixtures mesh with drugstore votives on black-lacquer tables; a plywood bench stretches the length of one wall. Most likely sound track: Bowie. Most likely clientele: thirtysomething music producers and art-gallery employees. Canadian art hangs on the walls. ✉ *1192 Queen St. W, at Gladstone, West Queen West* ☎ *416/537–2768* Ⓜ *501 Queen streetcar to Dufferin St.*

Gladstone Hotel. In a restored Victorian hotel, the Gladstone draws a young, arty-but-stylish crowd that appreciates the karaoke (Thursday through Saturday), the queer night on Wednesday, and frequent indie, jazz, or bluegrass bands, spoken word, and art shows. The ballroom café is the main space, with tall ceilings, exposed brick walls, and a long dark-wood bar—dinner is served until 10 PM. The Melody Bar hosts karaoke and bands. The tiny Art Bar has exhibitions, performances, and private events. The Ballroom is the large-event space. ✉ *1214 Queen St. W, West Queen West* ☎ *416/531–4635* ⊕ *www.gladstonehotel.com* Ⓜ *510 Queen streetcar to Dufferin St.*

Fodor's Choice
★ **The Paddock Tavern.** Hipsters and media-and-design professionals frequent this modern-day speakeasy all week to swill well-made classic martinis, cocktails, and premium beers—many from Ontario craft breweries—and sample the above-average fare from a seasonal menu that might include lamb burgers or wild mushroom risotto. A capacious bar fronted with riveted leather curves along two walls of the room, while semi-circular burgundy leather booths offer a little more privacy. Eclectic indie, soul, funk, or jazz plays most nights, but on Tuesday, pianist Kevin Quain—seemingly Tom Waits's vocal doppelgänger—is the long-standing entertainment. ✉ *178 Bathurst St., at Queen St., Queen West* ☎ *416/504–9997* ⊕ *www.thepaddock.ca* Ⓜ *501 Queen streetcar to Bathurst St.*

Reposado. The Toronto bar buzz is officially centered on Ossington Avenue, where watering holes, shops, and galleries are springing up like wildflowers. One of the first and still going strong is this classy tequila bar that opened in 2007. The dark wood, large windows, big back patio, and live jazz (most nights no cover) set the tone for a serious list of tequilas meant to be sipped, not slammed, and Mexican nibbles like tequila-cured salmon with crostini. ✉ *136 Ossington Ave., 2 blocks south of Dundas St. W, Queen West* ☎ *416/532–6474* ⊕ *www.reposadobar.com* Ⓜ *505 Dundas or 501 Queen streetcars.*

Ultra. At this contemporary and swanky bar and restaurant you can relax on a low chaise in the lounge with a fancy cocktail before tucking into Cuban-style chicken or hoisin-ginger salmon in the dining room. It has an undefined dress code; you should get by just fine with casual-chic, but suits and ties are common on weeknights. DJs spin Top 40, dance music, and mash-ups on Thursday, Friday, and Saturday to get people dancing. A C$10–C$20 cover is charged on weekends. The decor is *Sex and the City*–fabulous, and the rooftop patio is one of the city's best. If you don't want dinner, stick to the patio or lounge, where drinks and light snacks (fresh oysters, mini Kobe burgers) are served. ⊠ *314 Queen St. W, just east of Spadina, Queen West* ☎ *416/263–0330* ⊕ *www.ultratoronto.com* Ⓜ *Osgoode.*

> ### TORONTO COMEDIANS
>
> Since the Second City opened, Toronto has been a comedic hub. Gilda Radner, John Candy, Dan Aykroyd, Dave Thomas, Martin Short, Eugene Levy, Catherine O'Hara, and Rick Moranis each cut their teeth here or on SCTV, a TV offshoot. Toronto native Lorne Michaels hand-picked Aykroyd and Radner for the first season of *Saturday Night Live.* Mike Myers, Colin Mochrie (*Whose Line Is It, Anyway?*), and Dave Foley, Bruce McCulloch, and Mark McKinney (*Kids in the Hall*) performed at the Bad Dog Theatre early on. Jim Carrey and Howie Mandel debuted at Yuk Yuk's, and Samantha Bee frequented the Rivoli until joining *The Daily Show* in 2003.

COMEDY CLUBS

★ **The Rivoli.** Solid up-and-coming acts perform at the Monday ALTdot COMedy Lounge stand-up night or the Tuesday-night Sketch Comedy Lounge. The ratio of chuckles to groans is good. Some later-famous comedians (Mike Myers, Samantha Bee) have performed here. And it's free! ⊠ *332 Queen St. W, at Spadina Ave., Queen West* ☎ *416/596–1908* ⊕ *www.rivoli.ca* Ⓜ *Osgoode.*

Fodor'sChoice **The Second City.** Since it opened in 1973, Toronto's Second City—the
★ younger sibling of the Second City in Chicago—has been providing some of the best comedy in Canada. Regular features are sketch comedy, improv, revues. Weekend shows tend to sell out in summer. Tickets are C$12–C$28. ⊠ *51 Mercer St., Entertainment District* ☎ *416/343–0011* ⊕ *www.secondcity.com* Ⓜ *St. Andrew.*

Yuk Yuk's. Part of a Canadian comedy franchise, this giant venue headlines the best stand-ups, with covers between C$12 and C$19. Admission is C$3 on Tuesday, when amateurs and students from the Humber College Comedy School take the stage. Booking a dinner-and-show package guarantees you better seats. ⊠ *224 Richmond St. W, 1½ blocks west of University Ave., Entertainment District* ☎ *416/967–6425* ⊕ *www.yukyuks.com* Ⓜ *Osgoode.*

DANCE CLUBS

The majority of Toronto's many dance clubs and bars are centered in the Entertainment District, specifically along Richmond and Adelaide between University and Spadina. The club scene can be fickle, with new clubs opening and closing all the time. Our choices have been going strong for years, but for the flavor of the month and special events, check *NOW* (⊕ *www.nowtoronto.com*) and *Eye Weekly* (⊕ *www.eye-weekly.ca*). Some of the best DJs spin at bars or concert venues; check these weekly papers for details.

Calling ahead or going online to get on the guest list is usually worthwhile. Cover charges (C$5–C$10) are standard. Most clubs are open until 3 AM, but some stay open until 7 AM Sunday mornings. Dress codes are in effect but aren't over the top; avoid sneakers, shorts, and casual jeans and you should be fine.

★ **The Courthouse.** With its lofty ceilings, leather couches, professional pole dancers, and oversize fireplaces, this club above the Courthouse Market Grille—open to the public only on Saturday—is like a 1940s Hollywood mansion on acid. The cocktail crowd is upscale with many a guy in a tie (though a button-up will do) and ladies in heels, nice jeans, and tank tops. Stairs lead up to the second-story dance floor and to a mezzanine lounge that overlooks the scene. ⊠ *57 Adelaide St. E, between Yonge and Jarvis, Old Town* ☎ *416/214–9379* ⊕ *www.libertygroup. com* Ⓜ *King, Queen.*

The Fifth Social Club. This is what you get when you cross a New York–style warehouse loft with a disco playing Top 40, rock, R&B, Latin, and retro tunes. Professionals (ages 25 to 45), some dressed to the nines in Armani suits and Versace dresses (though jeans are permitted) provide the scenery. Couches tucked into corners create cozy conversation areas, and any empty spaces are frequently used for dancing. A menu of finger foods keeps dancers fueled throughout the night. It's open Thursday through Saturday; covers range from C$10 to C$15. ⊠ *225 Richmond St. W, 2 blocks west of University Ave., Entertainment District* ☎ *416/979–3000* ⊕ *www.thefifth.com* Ⓜ *Osgoode.*

Fodor'sChoice **The Guvernment Kool Haus Complex.** If you want to get your grind on in
★ a sea of revelers, this is the place. Each of the eight lounges and dance clubs in this complex has its own themed decor and DJ special events. In the main club, Dream Fridays and Spin Saturdays bring pulsing lasers and clouds of dry ice that float across 22,000 square feet of dance space. The chic rooftop Skybar has one of the city's best skyline views, whereas the mellower, glass-enclosed Deluxe overlooks the main dance floor. The club gets going after midnight. Kool Haus is the club's concert venue. Take a taxi to this one—it's a desolate after-hours walk. ⊠ *132 Queen's Quay E, at Jarvis, Harbourfront* ☎ *416/869–0045* ⊕ *www. theguvernment.com* Ⓜ *Union.*

This is London. Some balk at the pricey cover (usually C$15 Friday before 11, C$20 Saturday and Friday after 11) and the difficult doormen, but This is London remains extremely popular for its excellent homegrown and visiting DJs (Moby, Usher, Paris Hilton, and Girlicious have all done sets here), young-but-not-too-young clientele, and well-executed over-the-top baroque decor. Get on the guest list and dress to impress. ✉ *364 Richmond St. W, just east of Spadina Ave., entrance behind building, Entertainment District* ☎ *416/351–1100* ⊕ *www.thisislondonclub.com* Ⓜ *Osgoode.*

LATIN DANCE CLUBS

Salsa is to the new millennium what disco was to the '70s. Latin dance clubs have become the hangouts of choice for the club cognoscenti.

Babalúu. Truly the best of both worlds, this club and restaurant in the upscale Yorkville area combines the luxury of a tony lounge with the sizzle of sexy Latin rhythms. ■ **TIP➜ Free one-hour beginner salsa lessons are offered Tuesday through Saturday.** Cover prices vary (C$5–C$14); women occasionally get in free. ✉ *136 Yorkville Ave., lower level, just east of Avenue Rd., Yorkville* ☎ *416/515–0587* ⊕ *www.babaluu.com* Ⓜ *Bay.*

El Convento Rico. This slice of Latin America in the heart of Little Italy is seedy, steamy, and sticky. Toronto's Latin community comes here to play, as do many local gay men. The Friday and Saturday night drag shows, which start at 12:30 AM are good fun. Dancing starts at 9 PM Friday and Saturday. ✉ *750 College St., Little Italy* ☎ *416/588–7800* ⊕ *www.elconventorico.com* Ⓜ *506 College streetcar.*

Lula Lounge. There's no dress code, but Latin-music lovers of all ages dress up to get down to live Afro-Cuban, Brazilian, and salsa music at this Little Portugal hot spot. Tasty *mojitos* get you in the groove. Pop and rock musicians also perform sometimes; past shows have featured Sam Phillips and Jonathan Richmond. Salsa Saturdays combine dinner, salsa lessons, and live music. ✉ *1585 Dundas St. W, 1½ blocks west of Dufferin St., Greater Toronto* ☎ *416/588–0307* ⊕ *www.lula.ca* Ⓜ *506 College streetcar.*

GAY AND LESBIAN NIGHTLIFE

Much of Toronto's gay and lesbian nightlife is centered on Church and Wellesley streets. You can easily cruise up Church from Alexander to a couple of blocks north of Wellesley and pop into whichever bar is most happening that night.

DID YOU KNOW?

The Church–Wellesley neighborhood's gay roots go as far back as the early 1800s, when the land here was owned by (presumed gay) Toronto magistrate Alexander Wood. In those days, residents nicknamed the area Molly Woods Bush, "Molly" being a derogatory term for a gay man. The "gaybourhood" (as it's affectionately called) that we know today didn't develop until the 1970s.

There are plenty of LGTB-friendly places outside the Church Street strip. Queen Street West, for example, is sometimes called Queer West, due to the number of not-exclusively-gay-but-gay-friendly bars and restaurants like the Beaver, the Drake, the Gladstone, and Mitzi's Sister.

Publications catering to the gay community include *X-Tra* (⊕ *www.xtra.ca)*, free at various venues and at paper boxes around town, and *Fab* (⊕ *www. fabmagazine.com)*, a free monthly mag distributed at shops and restaurants. Both have information on nightlife, issues, and events.

BARS

Pegasus on Church. A mixed crowd of all different ages, styles, and genders comes to this second-floor lounge to meet, shoot pool, and, above all, play the interactive Internet game NTN Trivia. The music is mixed by the bartender of the day, and each one has a loyal following, and by DJs on weekends. ⊠ *489B Church St., just south of Wellesley, Church–Wellesley* ☎ *416/927–8832* ⊕ *www.pegasusonchurch.com* Ⓜ *Wellesley.*

Slack's. Toronto's only Lesbian bar, Slack's is both a casual restaurant and a dance bar in one open-concept space. Open for dinner (until 10 PM Tuesday and Sunday), the kitchen serves a creative variety of salads, pastas, and meats, and provides a friendly atmosphere with events that include bands, DJs, and featured artists. ⊠ *562 Church St., just north of Wellesley, Church–Wellesley* ☎ *416/928–2151* ⊕ *www.slacks.ca* Ⓜ *Wellesley.*

★ **Woody's.** A predominantly upscale, professional male crowd (twenties to forties) frequents this cavernous pub. DJs mix every night. Check out the Best Chest Contest (men competing only) on Thursday, the Best Butt Contest on Friday and Saturday, and the drag shows at 6 and 11 each Sunday. The exterior of Woody's was used as the popular hangout on the television show *Queer As Folk.* ⊠ *467 Church St., at Maitland St., Church–Wellesley* ☎ *416/972–0887* ⊕ *www.woodystoronto.com* Ⓜ *Wellesley.*

CLUBS

★ **Fly.** Some of the biggest and best DJs from around the world have spun records at the original "Babylon" from television's *Queer as Folk.* An impressive sound system, light show, and 10,000 square feet of space have won this queer-positive club several Best Dance Club in Toronto awards. The unofficial "shirts off after midnight" rule doesn't hurt, either. Cover ranges from C$10 before 11 PM some Fridays to C$30 after 1 AM on some Saturdays. ⊠ *8 Gloucester St., just east of Yonge St., Church–Wellesley* ☎ *416/410–5426* ⊕ *www.flynightclub. com* Ⓜ *Wellesley.*

Zipperz–Cellblock. This easygoing gay-and-lesbian bar caters to mixed age groups. At the piano bar in front you can join in on classic tunes; the dance club in the back rocks with a live DJ on weekends and drag shows some weekdays. No cover. ⊠ *72 Carlton St., at Church St., Church–Wellesley* ☎ *416/921–0066* ⊕ *www.zipperz-cellblock.ca* Ⓜ *College.*

MUSIC

Toronto is a regular stop for top musical performers, ranging from the Rolling Stones to Shania Twain to Justin Timberlake. Most clubs have covers that range from C$5 to C$10. Tickets are often available on Ticketmaster (⊕ *www.ticketmaster.ca*). Record shops Rotate This! (⊠ *801 Queen St. W* ☎ *416/504–8447* ⊕ *www.rotate.com*) and Soundscapes (⊠ *572 College St.* ☎ *416/537–1620* ⊕ *www.soundscapesmusic. com*) also sell tickets.

Each June, Toronto hosts **North by Northeast** (*NXNE* ☎ *416/863–6963* ⊕ *www.nxne.com*), an annual five-day festival that brings some 500 bands to the indoor and outdoor venues around the city. It's affiliated with the similar South by Southwest festival in Austin, Texas.

For large-venue shows ⇨ *See Arenas and Concert Halls, above.*

MIXED-GENRE VENUES

The Music Hall. A former vaudevillian hall was renovated in 2006 to become one of Toronto's top music venues, showcasing rock, pop, R&B, experimental, and world music. ⊠ *147 Danforth Ave., east of Broadview, The Danforth* ☎ *416/778–8163* ⊕ *www.themusichall.ca* Ⓜ *Broadview.*

The Molson Amphitheatre. Pop, rock, and country concerts take place at this amphitheater by the lake throughout the summer, at modest prices. The view of the skyline and the summer breezes make this one of the loveliest places to hear music in Toronto. ⊠ *909 Lake Shore Blvd. W, Harbourfront* ☎ *416/870–8000 Ticketmaster* ⊕ *www.molsonamp.com* Ⓜ *Union.*

The Phoenix Concert Theatre. A wide variety of music is presented at this two-room venue. Music airs live on local radio stations from the Main Room on Saturday; in the Parlour tunes from all genres can be enjoyed in a somewhat more intimate setting. ⊠ *410 Sherbourne St., between Wellesley and Carlton Sts., Cabbagetown, Greater Toronto* ☎ *416/323–1251* ⊕ *www.libertygroup.com* Ⓜ *Sherbourne; 506 Carlton streetcar.*

Sound Academy. This enormous venue on Lake Ontario opened in the former Docks dance club space in 2007 and has hosted popular bands such as Beck and Avenged Sevenfold. It's part of the Polson Pier entertainment complex, with lounges, video games, a drive-in movie theater, and outdoor billiard tables. When the entire space is used it holds 2,600 people. Some shows are all ages. ⊠ *Polson Pier, 11 Polson St., off Cherry St., just east of Parliament St., Harbourfront* ☎ *416/649–7437* ⊕ *www.sound-academy.com* Ⓜ *72 A bus.*

FOLK AND BLUES

Free Times Cafe. This restaurant specializes in vegetarian and organic Middle Eastern food (though meat is also served) and has acoustic and folk music every night of the week, plus a highly popular traditional Jewish brunch called "Bella! Did Ya Eat?," complete with live klezmer music every Sunday. ⊠ *320 College St., at Major St., Little Italy* ☎ *416/967–1078* ⊕ *freetimescafe.com* Ⓜ *Queen's Park.*

Grossman's Tavern. The old and raunchy vibe at Grossman's makes it ideal for the blues. There are R&B bands nightly and Dixieland jazz on Saturday afternoon. ⊠ *379 Spadina Ave., 1 block south of College St., Chinatown* ☎ *416/977–7000* ⊕ *www.grossmanstavern.com* Ⓜ *Queen's Park.*

★ **Hugh's Room.** The biggest names in folk, bluegrass, and blues music love to play this venue because the audiences here love to listen. The supperclub-like venue has a full menu at cabaret-style tables, but it's the intimate performances, not the mediocre food, that are the draw. Many shows sell out, so book early. The best tables are numbers 1–29, held for those who make dinner reservations. If you're not having dinner,

JAZZ FESTIVALS

Late June and early July bring music lovers to Toronto for the **Toronto Jazz Festival.** (☎ 416/928-2033 ⊕ www.torontojazz.com). The 2009 bill included Tony Bennett, Sonny Rollins, Melody Gardot, and Chris Hunter. Performances are at various venues around town. Concerts are priced individually, but you can buy a three- or five-show pass for a 15% or 20% discount on Mainstage shows.

One of Toronto's most popular summer events is **The Beaches International Jazz Festival** (☎ 416/698-2152 ⊕ www.beaches-jazz.com Ⓜ 501 Queen streetcar to Woodbine). Held in late July, the 10-day festival in the east Toronto Beaches neighborhood showcases jazz, R&B, funk, samba, and soul performers like (in 2009) blues guitarist Junior Watson and jazz singer Daniela Nardi at its Woodbine Park and Kew Gardens stages. More performers, and food vendors, line 2 km of Queen Street East, which is closed to traffic for the event. All performances are free.

arrive at least an hour early to snag one of the frontmost bar tables. The bar in back can get noisy during performances. ✉ *2261 Dundas St. W, just south of Bloor St. W, Greater Toronto* ☎ *416/531–6604* ⊕ *www. hughsroom.com* Ⓜ *Dundas West.*

The Silver Dollar Room. Some of the top blues acts around play here, as well as rock bands. The bar is dark and the viewing area narrow, but the blues-loving clientele is friendly, and you may strike up a conversation with the musicians between sets. ✉ *486 Spadina Ave., at College St., Chinatown* ☎ *416/763–9139* ⊕ *www.silverdollarroom.com* Ⓜ *Queen's Park.*

JAZZ, LATIN, AND FUNK

Lula Lounge (⇨ *Latin Dance Clubs, above*) is a great place to hear Latin music, even if you have two left feet.

The Orbit Room. At this icon on College Street you can drink by lava lamp at the bar or take a turn on the compact dance floor accompanied by jazz, jazzy rock, funk, roots reggae, and R&B. ✉ *580A College St., 2nd fl., Little Italy* ☎ *416/535–0613* ⊕ *www.orbitroom.ca* Ⓜ *506 College streetcar to Euclid.*

The Pilot Tavern. On Saturday from 3:30 to 6, this low-key (circa 1944) Toronto mainstay fills to the gills for mainstream and Dixieland jazz with a side of pints and pub grub. ✉ *22 Cumberland St., just west of Yonge St., Yorkville* ☎ *416/923–5716* ⊕ *www.thepilot.ca* Ⓜ *Bay.*

The Rex Hotel Jazz & Blues Bar. Legendary on the Toronto jazz circuit since it opened in the '80s, the Rex has two live shows every night plus afternoon shows on weekends. Most shows are free. The kitchen serves diner fare. ✉ *194 Queen St. W, at St. Patrick St., Queen West* ☎ *416/598–2475* ⊕ *www.therex.ca* Ⓜ *Osgoode.*

The Trane Studio. Always a worthwhile night out for jazz—occasionally with a Latin or Afro-Cuban bent—the intimate brick-walled Trane Studio features accomplished Canadian musicians as well as impressive upstarts. Caribbean-influenced snacks and dinners are served. ✉ *964 Bathurst St., 3 blocks north of Bloor St. W, The Annex* ☎ *416/913–8197* ⊕ *www. tranestudio.com* Ⓜ *Bathurst.*

POP AND ROCK

The Cameron Public House. A sign behind the bar here reads THIS IS PARADISE. If your idea of paradise is decorative cowboy boots hung from the ceiling, oversize papier-mâché ants on the walls, and grungy velvet sofas, well, sure. An eclectic bill of alt-rock, country, jazz, and everything in between is showcased in the cramped back room of this bar. Students at the nearby Ontario College of Art and Design frequent during the week. Crowds are heavy on weekends. ✉ *408 Queen St. W, at Cameron St., Queen West* ☎ *416/703–0811* ⊕ *www.thecameron.com* Ⓜ *Osgoode.*

★ **¿C'est What?** An eclectic mix of local bands—indie, pop, and jazz—plays almost every night at this tavernlike downtown club. But with six house beers and 35 Ontario (and a few Québec) microbrews on tap, it draws as many for the beer as for the bands. Good grub of the lamb burger or falafel variety soaks up brews like the house coffee porter. ✉ *67 Front St. E, at Church St., Entertainment District* ☎ *416/867–9499* ⊕ *www. cestwhat.com* Ⓜ *King.*

The Drake. A hotel, restaurant, art gallery, café, and music venue all in one, the Drake is high-style hip. The Underground, downstairs, fills with young, artsy types for the indie bands. The sound system is great, and the stark walls are usually decorated with art or projections. Live jazz is performed in the main-floor Drake Lounge, scenesters sip cocktails and order snacks or dinner. Escape to the rooftop Sky Yard for fresh air year-round. ✉ *1150 Queen St. W, 2 blocks east of Gladstone Ave., West Queen West* ☎ *416/531–5042* ⊕ *www.thedrakehotel.ca* Ⓜ *501 Queen streetcar.*

Fodor's Choice ★ **Horseshoe Tavern.** Since 1947, this has been known across the city as the tavern with entertainment, especially country music. Charlie Pride, Tex Ritter, Hank Williams, and Loretta Lynn all played here. Now the music is mostly new alternative rock, roots, blues, punk, and rockabilly bands, six nights a week. No food is served, but there's plenty of booze. ✉ *370 Queen St. W, at Spadina Ave., Queen West* ☎ *416/598–4753* ⊕ *www. horseshoetavern.com* Ⓜ *Osgoode.*

★ **Lee's Palace.** Some of the most exciting young bands in rock, indie, and punk are served up at this club with a psychedelic graffiti facade on the edge of the University of Toronto campus. Grab a table or watch the show from the sunken viewing area. Shows go from 8 PM on. ✉ *529 Bloor St. W, 1½ blocks east of Bathurst St., The Annex* ☎ *416/532–1598* ⊕ *www.leespalace.com* Ⓜ *Bathurst.*

Mitzi's Sister. It's a bit of a dive, and you'd feel out of place ordering anything but one of the local microbrews on tap, which makes Mitzi's the perfect venue for alt-, prog-, and folk rock, punk, and country bands. It's the sister restaurant of brunch fave Mitzi's Café, around the corner on Sorauren. ✉ *1554 Queen St. W, between Sorauren and Fuller Aves., West Queen West* ☎ *416/532–2570* ⊕ *www.mitzissister. com* Ⓜ *504 Queen streetcar.*

The Opera House. This large venue for live international acts is loud, wild, and a hot place for ravers. Past performers were Ill Bill, the Faint, and the Tokyo Police Club. ✉ *735 Queen St. E, Queen East* ☎ *416/466–0313* ⊕ *www.theoperahousetoronto.com* Ⓜ *504 Queen streetcar to Broadview Ave.*

Rivoli. Along the Queen Street strip, the Rivoli has long been a major showcase for the more daring arts in Toronto. A back room functions as a performance space, with progressive and indie rock, improvisational comedy troupes, and more. Bands have a cover charge, usually C$5–C$10. Asian-influenced cuisine and good steak are served in the dining room. The walls are lined with work (all for sale) by up-and-coming local artists. There's also a bar, and a pool hall upstairs. ✉ *332 Queen St. W, at Spadina Ave., Queen West* ☎ *416/596–1908 or 416/597–0794* ⊕ *www.rivoli.ca* Ⓜ *Osgoode.*

> ### TORONTO ARTS ILLUMINATED
>
> For 10 days in June, **Luminato** (⊕ *www.luminato.com*) packs in a hundred or more events spanning all the arts, from plays to tango lessons, from puppetry to poetry, and from art installations to funk bands. The festival attracts some big names such as Joni Mitchell, the Mark Morris Dance Group, and the Kronos Quartet.

5

Sports and the Outdoors

Updated by
Shannon Kelly

The city of Toronto enjoys a love-hate relationship with its professional sports teams, and fans can sometimes be accused of being fair-weather—except when it comes to hockey. In Toronto this national sport has always attracted rabid, sellout crowds, whether the Maple Leafs win, lose, or draw.

For participant activities, an extensive network of parks and trails provides opportunities to enjoy outdoor activities in Toronto year-round—biking, boating, hiking, or cross-country skiing. The parks of the Toronto Islands have spectacular views of the city skyline, and the Don Valley Trail System snakes from north of the city all the way down to Lake Ontario.

BEACHES

Lake Ontario is rarely warm enough for sustained swimming, except in late August, and is occasionally too polluted for any kind of dip. ■ TIP→ **Check** ⊕ **www.toronto.ca/beach for water-quality reports.** Still, it's fun to relax or take a stroll on one of the city's 11 sandy beaches.

☺ Once the site of a large, rollicking amusement park, **Sunnyside Park Beach,** west of downtown, is now a favorite place for a swim in the safe, heated water of the "tank" (a huge pool) or to grab a quick snack in the small restaurant inside the handsomely restored 1922 Sunnyside Bathing Pavilion. Also built in 1922 was the Sunnyside Amusement Park, created in the image of Coney Island. Much of the park was demolished in the 1950s with the expansion of Lake Shore Boulevard. One of the few remnants of the old amusement park is the **Palais Royale Ballroom** (www.palaisroyale.ca), where you can still catch live swing music occasionally. The Martin Goodman Trail passes along the waterfront here. Sir Casimir Gzowski Park borders Sunnyside Park to the west. ⊠ *Parkside Dr. and Lake Shore Blvd., south of High Park, Greater Toronto* ☎ *No phone* Ⓜ *Keele, then 80 Queensway bus south; 501 Queen streetcar; or 504 King streetcar.*

★ Toronto's **eastern waterfront** (east of Coxwell Avenue) has a string of beaches that are packed with sunbathers in summer. The beaches are connected by a continuous boardwalk that parallels the Martin Goodman Trail and really appear like one long beach. They're easily reached via a 20-minute ride east of downtown on the Queen streetcar (501), then a few blocks' walk south to the waterfront.

Woodbine Beach is the westernmost east-side beach. It has about 30 volleyball nets that are truly all used in summer and a playground. The beach shares a peninsula with Ashbridge's Bay Park. ■ TIP→ **One of the best views of Toronto is from the tip of Ashbridge's Bay Park. From here you can see the entire expanse of the city's coastline and beyond.** Of the three beaches, Woodbine cuts the deepest inland, meaning the boardwalk is farther away from the water. **Kew Beach** abuts Woodbine Beach east of Woodbine Avenue. It's more of the same sandy, rocky strip but narrower.

ADDITIONAL SPORTS RESOURCES

A number of agencies can help you find out more about sports and the outdoors in and around Toronto.

Tourism Toronto (☎ 416/203–2500 or 800/499–2514 ⊕ www.seetorontonow.com Ⓜ Union) has information on recreational and professional sports teams and outdoor recreation.

Toronto and Region Conservation (☎ 416/667–6295 ⊕ www.trca.on.ca) gives out a pamphlet on parks and trails and has a wealth of information about local natural areas on its Web site.

Toronto Parks, Forestry & Recreation (☎ 416/392–1111 ⊕ www.toronto.ca/parks Ⓜ Union) has maps of park biking and jogging paths and can provide information about public golf courses, tennis courts, and swimming pools.

On the mainland side of the boardwalk is Kew Gardens, with boccie courts and a playground. **Beaches Park** runs from Kew Beach (around Lee Avenue) to the end of the boardwalk at Victoria Avenue. ✉ *Along waterfront, from Coxwell Ave. to Victoria Park Ave., Beaches* ☎ *No phone* Ⓜ *Coxwell, then 22 Coxwell bus south; 501 Queen streetcar.*

The city's most pleasing beaches—and certainly the ones with the best views—are on the **Toronto Islands** (⊕ *www.toronto.ca/parks/island*), due south of downtown, across the Toronto Inner Harbour. The best beaches are those on the southeast tip of Ward's Island, Centre Island Beach, and the west side of Hanlan's Point. The most secluded and natural beach on the Islands is Hanlan's Beach, backed by a small dunes area, a portion of which is clothing-optional. Most families with kids head for Centre Island Beach. The Islands also have bike trails, picnic areas, snack stands, and boat rentals. To get here, take a ferry (C$6.50 round-trip) from the Harbour Square ferry terminal at Bay Street and Queens Quay East. Ferries leave every 15 to 30 minutes in summer; check the Islands Web site for current schedules.

PARKS

Toronto has more than 1,400 parks and plants about 8,000 trees per year.

Discovery Walks (☎ *311* ⊕ *www.toronto.ca/parks*) is a program of self-guided walks through ravines, parks, gardens, beaches, and neighborhoods. You can download brochures with information and maps online. There are also many DISCOVERY WALK signs throughout the city.

At close to 400 acres, forested **High Park** is the city's largest playground, great for hiking, biking, skating, sunning, and cross-country skiing. In summer, hordes descend to enjoy the outdoor activities here. Recreational facilities include a large public swimming pool, tennis courts, baseball and soccer fields, fitness trails, and walking paths. You can tour manicured rose gardens on the park's west side. In the southwest corner

Bringing Back the Don

The 15-km (9-mi) paved foot- and bike path that lines the Don River on Toronto's east side, which runs from the lakefront, where it connects with the Martin Goodman Trail, north to Edwards Gardens near Lawrence Avenue, is lovely in parts. However, the stagnant and polluted water, unsightly abandoned industrial areas, rickety bridges, poor signage, and a busy elevated highway along parts of the trail leave room for improvement.

In the 1800s, the Don River valley watershed area was cleared for settlement; by the early 20th century the Don Valley Brick Works was operating here and a railway had been built next to the river. In the 1950s the four-lane Don Valley Parkway was constructed along the river. Industry has taken its toll on the area. The river is polluted, and much of the old industrial land lies fallow.

Today devoted civic and government groups (⊕ www.toronto.ca/don) are working to revive the Don River valley.

Dams have been removed to allow fish to pass through again, dozens of wetlands areas have been restored, and tens of thousands of trees have been planted. Near the lakefront, an ongoing West Donlands naturalization and flood protection project will create a park and new trailhead.

A $55 million Evergreen Brick Works project (⊕ www.evergreen.ca/rethink-space) will transform the abandoned Don Valley Brick Works factory into an environmental community center with gardens, trails, educational programs, and a sustainable-food café by celebrity chef Jamie Kennedy. At this writing, the project is expected to be complete by Spring 2010. A Saturday farmers market (☉ May–Oct., 8–1) is already open. The site, on Bayview Avenue north of Bloor Street East, can be reached by bike, car (limited parking), bus 28A from the Davisville subway station, or Evergreen shuttle bus from the Broadview subway station (both buses Saturday only).

of the park is **Grenadier Pond,** home to thousands of migrating birds. In winter you can ice-skate on its frozen surface. The modest **High Park Zoo** is free to all and has domestic and exotic species including bison, emus, yaks, llamas, peacocks, and sheep. It's open year-round from 7 AM to dusk. The park hosts many summer special events, including professionally staged Shakespeare productions. To get here, take the TTC to the High Park station and walk south; the main entrance is off Bloor Street West at High Park Avenue. But you can also take the 506 College streetcar to the eastern entrance of the park, or explore from the south end of the park by taking the 501 Queen streetcar to Parkside Drive. ⊠ Bordered by Bloor St. W, Gardiner Expressway, Parkside Dr., and Ellis Park Rd., Greater Toronto ☎ 416/392–1111 ⊕ www.toronto.ca/parks/highpark.htm Ⓜ High Park.

☾ From **Sir Casimir Gzowski Park** there are marvelous views of the Toronto Islands, Ontario Place, and the downtown skyline. A portion of the paved Martin Goodman Trail—ideal for jogging, biking, and in-line skating—hugs the lakeshore. The park is accessible by the 501 Queen and 504 King streetcars and is right next to Sunnyside Park and Beach. ⌧ *Along Lake Shore Blvd. W, Greater Toronto.*

☾ A great way to spend a few hours is on the **Toronto Islands** (⇨ *Beaches, above)*, an easy 15-minute ferry trip from the Harbourfront. The Islands are car-free and have paved trails for biking, in-line skating, or strolling. Centre Island has an amusement park and is frequented by families with young kids. Ward's Island is primarily residential. Hanlan's Point is quiet and the least developed area on the Islands. If you want to see everything, the ideal way to get around is by bike (⇨ *Bicycling, below)*. But if you're headed to the Centre Island amusement park or beach, you won't need wheels. The islands also have sand dunes (at Hanlan's Point) and various green spaces for picnicking.

SPORTS AND FITNESS

With more pro sports teams than anywhere else in Canada, including the country's only NBA and MLB teams, and with notoriously die-hard fans—especially of the Leafs (hockey) and the FC (soccer)—Toronto is arguably the top destination for spectator sports north of the border.

And if you're keen on getting in on the action, T.O.'s 46 km (29 mi) of lakefront and 7,400 hectares (18,300 acres) of green space keep the options interesting. You can kayak, sail, bike, golf, skate, or work on your tennis serve, all within city limits.

6

BASEBALL

★ The **Toronto Blue Jays** (⌧ *Rogers Centre, 1 Blue Jays Way, Harbourfront* ☎ *416/341–1234* ⊕ *www.bluejays.com* Ⓜ *Union*) play April through September. Interest in the team has fallen since they won consecutive World Series championships in 1992 and 1993. Recent seasons have seen many young players trying to make their mark.

The spectacular Rogers Centre (formerly the SkyDome) has a fully retractable roof; some consider it to be one of the world's premier entertainment centers. Single-game tickets are C$9 to C$70.

Want local baseball without all the fuss? Intercounty team the **Toronto Maple Leafs** (⊕ *www.leafsbaseball.com*) plays home games at the north end of Christie Pits park—Bloor West at Christie Street. Admission is free.

BASKETBALL

The city's NBA franchise, the **Toronto Raptors** (⌧ *Air Canada Centre, 40 Bay St., at the Gardiner Expwy., Harbourfront* ☎ *416/815–5600, 416/872–5000 Ticketmaster* ⊕ *www.raptors.com* Ⓜ *Union*), played its first season in 1995–96. For several years they struggled mightily to win both games and fans in this hockey-mad city, but the Raptors have finally come into their own, and games often sell out. Single-game tickets are available beginning in September; the season is from October through April.

THE ORIGINAL MAPLE LEAFS

Before the Blue Jays (pre-1977), Toronto baseball meant the Maple Leafs, a AAA International League team that operated 1886–1967 and won several championships. And, for the record, they were the first Maple Leafs—the Toronto Arenas hockey team was renamed in 1927. Most successful from their inception to the mid-1920s, the Maple Leafs first played at a stadium on Hanlan's Point, in the Toronto Islands. At this stadium, on September 5, 1914, Babe Ruth hit his first professional home run, against the Leafs for the Providence Grays. A rookie Red Sox at the time, he had been optioned to the Grays. In 1926, a state-of-the-art stadium was built for the Leafs at Bathurst Street and Fleet Street (now Lake Shore Boulevard). It was demolished in 1968, a year after the Maple Leafs moved to Louisville, Kentucky. Today's Maple Leafs, an intercounty team, began play in 1969.

BICYCLING

More than 29 km (18 mi) of street bike routes cut across the city, and dozens more follow safer paths through Toronto's many parks, as well as across the islands. Both the Humber Valley Trail (west side) and the Don Valley Trail (east side) connect with the waterfront Martin Goodman Trail. Bike rentals are available in the city and on the Toronto Islands (⇨ *See Parks, above*).

■ TIP➔ The City of Toronto Web site ⊕ *www.toronto.ca/cycling* has info about biking in the city and a downloadable cycling map.

The 15-km **Don Valley Trail System** begins at Edward's Gardens near Lawrence Avenue and runs to the lake, where you can connect to the Martin Goodman Trail. Though cars noisily zoom by on the highways on the upper roadways and the stagnant river is no beauty, plenty of runners, bikers, and skaters take to the trail.

About 25 km (16 mi) of trails stretch along the **Humber River ravine** on the west side of the city, from Steeles Avenue south to Humber Bay Park, where the river flows quietly into Lake Ontario, not far from High Park.

★ The **Martin Goodman (Lakeshore) Trail** is a 19-km (12-mi) strip that runs along the waterfront all the way from the Balmy Beach Club in the east end out past the beaches southwest of High Park. It's easily the nicest bike ride in the city, but is best done heading east of Sherbourne Street or west of Bathurst Street, just outside the downtown core, since the trail runs along the congested Queens Quay between these points.

The car-free roads of the **Toronto Islands** (⇨ *See Beaches and Parks, above*) are ideal for biking. You can rent on Centre Island or take your bike over on the ferry.

BIKE RENTALS

Toronto Islands Bicycle Rentals (✉ *Centre Island pier, Toronto Islands* ☎ *416/203–0009*) has hourly or daily rentals for regular bikes (C$7 per hour/ C$30 per day), and tandem bikes (C$13 per hour/C$50 per day), and hourly rentals for covered two- or four-seater "quadricycles" (C$16 and C$29/hour), the largest of which can actually seat a family of six if two members are child-size.

Community Bicycle Network (⊠ 271 Queen St. W, at Euclid St., Queen West ☎ 416/504–2918 ⊕ communitybicyclenetwork.org) is a nonprofit bicycling advocacy organization that rents bikes for C$15 per day for the first day, C$10 per day thereafter, or C$50 per week. It's closed Sunday.

Wheel Excitement (⊠ 249 Queens Quay W, between Spadina and York Aves., Harbourfront ☎ 416/260–9000 ⊕ www.wheelexcitement.ca) rents bikes and in-line skates for C$30 per day or C$50 for a weekend. It's as central as you can get and allows you to easily head east or west on the Martin Goodman Trail.

CANOEING AND KAYAKING

From April to September you can rent canoes at Grenadier Pond in High Park, at the Harbourfront Centre, and in most of the conservation areas surrounding Toronto.

For paddling around the Toronto Islands, go to the **Harbourfront Canoe and Kayak Centre** (⊠ 283A Queen's Quay W, between Spadina and York Aves., Harbourfront ☎ 416/203–2277 or 800/960–8886 ⊕ www.paddletoronto.com Ⓜ 509 Harbourfront streetcar). It rents canoes for C$30 per hour or C$60 per day, single kayaks for C$30 per hour or C$70 per day, and tandem kayaks for C$40 per hour or C$85 per day. It also has lessons and group paddles.

Toronto Kayak & Canoe Adventures (☎ 416/536–2067 ⊕ www.toronto-adventures.ca) rents canoes and kayaks and leads guided trips on the Humber River, just west of High Park as well as on the Rouge River, at Cherry Beach, and more. Rentals are C$20 for two hours, C$25 for a guided tour, and C$35 with a shuttle from the end point (Sunnyside Park, on the waterfront) to the put-in point (near Bloor Street and Old Mill Road; take the Bloor subway line to Old Mill station). Reservations must be made by e-mail or via the Web site.

CAR RACING

At **Honda Indy** (⊠ Exhibition Place, Harbourfront ☎ 416/588–7223 Ⓜ Union, then 509 or 511 streetcar to Exhibition), formerly the Grand Prix of Toronto, cars roar around the roadways of the Canadian National Exhibition grounds and a portion of Lake Shore Boulevard. Local traffic is diverted.

Motorcycle and formula racing are held at **Mosport** (⊠ 3233 Concession Rd. 10, off RR 20, north of Hwy. 401, Exit 431, Bowmanville ☎ 905/983–9141 ⊕ www.mosport.com), about 100 km (60 mi) northeast of Toronto. Mosport is a multitrack facility, with a 4-km (2½-mi), 10-turn road course; a 1.4-km (.85-mi) paved oval; a 1-km (½-mi) kart track; and the Mosport Driver Development Centre. Races take place from May to September. To get here, take Exit 431 off Highway 401 at Bowmanville, head north on Rural Route 57, then east on Rural Route 20.

6

EQUESTRIAN EVENTS

The Fort Erie Race Track (⇨ *See Side Trips chapter*) is in the Niagara region, about 150 km (90 mi) south of Toronto.

The 10-day **Royal Agricultural Winter Fair** (✉ *Direct Energy Centre, Exhibition Place, Harbourfront* ☎ *416/263–3400* ⊕ *www.royalfair.org* Ⓜ *Union*) is a highlight of Canada's equestrian season each November, with jumping, dressage, and harness-racing competitions. General admission is C$18.

Woodbine Racetrack (✉ *555 Rexdale Blvd., at Hwy. 427, Rexdale* ☎ *888/675–7223* ⊕ *www.woodbineentertainment.com* Ⓜ *Islington, then 37 Islington bus*), a 30-minute drive northwest of downtown, near the airport, is the showplace of thoroughbred and harness racing in Canada. Events are year-round.

FOOTBALL

The Canadian Football League (CFL) has a healthy following across most of the country, even in Toronto, where the **Toronto Argonauts** (✉ *Rogers Centre, 1 Blue Jays Way, Harbourfront* ☎ *416/341–2746* ⊕ *www.argonauts.on.ca* Ⓜ *Union*) have struggled for fans against the Maple Leafs, Raptors, and Blue Jays. Tickets for home games are usually a cinch to get and range from C$33 to C$80. The season runs from June to November.

GOLF

PUBLIC COURSES

The golf season lasts only from April to late October. Discounted rates are usually available until mid-May and after Canadian Thanksgiving (early October). All courses are best reached by car.

★ Deemed Canada's best new course by *Golf Digest* when it opened in 1995, **Angus Glen Golf Club** (✉ *10080 Kennedy Rd., at Major McKenzie Dr. E, Markham* ☎ *905/887–0090, 905/887–5157 reservations* ⊕ *www.angusglen.com*) has remained one of the country's best places to play, hosting the Canadian Open in 2002 and 2007 on its par-72 South and North courses, respectively. Greens fees: C$175 (C$120 weekends after noon) including cart. You can book two months in advance.

Fodor's Choice The top course in Canada, the Jack Nicklaus–designed, 18-hole, par-73
★ **Glen Abbey Golf Club** (✉ *1333 Dorval Dr., just north of QEW, Oakville* ☎ *905/844–1800 information, 905/844–1811 reservations* ⊕ *www.clublink.ca*) is a real beauty. The Canadian Open was held here for the 25th time in 2009. Greens fees are C$235. Carts are C$18.

The **Don Valley Golf Course** (✉ *4200 Yonge St., south of Hwy. 401, North York* ☎ *416/392–2465* ⊕ *www.toronto.ca/parks/golf*) is a par-71, 18-hole municipal course. Greens fees are C$52 Monday to Thursday and C$59 Friday to Sunday; twilight rates are available for C$34 and C$37. Carts are an extra C$38. You can book up to five days in advance.

A creek runs through the **Royal Woodbine Golf Club** (✉ *195 Galaxy Blvd., off Hwy. 401 Dixon Rd. exit, Etobicoke* ☎ *416/674–4653*

CANADIAN FOOTBALL DIFFERENCES

American football fans who attend a CFL game discover a faster, more unpredictable and exciting contest than the American version. The longer, wider field means quarterbacks have to scramble more, a nifty thing to watch. Some differences between CFL and NFL football:

■ Field is slightly larger: 150 yards by 65 yards in the CFL, rather than 120 yards by 53⅓ yards in the NFL, with 20-yard-deep end zones.

■ The ultimate prize is the Grey Cup, which is both the yearly championship competition and the trophy awarded.

■ Only three downs are allowed to advance 10 yards.

■ A kicking team gains one point—called a rouge—if the ball cannot be returned out of the end zone.

■ A CFL team has 12 players rather than 11, with two slotbacks (offensive halfbacks) and without a tight end.

■ There are nine CFL teams (the NFL has 32).

■ The season is generally June through mid-November.

6

⊕ *www.royalwoodbine.com*) making for an interesting course (18 holes, par 71). Proximity to the international airport means some sound disturbances, but you can squeeze in a game before your flight. Greens fees range from C$75 for 18 holes (including cart) to C$125 for prime 10 AM–2 PM Friday and Saturday slots.

DRIVING RANGES AND VIRTUAL GOLF

At **InnerGolf** (⊠ *99 Sudbury St., Liberty Village* ☎ *416/538–4653* ⊕ *www. innergolf.ca*) more than 30 virtual courses based on real courses around the world are projected onto 9-foot screens. Nonvirtual CPGA golf pros are available. Rates are C$35 per hour or C$19.95 per hour (nonpeak) for the virtual driving range.

The 300-yard **Polson Pier Driving Range** (⊠ *11 Polson St., off Cherry St., just east of Parliament St., Harbourfront* ☎ *416/649–7437* ⊕ *www. polsonpier.com*) is open year-round. A bucket with 68 balls is C$13 on weekdays, C$15 on weekends.

EVENT

The **Canadian Open** (☎ *800/571–6736* ⊕ *www.rbccanadianopen.ca*), one of golf's Big Five tournaments, founded in 1904, is held in July, in most recent years at Glen Abbey or Angus Glen.

HOCKEY

The regular hockey season is October–mid-April.

Fodor's Choice ★ The **Toronto Maple Leafs** (⊠ *Air Canada Centre, 40 Bay St., at Gardiner Expwy., Harbourfront* ☎ *416/870–8000 Ticketmaster, 416/815–5700 information* ⊕ *www.mapleleafs.com* Ⓜ *Union*) share their venue with the National Basketball Association's Raptors. ■ TIP→ **Buy the tickets at least a few months in advance or risk the game's being sold out.** Whether the Leafs are on a winning or losing streak, their tickets are notoriously the toughest to score of any team in the National Hockey League.

The **Toronto Marlies** (✉ *Ricoh Coliseum, 100 Princes' Blvd., Exhibition Place, Harbourfront* ☎ *416/597–7825* ⊕ *www.torontomarlies.com* Ⓜ *509 Harbourfront or 511 Bathurst streetcar*) is the Leafs' AHL farm team.

ICE-SKATING

The City of Toronto operates 49 outdoor artificial rinks—and all are free. Skate rentals are generally not available. For details on city ice rinks, contact the **Toronto Parks, Forestry & Recreation Rink Hotline** (☎ *311 or 416/338–7465* ⊕ *www.toronto.ca/parks/recreation_facilities.htm*). Favorites are the rink in **High Park** and the tiny rink at **Nathan Phillips Square,** surrounded by towering skyscrapers in the heart of the Financial District.

The spacious rink at the **Harbourfront Centre** (✉ *235 Queens Quay W, at Lower Simcoe St., Harbourfront* ☎ *416/973–4866* ⊕ *www.harbourfrontcentre.com/skating* Ⓜ *Union*) is often voted the best in the city, due to its lakeside location and free DJ skate nights. Skate rentals are C$7, and the rink is open November through March.

JOGGING

Good places to jog are the boardwalk of the Beaches in the city's east end, High Park on the west side, the Toronto Islands, and the ravines or other public parks, many of which have jogging paths and trails. Toronto is generally safer than most American cities, but it's still wise to use normal prudence and avoid isolated spots.

★ The **Martin Goodman Trail** is a 19-km (12-mi) jogging route with an incredible view. The dirt and asphalt trails run along the waterfront from the Balmy Beach Club, at the end of Beech Avenue past the western beaches and High Park. It's popular with runners and it's especially busy on weekends. If you get out in the hours before work and after dinner, you're likely to catch some spectacular sunrises and sunsets.

LACROSSE

Lacrosse may not be the most popular of sports, but Toronto has Canada's only professional team, and when it comes to pro sports, the **Toronto Rock** (✉ *Air Canada Centre, 40 Bay St., at Gardiner Expwy., Harbourfront* ☎ *416/596–3075* ⊕ *www.torontorock.com* Ⓜ *Union*) has won more games than the beloved Maple Leafs, and, in fact, more than any other professional sports team in Canada.

SKIING AND SNOWBOARDING

CROSS-COUNTRY

Try Toronto's parks and ravines for cross-country skiing, especially **Earl Bales Park** (Bathurst Street near Sheppard Avenue), which has snowmaking facilities; High Park; the lakefront along the southern edge of the city; and, best of all, the Toronto Islands. All the trails in the parks and ravines are free.

The **Glen Eden Ski & Snowboard Centre** (⇨ *below*) is most popular for its downhill skiing but also has some challenging cross-country and snowshoeing trails.

The **Kortright Centre** (✉ *9550 Pine Valley Dr., Woodbridge off Hwy. 401 Major Mackenzie Dr. Exit, then 3 km [2 mi] west and left onto Pine Valley Dr.* ☎ *905/832–2289* ⊕ *www. kortright.org*), 35 km (22 mi) north of Toronto, has 16 km of trails available for skiing in winter. Admission is $6; equipment rentals are not available. It's open 10–4 daily.

DOWNHILL AND SNOWBOARDING

For serious skiing, Torontonians head north to the Collingwood, Muskoka, or Algonquin areas. Call Ontario Travel for **lift and surface conditions** (☎ *800/668–2746*) in the Greater Toronto Area.

The **Glen Eden Ski and Snowboard Centre** (✉ *Kelso Conservation Area, 5234 Kelso Rd., off Hwy. 401 Exit 320, Milton* ☎ *905/878–5011* ⊕ *www. gleneden.on.ca*), about 60 km (40 mi) west of Toronto, has a snowboarding half-pipe and quarter-pipe, four snow-tubing chutes, and a terrain park, in addition to 13 downhill ski runs. With only two black diamond runs, it's a good hill for beginning and moderate skiers.

The **Caledon Ski Club** (✉ *17431 Mississauga Rd., Caledon, 30 km [19 mi] north of Hwy. 401, Mississauga Rd. Exit* ☎ *519/927–5221* ⊕ *www. caledonskiclub.on.ca*), about 80 km (50 mi) northwest of Toronto, is a private ski club that's open Wednesday and Friday only for nonmembers. It's also closed to nonmembers for two weeks from late December to early January. It has 23 slopes, including nine for experts and a snowboard half-pipe.

Two quad chairs serve the 15 runs at the full-service **Hockley Valley Resort** (✉ *793522 Mono 3rd Line, RR1, at Hockley Valley Rd., 10 km [7 mi] east of Orangeville* ☎ *519/942–0754* ⊕ *www.hockley.com*), 80 km (50 mi) northwest of Toronto, which has six expert, five intermediate, and four beginner runs. There's also a hotel, spa, and golf course on-site.

SOCCER

The **Toronto FC** (✉ *BMO Field, 170 Princes' Blvd., Exhibition Place* Ⓜ *Union, then 509 Harbourfront streetcar west; 511 Bathurst streetcar south* ☎ *416/360–4625* ⊕ *www.torontofc.ca*), Toronto's first professional soccer team in years, and Canada's first Major League Soccer team, kicked off in 2006. The FC's new 20,000-seat stadium opened in April 2007. Games frequently sell out; single-game tickets go on sale a few days before the game.

SWIMMING

Public swimming is available at 39 indoor pools and 59 outdoor pools in parks and community centers throughout Toronto. For the latest information on city pools, contact **Toronto Parks & Recreation** (☎ *311 or 416/338–7665* ⊕ *www.toronto.ca/parks/recreation_facilities/swimming*).

TENNIS

Founded in 1881 and the third-oldest tennis tournament in the world, after Wimbledon and the U.S. Open, the **Rogers Cup** (⊠ *Rexall Centre, York University campus, 1 Shoreham Dr., off Jane St. north of Finch Ave., Greater Toronto* ☎ *416/665–9777 or 877/283–6647* ⊕ *www.rogerscup.com* Ⓜ *Downsview to 196 York University Rocket*), previously the Canadian Open, is an ATP Masters 1000 event for men and a Premier event for women. It's held in August, with the men's and women's events alternating between Toronto and Montréal each year.

The city has hundreds of courts, some free, open April through October daily from 7 AM to 11 PM (weather permitting). Parks with public courts include High Park on the west side of the city, Trinity-Bellwoods Park on Queen West (lighted), and Toronto Island Park (lighted). Contact the **Toronto Parks & Recreation** (☎ *311 or 416/392–1111* ⊕ *www.toronto.ca/parks/recreation/facilities/tennis*) for a pamphlet with a comprehensive list of courts.

Shopping

Updated by
Sarah Richards

Toronto prides itself on having some of the finest shopping in North America. Indeed, most of the world's name boutiques have branches here, especially in the Yorkville area, where you can find such designer labels as Hermès, Gucci, and Cartier. For those a little leaner of wallet, you can join in one of Torontonians' favorite pastimes: bargain hunting. Locals wear discount threads like badges of honor and stretch their dollar at Winners—where overstocked and liquidated designer pieces and last-season fashions are slashed to a fraction of their original retail prices.

Toronto has a large arts-and-crafts community, with numerous art galleries, custom jewelers, clothing designers, and artisans. Objets d'art like sophisticated glass sculpture and Inuit art are ideal as gifts or for your own home. Music stores all over Toronto stack shelves with international hits as well as homegrown talent like Alanis Morissette, Nickelback, Avril Lavigne, and a host of lesser-known pop, rap, hip-hop, folk, opera, and country artists. Bookstores such as Indigo have lounge areas where you can sip a coffee from the in-store café while perusing books by Canadian authors such as Barbara Gowdy, Ann-Marie McDonald, and Rohinton Mistry.

When it comes to department stores, all roads lead to Holt Renfrew on Bloor Street West, the epicenter of Toronto's designer shopping. A mere block east is the more mid-price department store the Bay. A second Bay can be found across from Eaton Centre, a sprawling shopping complex with multilevel parking in the heart of the city.

Most stores accept credit cards. U.S. currency generally is accepted, though not always at the most favorable rate of exchange. On Thursday and Friday most stores downtown stay open until 9 PM; on Sunday stores open at noon.

The biggest sale day of the year is Boxing Day, the first business day after Christmas, when nearly everything in the city is half price. In fact, clothing prices tend to drop even further as winter fades. Summer sales start in late June and continue through August.

Bear in mind that the national 5% Goods and Services Tax (GST) is added to the cost of your purchases at the cash register, in addition to the 8% Ontario sales tax.

DEPARTMENT STORES AND SHOPPING CENTERS

The Bay. The modern descendant of the Hudson's Bay Company, which was chartered in 1670 to explore and trade in furs, the Bay carries mid-price clothing, furnishings, housewares, and cosmetics, including designer names as well as the Bay's own lines. The southern end of the Yonge Street store connects to Eaton Centre by a covered skywalk over Queen Street. ⊠ *44 Bloor St. E, at Yonge St., Yorkville* ☎ *416/972–3333* Ⓜ *Bloor-Yonge* ⊠ *176 Yonge St., at Queen St., Dundas Square Area* ☎ *416/861–9111* Ⓜ *Queen.*

Fodor'sChoice
★ **Eaton Centre.** This block-long complex with exposed industrial-style ceilings is anchored at its northern end (Dundas Street) by the main branch of what used to be eatons and is now Sears, and at its southern end by the Bay. The Eaton Centre's northern end has a Times Square–style media tower on top of a gigantic anchor store, Sweden's popular H&M. ■ TIP➔ **Prices at Eaton Centre increase with altitude—Level 1 offers popularly priced merchandise, Level 2 is directed to the middle-income shopper, and Level 3 sells more expensive fashion and luxury goods.** Well-lighted parking garages can be found around the center, with spaces for nearly 2,000 cars. The complex is bordered by Yonge Street on the east, and James Street and Trinity Square on the west. ⊠ *220 Yonge St., Dundas Square Area* ☎ *416/598–8560* Ⓜ *Dundas, Queen.*

Fodor'sChoice
★ **Hazelton Lanes.** With more than 50 stores, a stroll through the two floors of Hazelton Lanes, the country's most upscale shopping mall, is an experience. Stores include Teatro Verde, the garden, home, and tabletop center; fashion-forward TNT Woman and Man (TNT is short for The Next Trend); Hugo Nicholson's exquisite, one-of-a-kind evening wear; Fabrice's unique, semiprecious jewelry, personally chosen and imported from Paris by the owner; as well as a restaurant with seating in an elegant courtyard. ⊠ *55 Avenue Rd., at Yorkville Ave., Yorkville* ☎ *416/968–8600* Ⓜ *Bay.*

Fodor'sChoice
★ **Holt Renfrew.** This multilevel national retail specialty store is the style leader in Canada. It is the headquarters for Burberry, Canali, Chanel, Karan, Armani, and Gucci as well as cosmetics and fragrances from London, New York, Paris, and Rome. ■ TIP➔ **Concierge service and personal shoppers are available, but just browsing makes for a rich experience.** ⊠ *50 Bloor St. W, at Bay St., Yorkville* ☎ *416/922–2333* Ⓜ *Bay.*

Queen's Quay Terminal. Incoming ships once unloaded their fishy cargo at the terminal, which now hosts a collection of unique boutiques, crafts stalls, food stores, and more. This is a great place to buy gifts. It's an easy walk from Union Station in summer, and a quick streetcar ride in winter. Parking is expensive, but there are some free spots in the area. ⊠ *207 Queen's Quay W, at York St., Harbourfront* ☎ *416/203–0510* Ⓜ *Union.*

7

TORONTO'S SHOPPING NEIGHBORHOODS

Whether you are interested in boutique-hopping in hip Queen Street West, bargain hunting in sprawling Kensington Market, or window-shopping in ritzy Bloor-Yorkville, read on to find the shopping neighborhood that is right for you.

THE ANNEX

The Annex, because of its proximity to the sprawling University of Toronto downtown campus, is home to academics, students, and aging hippies. Many of the houses have been restored, whereas others seem a bit seedy and run-down. All in all they serve as rooming houses, single-family dwellings, basement apartments, and expensive rentals for successful artists and writers. And these are the people who frequent the cafés and bistros, used-book and CD stores, and the occasional fashion boutique, like Risqué.

At the outer corner of the Annex—Bloor Street West and Bathurst—is Honest Ed's, a tacky discount store. It serves as the gateway to Mirvish Village, a one-block assortment of bookstores and boutiques on Markham Street south of Bloor Street. Local entrepreneur and theater mogul "Honest" Ed Mirvish was the brain behind the area's development.

CHINATOWN AND KENSINGTON MARKET

While the Chinese have made Spadina Avenue their own from Queen Street north to College Street, Spadina's basic bill of fare is still "bargains galore." The street, and the Kensington Market area tucked behind Spadina west to Bathurst Street, between Dundas and College streets, remains a collection of inexpensive vintage-clothing stores such as Courage My Love, Chinese clothing stores, Chinese restaurants, ethnic food and fruit shops, and eateries that give you your money's worth. International cheeses, fresh ocean fish, yards of fabric remnants, and designer clothes minus the labels in shops like Tom's Place are piled high. Be warned—this area can be extraordinarily crowded on weekends, when smart suburbanites head here for bargains. Take the College or Queen streetcar to Spadina Avenue.

ENTERTAINMENT DISTRICT

King Street East is tops for furniture hunters, beginning at Jarvis Street and continuing almost until the Don River. Sofas and chairs take center stage, seducing even the most mildly curious. Punctuated between the furniture stores are custom framing shops, art dealers, and cafés to refresh the weary shopper.

FINANCIAL DISTRICT

Toronto's Financial District has a vast underground maze of shopping warrens that burrow between and underneath its office towers. The tenants of this Underground City are mostly the usual assortment of chain stores, with an occasional surprise. Marked PATH, the walkways (the underground street system) make navigating the subterranean mall easy. The network runs roughly from the Fairmont Royal York hotel near Union Station north to the Atrium at Bay and Dundas.

GREATER TORONTO

Greater Toronto includes neighborhoods just outside central Toronto. The stretch of Yonge Street running between the Rosedale and Summerhill subway stops is the best place to find the most upscale antiques and interiors shops, such as Absolutely, purveyor of French-provincial wares. If the thought of freight charges dissuades you from serious spending, you can check out the trinkets at tiny shops like French Country and Word of Mouth, which carry every imaginable kitchen device. Also in Greater Toronto is the Danforth, which spans the long strip of Danforth Avenue between Broadview and Donlands subway stations. Here is a mishmash of health-conscious stores such as the Big Carrot Natural Food Market, and specialty kitchen shops such as the Cook's Place. Queen Street East from Pape Street to Jones Avenue is a bustling thoroughfare noted for its antiques and junk shops. A little farther east in The Beach, along Queen Street East starting at Woodbine Avenue, is a great spot for casual-clothing stores, gift and antiques shops, and bars and restaurants, all with a resort atmosphere.

QUEEN STREET WEST

If it's funky or fun, it's found on Queen West. The best shops are concentrated on both sides of Queen Street West from University Avenue to Spadina Avenue, with fashionable stores as far west as Bathurst Street and beyond. With its collection of vintage stores, Canadian designer boutiques, and bistros, this strip sets the pace for Toronto's street style. Come summer, street vendors and buskers create a carnival atmosphere. On Queen West vintage stores like Black Market and Preloved comfortably coexist with Fashion Crimes, which stocks Canadian designs with a bent for the street beat. Farther west on Queen, around Ossington Avenue, is a relatively new, even hipper area, where boutiques, galleries, and cafés are starting to flourish, called West Queen West.

YORKVILLE

In the 1960s Yorkville was Canada's hippie headquarters, a destination for runaways and folk musicians. Now gentrified, this area is *the* place to find the big fashion names, fine leather goods, upscale shoe stores, important jewelers, some of the top private art galleries, specialty bookstores, and crafts and home-decor shops—as well as eateries, from coffee shops to elegant Italian restaurants. Streets to explore include Cumberland Street, Yorkville Avenue, and Scollard Street, all running parallel to Bloor Street, east of Avenue Road.

Bloor Street West, from Yonge Street to Avenue Road, is a virtual runway for fashionistas. With the world's designer shops on both sides of the street, you might think you're on New York's Fifth Avenue. These boutiques are worth a visit for their architectural design alone. Several local shops are worth investigating also, including Royal de Versailles Jewelers, Bulgari, and Holt Renfrew, the ultimate designer and haute-couturier department store. Not to be missed is William Ashley, a china store like no other that ships worldwide. On Bellair, between Cumberland and Yorkville, are eye-popping shops with unusual accessories.

7

SPECIALTY SHOPS

Individual reviews are organized by type of merchandise, in alphabetical order by category. Dive in, and enjoy!

ANTIQUES AND INTERIORS

Absolutely. A mixture of whimsical trinkets as well as English sideboards and tables are sold at this shop. There's also an extensive collection of antique boxes made of materials ranging from horn to shagreen. ✉ *1132 Yonge St., at MacPherson Ave., Greater Toronto* ☎ *416/324-8351* Ⓜ *Summerhill.*

Belle Époque. Find very French, very *cher* antique and reproduction furnishings here. These days they're featuring what they call an "edgy Paris apartment aesthetic." In addition to home decor and garden ornaments, they also sell fashion accessories. ✉ *1066 Yonge St., at Roxborough St., Greater Toronto* ☎ *416/925-0066* Ⓜ *Rosedale.*

> ### SHOP AND GO
>
> Make a stop at the corner of Bellair and Cumberland Street for a snack at **MBCo.**—a cappuccino, perhaps, or a smoothie, fresh-fruit brioche, or delectable sandwich— to fuel your shopping adventures. ✉ *100 Bloor St. W, at Bellair St., Yorkville* ☎ *416/961-6266.*

French Country. Straight out of Provence, this delightful little shop carries food and wine-related furnishings and unique decorative arts that go perfectly with the rustic furniture inspired by the store's namesake. ✉ *6 Roxborough St. W, at Yonge St., Greater Toronto* ☎ *416/944-2204* Ⓜ *Rosedale.*

Putti. Sort through European and domestic antiques as well as bath and garden products at this luxurious store. Prices are a bit steep. ✉ *1104 Yonge St., at Roxborough St., Greater Toronto* ☎ *416/972-7652* Ⓜ *Rosedale.*

Quasi Modo. This quirky collection of 20th- and 21st-century furniture and design includes Herman Miller lounge chairs and Noguchi lamps, as well as pottery by Jonathan Adler. Normann Copenhagen rocking glasses are the current best sellers. ✉ *789 Queen St. W, at Bathurst St., Queen West* ☎ *416/703-8300* Ⓜ *Osgoode, then streetcar 501 west.*

Stanley Wagman Antiques. Stanley Wagman carries a large selection of art-deco pieces and lighting, as well as Louis XVI furniture and accessories. This is the place to find exquisite marble fireplaces, and it reputedly has the biggest selection of lighting in Canada. He ships worldwide. ✉ *224 Davenport Rd., Yorkville* ☎ *416/964-1047* Ⓜ *Dupont, Bay.*

Starr Howard & Co. Antiques. In this shop renowned for having the best selection of 18th-century English antiques in the city, collectors can find walnut Queen Anne chests, George III bookcases, George II carved mahogany games tables, and more. ✉ *100 Avenue Rd., at Boswell Ave., Yorkville* ☎ *416/922-7966* Ⓜ *Rosedale.*

Fodor's Choice
★ **Toronto Antiques on King.** The complex provides a host of choices, including dealers in furniture, dishes, jewelry, art, and carpets. It's open Tuesday through Sunday from 10 to 6, and busiest on days when there are matinees at nearby theaters. ✉ *276 King St. W, at Duncan St., Entertainment District* ☎ *416/345-9941* Ⓜ *St. Andrew.*

ART AND CRAFTS GALLERIES

Toronto is Canada's cosmopolitan art center, with a few hundred commercial art galleries carrying items as varied as glass sculpture, Inuit designs, and contemporary pieces. Queen West showcases edgy art installations; the Historic Distillery District offers more mainstream talent. Naturally, the area around the Art Gallery of Ontario is saturated with contemporary art galleries, most of which offer affordable pieces by Canadian artists.

To find out about special art exhibits, check the Saturday edition of the *Globe and Mail* entertainment section, as well as *NOW* and *Eye Weekly*—free weekly local newspapers on culture distributed on Thursday. *Toronto Life* magazine is also a good source of information on gallery happenings. ■ TIP➔ **Most galleries are open Tuesday through Saturday from 10 to 5 or 6, but call to confirm.**

Bau-Xi Gallery. Paul Wong, an artist and dealer from Vancouver, founded this gallery across the street from the Art Gallery of Ontario. The paintings and sculpture are a window on contemporary Canadian art, with a focus on Ontario. Much of the art is affordable. ✉ *340 Dundas St. W, at McCaul St. Chinatown* ☎ *416/977–0600* Ⓜ *St. Patrick.*

Corkin Gallery. With work by photographers such as André Kertesz and Richard Avedon, this gallery is one of the most fascinating in town. See hand-painted photos, documentary photos, fashion photography, and mixed-media art. ✉ *55 Mill St., Bldg. 61, Old Town* ☎ *416/304–1050* Ⓜ *King, then streetcar 504 east.*

Feheley Fine Arts. Browse Canadian Inuit and Northwest Coast art at this gallery started more than 40 years ago. ✉ *14 Hazelton Ave., at Yorkville Ave., Yorkville* ☎ *416/323–1373* Ⓜ *Bay.*

Gallery Moos. German-born Walter Moos opened his gallery in 1959 to promote Canadian and European art. He's a discerning, reliable dealer who's had Picassos, Chagalls, Mirós, and Dufys, as well as work by such internationally admired Canadians as Gershon Iskowitz, Ken Danby, Sorel Etrog, and Jean-Paul Riopelle. ✉ *622 Richmond St. W, at Bathurst St., Queen West* ☎ *416/504–5445* Ⓜ *Bathurst then streetcar 511 south.*

Loch Gallery. The intimate gallery in an old Victorian house almost exclusively exhibits representational and historic Canadian contemporary painting and sculpture. Artists include bronze sculptor Leo Mol and painters Jack Chambers and John Boyle. ✉ *16 Hazelton Ave., at Yorkville Ave., Yorkville* ☎ *416/964–9050* Ⓜ *Bay.*

Olga Korper Gallery. Many important artists, such as Lynne Cohen, Paterson Ewen, John McEwen, and Reinhard Reitzenstein, are represented by this trailblazing yet accessible gallery, which displays art from the 1960s on. It's a good place for beginning contemporary collectors. ✉ *17 Morrow Ave., at Roncesvalles Ave., Greater Toronto* ☎ *416/538–8220* Ⓜ *Dundas West, then streetcar east.*

Prime Gallery. Crafts from across Canada include avant-garde ceramics, wall sculpture, jewelry, and textiles. ✉ *52 McCaul St., at Queen St. W, Queen West* ☎ *416/593–5750* Ⓜ *Osgoode, then streetcar 501 west.*

7

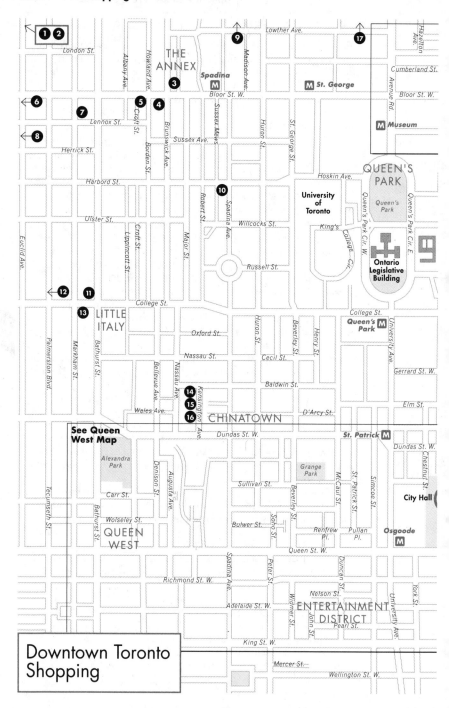

Downtown Toronto Shopping

7

Yorkville Shopping

Fodor'sChoice
★

Sandra Ainsley Gallery. The glass-sculpture gallery within the burgeoning Gooderham and Worts complex on Mill Street has large and small pieces. Rotating displays have included artists such as John Kuhn and Martin Blank. ⊠ *55 Mill St., Bldg. 32, Old Town* ☎ *416/214–9490* Ⓜ *King, then streetcar 504 east.*

Stephen Bulger. The photography gallery focuses on historical Canadian work, with Canadian and international artists such as Shelby Lee Adams and Larry Towell. ⊠ *1026 Queen St. W, at Shaw St., Queen West* ☎ *416/504–0575* Ⓜ *Osgoode, then streetcar 501 west.*

ART WALKS

To really get a sense of what is available in Toronto, the best thing to do is stroll around areas like Queen Street West and Yorkville. Some buildings are almost entirely dedicated to art galleries, like the building that houses YYZ at 401 Richmond Street West, and the redesigned Gooderham and Worts Historic Distillery District complex on Mill Street, in Old Town.

Wynick/Tuck Gallery. Many of the contemporary Canadian artists displayed here have become well established, attesting to this gallery's influence. ⊠ *401 Richmond W, at Spadina Ave., Queen West* ☎ *416/504–8716* Ⓜ *Osgoode, then streetcar 501 west.*

YYZ Artists' Outlet. There are two exhibition spaces here: one for visual art and one for time-based conceptions. The visual might contain two- and three-dimensional paintings and sculptures, whereas the time-based area might have performances, films, and videos. ⊠ *401 Richmond St. W, Suite 140, at Spadina Ave.Queen West* ☎ *416/598–4546* Ⓜ *Osgoode, then 501 streetcar west.*

AUCTIONS

Sotheby's. The Toronto outpost of the international auction house focuses entirely on Canadian art. Auctions happen twice yearly—the end of May and mid-November—at Ritchie's Auction House, 288 King Street East. ⊠ *9 Hazelton Ave., at Yorkville Ave., Yorkville* ☎ *416/926–1774 or 800/263–1774* Ⓜ *Bay.*

Waddington's. Canada's biggest auction house has more than 30 auctions every year, many of them prestigious collector and catalogue auctions. The auctions feature Canadian fine art, Inuit art, jewelry, and decorative arts. There are also themed collections such as smoking memorabilia or Moorcroft pottery. ⊠ *111 Bathurst St., at Adelaide St. W, Queen West* ☎ *416/504–9100 or 877/504–5700* Ⓜ *Bathurst, then 511 streetcar south.*

BOOKS

BMV. An impressive selection of new and used books is shelved side by side over two floors at BMV (which stands for "Books Magazines Video"). The staff is knowledgeable and helpful. ⊠ *2289 Yonge St., Greater Toronto* ☎ *416/482–6002* Ⓜ *Eglinton* ⊠ *10 Edward St., Dundas Square Area* ☎ *416/977–3087* Ⓜ *Dundas* ⊠ *471 Bloor St. W., at Brunswick Ave., The Annex* ☎ *416/967–5757* Ⓜ *Bathurst.*

7

Book City. Find good discounts—especially on publishers' remainders—a knowledgeable staff, and a fine choice of magazines at branches of this late-night Toronto chain, usually open until 10 or 11. Four locations are scattered throughout the city. ⊠ *501 Bloor St. W, at Brunswick Ave., The Annex* 🕾 *416/961–4496* Ⓜ *Bathurst, Spadina* ⊠ *2350 Bloor St. W, at Jane St., Greater Toronto* 🕾 *416/766–9412* Ⓜ *Jane* ⊠ *348 Danforth Ave., at Chester St., Greater Toronto* 🕾 *416/469–9997* Ⓜ *Chester* ⊠ *1430 Yonge St., at St. Clair St., Greater Toronto* 🕾 *416/961–1228* Ⓜ *St. Clair* ⊠ *1950 Queen St. E, east of Woodbine Ave., Greater Toronto* 🕾 *416/698–1444* Ⓜ *Queen, then streetcar 501 east.*

David Mirvish Books/Books on Art. Quality books and remainders fill this store, which specializes in books on visual arts, design, and architecture. They have the best price in town for the Sunday *New York Times.* ⊠ *596 Markham St., at Bloor St. W, The Annex* 🕾 *416/531–9975* Ⓜ *Bathurst.*

Indigo. A huge selection of books, magazines, and CDs is stocked at this store, which has a Starbucks and occasional live entertainment. ⊠ *55 Bloor St. W, Yorkville* 🕾 *416/925–3536* Ⓜ *Bay* ⊠ *2300 Yonge St., Greater Toronto* 🕾 *416/544–0049* Ⓜ *Eglinton.*

★ **Nicholas Hoare.** This bookstore is beloved by writers and readers alike and specializes in British authors, history, biography, and fiction. They occasionally have author appearances and book signings. ⊠ *45 Front St. E, at Church St., Old Town* 🕾 *416/777–2665* Ⓜ *King.*

★ **Pages Books and Magazines.** Shelves brim with international and small-press literature; fashion and design books and magazines; books on film, art, and literary criticism; and fiction. ⊠ *256 Queen St. W, at Beverley St., Queen West* 🕾 *416/598–1447* Ⓜ *Osgoode, then streetcar 501 west.*

This Ain't the Rosedale Library. In addition to stocking non-mainstream magazines and books, the store also offers a wide range of progressive nonfiction and works by local authors. ⊠ *86 Nassau St., at Bellevue St., Kensington Market* 🕾 *416/929–9912* Ⓜ *Queen's Park, then streetcar 506 west.*

SPECIAL-INTEREST BOOKSTORES

Ballenford Books. Architecture aficionados visit this store to browse through its huge selection of architecture titles. Sketches and drawings by local architects are exhibited regularly. ⊠ *600 Markham St., at Bloor St. W, The Annex* 🕾 *416/588–0800* Ⓜ *Bathurst.*

Cookbook Store. This store has the city's largest selection of books and magazines on cooking and wine. Book signings are frequently held here. Owners and staff are so knowledgeable they seem to have read every book on the shelves. ⊠ *850 Yonge St., at Yorkville Ave., Yorkville* 🕾 *416/920–2665 or 800/268–6018* Ⓜ *Bloor-Yonge.*

Israel's Judaica Centre. The Centre has the city's best selection of adult and children's books relating to Judaism in English, Hebrew, and Yiddish. Service is excellent. ⊠ *870 Eglinton Ave. W, at Bathurst St., Greater Toronto* 🕾 *416/256–1010* Ⓜ *Eglinton West.*

Open Air Books and Maps. More than 10,000 travel books, oodles of atlases and road maps, specialized travel books, and titles on nature and food make this the ideal place to feed your wanderlust. ⊠ *25 Toronto St., at Adelaide St. E, Entertainment District* 🕾 *416/363–0719* Ⓜ *King.*

Sleuth of Baker Street. Sleuth of Baker Street is the best place for mysteries and detective fiction, with an extensive collection of titles in both categories. Staff members are detective-fiction buffs themselves and can help you sleuth out the elusive noir book for which you've been hunting. The shop also puts out its own newsletter. ⊠ *1600 Bayview Ave., Greater Toronto* ☎ *416/483–3111* Ⓜ *Eglinton, then Eglinton East bus.*

Theatrebooks. An astounding collection of performing-arts books spans theater, film, opera, dance, television, and media studies. ⊠ *11 St. Thomas St., at Bloor St. W, Yorkville* ☎ *416/922–7175 or 800/361–3414* Ⓜ *Bay.*

THE GARMENT DISTRICT

Between Queen West and West Queen West, SoHo-style industrial lofts house a collection of textile shops stocking leathers, furs, and fabrics of every color under the sun. You can still see remnants of the goth fad that swept through this area in the 1990s with its smattering of macabre clubs and lounges.

Toronto Women's Bookstore. Titles focus on women and minorities and include the latest fiction by women, feminist works on women's political issues, literary criticism, and lesbian topics. ⊠ *73 Harbord St., at Spadina Ave., The Annex* ☎ *416/922–8744* Ⓜ *Spadina.*

CLOTHING

CHILDREN'S CLOTHING

Jacadi. The city's prettiest and priciest children's clothes are stocked here, in vibrant colors and fine fabrics from Paris. Three stylish French mothers are the design team. ⊠ *55 Avenue Rd., in Hazelton Lanes, Yorkville* ☎ *416/923–1717* Ⓜ *Bay.*

Kama Kazi Kids. This boutique specializes in European designer labels for kids such as red sound and Diesel, plus goodies for the mommy-to-be like Kors Maternity. ⊠ *744 Queen St. W, west of Bathurst St., Queen West* ☎ *416/703–0887* Ⓜ *Osgoode, then streetcar 501 west.*

MEN'S CLOTHING

Boomer. One of the best-kept secrets of Toronto men brings together tasteful yet trendy suitings and separates. ⊠ *309 Queen St. W, at John St., Queen West* ☎ *416/598–0013* Ⓜ *Osgoode, then streetcar 501 west.*

★ **Harry Rosen.** This miniature department store is dedicated to the finest men's fashions, with designers such as Hugo Boss, Armani, and Zegna. The casual section stocks preppy classics. ⊠ *82 Bloor St. W, at Yonge St., Yorkville* ☎ *416/972–0556* Ⓜ *Bloor-Yonge.*

Moore's the Suit People. Browse through thousands of discounted Canadian-made dress pants, sport coats, and suits, including many famous labels. Sizes run from extra short to extra tall and from regular to oversize; the quality is solid and the service is good. ⊠ *100 Yonge St., at Adelaide St., Financial District* ☎ *416/363–5442* Ⓜ *King.*

Perry's. These are the suit professionals. Have one custom-made from a broad range of fabrics, or buy off the rack from a collection of some of the finest ready-to-wear suits, which are made by Samuelsohn and Jack Victor (both from Montréal). ⊠ *1250 Bay St., at Cumberland St., Yorkville* ☎ *416/923–7397* Ⓜ *Bay.*

Stagioni. This 2,500-square-foot store has great deals on Italian designer suits, which the proprietors buy in bulk from factories in Italy. ⊠ *20 Toronto St., at Adelaide St. E, Financial District* ☎ *416/365–7777* Ⓜ *King.*

Stollerys. From wool to linen to salespeople with round spectacles holding measuring tapes, walking into this department store is like stepping into a tailor shop in 1900s England, only on a grander scale. Choose from four floors of carefully conservative clothing. ⊠ *1 Bloor St. W, at Yonge St., Yorkville* ☎ *416/922–6173* Ⓜ *Bloor-Yonge.*

Tom's Place. Find bargains aplenty on brand-name suits like Calvin Klein, Armani, and DKNY. Tom Mihalik, the store's owner, keeps his prices low. He carries some women's clothes as well. ⊠ *190 Baldwin St., at Augusta Ave., Kensington Market* ☎ *416/596–0297* Ⓜ *St. Patrick, then streetcar 505 west.*

MEN'S AND WOMEN'S CLOTHING

Club Monaco. The bright and airy flagship store of this successful chain, now owned by Ralph Lauren, has homegrown design basics: mid-price sportswear and career clothes. ⊠ *157 Bloor St. W, at Avenue Rd., Yorkville* ☎ *416/591–8837* Ⓜ *Museum.*

Fodor's Choice ★ **Kama Kazi.** Exclusive collections from Europe and the United Kingdom—including designs by Paris-based Cop.Copine and Christian Lacroix, tailored suits by London's Ozwald Boateng, combat military chic from Save The Queen, and activewear by Kama Kazi and Brazilian Blue Fish—line the shelves of this casually luxurious space. ⊠ *781 Queen St. W, west of Bathurst St., Queen West* ☎ *416/304–0887* Ⓜ *Osgoode, then streetcar 501 west.*

Lileo. Part emporium, part gallery, this is the place to go for forward-looking athletic fashion and lifestyle accessories designed to promote physical and spiritual well-being. ■ **TIP→ Stop by the juice and snack bar to keep your energy up while you shop.** ⊠ *55 Mill St., Bldg. 35, Old Town* ☎ *416/413–1410* Ⓜ *King, then streetcar 508 east.*

M0851. This is the place to go for all things leather. Sort through leather and denim jackets, pants, bags, and luggage. You can even have leather furniture, such as chairs and four-seater couches, made to order. ⊠ *23 St. Thomas St., at Bloor St. W, Yorkville* ☎ *416/920–4001* Ⓜ *Bay.*

Over the Rainbow. This denim center carries every variety of cut and flare: the trendy, the classic, and the questionable fill stacks of shelves. ⊠ *101 Yorkville Ave., at Hazelton Ave., Yorkville* ☎ *416/967–7448* Ⓜ *Bay.*

★ **Roots.** Torontonians' favorite leather jackets, bags, and basics come from this flagship store, which also manufactures Olympic uniforms for Canada, the United States, Barbados, and Great Britain. Branches are in several other Toronto neighborhoods, check out other locations at ⊕ *www.canadaroots.com.* ⊠ *100 Bloor St. W, at Yonge St., Yorkville* ☎ *416/323–3289* Ⓜ *Bay* ⊠ *1073 Yonge St., at Roxborough St., Greater Toronto* ☎ *416/927–1989* Ⓜ *Rosedale* ⊠ *1485 Yonge St., at St. Clair St., Greater Toronto* ☎ *416/967–4499* Ⓜ *St. Clair* ⊠ *356 Queen St. W, at Spadina Ave., Queen West* ☎ *416/977–0409* Ⓜ *Osgoode, then streetcar west* ⊠ *Eaton Centre, 220 Yonge St., Dundas Square Area* ☎ *416/593–9640* Ⓜ *Queen.*

Zara. The Spanish chain consistently attracts crowds craving gorgeous knockoffs of the hottest runway trends. There are currently four locations in Toronto, see others at ⊕ *www.zara.com.* ✉ *50 Bloor St. W, Yorkville* ☎ *416/916–2401* Ⓜ *Bay* ✉ *220 Yonge St., Dundas Square Area* ☎ *647/288–0333* Ⓜ *Bloor-Yonge* ✉ *341 Queen St. W, Queen West* ☎ *647/288-0545* Ⓜ *Osgoode, then streetcar 501 west* ✉ *3401 Dufferin St., in Yorkdale Mall, Greater Toronto* ☎ *647/288–7565* Ⓜ *Yorkdale.*

VINTAGE CLOTHING

Black Market. True vintage buffs hunt through the racks—very thrift shop—to uncover the best bargains. The second-floor shop overlooks Queen Street; a second, larger store across the street houses the biggest discounts. ✉ *319 Queen St. W, at John St., Queen West* ☎ *416/591–7945* Ⓜ *Osgoode, then streetcar 501 west* ✉ *256A Queen St. W, at John St., Queen West* ☎ *416/599–5858* Ⓜ *Osgoode, then streetcar 501 west.*

★ **Courage My Love.** The best vintage store in Kensington Market is crammed with the coolest retro stuff, from sunglasses to tuxedos. The in-house cat adds a nice touch. ✉ *14 Kensington Ave., at Dundas St. W, Kensington Market* ☎ *416/979–1992* Ⓜ *St. Patrick, then streetcar 504 west.*

Preloved. Former models and fashion insiders stock this shop by combing the vintage market and reconstructing their finds into unique designs. ✉ *613 Queen St. W, at Bathurst St., Queen West* ☎ *416/504–8704* Ⓜ *Osgoode, then streetcar 501 west.*

Tribal Rhythm. A horde of imported Thai and Indian trinkets, rows of quirky body jewelry, and vintage clothing are part of the charming and eclectic mix at this shop. ✉ *248 Queen St. W, at John St. Queen West* ☎ *416/595–5817* Ⓜ *Osgoode, then streetcar 501 west.*

WOMEN'S CLOTHING

Aritzia. Young urban women come here for modern funky pieces by lines such as Miss Sixty, Seven, and the house line Talula. There are other locations throughout the city. ✉ *280 Queen St. W, at John St., Queen West* ☎ *416/977–9919* Ⓜ *Osgoode, then streetcar 501 west* ✉ *Eaton Centre, 220 Yonge St., Dundas Square Area* ☎ *416/204–1318* Ⓜ *Queen* ✉ *50 Bloor St. W, at Bay St., Yorkville* ☎ *416/934–0935* Ⓜ *Bay.*

Chanel. Coco would have loved the largest Chanel boutique in Canada. The lush surroundings showcase most of the line, including the bags and accessories. ✉ *131 Bloor St. W, Yorkville* ☎ *416/925–2577* Ⓜ *Bay.*

Comrags. Designers Joyce Gunhouse and Judy Cornish have supplied the city with more than 20 years of sophisticated women's clothing designs. They aptly describe their store as "country farmhouse meets urban industrial." ✉ *654 Queen St. W, at Bathurst St., Queen West* ☎ *416/360–7249* Ⓜ *Osgoode, then 501 streetcar west.*

Corbò Boutique. Some of the most tasteful designers—Miu Miu, Prada, and Costume National, to name a few—are gathered here under one roof, along with some of the finest footwear in town. Did someone say Jimmy Choo or Ann Demeulemeester? This is upscale one-stop shopping. ✉ *119 Yorkville Ave., at Hazelton Ave., Yorkville* ☎ *416/928–0954* Ⓜ *Bay.*

Fashion Crimes. Part romantic, part funk, this Queen West haven of glam party dresses and dreamy designs has a display case packed full of elegant baubles and sparkling tiaras. Designer and owner Pam Chorley also has a pint-size label for girls called Misdemeanours. ✉ *322½ Queen St. W, at Spadina Ave., Queen West* ☎ *416/592–9001* Ⓜ *Osgoode, then streetcar 501 west.*

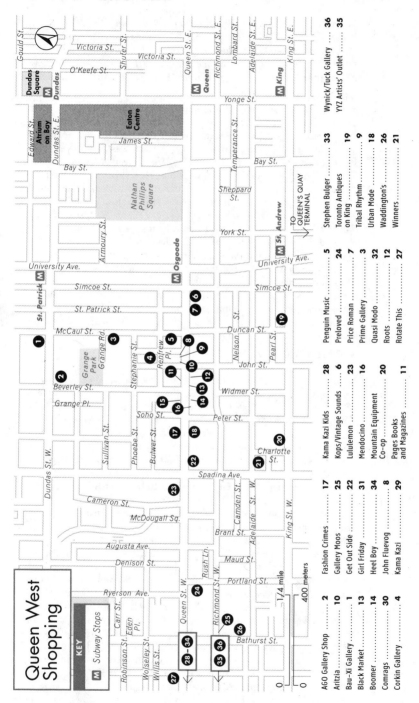

Queen West Shopping

KEY

Ⓜ Subway Stops

Girl Friday. Designer Rebecca Nixon sells sweet and stylish designs with a retro glam look. ✉ *776 College St., at Shaw St., Little Italy* ☎ *416/531–1036* Ⓜ *Queen's Park, then streetcar 501 west* ✉ *740 Queen St. W, west of Bathurst St., Queen West* ☎ *416/364–2511* Ⓜ *Osgoode, then streetcar 501 west.*

Hermès. The Parisian design house caters to the upscale horse- and hound-loving set, selling its classic sportswear, handbags, and accessories. ✉ *131 Bloor St. W, at Avenue Rd., Yorkville* ☎ *416/968–8626* Ⓜ *Museum.*

★ **Hugo Nicholson.** The selection of evening wear by Oscar, Valentino, Herrera, Galliano, and Nina Ricci is vast and exclusive. The service offered by the owners, the Rosenstein sisters, is old-school, with exacting alterations, a selection of accessories, and home delivery. ✉ *55 Avenue Rd., in Hazelton Lanes, Yorkville* ☎ *416/927–7714* Ⓜ *Bay.*

Kitsch Boutique. Pick out a loud Betsey Johnson evening dress or punky BCBG suit among these trendy pieces, many of which are imported from Miami, New York, Los Angeles, and France. ■TIP➜ Swing through the basement, where slow sellers are relegated until they're scooped up at half-price. ✉ *325 Lonsdale Rd., north of St. Clair St. W, Greater Toronto* ☎ *416/481–6712* Ⓜ *St. Clair West.*

Lilliput Hats. Wide-brimmed hats decorated with silk orchids in vibrant shades, close-fitting cloches, a practical straw hat that packs flat, outrageous or tailored hats—all can be found in handmade, off-the-rack, or to-order head coverings. Karyn Gingrais opened here in 1990 and has a huge following. Brides-to-be and their moms are well served. ✉ *462 College St., at Bathurst St., Little Italy* ☎ *416/536–5933* Ⓜ *Queen's Park, then streetcar 506 west.*

Lululemon. The bright and airy store is a perfect Zen match for items such as specialized yoga sports bras, top-of-the-line yoga mats, and stretchy yoga and gym togs. Check out other Toronto-area branches at ⊕ *www.lululemon.com.* ✉ *342 Queen W, at Spadina Ave., Queen West* ☎ *416/703–1399* Ⓜ *Osgoode, then streetcar 501 west.*

Mendocino. Score the best of the mid-price, super-trendy lines here— those polished looks you find in *In Style* magazine. This is a great stop if you have a limited amount of time and want to pack a lot in, since you can peruse the day and evening designs of a number of lines here. ✉ *294 Queen St. W, east of Spadina Ave., Queen West* ☎ *416/593–1011* Ⓜ *Osgoode, then streetcar 501 west.*

Paper Bag Princess. A vintage collection from the who's who of fashion includes Prada, Gucci, Chanel, and YSL. In this dramatic boutique with leopard-print carpet and glass chandeliers, statement-making selections of shoes and evening wear abound. ✉ *287 Davenport Rd., west of Avenue Rd., The Annex* ☎ *416/925–2603* Ⓜ *Dupont.*

Plaza Escada. The spacious store carries the designer Escada line of chic Italian creations. ✉ *110 Bloor St. W, at Bellair St., Yorkville* ☎ *416/964–2265* Ⓜ *Bay.*

7

Prada. The avant-garde designs are overshadowed only by the brilliant celadon interior of the store and the traffic-stopping window displays. ✉ *131 Bloor St. W, Unit 5, at Bellair St., Yorkville* ☎ *416/513–0400* Ⓜ *Museum.*

Price Roman. Edgy career and evening wear—think bias-cut dresses and asymmetrical hemlines—come in surprising fabric choices here, like Asian brocades and various silks. ✉ *267 Queen St. W, at McCaul St., Queen West* ☎ *416/979–7363* Ⓜ *Osgoode.*

Risqué. Shoppers find trendy clothes by Toronto designers as well as inexpensive accessories at this spot in the Annex. ✉ *404 Bloor St. W, at Brunswick Ave., The Annex* ☎ *416/960–3325* Ⓜ *St. George.*

San Remo. Find that ultrafeminine yet funky piece within this offbeat shop's lavender walls. ✉ *23 St. Thomas St., at Bloor St. W, Yorkville* ☎ *416/920–3195* Ⓜ *Bay.*

★ **Want.** With its inventory direct from Los Angeles, Want has goods you probably won't come across elsewhere in Toronto. The focus is on dresses, which run from fun and sporty to black-tie. ✉ *1454 Yonge St., at St. Clair St., Greater Toronto* ☎ *416/934–9268* Ⓜ *St. Clair* ✉ *1694 Avenue Rd., at Lawrence Ave., Greater Toronto* ☎ *416/256–9268* Ⓜ *Lawrence.*

★ **Winners.** Toronto's best bargain outlet has designer lines at rock-bottom prices. The Yonge Street branch, below the elegant Carlu event center, is enormous. ✉ *57 Spadina Ave., at King St. W, Entertainment District* ☎ *416/585–2052* Ⓜ *Union* ✉ *444 Yonge St., Dundas Square Area* ☎ *416/598–8800* Ⓜ *College* ✉ *110 Bloor St. W, at Bay St., Yorkville* ☎ *416/920–0193* Ⓜ *Bay.*

Wisteria Way. The casual clothing at this spot in the Beaches district is in line with the area's Coney Island atmosphere. Here's the place to find lines like Buffalo, Scooter, and Mexx—a combination of sporty and sexy. ✉ *1978 Queen St. E, east of Woodbine Ave., Greater Toronto* ☎ *416/693–6670* Ⓜ *Queen, then streetcar 501 west.*

FOOD

FOOD MARKETS

Fodor's Choice ★ **Kensington Market.** The outdoor market has a vibrant ethnic mix and charming restaurants, and sells everything from great cheese, coffee, nuts, and spices to natural foods, South American delicacies, and Portuguese baked goods. Vintage-clothing lovers delight in the shops tucked into houses lining the streets. ■ TIP➔ **Saturday is the best day to go, preferably by public transit; parking is difficult.** ✉ *Northwest of Dundas St. and Spadina Ave., Kensington Market* ☎ *No phone* Ⓜ *St. Patrick, then streetcar 504 west.*

St. Lawrence Market. Nearly 60 vendors occupy the historic permanent indoor market and sell items such as produce, caviar, and crafts. The building, on the south side of Front Street, was once Toronto's city hall. ■TIP➔ **The best time to visit is early on Saturday from 5 AM, when there's a farmers' market in the building on the north side.** ⊠ *92 Front St. E, at Jarvis St., Old Town* ☎ *416/392–7219* ☉ *Tues.–Thurs. 8–6, Fri. 8–7, Sat. 5–5; farmers' market Sat. 5–5* Ⓜ *Union.*

FOOD SHOPS

All the Best Fine Foods. Stop here for imported cheeses and good local breads, as well as high-quality prepared foods and condiments. ⊠ *1099 Yonge St., at Summerhill Ave., Greater Toronto* ☎ *416/928–3330* Ⓜ *Summerhill.*

Big Carrot Natural Food Market. This large health-food supermarket carries good selections of organic produce, health and beauty aids, and vitamins. There's a vegetarian café on-site and freshly prepared foods for takeout. ⊠ *348 Danforth Ave., at Broadview Ave., Greater Toronto* ☎ *416/466–2129* Ⓜ *Chester.*

Pusateri's. From humble beginnings as a Little Italy produce stand, Pusateri's has grown into Toronto's deluxe supermarket, with in-house prepared foods, local and imported delicacies, and desserts and breads from the city's best bakers. ⊠ *1539 Avenue Rd., at Lawrence Ave. W, Greater Toronto* ☎ *416/785–9100* Ⓜ *Lawrence* ⊠ *57 Yorkville Ave., at Bay St., Yorkville* ☎ *416/785–9100* Ⓜ *Bay.*

Soma. Satisfy your sweet tooth just by inhaling the delicate wafts of chocolate, dried fruits, and roasted nuts in this fair-trade, organic chocolate shop in the Historic Distillery District. Big sellers include crystallized Australian ginger dipped in dark Venezuelan chocolate and spiced Chai tea truffles. ⊠ *55 Mill St., Bldg. 48, Old Town* ☎ *416/815–7662* Ⓜ *King, then streetcar 508 east.*

Suckers Candy Co. It's like stepping into a comic book. More than 500 different suckers; retro and novelty candy from Canada, the United States, and the United Kingdom; gourmet cotton candy in eight different flavors; and custom-made loot bags and baskets will assuage any sweet tooth. This place is fun for all ages, and open until midnight on weekends. ⊠ *450 Danforth Ave., at Chester Ave., Greater Toronto* ☎ *416/405–8946* Ⓜ *Chester.*

Whole Foods. This vast, health-conscious high-end grocery store and café in the basement of Hazelton Lanes has mid- and high-priced items. While imported delicacies and the Yorkville address make it a haven for the well-off (here's where you can pay C$50 for chocolate-covered almonds or catch a celebrity in disguise), students and young professionals come for the organic produce and specialty vegetarian fare. Salad and pasta bars, freshly baked goods, and an impressive selection of prepared foods line one wall. ⊠ *55 Avenue Rd., in Hazelton Lanes, Yorkville* ☎ *416/944–0500* Ⓜ *Bay.*

HOME DECOR AND FURNISHINGS

AGO Gallery Shop. The store attached to the Art Gallery of Ontario has an overwhelming selection of curiosities, from books on maximal architecture to colorful dollhouses to prints of celebrated paintings. Adults and kids can shop side by side among the books and fun educational toys. ⊠ *317 Dundas St. W, at McCaul St., Chinatown* ☎ *416/979–6610* Ⓜ *St. Patrick.*

The Art Shoppe. The block-long, two-story shop is chock-full of eclectic highbrow furniture. ⊠ *2131 Yonge St., at Eglinton Ave., Greater Toronto* ☎ *416/487–3211* Ⓜ *Eglinton.*

Hollace Cluny. The shop sells mainly handmade modern furnishings and accents. ⊠ *1070 Yonge St., at Roxborough St., Greater Toronto* ☎ *416/968–7894* Ⓜ *Rosedale.*

Seagull Classics Ltd. Victorian and Tiffany-style lamps as well as art deco–inspired forms are among this store's unusual selection of lighting. ⊠ *1974 Queen St. E, at Waverley St., Greater Toronto* ☎ *416/690–5224* Ⓜ *Queen, then streetcar 501 east.*

★ **UpCountry.** The 12,000-square-foot store holds a unique mix of furniture collections that reflect leading-edge, solid design principles. Well made and reasonably priced, the upholstered sofas and chairs are built in small runs by Canadian manufacturers. ⊠ *310 King St. E, at Parliament St., Old Town* ☎ *416/366–7477* Ⓜ *King.*

Urban Mode. Modern and trend-oriented home accessories include colorful plastic desk accessories in interesting shapes, and funky wine racks and CD stands. Most are Canadian-designed. ⊠ *145 Tecumseth St., at Queen St. W, Queen West* ☎ *416/591–8834 or 877/265–5895* Ⓜ *Osgoode, then streetcar 501 west.*

JEWELRY

Cartier. The famous jewel box caters to Toronto's elite and has a good selection of the jewelry designer's creations, including the famous triple-gold-band Trinity Ring and the diamond-studded Torture watch. ⊠ *131 Bloor St. W, at Avenue Rd., Yorkville* ☎ *416/413–4929* Ⓜ *Bay.*

★ **Fabrice.** The owner of this shop has a good eye for pearls, semiprecious stones, and gold and silver designs. She lives in Paris and ships one-of-a-kind pieces from France and other fashion capitals to the delight of discerning Torontonians. ⊠ *55 Avenue Rd., in Hazelton Lanes, Yorkville* ☎ *416/967–6590* Ⓜ *Bay.*

Royal De Versailles. Don't let the front-door security scare you away from some of the most innovatively classic jewelry designs in town. ✉ *101 Bloor St. W, at Bay St., Yorkville* ☎ *416/967–7201* Ⓜ *Bay.*

Tiffany & Co. Tiffany is perfect for breakfast or anytime else. It's still the ultimate for variety and quality in classic jewelry. ✉ *85 Bloor St. W, at Bay St., Yorkville* ☎ *416/921–3900* Ⓜ *Bay.*

KITCHENWARE AND TABLETOP

The Cook's Place. Even the most cosmopolitan chef should find something to take home among this immense selection of cookware, including baking pans and hard-to-find gadgets and utensils. Don't miss the fascinating "wall of stuff." ✉ *501 Danforth Ave., Greater Toronto* ☎ *416/461–5211* Ⓜ *Chester.*

William Ashley. Ashley's has an extensive collection of china patterns and can often secure those it doesn't carry. Crystal and china are beautifully displayed, and prices are decent on expensive names such as Waterford. They are happy to pack and ship all over the world. ✉ *55 Bloor St. W, at Bay St., Yorkville* ☎ *416/964–2900* Ⓜ *Bay.*

Word Of Mouth. High-end kitchen appliances, accessories, and tools are priced very competitively, since this store imports directly. ✉ *1134 Yonge St., at Roxborough St., Greater Toronto* ☎ *416/929–6885* Ⓜ *Rosedale.*

MUSIC AND STEREO EQUIPMENT

Bay Bloor Radio. This stereo haven has the latest equipment and sound-sealed listening rooms that allow you to test-drive equipment. ✉ *Manulife Centre, 55 Bloor St. W, at Bay St., Yorkville* ☎ *416/967–1122* Ⓜ *Bay.*

CD Replay. This shop is about as *High Fidelity* (minus the vinyl) as they come. The staff is knowledgeable, and there are frequent deals on older CDs. They also sell new and used CDs and DVDs. ✉ *523 Bloor St. W, at Bathurst St., The Annex* ☎ *416/516–0606* Ⓜ *Bathurst.*

Kops/Vintage Sounds. This combo music shop is revered as the best used-records and -CD store in the city. Upstairs, Vintage Sounds sells vinyl—45s and LPs—from the '50s to '80s and CDs, whereas the downstairs Kops is more contemporary, with reggae, hip-hop, jazz, and soul. ■TIP→ The stores are independently owned, but you must walk through Kops to get to Vintage. ✉ *229 Queen St. W, at University Ave., Queen West* ☎ *416/598–4039* Ⓜ *Osgoode.*

Penguin Music. This slender little store packs a mighty wallop. Choose from a plethora of used indie-label CDs. ✉ *256A Queen St.W, at John St., Queen West* ☎ *416/597–1687* Ⓜ *Osgoode.*

Rotate This. Music buyers in the know come here for underground and independent music from Canada, the United States, and beyond. It has CDs, LPs, some magazines, concert tickets, and other treats. ✉ *801 Queen St. W, at Bathurst St., Queen West* ☎ *416/504–8447* Ⓜ *Osgoode, then streetcar 501 west.*

Song & Script. Broadway musicals are the specialty, and they carry CDs, songbooks, posters, and other paraphernalia. Personal service has been the key since it opened in 1964, and if what you're after isn't in stock, they will happily find and order it for you. ⊠ *2 Bloor St. W, at Bay St., Yorkville* ☎ *416/923–3044* Ⓜ *Bay.*

Soundscapes. Crammed with pop, rock, jazz, blues, folk, ambient, psychedelic, garage, avant-garde, and electronic titles, this shop satisfies the hip as well as fans of early Americana. Selections and organization reflect a love of music and its ever-expanding history. ⊠ *572 College St., at Manning Ave., Little Italy* ☎ *416/537–1620* Ⓜ *Queen's Park, then streetcar 506 west.*

SHOES

Brown's. The excellent selection of shoes here can make your heart race. At the Bloor store you can find the latest punky Steve Maddens next to a vampish Manolo Blahnik. Brown's also carries handbags and boots. ⊠ *Eaton Centre, Dundas Square Area* ☎ *416/979–9270* Ⓜ *Queen* ⊠ *55 Avenue Rd., in Hazelton Lanes, Yorkville* ☎ *416/968–1806* Ⓜ *Bay.*

David's. The collection is always elegant, if somewhat subdued—designers usually include Marc Jacobs, Kate Spade, Salvatore Ferragamo, and Lorenzo Banfi. ⊠ *66 Bloor St. W, at Bay St., Yorkville* ☎ *416/920–1000* Ⓜ *Bay.*

Get Out Side. Get your funky street-wear fix here. There are styles for men and women, as well as an entire wall of sneakers. ⊠ *437 Queen St. W, at Spadina Ave., Queen West* ☎ *416/593–5598* Ⓜ *Osgoode, then streetcar 501 west.*

Heel Boy. A number of well-known brand-name lines and a few edgier ones make this a popular shoe-shopping spot. ⊠ *682 Queen St. W, at Bathurst St., Queen West* ☎ *416/362–4335* Ⓜ *Osgoode, then streetcar 501 west.*

John Fluevog. Fluevog began in Vancouver, infusing good quality with fun, flair, and cutting-edge design, and is now an international shoe star. Stores can be found all over the United States, in Australia, and, luckily, also on Queen Street West. ⊠ *242 Queen St. W, at John St., Queen West* ☎ *416/581–1420* Ⓜ *Osgoode, then streetcar 501 west.*

Mephisto Boutique. These walking shoes have been around since the 1960s and are made entirely from natural materials. Passionate walkers swear by these shoes and claim they never, ever wear out—even on cross-Europe treks. ⊠ *1177 Yonge St., at Summerhill Ave., Greater Toronto* ☎ *416/968–7026* Ⓜ *Summerhill.*

Specchio. This is the place for fine Italian shoes and boots on the cutting edge of style, for every season, at surprisingly reasonable prices. They always seem to have your size in the back. ⊠ *1240 Bay St., at Cumberland St., Yorkville* ☎ *416/961–7989* Ⓜ *Bay.*

Town Shoes. Shoe-aholics have a field day in this reasonably priced, trendy shop, which carries house brands in casual, fashion, and sports shoes. The styles are cutting-edge for men and women. ⊠ *95 Bloor St. W, at Bellair St., Yorkville* ☎ *416/928–5062* Ⓜ *Bay.*

Zola. The store is tiny, but it's what's inside—a selection of women's shoes that includes the likes of Sigerson Morrison and Valentino—that counts. ⊠ *1726 Avenue Rd., at Lawrence Ave. W, Greater Toronto* ☎ *416/783–8688* Ⓜ *Lawrence* ☎ *416/922–8688* Ⓜ *Bay.*

SPORTING GOODS

Fodor's Choice ★ **Mountain Equipment Co-op.** MEC, the much-beloved Toronto spot for anyone remotely interested in camping, sells wares for minor and major expeditions. A baffling assortment of backpacks allows you to choose anything from a schoolbag to a globe-trotting sack. ■ TIP→ **Try out the rappelling goods on the climbing wall.** ⊠ *400 King St. W, at Spadina Ave., Entertainment District* ☎ *416/340–2667* Ⓜ *St. Andrew.*

★ **Nike.** The store's two floors display everything the famous brand-name has to offer, from athletic equipment to sneakers. ⊠ *110 Bloor St. W, at Bellair St., Yorkville* ☎ *416/921–6453* Ⓜ *Bay.*

Puma. Whether your sport is cricket, football, tennis, golf, or anything else, here is a complete selection of gear in seasonal colors and hot new styles by internationally known designers and a knowledgeable, sports-minded staff. A second store on Bloor Street is on the same block as Nike and Roots. ⊠ *2532 Yonge St., north of Eglinton Ave., Greater Toronto* ☎ *416/486–7862* Ⓜ *Eglinton* ⊠ *151 Bloor St. W, at Avenue Rd., Yorkville* ☎ *416/962–9155* Ⓜ *Bay.*

Running Room. The knowledgeable staff can guide you to the perfect pair of running shoes. Running Rooms have spawned a running community, and shops have sprouted up all over the city (the main branch is listed below); group runs commence every Wednesday evening and Sunday morning. ⊠ *55 Avenue Rd., in Hazelton Lanes, Yorkville* ☎ *416/960–3910* Ⓜ *Bay.*

Sporting Life. The first off the mark with the latest sportswear trends, this is the place to get couture labels like Juicy, La Coste, and Burberry—or to snag snowboard gear and poll the staff for advice on where to go to use it. A second "bikes and boards store" is down Yonge Street. ⊠ *2665 Yonge St., north of Eglinton Ave., Greater Toronto* ☎ *416/485–1611* Ⓜ *Eglinton* ⊠ *2454 Yonge St., north of Eglinton Ave., Greater Toronto* ☎ *416/485–4440* Ⓜ *Eglinton.*

7

Side Trips from Toronto

WORD OF MOUTH

"I guess NOTL is like a B&B and Niagara Falls is like a casino hotel—if you like 'quaint' and 'peaceful,' then NOTL is your best bet; if you like 'action' and 'bright lights,' then Niagara Falls is your best bet."

—toedtoes

Updated by
Shannon Kelly

The rush of 700,000 gallons of water a second. The divinely sweet, crisp taste of ice wine. The tug of a fish hooked under a layer of ice. Sure, the big-city scene in Toronto delivers the hustle and bustle you came for—but escaping the city can transport you to another world.

There's the mesmerizing and deservedly hyped Niagara Falls, acres of local vineyards in Niagara-on-the-Lake and the surrounding Wine Region, or the whimsical Cottage Country, with its quiet towns, challenging ski slopes, and lakefront resorts. Have an itch for the stage? Two major theater events, the Stratford Festival and the Shaw Festival, have long seasons with masterfully orchestrated plays by the bards, William Shakespeare and George Bernard Shaw. Or you can hit the outdoors on Bruce Trail, Canada's oldest and longest footpath, which winds from Niagara Falls to Tobermory 885 km (550 mi) north.

ORIENTATION AND PLANNING

GETTING ORIENTED

The Niagara Penninsula. South of Toronto, near the U.S. border, you'll find more than thundering Niagara Falls. Niagara-on-the-Lake and the wine region are stretched along the shores of Lake Ontario.

Stratford. Just under a two-hour drive west of Toronto, this town fills with Shakespeare fans every summer.

North of Toronto to the Lakes. It takes two to four hours of driving to reach the outdoor-oriented Simcoe County, Gravenhurst, Huntsville, and Algonquin Provincial Park.

PLANNING

WHEN TO GO

In winter Ontario's weather veers toward the severe, making road travel difficult away from major highways, and many museums and attractions are closed or have limited hours. If you like to ski, skate, snowmobile, or ice fish, there's no better time to visit. Otherwise it's best to visit from April through September, when the Stratford and Shaw festivals are in full swing and most sights are open longer. The warmer months also bring outdoor action, such as boating and hiking—or opportunities for resting on a beach or eating at an outdoor café. The increasingly popular Niagara Wine Festival takes place in late September.

TOP REASONS TO GO

Fruit-Picking: Many fruit farms on the Niagara Peninsula offer roadside stands and/or pick-your-own options. Here and around Stratford you can find an abundance of blueberries, peaches, and cherries, as well as late-summer vegetables like corn and field tomatoes. Get maps from 424 S. Service Road, Grimsby, or contact Tourism Niagara (☎ *800/263–2988*); Ontario Tourism (☎ *800/668–2746* ⊕ *www.ontario-travel.net*) or ⊕ *pickyourown.org*.

Hiking: The posted Bruce Trail stretches along the Niagara Escarpment from about St. Catherines 240 km (150 mi) north to the tip of the Bruce Peninsula, jutting into Lake Huron. The Niagara Parkway, which runs 56 km (35 mi) along the Niagara River, has easy walks and great water views. Many pleasant hiking trails can be found outside Stratford, and Algonquin Provincial Park has day-use and backcountry trails ranging from 6 to 88 km (4 to 55 mi).

Skiing: Blue Mountain, near Barrie, is popular, with 35 downhill trails and Ontario's largest ski resort. Horseshoe Resort, also near Barrie, offers downhill skiing (it has 25 alpine runs), as well as cross-country skiing, though skiers interested in lodge-to-lodge packages will want to check out Haliburton.

Theatergoing: A couple of long-dead British playwrights have managed to make two Ontario towns boom from May through October. The Shakespeare festival in Stratford and the Shaw festival in Niagara-on-the-Lake both enjoy great popular success as well as critical acclaim.

Wine-Tasting: One of the best regions—if not *the* best region—for wine production in Canada (Point Pelee, also in Ontario, and British Columbia's Okanagan Valley are others), the Niagara Peninsula has an unusually good microclimate for growing grapes. Many of the 60 or so wineries do tastings and/or tours.

GETTING HERE AND AROUND
AIR TRAVEL

Toronto's Pearson International Airport, 30 km (18 mi) north of downtown, is the most logical choice if you're heading directly to Stratford or regions north of Toronto, including Algonquin Provincial Park. The Niagara Falls International Airport in Niagara Falls, New York, is the closest air link to Niagara Falls, Ontario, and Niagara-on-the Lake. The larger Buffalo Niagara International Airport is 30 mi from Niagara Falls, Ontario. Other options are Toronto's downtown City Centre Airport, which serves only Porter Airlines, or the Hamilton International Airport, about halfway between Toronto and Niagara Falls, in Hamilton, Ontario.

Air Travel Contacts Buffalo Niagara International Airport (☎ *716/630–6000* ⊕ *www.buffaloairport.com*). **Hamilton International Airport** (☎ *905/679–1999* ⊕ *www.flyhi.ca*). **Niagara Falls International Airport** (☎ *716/297–4494* ⊕ *www.niagarafallsairport.com*). **Porter Airlines** (☎ *416/619–8622* or *888/619-8622* ⊕ *www.flyporter.com*). **Toronto Pearson International Airport** (☎ *416/776–3000* ⊕ *www.gtaa.com*).

CAR TRAVEL

A car is a necessity, except in downtown Niagara Falls and Stratford but is still recommended everywhere, as it allows much more flexibility.

If you are driving to your destination, the best time to leave Toronto is early- to mid-week; however, you should avoid the weekday rush hours of 7 to 9:30 AM and 4 to 6:30 PM. Toll highways and bridges are rare.

Car Contacts Toronto road-condition information (☎ 416/235–4686 or 800/268–4686).

TRAIN TRAVEL

It's easy to get to Niagara Falls and Stratford via train (on VIA Rail), and both are cities in which you can get by without wheels—just be sure to book a hotel close to the action. For other side trips, a car is necessary. Cross-Canada VIA Rail stops in Stratford, Niagara Falls, and other towns and cities in southern Ontario, and connects with Amtrak service at Niagara Falls, New York and Fort Erie in Buffalo, New York. Ontario Northland's Northlander line travels between Toronto and Bracebridge, Gravenhurst, Huntsville, and other northern points.

Train Contacts Amtrak (☎ 800/872–7245 ⊕ www.amtrak.com). **Ontario Northland** (☎ 800/461–8558 ⊕ www.ontarionorthland.ca). **VIA Rail** (☎ 888/842–7245 ⊕ www.viarail.ca).

RESTAURANTS

George Bernard Shaw once said, "No greater love hath man than the love of food," and Niagara-on-the-Lake, which hosts a festival devoted to the playwright, is a perfect place to indulge your epicurean desires. Many eateries serve fine produce and wines from the verdant Niagara Peninsula. In fact, Niagara wines make appearances on menus province-wide; try the sweet ice wine with dessert (or *as* dessert). Though Niagara-on-the-Lake appears to have changed little from its turn-of-the-20th-century style, the rebuilding and renovation of historical inns have brought this sleepy town into the first-class hospitality arena.

Expect a variety of cuisines across the province: fresh-caught fish in Cottage Country, home-style Canadian fare in small-town inns, or haute Canadian in Niagara Wine Region restaurants. Thanks to a long-standing British influence, there's plenty of roast beef, shepherd's pie, and rice pudding. Reservations at medium-price and upscale restaurants are recommended, particularly during peak season in the ski and festival towns and in Niagara Falls.

HOTELS

Reservations are strongly recommended everywhere during summer, and in ski areas in winter. Prices are comparable to those in the United States. All types of accommodations tend to be more expensive in tourist venues. In Niagara Falls, for example, hotel and motel rates are determined by proximity to the falls. Taxes are seldom included in quoted prices, but rates sometimes include food, especially in more remote areas such as Muskoka and Haliburton, where many resorts offer meal plans. Cottage rentals are available through local real-estate agents, tourism boards, or **At the Cottage** (⊕ www.atthecottage.com). **BBCanada.com** (☎ 800/239–1141 ⊕ www.bbcanada.com) can help you

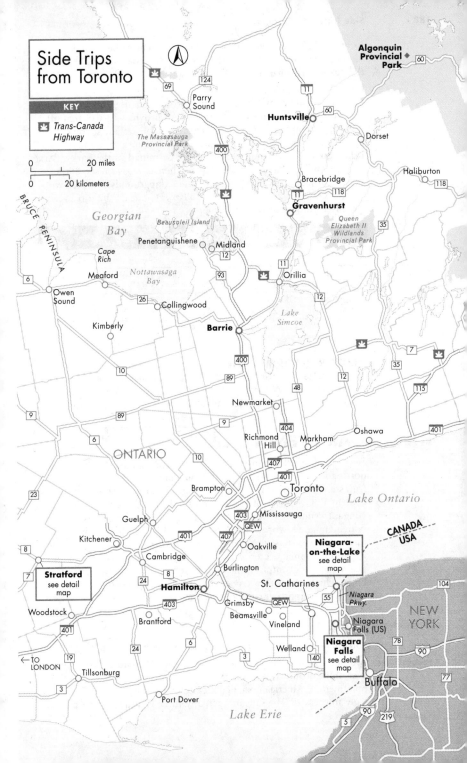

locate a B&B and reserve a room. A comprehensive B&B guide listing about 250 establishments is published by the **Federation of Ontario Bed & Breakfast Accommodations** (⊕ *www.fobba.com*).

CAMPING

Peak season in Ontario parks is June through August, and it is advised that you reserve a campsite if possible. All provincial parks that offer organized camping do have some sites available on a first-come, first-served basis. To prevent overcrowding, daily quotas have been established governing the number of people permitted in the parks. Park permits can be obtained ahead of time. There is a C$12 reservation fee. For detailed information on parks and campgrounds province-wide, contact Ontario Parks for the *Ontario Parks Guide* or Ontario Tourism for a free outdoor-adventure guide.

WHAT IT COSTS IN CANADIAN DOLLARS					
	¢	$	$$	$$$	$$$$
Restaurants	under C$8	C$8–C$12	C$13–C$20	C$21–C$30	over C$30
Hotels	under C$75	C$75–C$125	C$126–C$175	C$175–C$250	over C$250

Restaurant prices are per person for a main course at dinner. Hotel prices are for two people in a standard double room in high season, excluding 13% hotel tax.

VISITOR INFORMATION

Contacts **Ontario Tourism** (☎ *800/668–2746* ⊕ *www.ontariotravel.net*). **Ontario Parks** (☎ *800/668–2746 or 888/668–7275* ⊕ *www.ontarioparks.com*). **Tourism Niagara** (☎ *905/945–5444 or 800/263–2988* ⊕ *www.tourismniagara.com*).

THE NIAGARA PENINSULA

Within this small expanse of land, bordered by Lake Ontario to the north and Lake Erie to the south, you can stumble across a roadside fruit stand on a tour through rustic vineyards or gamble to your heart's content alongside one of nature's most beautiful displays of water. The Niagara Peninsula's various flavors make it a good place to entertain both high- and lowbrow interests. Niagara Falls, with its daring adventure tours, wax museums, and honeymoon certificates—not to mention its wildly popular water attraction—has a certain kitschy-and-glitzy quality. In stark contrast is the more tasteful and serene Niagara-on-the-Lake, which draws theatergoers to its annual Shaw Festival and wine lovers to the approximately 60 wineries and vineyards.

NIAGARA FALLS

130 km (81 mi) south of Toronto via the QEW (Queen Elizabeth Way).

Fodor's Choice ★   Although cynics have had a field day with **Niagara Falls**—calling it everything from "water on the rocks" to "the second major disappointment of American married life" (Oscar Wilde)—most visitors are truly impressed. The falls are actually three cataracts: the American

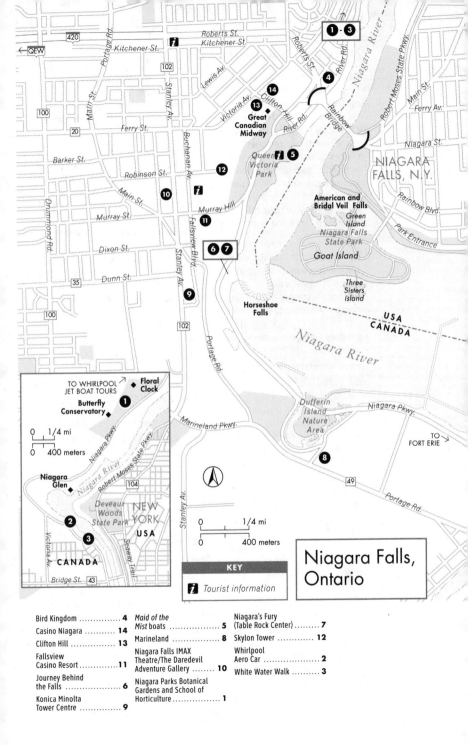

420

← QEW

100

20

35

100

102

102

49

43

104

Roberts St.
Roberts St.
Kitchener St.
Kitchener St.

Portage Rd.

Main St.

Stanley Av.

Ferry St.

Lewis Av.

Victoria Av.

Barker St.

Robinson St.

Main St.

Buchanan Av.

Fallsview Blvd.

Drummond Rd.

Murray St.

Murray Hill

Dixon St.

Dunn St.

Stanley Av.

Roberts St.

River Rd.

River Rd.

Niagara River

Robert Moses State Pkwy.

Main St.

Ferry Av.

Niagara St.

Rainbow Blvd.

Park Entrance

❶ · ❸

❹

Rainbow
Bridge

Clifton Hill
❶❹
❶❸
Great
Canadian
Midway

Queen ❼ ❺
Victoria
Park

NIAGARA
FALLS, N.Y.

❶❷

❶❶

❻❼

❾

American and
Bridal Veil Falls
Green
Island
Niagara Falls
State Park
Goat Island

Three
Sisters
Island

Horseshoe
Falls

USA
CANADA

Niagara River

Portage Rd.

Marineland Pkwy.

Dufferin
Island
Nature
Area

Niagara Pkwy.

TO
FORT ERIE →

❽

Portage Rd.

TO WHIRLPOOL → Floral
JET BOAT TOURS   Clock

Butterfly
Conservatory ▼

❶

0   1/4 mi

0   400 meters

Niagara Glen ◆

Niagara River

Robert Moses State Pkwy.

Deveaux
Woods
State Park

NEW
YORK
USA

❷

❸

Victoria Av.

Seaway Trail

CANADA

Bridge St.

Stanley Av.

0   1/4 mi

0   400 meters

KEY

🛈 *Tourist information*

Niagara Falls,
Ontario

NIAGARA FALLS HISTORY

Missionary and explorer Louis Hennepin, whose books were widely read across Europe, described the falls in 1678 as "an incredible Cataract or Waterfall which has no equal." Nearly two centuries later, Charles Dickens declared, "I seemed to be lifted from the earth and to be looking into Heaven." Henry James recorded in 1883 how one stands there "gazing your fill at the most beautiful object in the world."

These rave reviews lured countless daredevils to the falls. In 1859, 100,000 spectators watched as the French tightrope walker Blondin successfully crossed Niagara Gorge, from the American to the Canadian side, on a 3-inch-thick rope. From the early 18th century, dozens went over in boats and barrels. Nobody survived until 1901, when schoolteacher Annie Taylor emerged from her barrel and asked, "Did I go over the falls yet?" The stunts were finally outlawed in 1912.

The waterfall's colorful history began more than 10,000 years ago as a group of glaciers receded, diverting the waters of Lake Erie northward into Lake Ontario. The force and volume of the water as it flowed over the Niagara Escarpment created the thundering cataracts now known so well. The lure of Niagara Falls hasn't dimmed for those who want to marvel at a premier natural wonder; Niagara Falls, on the border of the United States and Canada, is one of the most famous tourist attractions in the world, and one of the most awe-inspiring.

and Bridal Veil Falls in New York State, and the Horseshoe Falls in Ontario. In terms of sheer volume of water—more than 700,000 gallons per second in summer—Niagara is unsurpassed in North America. On the American side you can park in the lot on Goat Island near the American Falls and walk along the path beside the Niagara River, which becomes more and more turbulent as it approaches the big drop-off of just over 200 feet.

After experiencing the falls from the U.S. side, you can walk or drive across Rainbow Bridge to the Canadian side, where you can get a far view of the American Falls and a close-up of the Horseshoe Falls. You can also park your car for the day in any of several lots on the Canadian side, and hop onto one of the People Mover buses, which run continuously to all the sights along the river. If you want to get close to the foot of the falls, the *Maid of the Mist* boat takes you close enough to get soaked in the spray.

The amusement parks and tacky souvenir shops that surround the falls attest to the area's history as a major tourist attraction. Most of the gaudiness is contained on Clifton Hill, Niagara Falls' toned-down Times Square. Despite these garish efforts to attract visitors, the landscaped grounds immediately bordering the falls are lovely and the beauty of the falls remains untouched.

One reason to spend the night here is to admire the falls illumination, which takes place every night of the year, from dusk until at least 10 PM (until as late as 1 AM during the summer). Even the most contemptuous observer will be mesmerized as the falls change from red to purple to blue to green to white, and finally all the colors of the rainbow in harmony.

GETTING HERE AND AROUND

Niagara Falls is accessible by bus or train, but a car is the best way to get around.

The Queen Elizabeth Way—better known as the QEW—was named for the wife of King George VI, the late Queen Mother, and runs from the U.S. border through the Niagara Region to Toronto. The four- to eight-lane freeway traverses—from south to north—Fort Erie, Niagara Falls, St. Catharines, and Hamilton, and ends in Toronto.

In Niagara Falls, in general, parking prices increase closer to the falls. The walk down to the falls is a steep one. You might want to take a taxi back up, or hop aboard the Falls Incline Railway, which operates between Portage Street and the Niagara Parkway. The trip takes about one minute and costs C$2.

The Niagara Transit Falls Shuttle travels along the Niagara Parkway as far north as the Whirlpool Aero Car entry area and as far south as Marineland, as well as taking major routes through town along Falls-view Boulevard, Stanley Avenue, and past the QEW on Ferry Street/Lundy's Lane. A day pass is C$6, single-trip fare is C$3.50.

From late April to mid-October, air-conditioned People Mover buses travel on a loop route between a public parking lot above the falls at Rapids View Terminal (next to Marineland, well marked) and the Whirlpool Aero Car parking lot about 9 km (6 mi) downriver and in summer as far as Queenston Heights Park, 15 km (9 mi) downriver. A day pass, available at any booth on the system, is C$7.50 per person per day. You can get on and off as many times as you wish at well-marked stops along the route.

DISCOUNTS AND DEALS

The following passes are available through the tourism board and also, generally, at ticket windows for specific sights.

The Clifton Hill Fun Pass includes entry to five Clifton Hill attractions for C$29.95 plus tax. The Midway Magic Pass includes two rides and 13 Midway tokens for C$14.99 plus tax.

The Niagara Falls and Great Gorge Adventure Pass (C$42.71, tax included) covers admission to Journey Behind the Falls, *Maid of the Mist*, White Water Walk, and the Butterfly Conservatory, plus a number of discount coupons and unlimited use of both the People Mover and the Falls Incline Railway. It's available from Niagara Parks.

Pick up the free Save-A-Buck coupon booklet for discounts on various tours, attractions, and restaurants.

TOURS

Double Deck Tours Tours operate daily from mid-May to mid-October and include most of the major sights of Niagara Falls. The fare includes admission to Journey Behind the Falls, *Maid of the Mist,* and the Whirlpool Aero Car. Tours depart at 11 from the *Maid of the Mist* building at the foot of Clifton Hill and run about four hours.

National Helicopters runs 20-minute tours that fly over the falls and wine country. Private (two-person) sunset tours, winery tours, and honeymoon packages are available at a slightly higher price.

★ Niagara Helicopters Ltd. takes you on a nine-minute flight over the giant whirlpool, up the Niagara Gorge, and past the American Falls, then banks around the curve of the Horseshoe Falls. ■TIP→ Get a C$10 discount coupon on the Web site. Special tour packages include flying to wineries and getting married in the sky.

Wet-and-wild Whirlpool Jet Boat Tours veer around and hurdle white-water rapids on a one-hour thrill ride that follows Niagara canyons up to the wall of rolling waters, just below the falls. Children must be at least six years old for the open-boat Wet Jet Tour and four years old for the covered-boat (dry!) Jet Dome Tour. From May to mid-June, September, and October, tours depart from Niagara-on-the-Lake. From mid-June to August, tours also leave from 3050 Niagara Parkway in Niagara Falls. Tours cost C$57. Reserve ahead and check the Web site for discounts.

> ## OFF TO THE RACES
>
> Beautifully landscaped with willows, manicured hedges and flower-bordered infield lakes, the **Fort Erie Race Track** (⊠ *230 Catherine St., off QEW Exit 2, Fort Erie* ☎ *905/871–3200* ⊕ *www.forterieracing.com*) has dirt and turf horse racing, with the year's highlight being the Prince of Wales Stakes, the second jewel in Canada's Triple Crown of Racing. It's open May through October, Sunday through Tuesday (and some Saturdays) for live races.

ESSENTIALS

Transportation Contacts Niagara Transit (☎ *905/356–1179* ⊕ *www.niagara-falls.ca*). **People Mover** (☎ *905/357–9340* ⊕ *www.niagaraparks.ca*).

Tour Contacts Double Deck Tours (☎ *905/374–7423* ⊕ *www.doubledecktours.com* ⊒ *C$60.50*). **National Helicopters** (⊠ *Niagara District Airport, 468 Niagara Stone Rd., Niagara-on-the-Lake* ☎ *905/641–2222 or 800/491–3117* ⊕ *www.nationalhelicopters.com* ⊒ *C$139/person, C$360 for a family of 4*). **Niagara Helicopters Ltd.** (⊠ *3731 Victoria Ave.* ☎ *905/357–5672 or 800/281–8034* ⊕ *www.niagara-helicopters.com* ⊒ *C$118*). **Whirlpool Jet Boat Tours** (⊠ *61 Melville St., Niagara-on-the-Lake* ☎ *905/468–4800 or 888/438–4444* ⊕ *www.whirlpooljet.com*).

Discounts and Deals Clifton Hill Fun Pass (⊕ *www.cliftonhill.com*) **Save-A-Buck coupon booklet** (⊕ *www.saveabuck.ca*)

Visitor Information Niagara Falls Tourism (⊠ *5515 Stanley Ave.* ☎ *905/356–6061 or 800/563–2557* ⊕ *www.niagarafallstourism.com*). **Niagara Parks** (☎ *905/371–0254 or 877/642–7275* ⊕ *www.niagaraparks.com*).

EXPLORING
TOP ATTRACTIONS

⑬ Clifton Hill. Undeniably the most crassly commercial district of Niagara Falls, you can't ignore the haunted houses, more wax museums than one usually sees in a lifetime, and fast-food chains. Attractions are typically open late (midnight–2 AM in summer, 11 PM off-season), with admission ranging from about C$5 to C$13. They include the 175-foot SkyWheel, refurbished in 2006, with enclosed, heated, and air-conditioned compartments; the **Great Canadian Midway** (☎ 905/358–3676), a 70,000 square-foot entertainment complex with an arcade, bowling alley, rides, and food; the **Guinness World Records Museum** (☎ 905/356–2299 ⊕ www.guinnessniagarafalls.com); **Ripley's Moving Theatre** in the **Ripley's Believe It or Not! Museum** (☎ 905/356–2299 ⊕ www.ripleysniagara.com), a 3-D movie, where the seats move with the picture; **the Movieland Wax Museum** (☎ 905/358–3676 ⊕ www.cliftonhill.com), with such lifelike characters as Indiana Jones and Snow White, and the **Hershey Store** (☎ 800/468–1714 ⊕ www.hersheycanada.com/en/discover), 7,000 square feet of truffles, fudge, cookbooks, and the trademark Kisses, marked by a six-story-high chocolate bar at the base of the hill (www.cliftonhill.com).

> ### NIGHT LIGHTS
>
> Adding to the ambience of nightly illumination are **Fireworks Over the Falls** displays every Friday and Sunday evening at 10 PM from late May to early September. Those staying in the neighborhood who don't have falls-view hotel rooms, or who can't bear to leave their slot machines for long, tend to gather at the patio of the Fallsview Casino Resort to watch the spectacle.
>
> Between November and early January, the **Winter Festival of Lights** (☎ 905/374–1616 ⊕ www.wfol.com) illuminates the entire Niagara Parkway, from the Whirlpool Bridge to the Dufferin Islands, with more than 1 million lights.

Clifton Hill and immediate surroundings are undergoing a C$100-million construction project, begun in 2005, aimed at creating a more modern, streamlined amusement center, with roller coasters (proposed), two water parks (one is already open), and a 28-story Comfort Suites hotel; the modernized SkyWheel was the first attraction completed. The entire project is projected to take up to 10 years to complete.

QUICK BITES

Skip the high-priced ice cream at DQ and Baskin Robbins and go for a cone, shake, or float from the '50s-soda-fountain-themed Always Refreshing Coke Shop inside the Coca-Cola store, which shares a building with the Hershey Store (✉ *5685 Falls Ave.*).

⑪ **Fallsview Casino Resort.** Canada's largest gaming and resort facility crowns the city's skyline, overlooking the Niagara Parks with picture-perfect views of both falls. Within the 30-story complex is Canada's only casino wedding chapel, a glitzy theater, spa, shops, and, for the gaming enthusiasts, 140 gaming tables, 3,000 slot machines, and plenty of restaurants. The Las Vegas–style Avalon Ballroom showcases a wide array of talents, from Reba McEntire to Brian Wilson to Jay Leno. ✉ *6380 Fallsview Blvd.* ☎ *888/325–5788 or 905/371–7505* ⊕ *www.fallsviewcasinoresort.com* ☉ *Daily 24 hrs.*

❺ **Fodor's Choice ★** *Maid of the Mist.* Boats have been operating for *Maid of the Mist* since 1846, when they were wooden-hulled, coal-fired steamboats. Today double-deck steel vessels tow fun-loving passengers on 30-minute journeys to the foot of the falls, where the spray is so heavy that ponchos must be distributed. From the observation areas along the falls, you can see those boarding the boats in their blue slickers. ✉ *Tickets and entrance at foot of Clifton Hill* 🗂 *Box 808, 5920 River Rd.* ☎ *905/358–0311* 🌐 *www.maidofthemist.com* 💲 *C$14.50* ⏱ *Departures every 15 min May–late Oct.; call or check Web site for details.*

8 Marineland. A theme park with a marine show, wildlife displays, rides, and aquariums—including a beluga whale habitat with underwater viewing areas—is 1½ km (1 mi) south of the falls. The daily marine shows include performing killer whales, dolphins, harbor seals, and sea lions. Children can pet and feed deer and get nose-to-nose with North American freshwater fish. Among the many rides is Dragon Mountain, the world's largest steel roller coaster. ✉ *7657 Portage Rd., off Niagara Parkway or QEW (McLeod Rd. exit)* ☎ *905/356–9565* 🌐 *www.marineland.ca* 💲 *C$39.95* ⏱ *Mid-May–June and mid-Sept.– mid-Oct., daily 10–dusk; July–mid-Sept. daily 9–dusk; ticket booth closes at 5.*

1 Niagara Parks Botanical Gardens and School of Horticulture. Professional gardeners have graduated from here since 1936; 100 acres of immaculately maintained gardens are open to the public. Within the Botanical Gardens is the **Niagara Parks Butterfly Conservatory,** housing one of North America's largest collections of free-flying butterflies—at least 2,000 butterflies from 50 species around the world are protected in a climate-controlled, rain forest–like conservatory. ✉ *2405 Niagara Pkwy.* ☎ *905/356–8554 or 877/642–7275* 🌐 *www.niagaraparks.com* 💲 *Gardens free, Butterfly Conservatory C$11.50* ⏱ *Gardens daily dawn–dusk; call or check Web site for Butterfly Conservatory hrs.*

12 Skylon Tower. Rising 775 feet above the falls, this is the best view of the great Niagara Gorge and the entire city. The indoor-outdoor observation deck has visibility up to 130 km (80 mi) on a clear day. Amusements for children plus a revolving dining room, a gaming arcade, and a 3-D theater, are other reasons to visit. ✉ *5200 Robinson St.* ☎ *905/356–2651 or 800/814–9577* 🌐 *www.skylon.com* 💲 *C$12.95* ⏱ *Mid-June–early Sept., daily 8 AM–midnight; early Sept.–mid June, 9 AM–10 PM most days.*

2 Whirlpool Aero Car. In operation since 1916, this antique cable car crosses the Whirlpool Basin in the Niagara Gorge. This trip is not for the fainthearted, but there's no better way to get an aerial view of the gorge, the whirlpool, the rapids, and the hydroelectric plants. ✉ *3850 Niagara Pkwy., 4½ km (3 mi) north of falls* ☎ *905/371–0254 or 877/642–7275* 🌐 *www.niagaraparks.com* 💲 *C$11.50* ⏱ *Mid-Mar.–mid-Nov., daily. Hrs vary; call or check Web site for details.*

3 White Water Walk. A self-guided route involves taking an elevator to the bottom of the Niagara Gorge, the narrow valley created by the Niagara Falls and River, where you can walk on a boardwalk beside the Class VI rapids of the Niagara River. The gorge is rimmed by sheer cliffs as it enters the giant whirlpool. ✉ *4330 Niagara Pkwy., 3 km (2 mi) north of falls* ☎ *905/371–0254 or 877/642–7275* 🌐 *www.niagaraparks.com* 💲 *C$8.75* ⏱ *Mid-Mar.–Nov. daily 9 AM–dusk, weather permitting; call or check Web site for hrs.*

WORTH NOTING

④ Bird Kingdom. A tropical respite from the crowds and Las Vegas–style attractions, Bird Kingdom is the world's largest indoor aviary, with more than 35 exotic-bird species in the 50,000-square-foot complex. For creepy-crawly lovers, there are also spiders, lizards, and snakes. ✉ *5651 River Rd.* ☎ *905/356–8888 or 866/994–0090* ⊕ *www.bird-kingdom.ca* 🎫 *$19.50* ⊙ *Oct.–June, daily 10–5; July and Aug., daily 9:30–6; Sept., weekdays 10–5, weekends 10–6.*

⑭ Casino Niagara. Slot machines, video-poker machines, and gambling tables, where games such as blackjack, roulette, and baccarat are played. Multisports wagering and off-track betting are available. Within the casino are several lounges, a Yuk Yuk's comedy club, and an all-you-can-eat buffet restaurant. Valet parking is available. ✉ *5705 Falls Ave.* ☎ *905/374–3598 or 888/946–3255* ⊕ *www.casinoniagara.com* ⊙ *Daily 24 hrs.*

⑥ Journey Behind the Falls. Here you can take an elevator to an observation deck that provides an eye-level view of the Canadian Horseshoe Falls and the Niagara River. From there a walk through tunnels cut into the rock takes you behind waterfalls where the roar is thunderous, and you can glimpse the backside of the crashing water through two portals cut in the rock face. ✉ *Tours begin at Table Rock Center, 6650 Niagara Pkwy.* ☎ *905/371–0254 or 877/642–7275* ⊕ *www.niagaraparks.com* 🎫 *Dec.–mid-Apr. C$9.50, mid-Apr.–Nov. C$12.50* ⊙ *Tours daily beginning at 9* AM; *hrs vary—call or check Web site for details.*

⑨ Konica Minolta Tower Centre. At 525 feet above the base of the falls, the tower affords panoramic views of the Horseshoe Falls and the area from its 25th-floor observation deck. ✉ *6732 Fallsview Blvd.* ☎ *905/356–1501 or 800/461–2492* ⊕ *www.niagaratower.com* 🎫 *C$5* ⊙ *Daily 7* AM–*11* PM*).*

⑩ Niagara Falls IMAX Theatre/The Daredevil Adventure Gallery. You can see the falls up close and travel back in time for a glimpse of its 12,000-year-old history with *Mysteries of the Great Lakes* or get the human story with *Niagara: Legends and Daredevils* on the six-story IMAX screen. The Daredevil Adventure Gallery chronicles the expeditions of those who have tackled the falls. ■TIP➔ Purchase tickets online for discounts. ✉ *6170 Fallsview Blvd.* ☎ *905/358–3611* ⊕ *www.imaxniagara.com* 🎫 *C$14.75* ⊙ *Shows on hr Nov.–Apr., daily; July and Aug., daily 9–9; May–Oct., daily 9–8.*

⑦ Niagara's Fury. New in summer 2008, Niagara's Fury is an interactive 4-D experience explaining how Niagara Falls formed over thousands of years. As you stand on a mesh platform surrounded by viewing screens, you feel snow falling, winds blowing, the floor rumbling, and waves crashing as you watch glaciers form, then collide, then melt, creating the falls as we know them today. ✉ *Table Rock Centre, 6650 Niagara Parkway* ☎ *905/371–0254 or 877/642–7275* ⊕ *www.niagaraparks.com* 🎫 *C$15* ⊙ *Showtimes vary.*

8

WHERE TO EAT

Dining in Niagara Falls is expensive. Even a meal at a fast-food joint will cost you a few bucks more than it would a few kilometers up the road. And while many of the priciest restaurants have fab views of the falls, their food pales in comparison to what you'd find in Niagara-on-the-Lake. Still, it can be worth it for the romance of a meal with a view.

> **WORD OF MOUTH**
>
> "The magnificent power of the Falls, lit up at night, with the sound and the mist and the multitude of angles at which it can be viewed, is awesome. *Maid of the Mist*, Journey behind the Falls, standing at the railing are great. But there is really a lot more."
>
> —Clasinvest

$$$$
CONTINENTAL
★

✕ **17 Noir.** A two-story restaurant within the Fallsview Casino complex, 17 Noir has the best food with a view in town. Start out with fresh oysters or lobster bisque, then move on to Canadian or USDA Prime steak, Dijon-crusted rack of lamb, or maple-miso-marinated Chilean sea bass. The tall space is dramatically modern, with a profusion of red, black and gold; for views of the falls, you can sit at a window-side table or on one of two patios. ⊠ *Fallsview Casino Resort, 6380 Fallsview Blvd.* ☎ *905/358–3255 or 888/325–5788* ⌚ *Reservations essential* ⊟ *AE, MC, V* ☾ *Closed Tues. No lunch.*

$$
ITALIAN

✕ **Capri.** Despite a down-at-the-heels exterior, this friendly, family-owned restaurant is casually elegant inside and serves huge, Italian-style platters of homemade pasta, such as linguine with chicken cacciatore. The three dining rooms, decorated in dark-wood paneling, draw families daily because of the half-dozen specially priced children's dishes and large menu. ⊠ *5438 Ferry St., near Stanley Ave.* ☎ *905/354–7519* ⊟ *AE, DC, MC, V.*

$$$
ITALIAN

✕ **Casa d'Oro.** Niagara kitsch is in full effect at this Italian restaurant operated by the Roberto family since 1971. Though it looks dated from the outside and like a Venetian castle estate sale inside, the ornate wall sconces and murals, fireplaces, wine casks, and huge faux-marble and bronze sculptures are somehow not out of place in Niagara Falls. Locals flock here for hearty entrées such as veal Oscar (breaded, topped with asparagus, crabmeat, and cream sauce, then baked), fettucine Alfredo, and penne bolognese, and the remarkable wine collection. Everything, including the pasta, is homemade. The patio fronts busy Victoria Avenue. ⊠ *5875 Victoria Ave.* ☎ *905/356–5646* ⊕ *www.thecasadoro.com* ⊟ *AE, DC, MC, V.*

$$$
ITALIAN
★

✕ **Casa Mia.** All the pasta is made in-house at this off-the-tourist-track Italian restaurant, a five-minute drive from the falls. (The restaurant has free shuttle service from local casinos and hotels.) Fresh-grated beets impart a shocking pink color to the gnocchi, divine with Gorgonzola sauce. If you've ever wondered what fresh cannelloni is like, try these pasta pancakes, filled with veal and spinach. The veal chop is pan-seared with sage and truffle oil. The wine cellar has more than 300 international labels, and weekends bring live music to the piano lounge. ⊠ *3518 Portage Rd.* ☎ *905/356–5410* ⊕ *www.casamiaristorante.com* ⊟ *AE, MC, V.*

$$ ✕ **Edgewaters Tap & Grill.** Inside this
AMERICAN former refectory building, this sec-
ond-floor restaurant operated by
Niagara Parks has a huge veranda
overlooking the falls across Niag-
ara Parkway. The short menu con-
sists of burgers, salads, pasta, and
steaks, but the reason to visit is
clearly the location, in the center
of the action beside the falls and
often with live amplified music
accompanying dinner in summer.
✉ *Niagara Pkwy. at Murray St.*
☎ *905/356–2217* ▤ *AE, MC, V.*

$$$ ✕ **Elements on the Falls.** The view's the thing here. Run by Niagara Parks,
CANADIAN Elements serves locally sourced Canadian fare. The setting is extraordi-
nary—you sit perched at the edge of Horseshoe Falls, from behind tall
windows or from the terrace. (Window seats can't be reserved, but most
tables have good views.) The dining room is contemporary and whimsical, with swooping blue ceilings that suggest waves and pillars that
look like birch bark. The changing menu might include slow-roasted
prime rib, Ontario chicken breast stuffed with Oka cheese, red pepper,
and basil, or a Caesar salad with lemon-pepper-garlic-grilled shrimp.
✉ *Table Rock Centre, 6650 Niagara Pkwy., just above Journey Behind
the Falls* ☎ *905/354–3631* ⊕ *www.niagaraparks.com* ⌦ *Reservations
essential* ▤ *AE, MC, V.*

$$–$$$ ✕ **Lucky's.** The insulated 1920s-style dining room, tucked away from
AMERICAN the crowds, is a quiet setting in which to take a break from the casino.
★ The dinner-only menu includes garlic-rubbed thin-crust pizza, jumbo
prawns, steaks, sandwiches, and burgers. ✉ *Casino Niagara, 5705 Falls
Ave.* ☎ *905/374–3598* ▤ *AE, DC, MC, V* ☺ *No lunch.*

$$$$ ✕ **Skylon Tower.** The view from the Revolving Dining Room, perched at
AMERICAN 520 feet overlooking the Horseshoe Falls, is breathtaking, but entrées,
such as grilled salmon with hollandaise and filet mignon with béarnaise
sauce—receive less glowing reports. A dinner here is about the experience, not the cuisine. The crowd is eclectic, with a couple in cocktail
wear seated (rather compactly) beside a family in casual clothes. Even
with a reservation, there may be a short wait. Plan on spending at least
C$45 per person to dine in the tower. The Summit Suite Dining Room,
an all-you-can-eat buffet restaurant one level up, doesn't revolve, but
has comparable views for less (about C$40 prix-fixe for dinner with
dessert) and serves a Sunday brunch year-round. A reservation at either
restaurant includes free admission to the observation deck. ✉ *5200
Robinson St.* ☎ *905/356–2651 or 800/814–9577* ⊕ *www.skylon.com*
⌦ *Reservations essential* ▤ *AE, D, DC, MC, V* ☺ *Summit Suite Dining
Room closed Sept.–late May.*

8

WHERE TO STAY

Though there is no shortage of B&Bs in Niagara Falls, those in Niagara-on-the-Lake are generally far superior. If you're going the B&B route, lay your head 20 km (12 mi) north in Niagara-on-the-Lake instead and make the falls a day trip.

$$$　⊡ **Country Inn & Suites.** If you're on a budget but not willing to stay at a dingy motor lodge, this seven-story hotel that opened in 2007 is probably your best choice. Guests rave about the friendly staff and the cleanliness of the rooms, which are decorated in the generic, contemporary style of a chain hotel but have the advantage of being fairly new. Some rooms have Jacuzzi tubs (right in the room, not in the bathroom). **Pros:** low-cost parking for $6 a day; within walking distance of Clifton Hill and falls. **Cons:** few rooms have views. ⊠ *5525 Victoria Ave.* ☎ *905/374–6040 or 888/201–1746* ⊕ *www.countryinns.com/niagarafallson* ⊃ *49 rooms, 59 suites ☖ In-room: refrigerator (some), Internet. In-hotel: pool, gym, laundry facilities, public Internet, parking (paid), no-smoking rooms* ☰ *AE, D, MC, V* ⦿⦿ *CP.*

$$$　⊡ **Crowne Plaza/Niagara Falls–Fallsview.** Since its opening as the Hotel General Brock in the 1920s, this grande dame of Niagara hotels has hosted royalty, prime ministers, and Hollywood stars. The imposing, stone-walled hotel still has some glamorous details—like an enormous chandelier above a sweeping staircase in the lobby—and is part of the Casino Niagara complex, with indoor access to gaming facilities, the Hard Rock Cafe, and the Rainbow Room Fallsview Restaurant overlooking the falls. In contrast with the historic public spaces, rooms are contemporary: deep colors and dark wooden fixtures blend with expansive windows that offer views of the falls from nearly every room. They underwent major refurbishment in 2008, after the Brock became a Crowne Plaza hotel. **Pros:** great deals in winter; old-fashioned sophistication. **Cons:** views from Fallsview Boulevard are better. ⊠ *5685 Falls Ave.* ☎ *905/374–4447 or 800/263–7135* ⊕ *www.niagarafallscrowneplazahotel.com* ⊃ *227 rooms, 7 suites ☖ In-room: refrigerators (some), Wi-Fi. In-hotel: restaurant, room service, bar, pool, concierge, Internet terminal, public Wi-Fi, parking (paid), no-smoking rooms* ☰ *AE, D, DC, MC, V.*

$$$$　⊡ **Fallsview Casino Resort.** The C$1 billion price tag of this casino-resort means there are touches of luxury everywhere: natural light streams through glass domes and floor-to-ceiling windows, chandeliers hang in grand hallways, and frescoes lend an aristocratic feel. All bright and colorful rooms in this 30-story hotel tower overlook the Horseshoe or American-side falls. VIP rooms have extra-large whirlpool tubs. The hotel is in a mall-casino-entertainment complex with restaurants, clothing stores, and the Avalon Ballroom, hosting big-name music and comedy acts. The romantic 17 Noir ($$$$) restaurant is one of Niagara Falls' best, but there are many other options in the Galleria mall in the same complex, such as the Grand Buffet with an all-you-can-eat dinner for C$22. The spa has a full range of massages and facials, as well as wraps and Vichy treatments. **Pros:** first-class accommodation; great entertainment; the most glamorous address in Niagara Falls. **Cons:** overwhelming popularity means rooms fill up fast. ⊠ *6380 Fallsview*

Blvd. ☎905/358–3255 or 888/946–3255 ⊕ www.fallsviewcasinoresort. com ↩289 rooms, 85 suites ☒ In-room: safe, kitchen (some), refrigerator (some), Internet. In-hotel: 12 restaurants, room service, pool, gym, spa, concierge, laundry service, executive floor, public Internet, Wi-Fi, parking (paid), no-smoking rooms ☰AE, MC, V.

$$$ ★ ☒ **Sheraton Fallsview Hotel and Conference Centre.** Most of the oversize guest rooms and suites in this upscale high-rise hotel have breathtaking views of the falls, and even basic family suites have wall-to-wall floor-to-ceiling windows that overlook the cascades. Loft Suites are spacious, and the Whirlpool Rooms have open whirlpool baths that look out to the bedroom and the falls beyond. A Cut Above Steakhouse has a daily breakfast buffet and à la carte lunch and dinner entrées. **Pros:** family rooms available; stellar views; convenient to Fallsview Casino. **Cons:** busy; impersonal service; daily charge for Internet. ⊠ *6755 Fallsview Blvd. ☎905/374–1077 or 800/618–9059 ⊕ www.fallsview.com ↩369 rooms, 38 suites ☒ In-room: safe (some), refrigerator, Internet terminal, public Wi-Fi. In-hotel: restaurant, bar, pool, gym, parking (paid), no-smoking rooms ☰AE, D, DC, MC, V.*

BIKING AND HIKING

The **Niagara Parks Commission** (☎905/371–0254 or 877/642–7275 ⊕ *www.niagaraparks.com*) has information on hiking and biking trails, local parks, and the Niagara Gorge. **Ontario Trails Council** (☎877/668–7245 or 613/389–7678 ⊕ *www.ontariotrails.on.ca*) has information and maps about hikes in the province.

★ The **Bruce Trail** stretches 885 km (550 mi) along the Niagara Escarpment, with an additional 400 km (250 mi) of side trails. It takes in scenery from the orchards and vineyards of the Niagara Escarpment—one of Canada's 15 UNESCO World Biosphere Reserves—to the craggy cliffs and bluffs at Tobermory, 370 km (230 mi) north of Niagara-on-the-Lake. You can access the hiking trail at just about any point along the route; the main trail is marked with white blazes, the side trails with blue blazes. Consult the *Bruce Trail Reference Guide*, available from the **Bruce Trail Conservancy** (☎905/529–6821 or 800/665–4453 ⊕ *www.brucetrail.org*) when hiking the trail. Northern parts of the trail are remote.

The 82.5-acre **Niagara Glen** (⊕ *www.niagaraparks.com/nature*) nature reserve has 4 km (2.5mi) of hiking trails through forested paths that pass giant boulders left behind as the falls eroded the land away thousands of years ago. Some trails are steep and rough, and the Glen has an elevation change of more than 200 feet.

The **Niagara Parkway & Niagara River Recreation Trail** (⊕ *www.niagaraparks.com/nature*) is 56 km (35 mi) of bicycle trails along the Niagara River from Fort Erie to Niagara-on-the-Lake. The terrain can be steep and rugged in parts.

8

NIAGARA-ON-THE-LAKE AND THE WINE REGION

15 km (9 mi) north of Niagara Falls and 130 km (80 mi) south of Toronto.

Ontarians have been growing Concord grapes for (sweet) wine in the Niagara region since the 1800s, but experiments with European *Vitis vinifera* species between the 1950s and '70s led to more serious wine production. As the quality of Ontario wines continues to improve and wines excel in international competitions, winemakers here have caught the attention of a growing number of wine lovers.

Today, the Niagara Peninsula is Canada's largest viticultural area, accounting for nearly 75% of the country's wine production and 85% of Ontario's VQA wines (⇨ *See Ontario Wine and "VQA" box*). The unique position of the Niagara appellation, wedged between Lake Ontario and the Niagara Escarpment, creates a microclimate that regulates the ground and air temperature. Winds blow off Lake Ontario and are reflected back by the escarpment, preventing cold air from settling. Heat stored in lake waters over the summer keeps ground temperatures warmer longer going into winter, and in spring, the cold waters keep the grounds from warming too fast and ruining buds with late-spring frosts. Some say that the slightly colder climate produces a more complex-tasting grape.

The hub of the Wine Region is the town of Niagara-on-the-Lake (NOTL). Since 1962 it has been considered the southern outpost of fine summer theater in Ontario because of its acclaimed Shaw Festival. But it offers more than Stratford, its older theatrical sister to the west. As one of the country's prettiest and best-preserved Victorian towns, Niagara-on-the-Lake has architectural sights, shops, flower-lined streets and plentiful ornamental gardens in summer, and quality theater nearly year-round. The town of 14,000 is worth a visit at any time of the year for its inns, restaurants, and proximity to the wineries, but the most compelling time to visit is from April through November, during the Shaw Festival. The majority of area wineries have tastings and tours, in addition to selling their products on-site. Though the retail stores may open as early as 10, tastings usually begin at 11.

GETTING HERE AND AROUND

From Buffalo or Toronto, Niagara-on-the-Lake is easily reached via the QEW. From Niagara Falls or Lewiston, take the Niagara Parkway.

Niagara-on-the-Lake is a very small town that can easily be explored on foot. Parking in downtown Niagara-on-the-Lake can be nightmarish if you aren't staying in a centrally located hotel or B&B with parking. Parking along the main streets is metered, at C$1 or C$1.50 per hour. Outside the historic downtown parking is free, but still limited.

The Niagara Peninsula's 60 wineries are found between Grimsby and Niagara-on-the-Lake, up to 16 km (10 mi) inland from Lake Ontario, but most are concentrated around Niagara-on-the-Lake or Vineland.

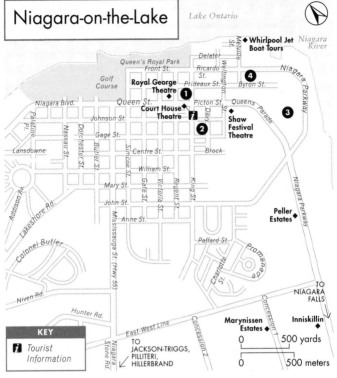

TOURS

Sentineal Carriages conducts year-round tours in and around Niagara-on-the-Lake. Catch a carriage at the Prince of Wales hotel or make a reservation for a pick-up. The private, narrated tours are C$45 for 15 minutes, C$65 for 30 minutes, and C$90 for 45 minutes (prices are per carriage).

BICYCLE TOURS Biking through the Niagara Region in any direction brings a touch of adventure as well as the opportunity to linger a while longer at each stop along the Wine Route. Bring sunscreen and sunglasses and be prepared for a few hills. Stiff-sole shoes for hard pedaling over rough terrain are recommended. Niagara Wine Tours International and Zoom rent bikes as well.

Niagara Wine Tours International leads several daylong and afternoon guided bike tours along the Wine Route for C$65–C$120. Bike rentals are C$30 per day; overnight packages are also offered.

Zoom Leisure runs several daylong winery tours—including a Beer & Wine Tour—ranging from C$69 to C$99 per person, and organizes custom guided and self-guided tours. Bike rentals are C$30 per day.

WINERY TOURS Many Niagara region hotels have wine-tour packages. Crush on Niagara packages include overnight stays, meals, and winery tours. Grape and Wine Tours runs day trips and one- and two-night packages.

CLOSE UP

Ontario's Ice Wines: Sweet Sippings

Ontario is the world's leading producer of ice wine, a product inspired by Niagara's hot late summers and bracing winters. Ice wine is produced from ripe grapes left on the vine into the winter. When the grapes start to freeze, most of the water in them turns solid, resulting in a fructose-laden, aromatic, and flavorful center. Temperatures must be -8°C (18°F) for at least 24 hours for this process to occur. Ice-wine grapes must be picked at freezing temperatures before sunrise and basket-pressed immediately to assure best results. The juice is allowed to settle for three to four days. Then it is clarified and slowly fermented using specially cultivated yeasts. By nature ice wine is sweet, but when well made, this nectar smells of dried fruits, apricots, and honey and finishes with a long, refreshing aftertaste.

For ice wine most Ontario winemakers prefer Vidal grapes, due to their thick skin and resistance to cracking in subzero temperatures. The thin-skinned Riesling yields better results but is susceptible to cracking and ripens much later than Vidal. Niagara wineries specializing in ice wine also use gewürztraminer, pinot noir, pinot gris, cabernet franc, chardonnay, gamay, merlot, and kerner.

Most experts advise drinking ice wine as a dessert or with a not-overly sweet dessert, though you might also try it with a strong cheese. But when it comes to ice wine, area entrepreneurs and chefs think outside the bottle as well, with ice-wine tea, chocolate, ice cream, and ice-wine sauces and glazes for meat and seafood.

ESSENTIALS

Tour Contacts Crush on Niagara (☎ 905/562–3373 or 866/408–9463 ⊕ www. crushtours.com). **Grape and Wine Tours** (☎ 905/562–9449 or 866/562–9449 ⊕ www.grapeandwinetours.com). **Niagara Wine Tours International** (✉ 92 Picton St., Niagara-on-the-Lake ☎ 905/468–1300 or 800/680–7006 ⊕ www. niagaraworldwinetours.com). **Sentineal Carriages** (☎ 905/468–4943 ⊕ www. sentinealcarriages.ca). **Zoom Leisure** (✉ 431 Mississauga St. ☎ 905/468–2366 or 866/811–6993 ⊕ www.zoomleisure.com).

Visitor Information Niagara-on-the-Lake Chamber of Commerce and Visitor & Convention Bureau (✉ 26 Queen St., Niagara-on-the-Lake ☎ 905/468–1950 ⊕ www.niagaraonthelake.com).

TOP EXPERIENCE: WINERIES

Niagara Wine Festival (☎ 905/688–0212 ⊕ www.niagarawinefestival.com). Several events honor Niagara's wine-making history: the 10-day **Niagara Ice Wine Festival, in** January; the two-weekend **Niagara New Vintage Festival** in June; and the 10-day Niagara Wine Festival, in late September. Festivals usually include gala events, food-and-wine pairings, tours and tastings, and musical performances. The Niagara Wine Festival has the biggest buzz: it honors the annual grape harvest and is one of Canada's largest annual celebrations, presenting more than 100 wine and culinary events, and attracting more than 500,000 people to the host city of St. Catharines and the adjoining Niagara Region.

Fodor's Choice   **Ontario Wine Route.** A well-marked strip of highway between Hamilton and
★   Niagara Falls takes you onto some secondary roads passing the region's
attractive scenery and through postcard-perfect small towns and villages.

From Toronto, take the QEW west and follow the signs for Niagara
Falls until just past Hamilton. Exit the QEW at 50 Road and follow
it south, turning east onto Highway 8, which becomes Regional Road
81. This route takes you past wineries, large and small, through the
towns of Grimsby, Beamsville, and the appropriately named town of
Vineland, as it climbs the Niagara Escarpment past woods and vineyards to the hamlet of Jordan (in addition to the wineries here, there
are antiques and specialty shops housed in historic buildings). East of
Jordan, the Wine Route turns south on 5th Street and then goes east on
8th Avenue to join Regional Road 89, which goes through the city of
St. Catharines before swinging north again on Four Mile Creek Road
toward Niagara-on-the-Lake. Several wineries have full-service upscale
restaurants. Some have patio wine bars and picnic facilities. ■ TIP➔ For
a full map of the wine route, pick up the free *Official Guide to the Wineries
of Ontario,* updated yearly, at the tourism board or at various attractions.
You can also download it or order it from the **Wine Council of Ontario**
(☎ 905/684–8070 ⊕ *www.winesofontario.org*).

Hillebrand Estates Winery. With more than 300 wine awards, this highly
commercial winery—one of Niagara's first—produces many excellent
varieties: small batches of pinot noir, chardonnay, ice wine, and more.
Its 2007 Trius brut has taken several top prizes at wine competitions.
After the half-hour cellar and vineyard tour for C$7 are three compli-
mentary tastings of this vintner's latest achievements. The upscale café
serves terrific meals. You can attend various themed seminars offered
daily for C$10–C$30 per seminar, including one in which you make
your own Trius red. ⊠ *1249 Niagara Stone Rd., Niagara-on-the-Lake*
☎ *905/468–7123 or 800/582–8412* ⊕ *www.hillebrand.com* ☉ *Oct.–May,
daily 10–7; June–Sept., daily 10–9. Tours daily every hr on hr: Nov.–Apr.
11–5; May, June, and Oct. 11–6; July–Sept. 11–8.*

Jackson-Triggs Niagara Estate Winery. An ultramodern facility blends state-
of-the-art wine-making technology with age-old, handcrafted enological
savvy. Prizes have included several bronze awards at the Decanter World
Wine Awards in 2008 (for a meritage, merlot, and sauvignon blanc)
and the Rosemount Estate Trophy for Best Shiraz award at the International Wines and Spirits competition in England in 2006. Its premium
VQA wines can be sipped in the tasting gallery and purchased in the
retail boutique. ■ TIP➔ If you're a wine-making newbie, Jackson-Triggs'
tour for C$5 might be one of the most informative around and is a good first
stop. The tour includes three tastings and a mini-lesson in wine tasting. ⊠ *2145 Niagara Stone Rd., Niagara-on-the-Lake* ☎ *905/468–4637
or 866/589–4637* ⊕ *www.jacksontriggswinery.com* ☉ *May–Oct., daily
10:30–6:30; Nov.–Apr., daily 10:30–5:30. Tours daily 10:30–5:30.*

Marynissen Estates. An in-the-know favorite in the small-scale winery
genre, this family-owned property is lauded for its affable service and
for its quality, good-value VQA wines, including a sauvignon blanc,
pinot gris, merlot, pinot noir, and cabernet blends. Though in town, the

8

winery and its single-story wooden provincial building is in a rural area. ⊠ *Concession Rd. 1, off East-West Line, between Line 3 and Larkin Rd.* ☎ *905/468-7270* ⊕ *www.marynis-sen.com* ⊙ *Daily 10–6.*

Pillitteri Estates Winery. This ice-wine producer with more than 400 medals in domestic and international competitions is also famous for its unique ice wine made from grapes harvested far later in winter than those of most other producers. With just 58 acres (compared to 800 acres for a large producer like Jackson-Triggs) of vineyards, Pillitteri is a mid-size family-owned operation. Free tours include two complimentary tastings. ⊠ *1696 Niagara Stone Rd.* ☎ *905/468-3147* ⊕ *www.pil-litteri.com* ⊙ *May 15–Oct. 15, daily 10–8; Oct. 16–May 14, daily 10–6. Tours daily at noon and 2.*

> ### ONTARIO WINE AND VQA
>
> Many Niagara wineries proudly declare their vintages "VQA," a designation awarded by the Vintners Quality Alliance of Ontario, the province's ultimate wine authority. VQA wines must meet rigorous standards that include being made entirely from fresh, quality-approved Ontario-grown grapes (no concentrates) and getting the green light by a panel of expert tasters prior to release. Look for the VQA stamp on the label.

★ **Vineland Estates Winery.** One of Ontario's most beautiful wineries occupies 75 acres that were once a Mennonite homestead established in 1845. The original buildings have been transformed into the visitor center and production complex. Several tour and tasting options are available, including wine and cheese tour and tasting for C$15. The excellent Restaurant@Vineland Estates Winery serves lunch and dinner, and the patio grill is open July through September. There is also a guesthouse and a bed-and-breakfast cottage on the property. ⊠ *3620 Moyer Rd., Vineland, 40 km (25 mi) west of Niagara-on-the-Lake* ☎ *905/562-7088 or 888/846-3526* ⊕ *www.vineland.com* ⊙ *Most days 10–6; call or check Web site for details. Public tours mid-May–Oct., daily at 11 and 3; Nov.–mid-May, weekends at 3. Private tours by request.*

EXPLORING

★ **Queen Street.** The core of the commercial portion; you can get a glimpse of the town's architectural history walking east along that single street, with Lake Ontario to your north. At No. 209 is the handsome Charles Inn, built in 1832 for a member of Parliament, with later additions at the end of the 19th century. No. 165 is an 1820 beauty, and No. 157 was built in 1817.

❶ **Niagara Apothecary.** Restored to look like a 19th-century pharmacy that opened here in 1869, glass-fronted walnut cabinets display vintage remedies such as Merrill's System Tonic (which "Purifies the Blood and Builds up the System"). Among the boxes and bottles is a rare collection of apothecary flasks. ⊠ *5 Queen St.* ☎ *905/468-3845* ⊕ *www. niagaraapothecary.ca* ⊠ *Free* ⊙ *Mid-May–June and early Sept., daily noon–6; July and Aug., daily 11–6, early Sept.–2nd Mon. in Oct., weekends noon–6.*

② Niagara Historical Society & Museum. In connected side-by-side buildings, one the 1875 former Niagara High School building and one the first building in Ontario to have been erected as a museum, in 1906, this extensive collection relates to the

WORD OF MOUTH

"Niagara-on-the-Lake is special in its own way. It is like stepping back in history." —prinret

often colorful history of the Niagara Peninsula from earliest times through the 19th century. The museum leads guided walking tours of the town (C$5). ⊠ *43 Castlereagh St.* ☎ *905/468–3912* ⊕ *www.niagarahistorical. museum* ⌸ *C$5* ⊙ *May–Oct., daily 10–5; Nov.–Apr., daily 1–5.*

❸ Fort George National Historic Site. On a wide stretch of parkland south of
♻ town sits the fort that was built in the 1790s but was lost to the Yan-
Fodor's Choice kees during the War of 1812. It was recaptured after the burning of the
★ town in 1813 and largely survived the war, only to fall into ruins by the 1830s. It was reconstructed a century later, and you can explore the officers' quarters, the barracks rooms of the common soldiers, the kitchen, and more. Staff in period uniform conduct tours and reenact 19th-century infantry and artillery drills. ⊠ *Queens Parade, Niagara Pkwy.* ☎ *905/468–4257* ⊕ *www.pc.gc.ca/lhn-nhs/on/fortgeorge* ⌸ *C$11.70* ⊙ *May–Oct., daily 10–5, Apr. and Nov. weekends 10–5.*

❹ St. Mark's Church. One of Ontario's oldest Anglican churches, built in 1804, St. Marks' parish is even older, formed in 1792. The stone church still houses the founding minister's original library of 1,500 books, brought from England. During the War of 1812, American soldiers used the church as a barracks, and still-visible rifle pits were dug in the cemetery. The church is open for concerts, lectures, and Sunday services only. ⊠ *41 Byron St.* ☎ *905/468–3123* ⊕ *www.stmarks1792.com.*

WHERE TO EAT

A number of wineries here have restaurants. Especially in summer, make reservations whenever possible. Many restaurants serve dinner only until 9 PM.

$$ ✕ **Fans Court.** Delicate Cantonese cuisine is prepared in an antiques-filled
CHINESE restaurant in a courtyard between an art gallery and a greenhouse. Miniature evergreens in urns stand at the entrance. In summer you can sit outdoors and sample such favorites as lemon chicken, black-pepper-and-garlic beef, and shrimp fried rice served in a pineapple. ⊠ *135 Queen St.* ☎ *905/468–4511* ⊟ *AE, MC, V.*

$$$$ ✕ **Hillebrand Winery Restaurant.** After a complimentary winery tour and
FRENCH tasting, you can settle down to a superb meal. Culinary masterpieces
★ have included Atlantic salt cod and potato ravioli or duck confit *rilette* and French green lentils with smoked bacon.The menu changes every six weeks. The tossed salad is a beautiful composition of organic greens, sundried blueberries, and roasted crisp garlic. Several tasting menus are available. The pastry chef's desserts, such as a dark-chocolate molten cake with double-chocolate ice-wine ice cream, are incredible, too. ⊠ *1249 Niagara Stone Rd., at Hwy. 55* ☎ *905/468–7123 or 800/582–8412* ⊕ *www.hillebrand.com* ⊟ *AE, DC, MC, V.*

8

$$$$ X **Inn on the Twenty Restaurant.** Regional
CONTINENTAL specialties and local and organic produce are emphasized on this season-
ally changing menu. Dine on grilled
Ontario striploin with Yukon-gold-
and-chive hash or fennel-pollen-and-
milk-poached whitefish with chant-
erelle risotto in an airy cottage-style
room with exposed beams, crisp
white linens, and huge windows.
Cave Spring Cellars, overlooking
Twenty Valley, provides many of the wines, including custom blends for
Inn on the Twenty. ✉ *3836 Main St., Jordan* ☎ *905/562–7313* ⊕ *www.*
innonthetwenty.com ⊟ *AE, MC, V.*

> **DID YOU KNOW?**
>
> The moderate climate of the Niag-
> ara region doesn't benefit only
> grapes: about 40% of Canada's
> apples and 70% of its peaches
> as well as berries, cherries, are
> grown in an area smaller than
> Rhode Island.

$$ X **Olde Angel Inn.** This British-style tavern inside Ontario's oldest operat-
CONTINENTAL ing inn sets out pub fare such as shepherd's pie, bangers and mash, and
★ steak Guinness with onion pie. Entrées include the house specialty prime
rib of beef au jus with Yorkshire pudding. Seating is in the dining room,
the pub, or the "snug" (lounge). Two-dozen domestic and imported
(European) brews are on tap. The pub has live music, ranging from
Celtic to '90s covers, on Friday and Saturday beginning at 9:30. ✉ *224*
Regent St. ☎ *905/468–3411* ⊕ *www.angel-inn.com* ⊟ *AE, D, MC, V.*

$$$$ X **Peller Estates Winery Restaurant.** Frequently cited as the best restaurant in
CONTINENTAL NOTL—an impressive feat in a town with many excellent restaurants—
★ Peller manages refinement without arrogance. The stately colonial revival
dining room is anchored by a huge fireplace at one end and has windows
running the length of the room overlooking a large patio and the estate
vineyards. A menu of ever-changing expertly prepared lunch and dinner
entrées has included succulently tender diver scallops with pancetta in a
tomato-and-tarragon sauce, cabernet-braised rib eye with lobster knuckles
and tomato risotto, and presalted grape-mustard-and-chervil-crusted lamb
with a goat-milk soufflé. Tasting menus are available at lunch and dinner.
Inventive desserts have included a honey-lemon soufflé with cardomom
crème anglaise. ✉ *290 John St. E* ☎ *905/468–4678* ⊕ *www.peller.com*
⌖ *Resevations essential* ⊟ *AE, D, DC, MC, V.*

$$$$ X **Restaurant @ Vineland Estates Winery.** Exquisite Italian food and vener-
CONTINENTAL able wines are served by an enthusiastic staff on the large outdoor patio
Fodor's Choice overlooking Lake Ontario or in the glassed-in restaurant, with a pan-
★ oramic view of the vineyard and lake. The menu is locally sourced and
seasonal; three-course dinners feature mushroom-and-thyme-chèvre
ravioli in truffle broth and a salad of peppery greens, Niagara dried
fruit, and pecorino. Feeling carnivorous? The chef might grill and ale-
braise an Ontario pork loin and serve it with a smoked bacon jus.
Desserts are a happy marriage of local fruits and an imaginative pastry
chef. The restaurant is in the Twenty Valley wine area, 40 km (25 mi)
west of Niagara-on-the-Lake. ✉ *3620 Moyer Rd., Vineland* ☎ *905/562–*
7088 Ext. 25 or 888/846–3526 ⊕ *www.vineland.com* ⊟ *AE, D, MC,*
V ☺ *Closed Mon. and Tues. Nov.–May.*

$$$$ X **Ristorante Giardino.** Italian marble combines with stainless steel and
ITALIAN rich colors to create a contemporary Italian setting on 19th-century

Queen Street. Italian-trained chefs produce antipasti such as thin-sliced smoked duck breast and classic Caprese salad. There's always fresh-made pasta, grilled fish, chicken, veal, and lamb. Make time to indulge in the kitchen's classic Italian desserts. The long wine list is worth a careful read. ⊠ *Gate House Hotel, 142 Queen St.* ☎ *905/468–3263* ⊕ *www. gatehouse-niagara.com* ⊟ *AE, DC, MC, V* ☺ *Closed Jan.–mid-Mar.*

$$$$
CANADIAN

✕ **Tiara Restaurant at Queen's Landing.** Overlooking the Niagara River, Tiara has an outstanding regional menu that makes good use of Niagara produce, in a room that is flattered by a stained-glass ceiling, near-panoramic windows, and warm amber hues. The chef's Europe-meets-West Coast menu features seafood, and sea bass is a specialty. Nearly every table has a water view. ⊠ *155 Byron St.* ☎ *905/468–2195 or 888/669–5566* ⊕ *www. vintage-inns.com* ⌂ *Reservations essential* ⊟ *AE, D, DC, MC, V.*

$$$$
ECLECTIC

✕ **Zee's Grill.** For alfresco dining, it's hard to beat Zee's huge wrap-around patio with heat lamps across from Shaw Festival Theatre. The seasonal, creative menu mixes homegrown comfort foods with global flavors in starters like *poutine* (fries, gravy, and cheese curds) with Nova Scotia lobster, grilled Ontario lamb sirloin with fresh mint and spring-pea risotto. Zee's is more informal than most similarly priced restaurants in NOTL. ⊠ *92 Picton St.* ☎ *905/468–5715* ⊕ *www.zees. ca* ⌂ *Reservations essential* ⊟ *AE, D, MC, V* ☺ *Closed Nov.–mid-Apr. No lunch weekdays.*

WHERE TO STAY

Though the Vintage Hotels (Queen's Landing, Prince of Wales, Pillar & Post) are some of the priciest in NOTL, they have excellent online deals and packages, sometimes shaving hundreds of dollars off the rate.

8

The Niagara Wine Region may be Canada's B&B capital, with more than 100 in Niagara-on-the-Lake alone. Their service and quality can rival some of the priciest hotels. For B&B listings, contact the **Niagara-on-the-Lake Bed & Breakfast Association** (☎ *905/468–0123 or 866/855– 0123* ⊕ *niagarabedandbreakfasts.com*). The **Niagara-on-the-Lake Historic Bed & Breakfasts** (⊕ *www.historicbb.com*) Web site maintains a list of historic B&Bs, all built before 1850 and all within two blocks from Queen–Picton Street, the center-of-town shopping and dining strip.

$$$$
★

▦ **The Charles Inn.** An air of old-fashioned civility permeates this 1832 Georgian gem. Spend summer evenings playing board games on the outdoor patio, and then dine on some of the best food to be found in the area. Wood-burning fireplaces, and a mixture of 19th-century antique and reproduction furniture add to the period charm of the large, bright rooms. Many rooms have doors onto the upper veranda. In the dining room, chef William Brunyansky crafts exquisite dishes. Many, such as pan-seared salmon Wellington with a wild mushroom tart and chive-and-white-wine cream, draw from the produce of the area. **Pros:** reliable lodging and dining; intimate and comfortable. **Cons:** some historic "quirks" like variable water temperature; some verandas are connected. ⊠ *209 Queen St.* ☎ *905/468–4588 or 866/556–8883* ⊕ *www.charles-inn.ca* ⤣ *12 rooms* ⌂ *In-room: Internet, Wi-Fi. In-hotel: restaurant, room service, no elevator, laundry service, parking (free), no-smoking rooms* ⊟ *AE, MC, V* ⊚⊫ *BP.*

$$$$ ⊡ **Harbour House.** A classy contemporary-cottage theme pervades this
Fodor's Choice luxurious boutique hotel one block from the Niagara River. The build-
★ ing's maritime, cedar-shingled look is topped off with a gambrel roof.
Spacious rooms have cozy touches like gas fireplaces, king-size feather-
top beds, and Frette robes, as well as DVD and CD players. You can
sample local preserves and homemade pastries at breakfast and attend
wine-and-cheese tastings in the afternoon. This is a good alternative to
the myriad B&Bs in town and the perfect place to splurge. **Pros:** staff
cater to every need; shared facilities (restaurant, spa, gym) with sister
properties Shaw Club and the Charles Inn. **Cons:** no restaurant, gym,
or spa on-site. ⊠ 85 Melville St. ☎ 905/468–4683 or 866/277–6677
⊕ www.harbourhousehotel.ca ⇨ 28 rooms, 3 suites ♿ In-room: Internet, Wi-Fi. In-hotel: public Internet, public Wi-Fi, parking (free), no-
smoking rooms ⊟ AE, MC, V ⟨○⟩ BP.

$$$$ ⊡ **Inn on the Twenty.** The inn is part of Leonard Pennachetti's Cave Spring
Cellars winery in the village of Jordan, a 30-minute drive from Niagara-
on-the-Lake. Suites have elegant 1920s mahogany headboards, whirlpool baths, and gas fireplaces; some have private gardens. Two suites
are in the separate clapboard Winemaker's Cottage, and two smaller
rooms are in the 1840 brick Vintage House, both just beside the inn.
The sophisticated restaurant ($$$$) has top-notch cuisine. **Pros:** rustic
allure; great service. **Cons:** a little away from the action. ⊠ 3845 Main
St., Jordan, off QEW Exit 55 or 57 ☎ 905/562–5336 or 800/701–8074
⊕ www.innonthetwenty.com ⇨ 2 rooms, 26 suites ♿ In-room: Internet, Wi-Fi (some). In-hotel: restaurant, Internet terminal, public Wi-Fi,
parking (free), no-smoking rooms ⊟ AE, DC, MC, V ⟨○⟩ CP.

$$$ ⊡ **Moffat Inn.** Some of the rooms at this charmer have original 1835 fire-
places, outdoor patios, brass beds, and wicker furniture. The indepen-
dent on-site restaurant, Tetley's, serves a variety of fondues, and meat or
seafood cooked on hot granite rocks. Vintage Hotels, which owns lux-
ury properties Prince of Wales and Queens Landing, purchased the Mof-
fat in late 2007; nondisruptive improvements are ongoing but pricing
will remain moderate. **Pros:** unpretentious; comfortable; clean. **Cons:**
rooms not as tony as other NOTL hotels; restaurant has erratic hours.
⊠ 60 Picton St. ☎ 905/468–4116 or 888/669–5566 ⊕ www.moffatinn.
com ⇨ 23 rooms, 1 apartment ♿ In-room: Wi-Fi. In-hotel: restaurant,
no elevator, parking (free), no-smoking rooms ⊟ AE, MC, V.

$$ ⊡ **Olde Angel Inn.** Though established in 1779, this coach-house inn
★ burned down during the War of 1812. Its current lemon-yellow incarna-
tion dates to 1816. Rooms have hardwood floors and rustic old-world
decor; two rooms have only a shower (no tub). The cottages, with
sofabeds, fireplaces, and kitchens, are the superior accommodations.
The English-style tavern ($$) sets out excellent British pub fare. **Pros:**
deservedly popular restaurant on-site; all rooms renovated in 2008.
Cons: parking for cottages only; historic nature of inn means poor
soundproofing (plan on staying up until the pub closes on weekends).
⊠ 224 Regent St. ☎ 905/468–3411 ⊕ www.angel-inn.com ⇨ 3 rooms,
2 suites, 2 cottages ♿ In-hotel: restaurant, bar, no elevator, no-smoking
rooms ⊟ AE, D, MC, V.

$$$$ ⛆ **Prince of Wales.** A visit from the Prince of Wales in 1901 inspired the
Fodor's Choice   name of this venerable hostelry that still welcomes the occasional royal
★   guest or film star (North American royalty). Designed in the style of an
upper-crust English manor house, the Prince of Wales is Victorian in flavor, complete with its own tearoom. All rooms have Tiffany lamps and
may be decked out with brocade draperies, four-poster beds, fireplaces,
and tufted Queen Anne chairs. There are plenty of ways to pamper
yourself too, such as with a green-tea-and-sugarcane pedicure in the
Secret Garden Spa, high tea in the Victorian-style Drawing Room, or
a meal at the highly acclaimed Escabèche restaurant. **Pros:** great range
of spa packages; beautiful facade. **Cons:** some rooms dark and small.
✉ *6 Picton St.* ☎ *905/468–3246 or 888/669–5566* ⊕ *www.vintage-
hotels.com* ⮑ *110 rooms* ☁ *In-room: safe, Wi-Fi. In-hotel: restaurant,
bar, room service, pool, gym, concierge, parking (paid), spa, some pets
allowed, no-smoking rooms* ▭ *AE, D, DC, MC, V.*

$$$$ ⛆ **Queen's Landing.** About half of the rooms at this Georgian-style mansion
have knockout views of the fields of historic Fort George or the marina—
ask for one when making a reservation. Rooms, renovated in 2008, are
elegant, with a contemporary waterfront decor; many have working fireplaces and jetted tubs. The Tiara Restaurant ($$$$) is excellent. **Pros:** great
location; classic lakeside views. **Cons:** pricey restaurant; some rooms have
parking lot views. ✉ *155 Byron St.* ☎ *905/468–2195 or 888/669–5566*
⊕ *www.vintage-hotels.com* ⮑ *142 rooms* ☁ *In-room: safe, Wi-Fi. In-
hotel: restaurant, bar, room service, pool, gym, concierge, parking (free),
some pets allowed, no-smoking rooms* ▭ *AE, D, DC, MC, V.*

$$$$ ⛆ **Riverbend Inn & Vineyard.** Surrounded by its own private vineyard,
★   this restored palatial 1860s Georgian-style mansion, opened in 2004,
was a local art gallery and still magnificently showcases some artful
gems. Gas fireplaces, dark woods, and rich tones of gold and wine add
to the upscale elegance of the suites and rooms. The airy, open restaurant overlooks the vineyard and relies heavily on fresh local ingredients. Sit back by the fireside and enjoy the formal but casual setting.
Pros: private vineyard adds character; all rooms have pleasant views
of the vineyards or front gardens. **Cons:** far from downtown; service in
the restaurant can be slow. ✉ *16104 Niagara Pkwy.* ☎ *905/468–8866
or 888/955–5553* ⊕ *www.riverbendinn.ca* ⮑ *19 rooms, 2 suites* ☁ *In-
room: Internet. In-hotel: restaurant, room service, bar, public Wi-Fi,
parking (free), no-smoking rooms* ▭ *AE, D, DC, MC, V.*

$$$$ ⛆ **Shaw Club Hotel & Spa.** Rooms at this contemporary boutique hotel,
many with fireplaces, are sleek and gorgeous, with oversize artwork. The
modern theme continues with iPod docks, bathrooms with TVs, 42-inch
plasma TVs in bedrooms, surround sound, and complimentary cappuccinos and Wi-Fi. Rooms in the Annex, next door, have a somewhat
less-impressive, contemporary decor but have fireplaces and Jacuzzi tubs
(albeit right in the bedroom). Standard rooms lack some perks, like plasma
TVs, and have an older, Victorian-style decor. The Shaw Festival Theatre is
right across the street. Zee's restaurant ($$$$) is popular, in particular for
its patio dining. **Pros:** dreamy beds; good restaurant; friendly staff. **Cons:**
standard and Annex rooms don't have the wow factor of other rooms
and public spaces. ✉ *92 Picton St.* ☎ *905/468–5711 or 800/511–7070*

8

⊕ *www.shawclub.com* ⤴ *30 rooms,
1 suite* ⌂ *In-rooms: refrigerator,
DVD, Internet (some), Wi-Fi. In-
hotel: gym, spa, public Internet, public Wi-Fi, parking (free), some pets
allowed, no-smoking rooms* ⊟ *AE,
D, DC, MC, V.*

NIGHTLIFE AND THE ARTS

Fodor's Choice
★

Niagara-on-the-Lake remained a
sleepy town until 1962, when local
lawyer Brian Doherty organized eight weekend performances of two
George Bernard Shaw plays, *Don Juan in Hell* and *Candida*. The next
year he helped found the **Shaw Festival,** whose mission is to perform
the works of Shaw and his contemporaries, who included Noël Cow-
ard, Bertolt Brecht, J.M. Barrie, J.M. Synge, and Chekov. The season
now runs from April through November with close to a dozen plays,
including some contemporary plays by Canadian playwrights, and one
or two musicals (which are performed un-miked). All are staged in one
of three theaters within a few blocks of one another. The handsome
Festival Theatre, the largest of the three, stands on Queen's Parade near
Wellington Street and houses the box office. The **Court House Theatre,**
on Queen Street between King and Regent streets, served as the town's
municipal offices from the 1840s until 1969, and is a national historic
site. At the corner of Queen and Victoria streets, the **Royal George Theatre** was originally built as a vaudeville house in 1915. ■ TIP→ **Regular-
price tickets cost C$30 to C$110, but discounts abound; see "Ways to Save"
on the Web site.** ⌖ *Shaw Festival Box Office, 10 Queen's Parade L0S
1J0* ☎ *905/468–2172 or 800/511–7429* ⊕ *www.shawfest.com.*

SHOPPING

Greaves Jams & Marmalades (✉ *55 Queen St., Niagara-on-the-Lake*
☎ *905/468–7831 or 800/515–9939* ⊕ *www.greavesjams.com*) makes
jams, jellies, and marmalades from mostly local produce using family
recipes, some of which have been around since the company began in
1927. The spreads have no preservatives, pectin, or additives.

**EN
ROUTE**

The Niagara Peninsula is Ontario's fruit basket. From midsummer to
late fall, roadside fruit and vegetable stands and farmers' markets are in
full bloom. Some of the best stands are on Highway 55, between Niagara-on-the-Lake and the QEW, and along Lakeshore Road, between
Niagara-on-the-Lake and St. Catharines.

Harvest Barn Country Markets (✉ *1822 Niagara Stone Rd./Hwy. 55, Niagara-on-the-Lake* ☎ *905/468–3224* ⊕ *www.harvestbarn.ca*), in a barn
with a red-and-white-striped awning, sells regional fruits and vegetables
and tempts with its baked goods: sausage rolls, bread, and fruit pies.
Join locals for lunch at the picnic tables.

Stratford,
Ontario

STRATFORD

145 km (90 mi) west of Toronto.

In July 1953 Alec Guinness, one of the world's greatest actors, joined with Tyrone Guthrie, probably the world's greatest Shakespearean director, beneath a hot, stuffy tent in a quiet town about a 90-minute drive from Toronto. This was the birth of the Stratford Shakespeare Festival, which now runs from April to early November and is one of the most successful and admired festivals of its kind.

The origins of Ontario's Stratford are modest. After the War of 1812, the British government granted a million acres of land along Lake Huron to the Canada Company, headed by a Scottish businessman. When the surveyors came to a marshy creek surrounded by a thick forest, they named it "Little Thames" and noted that it might make "a good mill-site." It was Thomas Mercer Jones, a director of the Canada Company, who decided to rename the river the Avon and the town Stratford. The year was 1832, 121 years before the concept of a theater festival would take flight and change Canadian culture.

For many years Stratford was considered a backwoods hamlet. Then came the first of two saviors of the city, both of them (undoubting) Thomases.

In 1904 an insurance broker named Tom Orr transformed Stratford's riverfront into a park. He also built a formal English garden, where flowers mentioned in the plays of Shakespeare—monkshood to sneezewort, bee balm to bachelor's button—blooms grandly to this day.

Next, Tom Patterson, a fourth-generation Stratfordian born in 1920, looked around; saw that the town wards and schools had names like Hamlet, Falstaff, and Romeo; and felt that some kind of drama festival might save his community from becoming a ghost town. The astonishing story of how he began in 1952 with C$125 (a "generous" grant from the Stratford City Council), tracked down Tyrone Guthrie and Alec Guinness, and somehow, in little more than a year, pasted together a long-standing theater festival is recounted in Patterson's memoirs, *First Stage: The Making of the Stratford Festival*.

Soon after it opened, it wowed critics from around the world with its professionalism, costumes, and daring thrust stage. The early years brought giants of world theater to the tiny town of some 20,000: James Mason, Alan Bates, Christopher Plummer, Jason Robards Jr., and Maggie Smith. Stratford's offerings are still among the best of their kind in the world, with at least a handful of productions every year that put most other summer arts festivals to shame. The *New York Times* always runs major write-ups, as do other newspapers and magazines in many American and Canadian cities.

Today Stratford is a city of 32,000 that welcomes more than 500,000 visitors annually for the Stratford Shakespeare Festival alone. Though some restaurants and other attractions are open only during the April-to-November festival season, there are quieter things to do when the theaters close. Art galleries remain open throughout winter. Shopping is good off-season, and those who love peaceful walks can stroll along the Avon. Many concerts are scheduled in the off-season, too.

GETTING HERE AND AROUND

Ontario's main east-west highway, the 401, which traverses the province all the way from the Michigan to Quebec borders, is the main route from Toronto to Kitchener-Waterloo; from there, Highway 7/8 heads to Stratford.

Stratford is an ideal town for crusing via bicycle. Totally Spoke'd rents cruisers and mountain bikes for C$35 per day and tandem bikes for C$45 per day.

ESSENTIALS

Bicycle Rental Totally Spoke'd (⊠ *29 Ontario St.* ☎ *519/273–2001* ⊕ *www.totallyspoked.ca*).

Visitor Information The Stratford Festival (⊠ *55 Queen St.* ☎ *519/273–1600 or 800/567–1600* ⊕ *www.stratfordfestival.ca*). **Stratford Tourism Alliance** (⊠ *47 Downie St.* ☎ *519/271–5140 or 800/561–7926* ⊕ *www.welcometo-stratford.com*).

EXPLORING

Gallery Stratford. Regular exhibits of Canadian visual art (some for sale) and, in summer, of theater arts are displayed here. ⌧ *54 Romeo St.* ☎ *519/271–5271* ⊕ *www.gallerystratford.on.ca* ⌧ *C$5* ☉ *Mid-Apr.– mid-Nov., Tues.–Sun. 10–5; mid-Nov.–mid-Apr., Tues.–Sun. noon–4.*

★ **Stratford Perth Museum.** You can brush up on Stratford and Perth County history with permanent displays and changing exhibits that cover such topics as hockey in Stratford, the city's railroad, and the settlement of the area in the early 1800s. There are hiking trails on the property. ⌧ *4275 Huron Rd.* ☎ *519/271–5311* ⊕ *www.stratfordperthmuseum.ca* ⌧ *By donation* ☉ *May–Aug., Tues.–Sat. 10–5, Sun. and Mon. noon–5; Sept.–Apr., Tues.–Sat. 10–4.*

WHERE TO EAT

$$ ✕ **Bentley's.** The well-stocked bar at this long and narrow British-style
BRITISH   pub divides the room into two equal halves, with the locals hovering on the east side. The pub fare has staples such as fish-and-chips, grilled steak and fries, and a few vegetarian options such as vegetable ravioli in roasted-red-pepper cream sauce. Regulars to this watering hole say they come for the imported, domestic, and microbrew beers, 18 of which are on tap—the easygoing clientele and camaraderie are bonuses. ⌧ *99 Ontario St.* ☎ *519/271–1121* ⊕ *www.bentleys-annex. com* ▭ *AE, MC, V.*

$$$$ ✕ **Bijou.** A husband-and-wife team, both Stratford Chefs School grads,
FRENCH   operates this small, self-professed "culinary gem," whose chalkboard menu changes daily. Modern French two- or three-course prix-fixe (for dinner) meals have an Asian twist: duck confit steamed in cabbage leaves with French lentils and bok choy may be an option for your main course. For dessert, there might be a banana tart tatin with black-pepper ice cream and caramel sauce. The entrance is a bit hidden, next to the Stratford Hotel, across a parking lot on Erie Street, or through Allen's Alley, off Wellington Street. ⌧ *105 Erie St.* ☎ *519/273–5000* ⊕ *www. bijourestaurant.com* ⌕ *Reservations essential* ▭ *AE, MC, V* ☉ *Closed Mon. No lunch Tues.–Thurs. or Nov.–May.*

¢   ✕ **Boomer's Gourmet Fries.** No time for leisurely dining? Boomer's,
AMERICAN   equipped with a take-out window and a handful of stools at a counter, speedily serves fries of every ilk (all cooked in canola oil with no preservatives), a dozen varieties of burgers, and scrumptious fish-and-chips year-round. Try one of the many unique and delicious takes on a Canadian "delicacy," *poutine:* the traditional version is fries topped with cheese curds and gravy. ⌧ *26 Erie St.* ☎ *519/275–3147* ⊕ *www. boomersgourmetfries.ca* ▭ *No credit cards* ☉ *Closed Sun. Nov.–Mar. and Mon. Nov.–Apr.*

$$$$ ✕ **Church Restaurant and Belfry.** It was constructed in 1873 as a Congre-
CANADIAN   gational church, but today white tablecloths gleam in the afternoon
★   light that pours through the stained-glass windows. Meals here are production numbers: porcini risotto, steak frites, thin-crust pizzas, and a burger with house barbecue sauce. The Belfry, upstairs, uses the same excellent kitchen, but the setting is casual, with small plates of veggie, meat, pasta, and fish dishes, such as miso-carmelized sablefish that can be combined, tapaslike. ⌧ *70 Brunswick St.* ☎ *519/273–3424*

8

🌐 *www.churchrestaurant.com* 🍴 *Reservations essential* 🗖 *AE, MC, V*
🕙 *Church closed Mon. and Jan.–Mar. Belfry closed Sun. and Mon. and*
Jan.–Mar.

$$–$$$ ✕ **Down the Street Bar and Restaurant.** Funky and informal, this bistro–bar
CANADIAN   is the hottest place in town, and a popular spot for the post-theater
crowd. Entrées on the seasonal menu, such as apple-brined pork chops,
make for delicious casual dining. Appetizers and entrées are served till
midnight. A comprehensive selection of imported and microbrew beers
is on tap. ⊠ *30 Ontario St.* ☎ *519/273–5886* 🍴 *Reservations essential*
🗖 *AE, MC, V* 🕙 *Closed Mon. Closed Sun. mid-Oct.–mid-June. No
lunch mid-Oct.–mid-May.*

$$$$ ✕ **The Old Prune.** A converted Victorian house holds a number of charm-
CANADIAN   ing dining rooms and a glass-enclosed conservatory surrounded by a
tidy courtyard. Chef Bryan Steele coaxes fresh local ingredients into
innovative dishes with the best of what's available globally: grilled
Clare Island salmon with white asparagus and a mint-and-mustard-
seed hollandaise, or locally raised beef rib eye with an artichoke-and-
tomato gratin. Desserts are baked fresh for each meal. ⊠ *151 Albert
St.* ☎ *519/271–5052* 🍴 *Reservations essential* 🌐 *www.oldprune.on.ca*
🗖 *AE, MC, V* 🕙 *Closed Nov.–mid-May and Mon. No lunch.*

$$–$$$ ✕ **Pazzo Ristorante and Pizzeria.** Stratford's main corner is home to one
ITALIAN   of the city's best Italian restaurants. Have a drink and people-watch at
the bar or patio. Upstairs is the Ristorante, with hearty regional-Italian
mains and homemade pastas such as spaghetti with mussels, artichokes,
and garlic. The three-course lunch for about C$20 is a steal. Down-
stairs, in the partially subterranean bar and pizzeria, munch on pasta,
equally well-prepared thin-crust pizzas—try the Soprano, with cala-
brese, Portobello mushrooms, and Asiago. It's a popular meeting place
after the play, and the service is quick and friendly. ⊠ *70 Ontario St.*
☎ *519/273–6666* 🌐 *www.pazzo.ca* 🗖 *AE, MC, V* 🕙 *Ristorante closed
Mon. and Nov.–mid-May (pizzeria open year-round).*

$$$$ ✕ **Rundles Restaurant.** At Stratford's top choice for sophisticated haute cui-
CONTINENTAL   sine the look is summery and modern: brick is exposed, windows are
Fodor's Choice   unadorned and panoramic, and, with a theatrical flourish, flowing white
★   silk scarves hang from primitive stone masks. Diners have five to seven
choices for each course (appetizer, entrée, and dessert) on the prix-fixe
menu. Offerings change frequently, but regulars would protest the removal
of the braised duck confit or, for dessert, the lemon tart with orange sorbet.
In 2008 Rundles introduced the slightly less-expensive and more relaxed
Sophisto-Bistro, at the same location, whose three- and four-course dinners might include roasted skate wing with chorizo broth or for dessert
chilled rhubarb soup with rhubarb sorbet. Considerable artistry is lavished on preparation and presentation. ⊠ *9 Cobourg St.* ☎ *519/271–6442*
🌐 *www.rundlesrestaurant.com* 🍴 *Reservations essential* 🗖 *AE, MC, V*
🕙 *Closed mid-Oct.–late May and Mon. No lunch weekdays.*

$$ ✕ **Sun Room.** Locals know the Sun Room well for the best stir-fries in
ECLECTIC   town and its various Szechuan noodle dishes. But you can also go for
★   entrées like Perth County pan-seared pork tenderloin. Save room for
desserts: the popular sundried cherry crème brûlée is always on the
menu. The dining room is casual, with tile floors, cane chairs, and green

pub-style lanterns, and the service is very welcoming. ⊠ *55 George St.* ☎ *519/273–0331* ⊕ *www.sunroomstratford.com* ⌁ *Reservations essential* ⊟ *AE, MC, V* ⊘ *Closed Sun. No lunch Mon.*

$$ ✕**York Street Kitchen.** Locals come to this casual spot across from the
CAFÉ   waterfront for the signature thick and juicy sandwiches and, for dinner,
★   homemade comfort dishes, such as meat loaf with Yukon-gold mashed potatoes or barbecue chicken, but especially for the breakfasts served daily: favorites are the French toast with homemade apple compote and the Canadiana sandwich with peameal bacon, mustard, tomato, and egg on a Kaiser roll. A build-your-own sandwich menu (¢) is available for lunch and at the take-out window in summer. The funky dining room is decorated with turquoise exposed-brick walls and bright patterned vinyl tablecloths. During festival season the lines form early. ⊠ *41 York St.* ☎ *519/273–7041* ⊕ *www.yorkstreetkitchen.com* ⊟ *MC, V.*

WHERE TO STAY

Stratford has a wide range of atmospheric bed-and-breakfasts on the outskirts of downtown, while more trendy boutique hotels are scattered around the center. The majority of characterless big chain hotels are not worth the price. Keep in mind that room rates are discounted substantially in winter, sometimes by more than 50%. The **Stratford Area Bed & Breakfast Association** (☎ *519/272–2961* ⊕ *www.sabba.ca*) conducts regular inspections of area B&Bs and maintains a list of those that pass muster.

$$ ☶**Festival Inn.** This is Stratford's largest hotel, east of town in a commercial area, a 10-minute drive from the theaters. Most rooms (120) and public spaces were renovated in 2009. The remaining rooms will be renovated in 2010, and a restaurant will be added. Rooms have coffeemakers and either one king or queen or two double beds. Four have double Jacuzzi tubs. The annex rooms are the newest, constructed in 1996, and the most recently updated. **Pros:** inexpensive and decent rooms; exceptional staff. **Cons:** slightly out of town; some rooms need renovating. ⊠ *1144 Ontario St.* ☎ *519/273–1150 or 800/463–3581* ⊕ *www.festivalinnstratford.com* ⤶ *169 rooms* ⌂ *In-room: refrigerator, Internet. In-hotel: restaurant, bar, pool, public Wi-Fi, parking (free), no-smoking rooms* ⊟ *AE, MC, V* ⦿❘ *CP.*

$$ ☶**Foster's Inn.** Two doors away from the Avon and Studio theaters, this
★   brick building dates to 1906 and has a bit of history—it once housed the International Order of Odd Fellows, a fraternal organization that started in the United Kingdom. Brightly painted rooms, on the second and third floors, are comfortable if basic, with queen-size beds and wood floors. The hotel's street-level bar and restaurant attract a lively mix of patrons. Though guest rooms are above the bar and restaurant, noise isn't a problem. The dining room offers a broad menu and the most delicious steaks in town. **Pros:** great deals in winter; excellent locale. **Cons:** fills up fast in summer. ⊠ *111 Downie St.* ☎ *519/271–1119 or 888/728–5555* ⊕ *www.fostersinn.com* ⤶ *9 rooms* ⌂ *In-room: Internet, Wi-Fi (some). In-hotel: restaurant, room service, bar, public Wi-Fi, no-smoking rooms* ⊟ *AE, MC, V.*

$$$$ ☶**Stewart House Inn.** The interior of this elegant 1870s home draws on
★   the Victorian period but with a modern touch. Each of the six guest

8

rooms has a Victorian-inspired theme, from the soft green Georgian Room with Egyptian linens to the extra-large Regency Room, with a king canopy bed and double soaker tub. All the bathrooms have heated tiles. You can start the day on the right foot with coffee or tea service requested via the house's original call system, followed by a grand complimentary breakfast. The hotel discourages children under 10, and the owner has two miniature schnauzers. **Pros:** exceptional service; in-house massage. **Cons:** not in a central location; ground-floor Garden Room available only in summer. ⊠ *62 John St. N* ☏ *519/271–4576 or 866/826–7772* ⊕ *www.stewarthouseinn.com* ⤳ *6 rooms* ⏦ *In-room: DVD, Wi-Fi. In-hotel: pool, no elevator, laundry service, public Wi-Fi, parking (free), no-smoking rooms* ⊟ *AE, MC, V* ⊺ *BP.*

$ 🖼 **Swan Motel.** The original 1960s motel sign still marks this single-story white-brick motel 3 km (2 mi) south of downtown, but inside, rooms are updated regularly and outside flowering plants and trees sprawl across the generous, nicely landscaped grounds with a large pool. Free coffee, tea, and muffins await guests in the morning. **Pros:** one of the best deals in town; friendly hosts. **Cons:** a 25-minute walk to downtown; stark rooms. ⊠ *960 Downie St.* ☏ *519/271–6376* ⊕ *www. swanmotel.on.ca* ⤳ *24 rooms* ⏦ *In-room: refrigerator, Internet, Wi-Fi. In-hotel: pool, public Wi-Fi, parking (free), no-smoking rooms* ⊟ *MC, V* ⊘ *Closed Nov.–late Apr.* ⊺ *CP.*

$$$$ 🖼 **The Three Houses.** On a quiet residential street, this elegant and taste-
★   fully decorated trio of two Edwardian houses and one Victorian has been frequented by the likes of Kevin Spacey, Julie Andrews, and Christopher Plummer. The suites are spread over three floors and are packed with original art, and all have a private balcony or veranda. The Garden House, in an 1870s coach carriage house offers a quiet retreat and a four-poster bed—popular with couples on honeymoons. Breakfasts are three courses: fruit, eggs, and baked goods. Dinner is served on request. The gracious host, David, speaks a multitude of foreign languages, mostly to accommodate his influx of European visitors. **Pros:** star appeal; exquisite decorative taste; heated pool. **Cons:** irregular hours in winter; sometimes entire house is rented out to film crews. ⊠ *100 Brunswick St.* ☏ *519/272–0722* ⊕ *www.thethreehouses. com* ⤳ *6 suites* ⏦ *In-room: refrigerator, DVD, Wi-Fi. In-hotel: pool, no elevator, laundry service, public Wi-Fi, parking (free), no-smoking rooms* ⊟ *AE, D, DC, MC, V* ⊺ *BP.*

$$$$ 🖼 **XIS.** A married couple whose backgrounds are in accounting and
Fodor's Choice   pharmacy transformed this former downtown bank building into an
★   exquisite, ultrachic inn (XIS is pronounced *zees*). White-leather chairs and sleek, shojilike wood-and-glass panels in the rooms might help you sink into a Zen-like mood. You can pamper yourself with Bulgari bath products and Frette linens or treat yourself to cashews and Evian water. A complimentary glass of wine greets you on arrival; coffee, tea, cappuccino, and espresso are delivered upon request. The huge Continental breakfasts include homemade pastries and granola, yogurt, fruit, soft-boiled eggs, freshly baked bread, and Québec cheeses. **Pros:** Stratford's slickest lodging; spa next door. **Cons:** closed in winter; doesn't come cheap. ⊠ *6 Wellington St.* ☏ *519/273–9248* ⊕ *www.xis-stratford.com*

➦ 6 rooms ☖ In-room: safe, DVD, Internet. In-hotel: laundry service, parking (free), no-smoking rooms ▤ AE, MC, V ☺ Closed Nov.–mid-May ⦿ CP.

THE ARTS

In July and August, **Stratford Summer Music** (☎ 519/271–2101 ⊕ www. stratfordsummermusic.ca) brings musicians—from string quartets to Mexican mariachi bands—to several indoor and outdoor venues around town.

Fodor's Choice ★ Stratford Festival. A mix of Shakespeare, works by other dramatists, and popular musical performances take place in four theaters, each in its own building and each with distinct physical aspects (size, stage configuration, technical support) that favor different types of productions. At the height of the festival in July and August you may be able to choose between four simultaneous performances from among the 15 different productions mounted during the season. The Festival also offers numerous non-play concerts, workshops, tours, lectures, and talks, such as Meet the Festival, where the public can ask questions of actors and artists.

The **Festival Theatre** (⊠ 55 Queen St.), the original and the largest of Stratford's theaters, has a thrust stage that brings the action deep into the audience space. Try for fairly central seats in this theater. The open-air **Festival Pavilion,** just beside the Festival Theatre, was launched in 2008, hosting one production per season at off-hours 11:30 AM and 5:30 PM. **The Avon** (⊠ 99 Downie St.) has a traditional proscenium stage, good sight lines, and elevators to each level. The **Tom Patterson Theatre** (⊠ 111 Lakeside Dr.) has a long, narrow runway thrust stage and 480 steeply stacked seats. The **Studio Theatre** (⊠ 34 George St. E), the most intimate of the festival venues, with only 260 seats, has a modified thrust stage and specializes in experimental and new works. The Festival and the Avon theaters are open from late April to early November. The Tom Patterson and Studio productions start in May and close by the end of September. Matinee and evening performances run Tuesday through Saturday; Sunday has regular matinee and occasional evening shows. Theaters are closed Monday.

For tickets, information, and accommodations, contact the festival office directly. ⊠ 55 Queen St. ☎ 519/273–1600 or 800/567–1600 ⊕ www.stratfordfestival.ca.

EN ROUTE
The tiny village of St. Jacobs, in Mennonite country 50 km (30 mi) northeast of Stratford, has a main street lined with quilt shops, fresh-from-the-farm food stores, and restaurants whose menus feature locally raised and -grown meat and produce. The **St. Jacobs Farmers' Markets** (⊠ Farmers' Market Rd., at Weber St. N, off Rte. 15 ☎ 519/747–1830

DISCOUNT TICKETS

Regular Stratford Festival tickets are around C$50 to C$110, but there are many ways to pay less. Spring previews and select fall performances are discounted 30%. Savings of 30% to 50% can be had for students and seniors, and theatergoers aged 18 to 29 can buy seats online for C$25 for select performances two weeks prior to performances. Also available are early-ordering discounts, rush seats, and family and group discounts.

8

⊙ *Sept.–mid-June Thurs. and Sat. 7–3:30; mid-June–Aug. Tues. 8–3, Thurs. and Sat. 7–3:30, Sun. 10–4)*, just outside of town, has hundreds of indoor and outdoor booths with homemade foods straight from the farm: preserves, pies, smoked meats, and cheeses. Don't miss the hot apple fritters, a treat worth queuing for: the apples are peeled and fried while you wait.

NORTH OF TORONTO TO THE LAKES

Outcroppings of pink and gray granite mark the rustic area in the Canadian Shield known to locals as Cottage Country. Drumlins of conifer and deciduous forest punctuate 100,000 freshwater lakes formed from glaciers during the Ice Age. Place-names such as Orillia, the Muskokas, Gravenhurst, Haliburton, and Algonquin reveal the history of the land's inhabitants, from Algonquin tribes to European explorers to fur traders. The area became a haven for the summering rich and famous during the mid-19th century, when lumber barons who were harvesting near port towns set up steamship and rail lines, making travel to the area possible. Since then, Cottage Country has attracted urbanites who make the pilgrimage to hear the call of the loon or swat incessant mosquitoes and black flies. "Cottages" is a broadly used term that includes log cabins as well as palatial homes that wouldn't look out of place in a wealthy urban neighborhood. For the cottageless, overnight seasonal camping in a provincial park is an option, as is a stay in a rustic lodge or posh resort.

To reach this area, take Highway 400 north, which intersects with the highly traveled and often congested Highway 11. Highway 60 is less traveled and cuts across the province through Algonquin Provincial Park. ■TIP→ If you are heading north or west of Barrie in winter, go with a four-wheel-drive vehicle. Resorts, especially, are usually well off the highway and may require navigating twisting backcountry routes.

These towns and regions are two to four hours from Toronto and are generally weekend or even weeklong trips from the city. Algonquin Provincial Park can be done in a weekend, but four days is the average stay as there's a lot of ground to cover.

After Labor Day and before mid-May, few tourist attractions apart from Algonquin Park and ski resorts are open. Ski Ontario has information on the condition of slopes across the province.

Fishing licenses are required for Ontario and may be purchased from Ministry of Natural Resources offices and from most sporting-goods stores, outfitters, and resorts—one-day passes cost C$16; one-year is C$61. Restrictions are published in *Recreational Fishing Regulations Summary,* free from the Ministry. Ontario Tourism publishes a free catalog of about 500 fishing resorts and lodges. These establishments are not hotels near bodies of water that contain fish but businesses designed to make sport fishing available to their guests. Each offers all the accoutrements, including boats, motors, guides, floatplanes, and freezers. Rates at these lodges are hefty.

ESSENTIALS

Fishing Contacts Ministry of Natural Resources (☎ *800/667–1940 or 705/755–2000* ⊕ *www.mnr.gov.on.ca).*

Ski Information Ski Ontario (☎ *705/443–5450* ⊕ *www.skiontario.on.ca).*

Tourism Information Georgian Bay Tourism (✉ *208 King St., Midland* ☎ *705/526–7884 or 800/263–7745* ⊕ *www.georgianbaytourism.on.ca).* **Haliburton County Tourism** (✉ *12340 Hwy. 35 , Minden* ☎ *705/296–1777 or 800/461–7677* ⊕ *www.haliburtoncounty.com/tourism).* **Muskoka Tourism** (✉ *1342 Hwy. 11 N, R.R. 2, Kilworthy* ☎ *705/689–0660 or 800/267–9700* ⊕ *www.discovermuskoka.ca).*

SIMCOE COUNTY

Barrie is 90 km (56 mi) north of Toronto on Hwy. 400. Collingwood is 150 km (90 mi) north of Toronto on Hwys. 400 and 26; 55 km (35 mi) west of Barrie on Hwy. 26. Midland is 50 km (30 mi) north of Barrie on Hwys. 400 and 93.

Wedged between the southern Georgian Bay area on Lake Huron and the 743-square-km Lake Simcoe in the east, Simcoe County is home to ski resorts, waterfront towns, and historic sites. The county's largest city, Barrie (population 130,000), on the shore of Lake Simcoe, was originally a landing place for the area's aboriginal inhabitants and, later, for fur traders. The quiet towns of Midland and Penetanguishene (also called Penetang by locals) occupy a small corner of northern Simcoe County known as Huronia, on a snug harbor at the foot of Georgian Bay's Severn Sound. To the west, the more attractive harbor town of Collingwood, on Nottawasaga Bay, is at the foot of Blue Mountain, the largest ski hill in the province.

8

EXPLORING

★ **Sainte-Marie among the Hurons.** A Jesuit mission was originally built on this spot in 1639. The reconstructed village, which was once home to a fifth of the European population of New France, was the site of the European settlers' first hospital, farm, school, and social service center in Ontario. Villagers also constructed a canal from the Wye River. A combination of disease and Iroquois attacks led to the mission's demise. Twenty-two structures, including a native longhouse and wigwam, have been faithfully reproduced from a scientific excavation. Staff members in period costume saw timber, repair shoes, sew clothes, and grow vegetables—keeping the working village alive. ✉ *Hwy. 12 E, Midland, 5 km (3 mi) east of Rte. 93* ☎ *705/526–7838* ⊕ *www.saintemarieamongthehurons.on.ca* 🎟 *Late-Apr.–mid-May and mid–late Oct., C$9.25; mid-May–mid-Oct., C$11.25* ⊙ *Late Apr.–mid-May and mid–late Oct., weekdays 10–5; mid-May–mid-Oct., daily 10–5; last entry at 4:45.*

Martyrs' Shrine. On a hill overlooking Sainte-Marie among the Hurons, a twin-spired stone cathedral was built in 1926 to honor the eight missionaries who died in Huronia; in 1930, five of the priests were canonized by the Roman Catholic Church. ✉ *Off Hwy. 12 E* ☎ *705/526–3788* ⊕ *www.martyrs-shrine.com* 🎟 *C$3* ⊙ *Mid-May–mid-Oct., daily 8:30–8:30.*

Georgian Bay Islands National Park. A series of 59 islands in Lake Huron's Georgian Bay, the park can only be visited via boat. Cruises leave from the town docks in Midland and Penetang from May through October. The 300-passenger *Miss Midland*, operated by **Midland Tours** (☎ 888/833–2628 ⊕ *www.midlandtours.com* ✉ C$24), leaves from the Midland town dock and offers 2½-hour sightseeing cruises daily mid-May to mid-October. The company can arrange departures from Toronto (via bus, with hotel pickup), which includes time to explore the town of Midland. From the Penetang town dock, **Georgian Bay Cruises** (☎ 705/549–7795 *or* 800/363–7447 ⊕ *www.georgianbaycruises.com* ✉ C$18–C$25) takes passengers on tours ranging from 1½- to 3½-hour tours of Penetanguishene Harbour and the Georgian Bay islands on its 200-passenger MS *Georgian Queen.* Also available are 2½-hour dinner cruises. Cruises depart once daily in July and August; less frequently in May, June, September, and October.

The park's own boat, the *Daytripper* (☎ 705/526–8907 ✉ C$16 ☽ *July and Aug., Thurs.–Mon.*), makes the 15-minute trip to Beausoleil Island, which has hiking trails and beaches, from Honey Harbour. ⊠ *Welcome center: off Hwy. 400 Exit 153 or 156, Port Severn ⌂ 901 Wye Valley Rd., Box 9, Midland L4R 4K6* ☎ *705/526–9804* ⊕ *www.pc.gc.ca/georgianbay* ✉ *C$5.80* ☽ *Mid-June–early Oct.*

WHERE TO STAY

$$$ 🏨 **Blue Mountain Resort.** The largest ski resort in Ontario, and only getting bigger, this huge property near Collingwood revolves around its brightly painted Scandinavian-style alpine "village" with several blocks of shops, restaurants, bars, a grocery, and a plaza with live music. Aside from the slopes, it has an outstanding 18-hole golf course, a spa with thermal waterfalls, mountain biking, a lakeside beach, and an aquatic park. Myriad lodging choices include the modestly priced (and somewhat shabby) **Blue Mountain Inn,** the Swiss-chalet-style **Westin Trillium House,** the studios and one- or two-bedroom of the **Village Suites** or **Mosaïc** complex. You can also reserve a condo or even an entire house. The 13 restaurants include fine dining, such as the Continental 3 Guys and a Stove, as well as pizzerias, pubs, and sandwich shops. **Pros:** wide range of accommodation, excellent skiing, complimentary shuttle bus. **Cons:** Blue Mountain Inn needs renovation. ⊠ *Off Hwy. 26, follow signs 7 km (4 mi) west of Collingwood ⌂ 108 Jozo Weider Blvd., Collingwood L9Y 3Z2* ☎ *705/445–0231 or 877/445–0231* ⊕ *www.bluemountain.ca* ⌂ *Blue Mountain Inn: 93 rooms, 2 suites; Westine Trillium House: 222 suites; Mosaïc: 85 suites; Village Suites: 447 suites.* ⌂ *In-room: safe (some), DVD (some), kitchen (some), refrigerator (some), Internet, Wi-Fi (some). In-hotel: 13 restaurants, room service, bars, golf course, tennis courts, pool, gym, spa, beachfront, water sports, bicycles, children's programs (ages 2–17), public Internet, parking (free and paid), no-smoking rooms* ☐ *AE, DC, MC, V.*

Fodor'sChoice
★

$$$ 🏨 **Horseshoe Resort.** Modern guest rooms at this lodge on a 1,600-acre property have down comforters (most) and some have views of the valley and golf course. Many suites have sunken living rooms, electric fireplaces, and whirlpool baths. In winter, nonski activities include dogsledding and snow tubing. In the summer season, the focus is most

decidedly golf but the resort also has 35 km (22 mi) of trails for hiking, biking, and four-wheeling and can arrange everything from off-road 4WD tours and zip-lining to hot-air ballooning. Dining options include formal Silks for dinner with a menu of local and seasonal dishes, such as porcini-crusted chicken, and casual offerings of burgers, pizza, and ribs at the pub-style Crazy Horse Saloon. **Pros:** free Wi-Fi; fun programs for kids. **Cons:** dull and outdated room decor. ⊠ *East of Hwy. 400 Exit 117* ⌂ *1101 Horseshoe Valley Rd., Comp. 10, R.R. 1, Barrie L4M 4Y8* ☎ *705/835–2790 or 800/461–5627* ⊕ *www.horseshoeresort.com* ⇨ *56 rooms, 45 suites* ⌂ *In-room: refrigerator (some), Wi-Fi. In-hotel: 3 restaurants, room service, bar, golf courses, tennis courts, pools, gym, spa, bicycles, children's programs (ages 5–12), public Wi-Fi, parking (free), no-smoking rooms* ▤ *AE, MC, V* ⎮◯⎮ *BP.*

$$ ⊡ **Talisman Resort.** Open since 1963, this small Austrian chalet–style resort has a ski hill abutting the lodge and a lovely golf course leading up to the resort. Rooms have views of either the Beaver Valley or Talisman Mountain; decor is unremarkable but some suites have oversize leather sofas and stone fireplaces. Outdoor hot tubs, a spa, and yoga classes can help you relax after hitting the ski slopes. The rural setting, among hills and trees, is beautiful, and easily enjoyed via the 79 km (50 mi) of hiking trails. The main dining room, the Terrace, serves Canadian Continental dishes. Talisman has plans to eventually build a new resort village with luxury condos. **Pros:** affordable prices; outdoor hot tubs; Kids Klub ski school. **Cons:** small rooms with dated decor; not much to offer advanced skiers. ⊠ *150 Talisman Mountain Dr., Kimberley* ☎ *519/599–2520 or 800/265–3759* ⊕ *www.talisman.ca* ⇨ *85 rooms, 8 suites* ⌂ *In-room: refrigerator, Internet, Wi-Fi. In-hotel: 4 restaurants, golf course, tennis court, pool, gym, spa, bicycles, children's programs (ages 2–12), parking (free), no-smoking rooms* ▤ *AE, D, MC, V* ⊙ *Closed mid-Mar.–late June and early Sept.–mid-Dec.*

SPORTS AND THE OUTDOORS

Most ski resorts have a multitude of summer activities, such as mountain biking, golf, and adventure camps.

Fodor's Choice The province's highest vertical drop, of 720 feet, is at **Blue Mountain** ★ **Resort** (⊠ *Off Hwy. 26, follow signs 7 km (4 mi) west of Collingwood, Collingwood* ☎ *705/445–0231, 416/869–3799 from Toronto* ⊕ *www.bluemountain.ca*), 11 km (7 mi) west of Collingwood, off Highway 26. Ontario's most extensively developed and heavily used ski area has 35 trails served by six high-speed six-person lifts, one quad, two triple chairs, three double chairs, and five magic carpets.

One of the few resorts to offer snowboarding, tubing, snowmobiling, snowshoeing, and cross-country and downhill skiing trails and facilities is **Horseshoe Resort** (⊠ *Horseshoe Valley Rd., R.R. 1,* ☎ *705/835–2790 or 800/461–5627* ⊕ *www.horseshoeresort.com*), 50 km (31½ mi) north of Barrie, off Highway 400. The resort has 25 alpine runs, 15 of which are lit at night, served by six lifts, a handle tow, and a Magic Carpet. The vertical drop is only 304 feet, but several of the runs are rated for advanced skiers.

8

Skiers and snowboarders can take advantage of 40 runs at **Mount St. Louis Moonstone** (✉ *Off Hwy. 400 Exit 131, 24 Mount St. Louis Rd., R.R. 4, Coldwater* ☎ *705/835–2112 or 877/835–2112* ⊕ *www.mslm.on.ca*), 26 km (16 mi) north of Barrie. The majority of slopes are for beginner and intermediate skiers, though there's a sprinkling of advanced runs. The resort's Kids Camp, a day-care and ski-school combination, attracts families. Inexpensive cafeterias within the two chalets serve decent meals. No overnight lodging is available. Nestled at the base of Mt. Talisman in the heart of Beaver Valley is the Tyrolean-inspired **Talisman Resort** (✉ *150 Talisman Dr., Kimberley* ☎ *519/599–2520 or 800/265–3759* ⊕ *www. talisman.ca*) with 17 downhill runs ranging from beginner to intermediate, plus one magic carpet and five chair lifts. Families like the resort for its popular Kids Klub, a program in which children are placed into age-based ski groups for daily activities.

GRAVENHURST

74 km (46 mi) north of Barrie on Hwy. 11.

North along Highway 11, rolling farmland gradually changes to lakes and pine trees amid granite outcrops of the Canadian Shield. This region, called Muskoka for Lake Muskoka, the largest of some 1,600 lakes in the area, is a favorite playground of people who live in and around Toronto.

Gravenhurst is a town of approximately 10,000 and the birthplace of Norman Bethune, regarded as a Canadian hero. The heart of town is the colorful Muskoka Wharf, the result of a C$170 million overhaul completed in 2008, with its boardwalk along the water, restaurants, steamship docks, vacation condos, and plaza that hosts festivals and a Wednesday farmers' market from Late May to early October. Still, Gravenhurst is a tiny town and can be seen in a day or even an afternoon.

EXPLORING

Bethune Memorial House. An 1880-vintage frame structure, this National Historic Site honors the heroic efforts of field surgeon and medical educator Henry Norman Bethune (1830–1939), who worked in China during the Sino-Japanese War in the 1930s and trained thousands to become medics and doctors. There are period rooms and an exhibit tracing the highlights of his life. The house has become a shrine of sorts for Chinese diplomats visiting North America. ✉ *235 John St. N* ☎ *705/687–4261* ⊕ *www.pc.gc.ca/lhn-nhs/on/bethune/index.aspx* 🎫 *C$3.90* ⏱ *June–Labor Day, daily 10–4; day after Labor Day–Oct., Sat.–Wed. 10–4; Nov.–May, by appointment.*

★ **Muskoka Steamships.** From June to mid-October, cruises tour Muskoka Lakes. Excursions include lunch and dinner cruises (C$49–C$83) or one- to four-hour afternoon cruises ($C18–C$49). Reservations are required. The restored 128-foot-long, 99-passenger *RMS Segwun* (the initials stand for Royal Mail Ship) is North America's oldest operating steamship, built in 1887, and is the sole survivor of a fleet that provided transportation through the Muskoka Lakes. The 200-passenger

Wenonah II is a 1907-inspired vessel with modern technology. The 1915 *Wanda III* steam yacht is available for private cruises only. ✉ *185 Cherokee La., Muskoka Wharf* ☎ *705/687–6667 or 866/687–6667* ⊕ *www.realmuskoka.com*

Muskoka Boat & Heritage Centre. Learn about steamboat technology in this museum with restored historic boats, including a 1924 propeller boat, a 30-foot 1894 steamboat, and gleaming wooden

speedboats. ✉ *275 Steamship Bay Rd., Muskoka Wharf* ☎ *705/687–2115 or 866/687–6667* ⊕ *www.realmuksoka.com* ☜ *C$6.80* ☉ *Late June–mid-Oct., daily 10–6; mid-Oct.–late June, Tues.–Sat. 10–4.*

WHERE TO EAT

$$ ✕**Blue Willow Tea Shop.** Afternoon tea is served at this cozy room over-
CAFÉ looking Muskoka Bay, every day from 2 PM to 4 PM. It includes a three-tier platter of shortbread, scones with Devonshire cream, and savory finger sandwiches, plus a pot of tea per person. The dozen or so petite tables are set with blue-willow-pattern china. Lunches are sandwiches, such as grilled bacon and Brie, quiches, and specials like homemade stews. Dinner choices are limited to five or six options; roast beef and Yorkshire pudding is a popular Wednesday-night special. The attached shop sells loose teas, baked goods, teapots, and Devonshire cream. ✉ *900 Bay St., Muskoka Wharf* ☎ *705/687–2597* ▭ *MC, V* ☉ *Closed Mon. Oct.–June. No dinner Mon., Tues., Thurs., Sun.*

$$$$ ✕**Elements.** At the Taboo Resort, Elements offers contemporary Canadian
CANADIAN entrées like grilled beef tenderloin served with a flageolet cassoulet, oven-dried cherry tomatoes, and smoked bacon, and seafood ravioli. A sushi menu is also available. Desserts such as roasted honey crème caramel with fresh berries, may be the highlight. At the highly acclaimed Culinary Theatre (C$95/person), in the same dining room, 18 bar stools surround the chef's station, giving you an up-close view of the preparation of your Asian-influenced six-course menu. The look is formal, modern, and subdued, with sleek black wood veneers, hardwood floors, and a wall of lakefront windows. ✉ *1209 Muskoka Beach Rd.* ☎ *705/687–2233 or 800/461–0236* ⊕ *www.tabooresort.com* ☎ *705/687–2233* ☜ *Reservations essential* ▭ *AE, MC, V* ☉ *Closed 2nd wk of Dec.–Apr.*

$$$ ✕**North.** When it opened in 2007, North quickly became the best in-town
CANADIAN restaurant, serving hearty Canadian fare that makes good use of local
★ produce. The menu changes seasonally but has featured roasted halibut with leek-and-couscous risotto and elk tenderloin with blackberry jus. In the sophisticated dining room high-backed dark leather chairs and white tablecloths are paired with rustic-looking stained pine floors. Though it's one of the classiest establishments in town, the service and atmosphere is relaxed and approachable. ✉ *530 Muskoka Rd. N* ☎ *705/687–8618* ▭ *AE, MC, V* ☉ *Closed Sun. Call for hrs in Nov.–Apr.*

8

WHERE TO STAY

$$$$ 🔲 **Bayview-Wildwood Resort.** Seemingly far from civilization but truly only
☉   a 20-minute drive south of Gravenhurst, this all-inclusive lakeside resort
dates to 1898, and is particularly geared to outdoor types and families.
It's the kind of casual place where guests chat into the evening, loung-
ing in Adirondack chairs around a fire pit. Canoeing and kayaking are
popular; floatplane excursions and golf can also be arranged. In winter,
gear up for tobogganing, sleigh rides, and snowshoeing. Most rooms
have fireplaces and some have whirlpool baths; all but a few have views
over Sparrow Lake. You can also book private cottages with decks. There
are great deals on family vacations and weekend packages. **Pros:** great
for families; casual atmosphere; free activities for kids. **Cons:** strict meal
times; room decor is passé; noisy cargo trains pass by throughout the day
and night. ⊠ *1500 Port Stanton Pkwy., R.R. 1, Severn Bridge, 25 km (16
mi) south of Gravenhurst* ☎ *705/689–2338 or 800/461–0243* ⊕ *www.
bayviewwildwood.com* ⤙ *36 rooms, 26 suites, 22 cottages, 3 houses*
⚴ *In-room: refrigerator, kitchen (some), Wi-Fi (some). In-hotel: restaurant, bar, tennis courts, pools, gym, beachfront, water sports, bicycles,
no elevator, children's programs (ages infant–17 yrs), laundry facilities,
public Wi-Fi, parking (free), no-smoking rooms* ⊟ *AE, MC, V* �‖❙ *AI.*

$$$$ 🔲 **Taboo Resort, Golf and Spa.** A magnificent 1,000-acre landscape of
Fodor's Choice   rocky outcrops and windswept trees typical of the Muskoka region
★   surrounds this luxury resort. All kinds of diversions are available, from
a highly rated golf course to mountain biking. The resort borders Lake
Muskoka; guests enjoy boat rentals from canoes and kayaks to small
powerboats. The building exteriors resemble a traditional northern
Canadian lodge, but the Signature rooms and suites and Cottage Chalets have a sleek design with walnut-wood furnishings and crisp, white
linens. The lowest-tier Classic and Deluxe rooms are more traditional in
design. Every room has a balcony, most with forest and lake views, and
more than half have a gas or wood fireplace. The menu of traditional
spa offerings is peppered with unique treatments like a cranberry body
polish and a rejuvenating red-grape wrap. Dining options include the
überchic Elements ($$$$), the modern lobby lounge, with amazing lake
view through wraparound picture windows, and the waterfront Boat-
house Bar & Grill. **Pros:** charming locale; excellent golfing facilities.
Cons: expensive; tiny bathrooms in Signature rooms. ⊠ *1209 Muskoka
Beach Rd.* ☎ *705/687–2233 or 800/461–0236* ⊕ *www.tabooresort.com*
⤙ *79 rooms, 22 suites, 15 Cottage Chalets* ⚴ *In-room: kitchen (some),
refrigerator, Internet (some), Wi-Fi (some). In-hotel: 5 restaurants, room
service, bars, golf courses, tennis courts, pools, gym, spa, beachfront,
water sports, bicycles, laundry service, public Wi-Fi, parking (free), no-
smoking rooms* ⊟ *AE, MC, V* ☉ *Closed mid-Dec.–Apr.*

HUNTSVILLE

51 km (32 mi) north of Gravenhurst on Hwy. 11.

Muskoka's Huntsville region is filled with lakes and streams, strands of
virgin birch and pine, and deer—and no shortage of year-round resorts.
It is usually the cross-country skier's best bet for an abundance of natural snow in southern Ontario. All resorts have trails.

WHERE TO EAT

$$$

CANADIAN

★

✕**The Norsemen Restaurant.** Generations of devotees have returned to this restaurant in the wooded hills above Huntsville for the warm hospitality and a tempting Canadian harvest with European (largely French) flair. Past menus have included seared escallops of venison with a juniper-gin sauce and the cassoulet with duck, sausage, and lamb. Built in the 1920s, the lodge became a restaurant in 1975 and is unabashedly rustic and homey, with a double-sided stone fireplace, locally harvested beams overhead, and oxbows over the doorways. The extensive wine list is a point of pride. Tables on the screened-in porch have lake views. Seatings are between 6 and 9:30; plan on a leisurely dinner. ✉ 1040 Walker Lake Dr., 2 km (1 mi) north of Hwy. 60 ☎ 705/635–2473 or 800/565–3856 ☰ AE, MC, V ☯ Jan.–Mar. closed Mon.–Thurs.; Apr.–May and Sept.–Dec. closed Mon. and Tues.; June–Aug. closed Mon., call to confirm. No lunch.

> ### BLACK FLY SEASON: WHAT'S THE BUZZ?
>
> For a week or two in May or early June, "blackfly season" hits Muskoka, and the mosquitoes follow in the heat of summer. Most Muskoka lodges and restaurants are prepared, with screened-in porches and such. Bites are itchy and annoying, but the insects aren't disease-carrying. Use insect repellant with DEET, wear long sleeves and pants, wear light clothing, and stay indoors during early morning and late afternoon/evening, when flies are most active.

WHERE TO STAY

$$$$

🏨**Deerhurst Resort.** This ultradeluxe-but-not-stuffy resort spread along Peninsula Lake is a 780-acre, self-contained community with restaurants and lodgings to fit every budget. The flavor is largely modern, although the main lodge with huge flagstone pillars dates from 1896. The resort's Pavilion wing is four stories high, embellished with an octagonal tower and decorative gables; its rooms are done in a floral-and-stripe combination and have large windows with views of the grounds and lakefront. The beautiful golf courses are studded with pines and lakes. Other activities include parasailing and water skiing in summer and sleigh rides and snow tubing in winter; the resort also arranges various Algonquin Park tours. The casual Maple restaurant, opened in 2009, serves an eclectic mix of sushi, home-style Canadian fare, and the more upscale Eclipse serves Canadian specialties, such as Ontario lamb, Alberta beef, and rainbow trout. **Pros:** top-notch facilities; nice rooms; a multitude of activities. **Cons:** some rooms need updating. ✉ 1235 Deerhurst Dr., just south of Rte. 60 ☎ 705/789–6411 or 800/461–4393 ⊕ www.deerhurstresort.com ⇥ 400 rooms ⌂ In-room: DVD (some), Internet (some), Wi-Fi (some). In-hotel: 3 restaurants, bar, golf courses, tennis courts, pools, gym, spa, water sports, laundry service, parking (free), no-smoking rooms ☰ AE, MC, V.

$$

🏨**Portage Inn.** Stay near pine trees, ski runs, and snowmobile trails at this country-style 1889 home, which is open year-round. Rooms have great views of the lake; three bedrooms have en suite hot tubs, and one has a fireplace. There are two luxurious cottages, which are a great deal at $250–$300 per night. The inn has snowshoeing in winter and canoeing and kayaking in summer and a hot tub for all to use. There's a minimum two-night stay on weekends. **Pros:** affordable peace and quiet; hot tubs in rooms; close to Hidden Valley. **Cons:** some rooms don't have TVs; far from town. ⊠ *1563 N. Portage Rd., Lake of Bays, off Rte. 23, 13 km east of Huntsville* ☎ *705/788–7171 or 888/418–5555* ⊕ *www.portageinn.com* ⟋ *6 rooms, 2 cottages* ⟐ *In-room: no a/c, no TV (some). In-hotel: tennis court, bicycles* ▤ *MC, V* ❘◯❘ *BP.*

SKIING

Hidden Valley Highlands Ski Area (⊠ *1655 Hidden Valley Rd., off Hwy. 60, 8 km east of town* ☎ *705/789–1773* ⊕ *www.skihiddenvalley.on.ca*) has 35 skiable acres with 14 hills and three quad lifts. It's great for beginner and intermediate skiers, with a couple of black-diamond runs for daredevils.

ALGONQUIN PROVINCIAL PARK

35 km (23 mi) east of Huntsville on Hwy. 60.

GETTING HERE AND AROUND

The huge park has 29 different access points, so do call ahead to devise the best plan of attack for your visit based on your interests. The most popular entry points are along the Highway 60 corridor, where you'll find all the conventional campgrounds. If you're heading into the park's interior, spring for the detailed Algonquin Canoe Routes Map (C$4.95), available on the park Web site. The visitor center, at the park gates or bookstore, or on the Highway 60 corridor, 43 km east of the West Gate, has information on park programs, a bookstore, a restaurant, and a panoramic-viewing deck.

EXPLORING

★ **Algonquin Provincial Park** stretches across 7,650 square km (2,954 square mi), containing nearly 2,500 lakes, 272 bird species, 45 species of mammals, 50 species of fish, and encompassing forests, rivers, and cliffs. The typical visitor is a hiker, canoeist, camper—or all three. But don't be put off if you're not the athletic or outdoorsy sort. About a third of Algonquin's visitors come for the day to walk one of the 17 well-groomed and well-signed interpretive trails, or enjoy a swim or a picnic. Swimming is especially good at the Lake of Two Rivers, halfway between the west and east gates along Highway 60. Spring, when the moose head north, is the best time to catch a glimpse of North America's largest land mammal. Getting up at the crack of dawn gives you the best chance of seeing the park's wildlife. Park naturalists give talks on area wildflowers, animals, and birds, and you can book a guided hike or canoe trip. Expeditions to hear wolf howling take place in late summer and early autumn. The park's **Algonquin Logging Museum** (⊙ *Mid-May–mid Oct., daily 9–5*) depicts life at an early Canadian logging camp. ⊠ *Hwy. 60; main and east gate is west of town of Whitney; west gate is east of town of Dwight, Whitney* ☎ *705/633–5572* ⊕ *www. algonquinpark.on.ca* ⟐ *C$11.85 per vehicle* ⊙ *Apr.–mid-Oct., daily 8 AM–10 PM; mid-Oct.–Mar., daily 9–5. Park attractions may have their own operating hrs; call ahead.*

WHERE TO EAT

■ **TIP→** If you'd like wine with dinner, bring your own: park restrictions prohibit the sale of alcohol here.

$$$$ ✕**Arowhon Pines Restaurant.** A meal
CANADIAN   at this circular log-cabin restaurant
Fodor's Choice   in the heart of Algonquin Park is
★   the highlight of many visits. Window-side tables have lake views, but a towering, double-sided stone fireplace in the center of the room is an attraction, too. Menus, which change daily, focus on Ontario's seasonal ingredients and might include grilled tarragon-scented trout in a cornmeal crust, bacon-wrapped filet mignon in a wild mushroom sauce, or smoked baked ham with a maple glaze and mango chutney. The menu always includes two to four vegetarian options, and other diets are readily accommodated. Dinners are C$70 prix-fixe for nonguests. Lunch and breakfast are also served. ✉ *Algonquin Provincial Park, near west entrance, 8 km north of Hwy. 60* ♉ *Algonquin Park, Box 10001 Huntsville* ☎ *705/633–5661 or 866/633–5661* ⊕ *www.arowhonpines.com* ♦ *Reservations essential* ⏰ *BYOB* ▤ *MC, V* ⊗ *Closed mid-Oct.–late-May.*

$$$$ ✕**Bartlett Lodge Restaurant.** In the original 1917 lodge building, this small
CANADIAN   lakeside pine dining room offers an ever-changing menu of traditional
★   Canadian breakfasts (C$15 prix-fixe for staples like eggs Benedict and blueberry pancakes) and five-course dinners (C$55 prix-fixe), which might kick off with seared scallops and move on to seared duck breast with a star-anise rub or the house specialty, beef tenderloin. Fish and vegetarian options, such as sweet-potato gnocchi with shaved Gruyère, are always available. Desserts, all made on-site, will include a cheesecake and a crème brûlée (perhaps a chocolate-chili version). Breakfast is served from 8 to 9:30 and dinner seatings are at 6 and 8 only. ✉ *Algonquin Park, by boat from Cache Lake Landing, just south of Hwy. 60, Huntsville* ☎ *705/633–5543* ⊕ *www.bartlettlodge.com* ♦ *Reservations essential* ⏰ *BYOB* ▤ *MC, V* ⊗ *Closed mid-Oct.–mid-May. No lunch.*

WHERE TO STAY

$$$$ 🏨**Arowhon Pines.** The stuff of local legend, Arowhon is a family-run wilderness retreat deep in Algonquin Provincial Park known for unpretentious rustic "luxury" and superb dining. One- to 12-bedroom log cabins are decorated with antique pine furnishings. Every cabin has a fireplace, though unless you book a private cabin, you must share it with other lodgers. Every room has a private bath, however. Room rates include three daily meals in the dining room ($$$$) overlooking the lake and a park permit. **Pros:** all-inclusive swimming, sailing, hiking, and birding on a private lake in a gorgeous setting; excellent restaurant. **Cons:** limited menu; pricey considering rusticity of cabins; only half of the rooms have water views. ✉ *Algonquin Park, near*

8

west entrance, 8 km north of Hwy. 60 ⊕ *Algonquin Park, Box 10001, Huntsville* ☎ *705/633–5661 or 866/633–5661 toll-free year-round* ⊕ *www.arowhonpines.ca* ⇘ *50 rooms in 13 cabins* ⚐ *In-room: no a/c, no phone, no TV. In-hotel: restaurant, beachfront, water sports, tennis court, no elevator, laundry service, parking (free), no-smoking rooms* ⊟ *MC, V* ⊙ *Closed mid-Oct.–late May* ⦿ *AI.*

$$$$ ⊞ **Bartlett Lodge.** Smack in the center
★   of Algonquin Provincial park, this impressive 1917 resort is reached by a short boat ride on Cache Lake (just make your reservation and use the phone at the landing to call the lodge when you arrive). The immaculate one- to three-bedroom private log cabins, each with its own canoe and a screened porch facing the lake, have gleaming hardwood floors and king-size beds with patchwork quilts. Some have wood stoves. Solar power is used when possible and one cabin is completely "off the grid." (The lodge is working toward being completely energy independent.) Quiet reigns: no waterskiing, Jet Skiing, or motors over 10 horsepower are allowed on the lake (but you can take out a canoe); and you won't find radios, phones, or TVs in the cabins. Platform tents have king-size or two single beds and include breakfast only. The restaurant ($$$$) is excellent but does not serve lunch, though preordered picnic lunches are available. **Pros:** eco-friendly; boat-only access means total seclusion; authentic "cottage" experience. **Cons:** strict meal times. ✉ *Algonquin Park, by boat from Cache Lake Landing, just south of Hwy. 60* ⊕ *Box 10004, Algonquin Park, Huntsville P1H 2G8* ☎ *705/633–5543, 905/338–8908 in winter* ⊕ *www.bartlettlodge.com* ⇘ *12 cabins, 2 platform tents* ⚐ *In-room: no a/c, no phone, refrigerator, no TV. In-hotel: restaurant, water sports, bicycles, no elevator, parking (free), no-smoking rooms* ⊟ *MC, V* ⊙ *Closed late Oct.–early May* ⦿ *MAP.*

ALGONQUIN TOURS: TEA WITH MOOSE?

Northern Edge Algonquin (☎ *800/953–3343* ⊕ *www. northernedgealgonquin.com*) eco-adventure company provides educational and adventurous ways to explore the region. On the Morning Tea with Moose canoe trip, sip a cuppa while observing the plentitude of wildlife on the banks of the region's windy rivers and lily-filled bays. Other retreat and learning vacation themes include wilderness survival, sea-kayaking, yoga, shamanism, dogsledding, and a number of women-only weekends.

CAMPING   Algonquin has three styles of camping available. Along the parkway
AND CABINS   corridor, a 56-km (35-mi) stretch of Highway 60, are eight organized campgrounds. Prices range from C$30.25 to C$40 depending on the campground and whether you require electricity. Within the vast park interior you won't find any organized campsites (and the purists love it that way). Interior camping permits are C$11 per person, available from Ontario Parks. Contact Algonquin Park's main number (☎ *705/633–5572*) to hash out the details of interior camping before calling Ontario Parks to reserve. In between the extremes of the corridor campgrounds and interior camping are the lesser-known peripheral campgrounds—Kiosk, Brent, and Achray—in the northern and eastern reaches of the park, which you access by long, dusty roads.

These sites do not have showers, and Brent has only pit toilets. The Highway 60 corridor campsites have showers, picnic tables, and, in some cases, RV hookups.

Reservations are required for all campsites, cabins, and for interior camping; call **Ontario Parks** (☎ *888/668–7275* ⊕ *www.ontarioparks.com*).

A bit less extreme than pitching a tent in Algonquin's interior, but just as remote, is a stay in one of the park-run ranger cabins (C$54–C$125 per person, C$11 each additional adult), which have woodstove or propane heat and, in some cases, mattresses and electricity. Four of the 13 cabins are accessible by car; the rest are reached by canoe, which can take from one hour to two days.

SPORTS AND THE OUTDOORS

OUTFITTERS **Algonquin Outfitters** (☎ *705/635–2243 or 800/469–4948* ⊕ *www.algonquinoutfitters.com*) has four store locations in and around the park—Oxtongue Lake, Huntsville, Opeongo Lake, and Brent Base on Cedar Lake—specializing in canoe rentals, outfitting and camping services, sea kayaking, and a water-taxi service to the park's central areas. Call to confirm equipment rentals and tour availability.

If you plan to camp in the park, you may want to contact the **Portage Store** (✉ *Hwy. 60, Canoe Lake, Algonquin Park* ☎ *705/663–5622 in summer, 705/789–3645 in winter* ⊕ *www.portagestore.com*), which provides extensive outfitting services. They have packages that might include permits, canoes, and food supplies, as well as maps and detailed information about routes and wildlife.

GUIDED TOURS **Call of the Wild** (☎ *905/471–9453 or 800/776–9453* ⊕ *www.callofthewild.ca*) offers guided trips of different lengths—dogsledding and snowmobiling in winter, canoeing and hiking in summer—in the park. Transportation from Toronto can be arranged with every package.

Voyageur Quest (☎ *416/486–3605 or 800/794–9660* ⊕ *www.voyageurquest.com*) provides Canadian wilderness trips year-round in Algonquin Park and throughout northern Ontario.

Winterdance Dogsled Tours (☎ *705/457–5281* ⊕ *www.winterdance.com*) takes you on afternoon, multiday, and moonlight dogsledding adventures in Haliburton and Algonquin Provincial Park. Canoe tours are available in summer.

8

Travel Smart Toronto

WORD OF MOUTH

"If the weather is poor, there is also an extensive underground pedestrian system called PATH. Lined with shops, it runs through the downtown core up to about the Eaton Centre. It's heavily used by commuters, as you'll discover if you're travelling against the flow at rush hour."

—QueScaisJe

GETTING HERE & AROUND

Most of the action in Toronto happens between just north of Bloor and south to the waterfront, and from High Park in the west to the Beaches in the east. It's easy to get around this area via subway, streetcar, and bus. Service is frequent.

Yonge Street (pronounced "young") is the official dividing line between east and west streets. It's a north–south street that stretches from the waterfront up through the city. Street numbers increase heading away from Yonge in either direction. North–south street numbers increase heading north from the lake.

▮ AIR TRAVEL

Flying time to Toronto is 1½ hours from New York and Chicago and 5 hours from Los Angeles. Nonstop to Toronto from London is about 7 hours.

Most airlines serving Toronto have numerous daily trips. Allow extra time for passing through customs and immigration, which are required for all passengers, including Canadians. The 2½-hour advance boarding time recommended for international flights is applied to Canada. The Toronto airport has check-in kiosks for Air Canada flights, which cut back on time spent in line.

Note that weather conditions can affect whether or not your plane to and from Toronto will leave on time. Brace yourself for the possibilities of delays in winter.

All travelers must have a passport to enter or reenter the United States. U.S. Customs and Immigration maintains offices at Pearson International Airport in Toronto; U.S.-bound passengers should arrive early enough to clear customs before their flight.

Security measures at Canadian airports are similar to those in the United States. Be sure you're not carrying anything that could be construed as a weapon: a letter opener, Swiss Army knife, or a toy

---

NAVIGATING TORONTO

■ The CN Tower can be seen from most anywhere in the city except on very cloudy days. Remember its location (Front and John streets) to get your bearings.

■ Lake Ontario is the ultimate landmark. It's always south, no matter where you are.

■ The subway is the fastest way to get around the city. Stay at a hotel near a subway line to make navigating the city easier.

■ The streetcar and bus signs can be easy to miss. Look for the red, white, and blue signs with a black streetcar picture on electrical poles near street corners every five blocks or so along the route.

■ Carry a map with you, and don't hesitate to ask for directions.

---

weapon, for example. Arriving passengers from overseas flights might find a beagle in a green coat sniffing their luggage; he's looking for forbidden agricultural products, including illegal drugs.

None of the major airlines or charter lines permits smoking.

Airlines and Airports Airline and Airport Links.com (⊕ www.airlineandairportlinks.com) has links to many of the world's airlines and airports.

Airline Security Issues Transportation Security Administration (⊕ www.tsa.gov) has answers for almost every question that might come up.

Air Travel Resources in Toronto Canadian Transportation Agency (☎ 888/222–2592 ⊕ www.cta-otc.gc.ca).

AIRPORTS

Flights into Toronto land at Terminals 1 and 3 of Lester B. Pearson International Airport (YYZ), 32 km (20 mi) northwest of downtown. There are two main terminals, so check in advance which one your flight leaves from to save hassles. The automated LINK cable-line shuttle system moves passengers almost noiselessly between Terminals 1 and 3 and the GTAA Reduced Rate Parking Lot.

Internet access is available for C$10 per day in Terminal 1, or for free in Air Canada's Maple Leaf Lounge (for executive-class passengers). There are several chain hotels at the airport.

The airport departure tax from Pearson International is C$20 per person (C$8 for connecting passengers) included in the price of your airline ticket.

Porter Airlines—which flies to Halifax, Montréal, Newark, Quebec City, and Ottawa—is the only airline operating from Toronto City Centre Airport (YTZ), often called the Island Airport, in the Toronto Islands. The airport departure tax from City Centre is C$15 per person and is also included in the ticket price. There are few amenities at this smaller airport, but it is very convenient to downtown.

Airport Information Lester B. Pearson International Airport (☎ 416/776–3000 ⊕ www.gtaa.com). **Toronto City Centre Airport** (☎ 416/203–6942 ⊕ www.torontoport. com/airport.asp).

GROUND TRANSPORTATION

Although Pearson International Airport is not far from downtown, the drive can take well over an hour during weekday rush hours (6:30–9:30 AM and 3:30–6:30 PM). Taxis to a hotel or attraction near the lake cost C$45 or more and have fixed rates to different parts of the city. (Check fixed-rate maps at ⊕ www.gtaa.com.) You must pay the full fare from the airport, but it's often possible to negotiate a lower fare going to the airport from downtown with regular city cabs. It's illegal for city cabs to pick up passengers at the airport, unless they are called—a time-consuming process, but sometimes worth the wait for the lower fare. Likewise, airport taxis cannot pick up passengers going to the airport, only regular taxis can be hailed or called to go to the airport.

Pacific Western Transportation offers 24-hour Airport Express coach service daily to several major downtown hotels and the Toronto Coach Terminal (Bay and Dundas streets). It costs C$19.50 one-way, C$32.95 round trip. Pickups are from the Arrivals levels of the terminals at Pearson. Look for the curbside bus shelter, where tickets are sold.

GO Transit interregional buses transport passengers to the Yorkdale and York Mills subway stations from the arrivals levels. Service can be irregular (once per hour) and luggage space limited, but at C$4.45 it is the least expensive way to get to the city's northern suburbs.

Two Toronto Transit Commission (TTC) buses run from any of the airport terminals to the subway system. Bus 192 (Airport Rocket bus) connects to the Kipling subway station; Bus 58 Malton links to the Lawrence West station. Luggage space is limited and no assistance is given, but the price is only C$2.75 in exact change (⇨ See *Bus Travel*).

If you rent a car at the airport, ask for a street map of the city. Highway 427 runs south some 6 km (4 mi) to the lakeshore. Here you pick up the Queen Elizabeth Way (QEW) east to the Gardiner Expressway, which runs east into the heart of downtown. If you take the QEW west, you'll find yourself swinging around Lake Ontario, toward Hamilton, Niagara-on-the-Lake, and Niagara Falls.

From City Centre a free ferry operates to the terminal at the base of Bathurst Street; the trip takes less than 10 minutes. Porter Airlines also runs a free shuttle from Union Station to the ferry terminal.

Contacts Go Transit (☎ 416/869–3200 or 888/438–6646 ⊕ www.gotransit.com). **Pacific Western Transportation** (☎ 905/564–6333 or 800/387–6787 ⊕ www.torontoairportexpress. com). **Toronto Transit Commission or TTC** (☎ 416/393–4636 ⊕ www.ttc.ca).

TRAVEL TO DOWNTOWN TORONTO FROM PEARSON AIRPORT		
Mode of Transport	Duration	Price
Taxi	45–90 min	C$45
Airport Express bus	45–90 min	C$19.50
GO train	40 min	C$4.45
Car	45–90 min	NA
TTC	40 min	C$2.75

FLIGHTS

Toronto is served by American, Continental, Delta, Northwest, United, US Airways, and Air Canada, as well as more than a dozen European and Asian carriers with easy connections to many U.S. cities. Toronto is also served within Canada by Air Canada Jazz, WestJet, Porter, and Air Transat, a charter airline.

Airline Contacts **Air Canada** (☎ 888/247-2262 or 514/393-3333 ⊕ www.aircanada. com). **Air Canada Jazz** (☎ 888/247-2262 or 514/393-3333 ⊕ www.flyjazz.ca). **Air Transat** (☎ 877/872-6728 ⊕ www.airtransat. ca). **American Airlines** (☎ 800/433-7300 ⊕ www.aa.com). **Continental Airlines** (☎ 800/523-3273 for U.S. and Mexico reservations, 800/231-0856 for international reservations ⊕ www.continental.com). **Delta Airlines** (☎ 800/221-1212 for U.S. reservations, 800/241-4141 for international reservations ⊕ www.delta.com). **Northwest Airlines** (☎ 800/225-2525 ⊕ www.nwa.com). **Porter Airlines** (☎ 888/619-8622 or 416/619-8622 ⊕ www.flyporter.com). **United Airlines** (☎ 800/864-8331 for U.S. reservations, 800/538-2929 for international reservations ⊕ www.united.com). **US Airways** (☎ 800/428-4322 for U.S. and Canada reservations, 800/622-1015 for international reservations ⊕ www.usairways.com). **WestJet** (☎ 888/937-8538 ⊕ www.westjet.com).

■ BOAT TRAVEL

Frequent ferries connect downtown Toronto with the Toronto Islands. In summer, ferries leave every 15 to 30 minutes for Ward's Island, every hour for Centre Island, and every 30 to 45 minutes for Harlan's Point. Ferries begin operation between 6:30 and 9 AM and end between 10 and 11:45 PM. Fares are C$6.50 round-trip.

Boat Information **Toronto Islands Ferry** (☎ 416/392-8193 ⊕ www.toronto.ca/parks/island).

■ BUS TRAVEL

ARRIVING AND DEPARTING

Most buses arrive at the Toronto Coach Terminal, which serves a number of lines, including Greyhound (which has regular service to Toronto from all over the United States), Coach Canada, Ontario Northland, and Can-AR. The trip takes six hours from Detroit, three hours from Buffalo, and 11 hours from Chicago and New York City. During busy times, such as around holidays, border crossings can add an hour or more to your trip since every passenger must disembark and be questioned.

Information on fares and departure times is available online or by phone. Tickets are purchased at the Toronto Coach Terminal before boarding the buses.

Some Canadian bus lines do not accept reservations, but Coach Canada and Greyhound Canada allow online ticket purchases, which can then be printed out on your computer or picked up at the station. On most lines, there are discounts for senior citizens (over 60), children (under 12) and students (with ISIC cards). Purchase your tickets as far ahead as possible, especially for holiday travel. Seating is first-come, first-served; arriving 45 minutes before your bus's scheduled departure time usually gets you near the front of the line.

A low-cost bus company, Megabus, runs from Buffalo, New York, to Toronto through Niagara Falls. The further in advance tickets are purchased, the less expensive they are.

WITHIN TORONTO

Toronto Transit Commission (TTC) buses and streetcars link with every subway station to cover all points of the city. ⇨ *See Public Transportation Travel below.*

Bus Information Can-AR (📞 905/564–1242 ⊕ www.can-arcoach.com). **Coach Canada** (📞 800/461–7661 ⊕ www.coachcanada. com). **Greyhound Lines of Canada Ltd.** (📞 416/594–1010 or 800/661–8747 ⊕ www. greyhound.ca). **Megabus** (⊕ www.megabus. com). **Ontario Northland** (📞 705/472–4500 or 800/363–7512 ⊕ www.ontc.on.ca). **Toronto Coach Terminal** (✉ 610 Bay St., just north of Dundas St. W, Dundas Square Area 📞 800/461–8558).

▌ CAR TRAVEL

Given the relatively high price of gas, Toronto's notoriously terrible traffic, and the ease of Toronto's public transportation system, car travel is recommended only for those who wish to drive to sites and attractions outside the city, such as the Niagara Wine Region, Niagara Falls, and live theater at Stratford or Niagara-on-the-Lake. The city of Toronto has an excellent transit system that is inexpensive, clean, and safe, and cabs are plentiful.

In Canada your own driver's license is acceptable for a stay of up to three months. In Ontario, drivers must be 21 to drive a rental car. There may be a surcharge of C$10–C$30 per day if you are between 21 and 25. Agreements may require that the car not be taken out of Canada, including the U.S. side of Niagara Falls; check when booking.

CAR RENTAL

Rates in Toronto begin at C$30 a day and C$150 a week for an economy car with unlimited mileage. This does not include tax, which is 13%. If you prefer a manual-transmission car, check whether the rental agency of your choice offers it; some companies don't in Canada. All of the major chains listed below have branches both downtown and at Pearson International Airport.

Contacts Alamo (📞 800/522–9696 ⊕ www. alamo.com). **Avis** (📞 800/331–1084 ⊕ www. avis.com). **Budget** (📞 800/472–3325 ⊕ www. budget.com). **Discount Car and Truck Rental** (📞 416/249–5800 in Toronto, 888/820–7378 in Ontario, 800/263–2355 outside Ontario or in U.S. ⊕ www.discountcar.com). **Enterprise** (📞 416/798–1465 or 800/261–7331 ⊕ www. enterprise.com). **Hertz** (📞 800/654–3001 ⊕ www.hertz.com). **National Car Rental** (📞 800/227–7368 ⊕ www.nationalcar.com).

GASOLINE

Distances are always shown in kilometers, and gasoline is always sold in liters. (A gallon has 3.8 liters.)

Gas prices in Canada are higher than in the United States and have been on the rise. At this writing, the per-liter price is between C$0.89 and C$1.28 (US$3.38–$4.80 per gallon). Gas stations are plentiful; many are self-service and part of small convenience stores. Large stations are open 24 hours; smaller ones close after the dinner rush. For up-to-date prices and where to find the cheapest gas in the city (updated daily), go to ⊕ *www.toronto-gasprices.com.*

PARKING

Toronto has green parking-meter boxes everywhere. Parking tickets net the city C$50 million annually, so they are frequently given out. Boxes are computerized; one hour costs C$2, payable with coins—the dollar coin, the two dollar coin, and nickels, dimes, and quarters are accepted—or a credit card (AE, MC, or V). Parking lots are found under office buildings, or on side streets near main thoroughfares. Regular rates are between C$1.50 and C$2.50 per half-hour.

ROAD CONDITIONS

Rush hours in Toronto (6:30 to 9:30 AM and 3:30 to 6:30 PM) are bumper to bumper, especially on the 401 and Gardiner Expressway. Avoid rush hours like the plague, particularly when coming into or leaving the city.

ROADSIDE EMERGENCIES

The American Automobile Association (AAA) has 24-hour road service in Canada, provided via a partnership with the Canadian Automobile Association (CAA).

Emergency Services **Canadian Automobile Association** (☎ 416/221–4300 or 800/268–3750 ⊕ www.caa.ca).

RULES OF THE ROAD

By law, you are required to wear seat belts and to use infant seats in Ontario. Fines can be steep. Right turns are permitted on red signals unless otherwise posted. You must come to a complete stop before making a right turn on red. Pedestrian crosswalks are sprinkled throughout the city, marked clearly by overhead signs and very large painted yellow Xs. Pedestrians have the right of way in these crosswalks. However, Toronto residents rarely heed crosswalk signals, so use caution in driving along downtown streets. The speed limit in most areas of the city is 50 kph (30 mph) and usually within the 90–110 kph (50–68 mph) range outside the city.

Watch out for streetcars stopped at intersections. Look to your right for a streetcar stop sign (red, white, and blue signs on electrical poles). ⚠ **It's illegal to pass or pull up alongside a streetcar stopped here— even if its doors aren't open—since it might be about to pick up or drop off passengers.** Stop behind the streetcar and wait for it to proceed.

Ontario is a no-fault province, and minimum liability insurance is C$200,000. If you're driving across the Ontario border, bring the policy or the vehicle-registration forms and a free Canadian Non-Resident Insurance Card from your insurance agent. If you're driving a borrowed car, also bring a letter of permission signed by the owner.

Driving motorized vehicles while impaired by alcohol is taken seriously in Ontario and results in heavy fines, imprisonment, or both. It's illegal to refuse to take a Breathalyzer test. The possession of radar-detection devices in a car, even if they are not in operation, is illegal in Ontario. Studded tires and window coatings that do not allow a clear view of the vehicle interior are forbidden.

FROM THE U.S.

Expect a wait at major border crossings. The wait at peak visiting times can be 60 minutes. If you can, avoid crossing on weekends and holidays at Detroit–Windsor, Buffalo–Fort Erie, and Niagara Falls, New York–Niagara Falls, Ontario, when the wait can be even longer.

Highway 401, which can stretch to 16 lanes in metropolitan Toronto, is the major link between Windsor, Ontario (and Detroit), and Montréal, Québec. There are no tolls anywhere along it, but you should be warned: between 6:30 and 9:30 each weekday morning and from 3:30 to 6:30 each afternoon, the 401 can become very crowded, even stop-and-go; plan your trip to avoid rush hours. A toll highway, the 407, offers quicker travel; there are no tollbooths, but cameras photograph license plates and the system bills you, if it has your address. They have access to plates registered in Georgia, Maryland, Maine, Michigan, New York, Ohio, Ontario, Quebec, and Wisconsin. If you are not identified then you don't have to pay. The 407 runs roughly parallel to the 401 for a 65-km (40-mi) stretch immediately north of Toronto.

If you're driving from Niagara Falls (U.S. or Canada) or Buffalo, New York, take the Queen Elizabeth Way, which curves along the western shore of Lake Ontario and eventually turns into the Gardiner Expressway, which flows right into downtown.

Insurance Information **Insurance Bureau of Canada** (☎ 416/362–2031 ⊕ www.ibc.ca).

■ PUBLIC TRANSPORTATION

The Toronto Transit Commission (TTC), which operates the buses, streetcars, and subways, is safe, clean, and reliable. There are three subway lines, with 65 stations along the way: the Bloor–Danforth line, which crosses Toronto about 5 km (3 mi) north of the lakefront, from east to west, and Yonge–University line, which loops north and south like a giant "U," with the bottom of the "U" at Union Station, and the Sheppard line, which covers the northeastern section of the city. A light rapid transit (LRT) line extends service to Harbourfront along Queen's Quay.

From Union Station you can walk underground (or via the Skywalk) to the Metro Toronto Convention Centre and to many hotels, including the InterContinental Toronto Centre, the Fairmont Royal York, Toronto Hilton, and Sheraton Centre—a real boon in inclement weather.

Buses and streetcars link with every subway station to cover all points of the city. Service is generally excellent, with buses and streetcars covering major city thoroughfares about every 10 minutes; suburban service is less frequent. All buses, subways, and streetcars accept exact change, tickets, tokens, or monthly Metropass swipecards. (Note that with tickets or exact change on the subway, you must use the turnstile closest to the station agent window and drop the ticket into the clear receptacle, whereas a token or swipecard can be used at any turnstile.) Paper transfers are free; pick one up from the driver when you pay your fare on the bus or streetcar or get one from the transfer machines just past the turnstiles in the subway, then give the driver or station agent the transfer on the next leg of your journey. If you have a monthly pass, just show the card to the driver or station agent.

The single fare for subways, buses, and streetcars is C$2.75. An all-day unlimited-use pass (valid for 24 hours beginning at the start of service on the day purchased) is C$9; five tickets or tokens are available for C$11.25; 10 tickets or tokens are C$22.50. ■ TIP→ **On weekends and holidays, up to two adults and four children can use the C$9 day pass—an excellent savings.** Tokens and tickets are sold in each subway station and many convenience stores. All vehicles accept tickets, tokens, or exact change, but you must buy tickets and tokens before you board. Note that transfers are time-sensitive from your start point, and TTC staff know how long it takes to get to your transfer point to prevent misuse.

If you plan to stay in Toronto for a month or longer, consider the Metropass, a prepaid card (C$109) that allows unlimited rides during one calendar month.

The free *Ride Guide,* published annually by the TTC, is available in most subways. It shows nearly every major place of interest in the city and how to reach it by public transit. The TTC's telephone information line provides directions in 20 languages.

Subway trains run from approximately 6 AM to 1:30 AM Monday through Saturday and from 9 AM to 1:30 AM Sunday; holiday schedules vary. Subway service is frequent, with trains arriving every two to five minutes. Most buses and streetcars operate on the same schedules. On weekdays, subway trains get very crowded (especially on the Yonge–University line northbound and the Bloor–Danforth line eastbound) from 8 to 10 AM and 5 to 7 PM.

Late-night buses along Bloor and Yonge streets, and as far north on Yonge as Steeles Avenue, run from 1 AM to 5:30 AM. Streetcars that run 24 hours include those on King Street, Queen Street, and College Street. Late-night service is slower, with buses or streetcars arriving every 30 minutes or so. All-night transit-stop signs are marked with reflective blue bands.

Streetcar lines, especially the King line, are interesting rides with frequent service.

Riding the city's streetcars is a great way to capture the flavor of the city, since you pass through many neighborhoods.

Streetcar stops have a red pole with a picture of a streetcar on it. Bus stops usually have shelters and gray poles with bus numbers and route maps posted. Both buses and streetcars have their final destination and their number on both the front and back and side windows. The drivers are friendly and will be able to help tourists with their questions.

Smoking is prohibited on all subway trains, buses, and streetcars, and is a rule that is strictly enforced.

TTC TICKET/PASS	PRICE
Single Fare	$2.75
Day Pass	$9
5-Ticket or -Token Pack	$11.25
10-Ticket or -Token Pack	$22.50
Monthly Unlimited Pass	$109

Subway and Streetcar Information Toronto Transit Commission or TTC (☎ 416/393-4636, 416/393-4100 for lost and found ⊕ www.ttc.ca).

▮ TAXI TRAVEL

Taxis can be hailed on the street, but if you need to make an appointment (e.g., for an early-morning airport run), or if you are in a residential neighborhood, it's necessary to call ahead. Taxi stands are rare, and usually located only at hotels and at the airport.

Taxi fares are C$4 for the first 0.155 km and C$0.25 for each 31 seconds not in motion and for each additional 0.155 kilometers. A C$0.25 surcharge is added for each passenger in excess of four. The average fare to take a cab across downtown is C$8–C$9, plus a roughly 15% tip (⇨ see Tipping), when the traffic is flowing normally. The largest companies are Beck, Co-op, Diamond, Metro, and Royal.

▮TIP➔ By calling ☎ 416/829-4222, you can be connected to one of many taxi companies for free via an automated system.

Taxi Companies Beck (☎ 416/751-5555). **Co-op** (☎ 416/504-2667). **Diamond** (☎ 416/366-6868). **Metro** (☎ 416/504-8294). **Royal** (☎ 416/785-3322).

▮ TRAIN TRAVEL

Amtrak has service from New York and Chicago to Toronto (both 12 hours), providing connections between Amtrak's U.S.-wide network and VIA Rail's Canadian routes. VIA Rail runs trains to most major Canadian cities; travel along the Windsor–Québec City corridor is particularly well served. Amtrak and Via Rail operate from Union Station on Front Street between Bay and York streets. You can walk underground to a number of hotels from the station. There is a cab stand outside the main entrance of the station.

Trains to Toronto may have two tiers of service, business class and reserved coach class. Business class is usually limited to one car, and benefits include more legroom, meals, and complimentary alcoholic beverages.

To save money, look into rail passes. But be aware that if you don't plan to cover many miles, you may come out ahead by buying individual tickets.

If you're planning to travel a lot by train, look into VIA Rail's Canrail pass. It allows 12 days of coach-class travel within a 30-day period; sleeping cars are available, but they sell out very early and must be reserved at least a month in advance during high season (June through mid-October), when the pass is C$923 (discounts for youths and senior citizens aged 60 and over). Low-season rate (mid-October through May) is C$576.

Children under two travel for free in a parent's seat; and children up to 11 can get their own seat for roughly half the price of an adult ticket.

Major credit cards, debit cards, and cash are accepted. Traveler's checks are accepted in Canadian and U.S. currencies; for others, go to the Currency Exchange kiosk on the main level of the station.

Reservations are strongly urged for intercity and interprovincial travel and for journeys to and from the United States. If your ticket is lost, it is like losing cash, so guard it closely. If you lose your reservation number, your seat can still be accessed by using your name or the train you have been booked on.

GO Transit is the Greater Toronto Area's commuter rail. (It also runs buses.) The double-decker trains are comfortable and have restrooms.

Train Contacts Amtrak (☎ *800/872-7245* ⊕ *www.amtrak.com*). **GO Transit** (☎ *416/869-3200 or 888/438-6646* ⊕ *www.gotransit.com*). **Union Station** (✉ *65-75 Front St., between Bay and York Sts.* ☎ *416/366-8411*). **VIA Rail Canada** (☎ *888/842-7245* ⊕ *www.viarail.ca*).

ESSENTIALS

▮ BUSINESS SERVICES AND FACILITIES

FedEx Office—where you can fax, copy, print, and rent computers—has several locations in Toronto.

Contacts FedEx Kinko's (✉ *357 Bay St., at Temperance St., Financial District* ☎ *416/363–2705* ✉ *505 University Ave., at Dundas St. W, Chinatown* ☎ *416/979–8447* ✉ *459 Bloor St. W, at Major St., The Annex* ☎ *416/928–0110* ⊕ *www.kinkos.ca).*

▮ COMMUNICATIONS

INTERNET

Most hotels in Toronto have some Internet access, and more and more are offering Wi-Fi. There are many designated Internet cafés around town, or cafés that provide Wi-Fi for customers.

Note that cybercafés frequently change hands and names but often stay in the same location. Rates are usually C$2–C$3 per hour. Two areas are hubs for 24-hour cybercafés: Bloor and Bathurst (heading east) and Church–Wellesley on Yonge. Cybercafes lists more than 4,000 Internet cafés worldwide.

Contacts Cybercafes (⊕ *www.cybercafes. com)*

Internet Cafés iKlick (✉ *614 Yonge St., at Wellesley St., Church-Wellesley* ☎ *416/922–0852* ✉ *1453 Queen St. W, at Lansdowne Ave., Queen West* ☎ *416/538–3317).* **Netropass** (✉ *836 Yonge St., at Cumberland St., Bloor-Yonge* ☎ *416/323–3177* ✉ *767 Yonge St. Bloor-Yonge* ☎ *416/923–3737* ⊕ *www.netropass.com).* **Internet Mart** (✉ *519 Bloor St. W, at Bathurst St., The Annex* ☎ *416/538–1498).*

PHONES

The good news is that you can now make a direct-dial telephone call from virtually any point on earth. The bad news? You can't always do so cheaply. Calling from a hotel is almost always the most expensive option; hotels usually add huge surcharges to all calls, particularly international ones. Calling cards usually keep costs to a minimum, but only if you purchase them locally. And then there are mobile phones, which are sometimes more prevalent—particularly in the developing world—than landlines; as expensive as mobile phone calls can be, they are still usually a much cheaper option than calling from your hotel.

When you are calling Canada, the country code is 1. The country code is 1 for the United States as well, so dialing a Canadian number is like dialing a number long distance in the U.S.—dial 1, followed by the 10-digit number.

CALLING WITHIN CANADA

Local calls in Canada are exactly the same as local calls in the United States. Pay phones are every few blocks and take quarters (C50¢ for the first three minutes). Ask at your hotel whether local calls are free—there may be hefty charges for phone use. Buying a prepaid calling card or renting a cell phone may be worthwhile if you plan to make many local calls.

CALLING OUTSIDE CANADA

Calling to the United States from Canada is billed as an international call, even though you don't have to dial anything but 1 and the 10-digit number. Charges can be $1 per minute or more on cell phones. Prepaid calling cards are the best option.

CALLING CARDS

Prepaid phone cards, which can be purchased at convenience stores, are generally the cheapest way to call the United States. You can find cards for as little as C$5 for eight hours of talk time. With these cards, you call a toll-free number, then enter the code from the back of the card. You can buy the cards online before you leave home.

MOBILE PHONES

Some countries use different frequencies than what's used in the United States. If you have a multiband phone (and your service provider uses the world-standard GSM network (as do T-Mobile, AT&T, and Verizon), you can probably use your phone abroad. Roaming fees can be steep, however: 99¢ a minute is considered reasonable. And overseas you normally pay the toll charges for incoming calls. It's almost always cheaper to send a text message than to make a call, since text messages have a very low set fee (often less than C5¢).

If you just want to make local calls, consider buying a new SIM card (note that your provider may have to unlock your phone for you to use a different SIM card) and a prepaid service plan in the destination. You'll then have a local number and can make local calls at local rates. If your trip is extensive, you could also simply buy a new cell phone in your destination, as the initial cost will be offset over time. Fido, a Canadian cell-phone company, sells prepaid SIM cards with a 30¢-per-minute rate to the U.S. and long-distance in Canada. You have to go to a Fido store to buy and install the card, however.

■TIP➜ If you travel internationally frequently, save one of your old mobile phones or buy a cheap one on the Internet; ask your cell phone company to unlock it for you, and take it with you as a travel phone, buying a new SIM card with pay-as-you-go service in each destination.

You can rent cell phones for as little as US$30 per week with Cellular Abroad, but international rates to the U.S. are 57¢ per minute.

All of the suppliers in Canada support GSM 1900, so if your U.S. mobile phone has a dual-band that includes 1900 Mhz, it should work in Toronto. There are plenty of mobile-phone stores in downtown Toronto for renting phones.

Cellular Abroad rents and sells GMS phones and sells SIM cards that work in many countries. Mobal rents mobiles and sells GSM phones (starting at US$49) that will operate in 140 countries. Per-call rates vary throughout the world. Planet Fone rents cell phones, but the per-minute rates are expensive.

Contacts **Cellular Abroad** (☎ 800/287–5072 ⊕ www.cellularabroad.com). **Fido** (✉ 218 Yonge St., between Queen and Dundas, Dundas Square Area ☎ 416/597–1436 ✉ 100 Kings St. W., Financial District ☎ 416/534–5347 ⊕ fido.ca). **Mobal** (☎ 888/888–9162 ⊕ www. mobalrental.com). **Planet Fone** (☎ 888/988–4777 ⊕ www.planetfone.com).

∎ CUSTOMS AND DUTIES

You're always allowed to bring goods of a certain value back home without having to pay any duty or import tax. But there's a limit on the amount of tobacco and liquor you can bring back duty-free, and some countries have separate limits for perfumes; for exact figures, check with your customs department. The values of so-called "duty-free" goods are included in these amounts. When you shop abroad, save all your receipts, as customs inspectors may ask to see them as well as the items you purchased. If the total value of your goods is more than the duty-free limit, you'll have to pay a tax (most often a flat percentage) on the value of everything beyond that limit.

Clearing customs is fastest if you're driving over the border. Unless you're pulled aside or traffic is backed up, you'll be through in a matter of minutes. When arriving by air, wait times can be lengthy—plan on at least 45 minutes. If you're traveling by bus, customs is a slow process as all passengers must disembark, remove their luggage from the bus, and be questioned. Make sure all prescription drugs are clearly labeled or bring a copy of the prescription with you.

American and British visitors may bring in the following items duty-free: 200 cigarettes, 50 cigars, and 7 ounces of tobacco; 1 bottle (1.5 liters or 53 imperial ounces) of wine, 1.14 liters (40 ounces) of liquor, or 24 355-milliliter (12-ounce) bottles or cans of beer for personal consumption. Any alcohol and tobacco products in excess of these amounts are subject to duty fees, provincial fees, and taxes. You can also bring in gifts of no more than C$60 in value per gift.

A deposit is sometimes required for trailers, which is refunded upon return. Cats and dogs must have a certificate issued by a licensed veterinarian that clearly identifies the animal and certifies that it has been vaccinated against rabies during the preceding 36 months. Certified assistance dogs are allowed into Canada without restriction. Plant material must be declared and inspected. There may be restrictions on some live plants, bulbs, and seeds. With certain restrictions or prohibitions on some fruits and vegetables—including oranges, apples, and bananas—visitors may bring food with them for their own use, provided the quantity is consistent with the duration of the visit.

Canada's firearms laws are significantly stricter than those in the United States. All handguns and semiautomatic and fully automatic weapons are prohibited and cannot be brought into the country. Sporting rifles and shotguns may be imported provided they are to be used for sporting, hunting, or competing while in Canada. All firearms must be declared to Canada Customs at the first point of entry. Failure to declare firearms will result in their seizure, and criminal charges may be made. Regulations require visitors to have a confirmed "Firearms Declaration" to bring any guns for sporting, hunting, or competition into Canada; a fee of C$25 applies, good for 60 days. For more information, contact the Canadian Firearms Centre.

Information in Canada Canada Revenue Agency (☎ 800/267–5177 for international and nonresident inquiries ⊕ www.cra.gc.ca). **Canadian Firearms Centre** (☎ 800/731–4000 ⊕ www.cfc-cafc.gc.ca).

DID YOU KNOW?

Though Canada is a bilingual country—it has two official languages, French and English—Toronto is the Anglophone center of Canada, and 99% of the people living here will speak to you in English. By law, product labels must also be in French, but you won't find French road signs or hear much French here.

U.S. Information U.S. Customs and Border Protection (⊕ www.cbp.gov).

▌ ELECTRICITY

Canada's electrical capabilities and outlet types are no different from those in the United States. Residents of the United Kingdom, Australia, and New Zealand will need adapters to type A (not grounded) or type B (grounded) plugs. Voltage in Canada is 110, which differs from the United Kingdom, Australia, and New Zealand. Newer appliances should be fine, but check with the manufacturer and buy a voltage converter if necessary.

▌ EMERGENCIES

For a complete listing of emergency services, you can always check the Yellow Pages or ask for assistance at your hotel desk. The Dental Emergency Clinic operates from 8 AM to midnight. Many Pharma Plus Drugmarts are open until midnight; some branches of Shoppers Drug Mart are open 24 hours.

All international embassies are in Ottawa; there are some consulates in Toronto, including a U.S. consulate. The consulate is open weekdays 8:30–3, but most services are offered only before noon.

Doctors and Dentists Dental Emergency Clinic (✉ 1650 Yonge St., Greater Toronto ☎ 416/485–7121).

Foreign Consulates Consulate General of the United States (✉ 360 University Ave.,

Queen West ☎ 416/595-1700 ⊕ toronto. usconsulate.gov).

General Emergency Contacts Police and ambulance (☎ 911).

Hospitals and Clinics St. Michael's Hospital (✉ 30 Bond St., near Sherbourne and Queen Sts., Dundas Square Area ☎ 416/360-4000 ⊕ www.stmichaelshospital.com). **Toronto General Hospital** (✉ 200 Elizabeth St., Queen's Park ☎ 416/340-4800, 416/340-3946 for emergencies ⊕ www.uhn.ca).

Hotlines Ambulance, fire, and police (☎ 911).

Pet Care Veterinary Emergency Clinic (✉ 920 Yonge St., just north of Bloor St., Yorkville ☎ 416/920-2002 ⊕ www.vectoronto. com ⊙ Open 24 hrs).

24-Hour and Late-Night Pharmacies Pharma Plus (✉ 777 Bay St., at College St., Dundas Square Area ☎ 416/977-5824 ⊕ www.rexall.ca ⊙ Daily 8 AM–midnight ✉ 63 Wellesley St., at Church St., Church-Wellesley ☎ 416/924-7760 ⊙ Daily 8 AM–midnight). **Shoppers Drug Mart** (✉ 465 Yonge St., at College St., Dundas Square Area ☎ 416/979-2424 ⊙ 24 hrs ✉ 388 King St. W, at Spadina Ave., Entertainment District ☎ 416/597-6550 ⊙ Daily 8 AM–midnight ✉ 390 Queen's Quay W, at Spadina Ave., Harbourfront ☎ 416/260-2766 ⊙ Daily 8 AM–midnight ⊕ www.shoppers-drugmart.ca).

▌HEALTH

Toronto does not have any unique health concerns. It is safe to drink tap water. Pollution in the city is generally rated Good to Moderate on the international Air Quality Index. However, smog advisories are listed by the Ontario Ministry of the Environment at ⊕ *www.airqualityontario. com.*

HEALTH CARE

Consider buying trip insurance with medical-only coverage. Neither Medicare nor some private insurers cover medical expenses anywhere outside of the United States. Medical-only policies typically reimburse you for medical care (excluding that related to preexisting conditions) and hospitalization abroad, and provide for evacuation. You still have to pay the bills and await reimbursement from the insurer, though.

Another option is to sign up with a medical-evacuation assistance company. A membership in one of these companies gets you doctor referrals, emergency evacuation or repatriation, 24-hour hotlines for medical consultation, and other assistance. International SOS Assistance Emergency and AirMed International provide evacuation services and medical referrals. MedjetAssist offers medical evacuation.

Medical Assistance Companies AirMed International (⊕ www.airmed.com). **International SOS Assistance Emergency** (⊕ www. intsos.com). **MedjetAssist** (⊕ www.medjet-assist.com).

Medical-Only Insurers International Medical Group (⊕ www.imglobal.com). **International SOS** (⊕ www.internationalsos.com). **Wallach & Company** (⊕ www.wallach.com).

OVER-THE-COUNTER REMEDIES

OTC medications available in Canada are nearly identical to those available in the United States. In some cases, brand names are different, but you'll recognize common brands like Tylenol, Midol, and Advil. Nonprescription medications can be found at drugstores and in some grocery and convenience stores.

▌HOURS OF OPERATION

Post offices are closed weekends, but post-office service counters in drugstores are usually open on Sunday. There is no mail delivery on weekends. When open, hours are generally 8 to 6 or 9 to 7. The Beer Store and the LCBO (Liquor Control Board of Ontario), which sell beer and wine and liquor, respectively, close on holidays.

Most banks are open Monday through Thursday 10 to 5 and Friday 10 to 6. Some banks are open longer hours and also on Saturday. All banks are closed on national holidays. Most banks have ATMs that are accessible around the clock.

As in most large North American urban areas, many highway and city gas stations in and around Toronto are open 24 hours daily, although there's rarely a mechanic on duty Sunday. Smaller stations close at 7 PM.

The variety of museums in Toronto also reflects opening and closing times: none are consistent, and it is best to phone ahead or check a museum's Web site. Opening hours of sites and attractions are denoted by a clock icon.

The two main pharmacy chains, Shoppers Drug Mart and Pharma Plus, have several locations throughout the city that are open either until midnight or open 24 hours.

Most retail stores are open Monday through Saturday 10 to 6, and many now open on Sunday (generally noon to 5) as well. Downtown stores are usually open until 9 PM seven days a week. Some shops are open Thursday and Friday evenings, too. Shopping malls tend to be open weekdays from 9 or 10 AM to 10 PM, Saturday from 9 AM to 6 PM, and Sunday from noon to 5 PM although many malls extend their hours pre-Christmas. Corner convenience stores are often open 24 hours, seven days a week.

HOLIDAYS

Standard Canadian national holidays are New Year's Day, Good Friday, Easter Monday, Victoria Day (Monday preceding May 25), Canada Day (July 1), Civic Day aka Simcoe Day in Toronto (first Monday in August), Labour Day (first Monday in September), Thanksgiving (second Monday in October), Remembrance Day (November 11), Christmas, and Boxing Day (December 26).

▌ MAIL

Canada's national postal system is called Canada Post. There are few actual post-office buildings in Toronto. Instead, many drugstores have post-office counters that offer full mail services. Check the Canada Post Web site for locations; a red, blue, and white Canada Post sign will also be affixed to the storefront. Post offices are closed weekends, and there is no mail delivery on Saturday. During the week most post offices are open from 8 to 6, or from 9 to 7.

In Canada you can buy stamps at the post office or from vending machines in most hotel lobbies, railway stations, airports, bus terminals, many retail outlets, and some newsstands. Letters can be dropped into red Canada Post boxes on the street or mailed from Canada Post counters in drugstores or at actual post office locations. If you're sending mail to or within Canada, be sure to include the postal code—six digits and letters. Note that the suite number may appear before the street number in an address, followed by a hyphen. The postal abbreviation for Ontario is ON.

Main postal outlets for products and services in the downtown area are the Adelaide Street Post Office; the Atrium on Bay Post Office near the Marriott, the Delta Chelsea Hotel, and the Eaton Centre; and Postal Station "F," one block southeast of the major Bloor-Yonge intersection.

The Canadian postal system is almost identical to the U.S. system. To send regular letters within Canada, just ask for a letter stamp, which is C54¢. Stamps for letters to the United States are C98¢. Ask for a U.S. stamp. Stamps for letters to countries other than the United States are C$1.65. Ask for an international stamp. Envelopes that exceed 30 grams (1 ounce) or are oversized cost incrementally more. Letter stamps are also sold in books of 10 or rolls of 100 for domestic, or books of six or rolls of 50 for international.

When sending mail other than a letter weighing fewer than 30 grams, take your envelope or package to a postal counter in a drugstore or to the post office to have it weighed and priced accordingly.

Mail may be sent to you care of General Delivery, Toronto Adelaide Street Post Office, 36 Adelaide Street East, Toronto, ON M5C 1J0.

Information **Canada Post** (☎ 416/979–8822, 866/607–6301 in Canada ⊕ www.canadapost. ca).

Main Branches **Adelaide Street Post Office** (✉ 31 Adelaide St. E, Financial District ☎ 416/214–2352). **Atrium on Bay Post Office** (✉ 595 Bay St., Dundas Square Area ☎ 416/506–0911). **Postal Station "F"** (✉ 50 Charles St. E, Yorkville ☎ 416/413–4815).

SHIPPING PACKAGES

Customs forms are required with international parcels. Parcels sent regular post typically take up to two weeks. The fastest service is FedEx, which has 24-hour locations at University and Dundas and at Bloor and Spadina. "Overnight" service with Canada Post usually takes two days.

Express Services **FedEx** (✉ 505 University Ave., at Dundas St. W, Chinatown ☎ 416/979–8447 ⊕ www.fedex.ca ✉ 459 Bloor St. W, at Major St., Annex ☎ 416/928–0110 ✉ 357 Bay St., at Temperance St., Entertainment District ☎ 416/363–2705).

▌MONEY

Unless otherwise stated, all prices, including dining and lodging, are given in Canadian dollars. Toronto is the country's most expensive city.

Prices throughout this guide are given for adults. Substantially reduced fees are almost always available for children, students, and senior citizens.

ATMS AND BANKS

Your own bank will probably charge a fee for using ATMs abroad; the foreign bank you use may also charge a fee.

Nevertheless, you'll usually get a better rate of exchange at an ATM than at a currency-exchange office or even when changing money in a bank. And extracting funds as you need them is a safer option than carrying around a large amount of cash.

■**TIP**➔ PIN numbers with more than four digits are not recognized at ATMs in many countries. If yours has five or more, remember to change it before you leave.

ATMs are available in most bank, trust-company, and credit-union branches across the country, as well as in many convenience stores, malls, and gas stations. The major banks in Toronto are Scotiabank, CIBC, HSBC, Royal Bank of Canada, the Bank of Montréal, and TD Canada Trust.

ITEM	AVERAGE COST
Cup of Coffee	C$1.50
Glass of Wine	C$6–C$9
Glass of Beer	C$3–C$6
Sandwich	C$6–C$8
One-Mile Taxi Ride in Capital City	C$2.50 (plus initial C$2.75)
Museum Admission	C$8–C$20

CREDIT CARDS

Throughout this guide, the following abbreviations are used: **AE,** American Express; **D,** Discover; **DC,** Diners Club; **MC,** MasterCard; and **V,** Visa.

It's a good idea to inform your credit-card company before you travel, especially if you're going abroad and don't travel internationally very often. Otherwise, the credit-card company might put a hold on your card owing to unusual activity—not a good thing halfway through your trip. Record all your credit-card numbers—as well as the phone numbers to call if your cards are lost or stolen—in a safe place, so you're prepared should something go wrong. Both MasterCard and

Visa have general numbers you can call (collect if you're abroad) if your card is lost, but you're better off calling the number of your issuing bank, since Master-Card and Visa usually just transfer you to your bank; your bank's number is usually printed on your card.

If you plan to use your credit card for cash advances, you'll need to apply for a PIN at least two weeks before your trip. Although it's usually cheaper and safer to use a credit card abroad for large purchases (so you can cancel payments or be reimbursed if there's a problem), note that some credit-card companies *and* the banks that issue them add substantial percentages to all foreign transactions, whether they're in a foreign currency or not. Check on these fees before leaving home, so there won't be any surprises when you get the bill.

■ TIP➔ **Before you charge something, ask the merchant whether or not he or she plans to do a dynamic currency conversion (DCC). In such a transaction the credit-card** *processor* **(shop, restaurant, or hotel, not Visa or MasterCard) converts the currency and charges you in dollars. In most cases you'll pay the merchant a 3% fee for this service in addition to any credit-card company and issuing-bank foreign-transaction surcharges.**

Dynamic currency conversion programs are becoming increasingly widespread. Merchants who participate in them are supposed to ask whether you want to be charged in dollars or the local currency, but they don't always do so. And even if they do offer you a choice, they may well avoid mentioning the additional surcharges. The good news is that you *do* have a choice. And if this practice really gets your goat, you can avoid it entirely thanks to American Express; with its cards, DCC simply isn't an option.

Reporting Lost Cards American Express (☎ 800/992–3404 in the U.S. or 336/393–1111 collect from abroad ⊕ www.americanexpress.com). **Diners Club** (☎ 800/234–6377

in the U.S. or 303/799–1504 collect from abroad ⊕ www.dinersclub.com). **Discover** (☎ 800/347–2683 in the U.S. or 801/902–3100 collect from abroad ⊕ www.discovercard.com). **MasterCard** (☎ 800/622–7747 in the U.S. or 636/722–7111 collect from abroad ⊕ www.mastercard.com). **Visa** (☎ 800/847–2911 in the U.S. or 410/581–9994 collect from abroad ⊕ www.visa.com).

CURRENCY AND EXCHANGE

U.S. dollars are sometimes accepted—more commonly in the Niagara region close to the border than in Toronto. Some hotels, restaurants, and stores are skittish about accepting Canadian currency over $20 due to counterfeiting, so be sure to get small bills when you exchange money or visit an ATM. Major U.S. credit cards and debit or check cards with a credit-card logo are accepted in most areas. Your credit-card-logo debit card will be charged as a credit card.

The units of currency in Canada are the Canadian dollar (C$) and the cent, in almost the same denominations as U.S. currency ($5, $10, $20, 1¢, 5¢, 10¢, 25¢, etc.). The $1 and $2 bill are no longer used; they have been replaced by $1 and $2 coins (known as a "loonie," because of the loon that appears on the coin, and a "toonie," respectively). At this writing the exchange rate is US$0.851 to C$1.

Google does currency conversion. Just type in the amount you want to convert and an explanation of how you want it converted (e.g., "14 Swiss francs in dollars"), and then voilà. Oanda.com also allows you to print out a handy table with the current day's conversion rates. XE.com is a good currency conversion Web site.

Conversion sites Google (⊕ *www.google. com*). **Oanda.com** (⊕ *www.oanda.com*). **XE.com** (⊕ *www.xe.com*).

■ **TIP→** Even if a currency-exchange booth has a sign promising no commission, rest assured that there's some kind of huge, hidden fee. (Oh . . . that's right. The sign didn't say no *fee*.) And as for rates, you're almost always better off getting foreign currency at an ATM or exchanging money at a bank.

■ PACKING

You may want to pack light because airline luggage restrictions are tight. For winter, you need your warmest clothes, in many layers, and waterproof boots. A scarf that covers your face is a good idea—winds can be brutal. In summer, loose-fitting, casual clothing will see you through both day and evening events. It's a good idea to pack a sweater or shawl for cool evenings or restaurants that run their air conditioners full blast. Men will need a jacket and tie for the better restaurants and many of the nightspots. Jeans are as popular in Toronto as they are elsewhere and are perfectly acceptable for sightseeing and informal dining. Be sure to bring comfortable walking shoes. Consider packing a bathing suit for your hotel pool and a small umbrella.

■ PASSPORTS AND VISAS

Anyone who is not a Canadian citizen or Canadian permanent resident must have a passport to enter Canada. Passport requirements apply to minors as well. Anyone under 18 traveling alone or with only one parent should carry a signed and notarized letter from both parents or from all legal guardians authorizing the trip. It's also a good idea to include a copy of the child's birth certificate, custody documents if applicable, and death certificates of one or both parents, if applicable. (Most airlines do not allow children under age five to travel alone, and on Air Canada, for example, children under age 12 are allowed to travel unaccompanied only on nonstop flights. Consult the airline, bus line, or train service for specific regulations if using public transport.) Citizens of the United States, United Kingdom, Australia, and New Zealand do not need visas to enter Canada for a period of six months or less.

PASSPORTS

U.S. passports are valid for 10 years. You must apply in person if you're getting a passport for the first time; if your previous passport was lost, stolen, or damaged; or if your previous passport has expired and was issued more than 15 years ago or when you were under 16. All children under 18 must appear in person to apply for or renew a passport. Both parents must accompany any child under 16 (or send a notarized statement with their permission) and provide proof of their relationship to the child.

■ **TIP→** Before your trip, make two copies of your passport's data page (one for someone at home and another for you to carry separately). Or scan the page and e-mail it to someone at home and yourself.

If you're renewing a passport, you can do so by mail. Forms are available at passport acceptance facilities and online. The cost to apply for a new passport is $100 for adults, $85 for children under 16; renewals are $75. Allow six weeks for processing, both for first-time passports and renewals. For an expediting fee of $60 you can reduce this time to about two weeks. If your trip is less than two weeks away, you can get a passport even more rapidly by going to a passport office with the necessary documentation. Private expediters can get things done in as little as 48 hours.

U.S. Passport Information U.S. Department of State (☎ 877/487–2778 ⊕ travel.state.gov/ passport).

U.S. Passport and Visa Expediters
A. Briggs Passport & Visa Expediters (☎ 800/806–0581 or 202/464–3000 ⊕ www. abriggs.com). **American Passport Express** (☎ 800/455–5166 or 603/559–9888 ⊕ www. americanpassport.com). **Passport Express** (☎ 800/362–8196 or 401/272–4612 ⊕ www. passportexpress.com). **Travel Document Systems** (☎ 800/874–5100 or 202/638–3800 ⊕ www.traveldocs.com).

■ RESTROOMS

Toronto is often noted for its cleanliness, which extends to its public restrooms. In the downtown shopping areas, large chain bookstores and department stores are good places to stop. If you dart into a coffee shop, you may be expected to make a purchase. Gas stations downtown do not typically have restrooms. Only a few subway stations have public restrooms; their locations are noted on the subway map posted above the doors in each car on the train.

■ SAFETY

Toronto is renowned as a safe city, but you should still be careful with your valuables—keep them in a hotel safe when you're not wearing them. Downtown areas are generally safe at night, even for women alone. Most of the seedier parts of the city are on its fringes. However, areas east of Dufferin on Queen Street, College, or Bloor can feel desolate after dark as can most of Dundas Street, though a few pioneer hipster bars are popping up in these areas.

Panhandling happens in Toronto, especially in Queen West and Kensington Market. Jaywalking is not illegal in Toronto and it happens frequently. Be alert when driving or walking—streetcars, jaywalkers, and the plentiful bicyclists make downtown navigation somewhat hazardous.

■TIP➔ **Distribute your cash, credit cards, IDs, and other valuables between a deep front pocket, an inside jacket or vest pocket, and a hidden money pouch. Don't reach for the money pouch once you're in public.**

Advisories U.S. Department of State (⊕ travel.state.gov).

■ TAXES

A Goods and Services Tax (GST) of 5% applies on virtually every transaction in Canada except for the purchase of basic groceries.

In addition to imposing the GST, Ontario levies a Provincial Sales Tax (PST) of 8% on most items purchased in shops and on restaurant meals. (Be aware that taxes and tip add at least 30% to your food and beverage total when dining out.) Toronto has a 5% hotel tax plus, at most properties, a 3% destination marketing fee, but the PST does not apply to lodging (so total tax on lodging is 13%).

Alcohol purchased at Liquor Control Board of Ontario (LCBO) stores is taxed at 12% by the province, so you'll pay a total of 17% tax. Prices displayed in LCBO stores include tax, so you won't see the extra taxes levied at the register. Other stores that sell wine charge only GST, but since they have to pay the LCBO a 10% tax, it's fair to assume they've marked up their prices accordingly.

■ TIME

Toronto is on Eastern Standard Time (EST), the same as New York. The city is three hours ahead of Pacific Standard Time (PST), which includes Vancouver and Los Angeles, and is one hour behind Atlantic Standard Time, which is found in the Maritime Provinces. The Province of Newfoundland and Labrador is 1½ hours ahead of Toronto.

Timeanddate.com can help you figure out the correct time anywhere.

Time Zones Timeanddate.com (⊕ *www.time-anddate.com/worldclock*).

■ TIPPING

Tips and service charges are not usually added to a bill in Toronto. In general, tip 15% of the total bill. This goes for food servers, barbers and hairdressers, and taxi drivers. Porters and doormen should get about C$2 a bag. For maid service, leave C$2–C$5 per person a day.

■ VISITOR INFORMATION

The Web site of the City of Toronto has helpful material about everything from local politics to public transit. The monthly magazine *Toronto Life* and the weekly alternative papers *Now* and *Eye Weekly* list the latest art and nightlife events and carry information about dining, shopping, and more. Another site, ⊕ *www.toronto.com*, is one-stop shopping for nuts-and-bolts info like traffic or transportation, as well as for cultural events and links to lots of other Toronto Web sites and blogs.

Written by locals, for locals, Blog To includes commentary on Toronto life and upcoming cultural events.

Official Web sites Canadian Tourism Commission (☎ *604/638–8300* ⊕ *www.canadatourism.com*. **City of Toronto** (⊕ *www.toronto.ca*).**Ontario Travel** (☎ *800/668–2746* ⊕ *www.ontariotravel.net*). **Tourism Toronto** (☎ *416/203–2600 or 800/499–2514* ⊕ *www.seetorontonow.com*).

Other Helpful Web sites Toronto Life (⊕ *www.torontolife.com*). **NOW** (⊕ *www.now-toronto.com*)**Eye Weekly** (⊕ *wwweyeweekly.com*). **Blog TO** (⊕ *www.blogto.com*).

INDEX

PHOTO CREDITS

9 (left), Sylvain Grandadam/age fotostock. 9 (right), PCL/Alamy. 12, Icon Sports Media Inc. 13 and 15 (left and right), Bill Brooks/Alamy. 17 (left), PCL/Alamy. 17 (right), Atlantide S.N.C./age fotostock.

ABOUT OUR WRITERS

Freelance writer/editor and former Fodor's staffer Shannon Kelly has contributed to many Fodor's guides, including *San Francisco, Brazil*, and *New York City*. After two cross-continent moves, she has spent the last several years firmly rooted in Toronto, exploring the city and the province of Ontario from top to bottom.

Sarah Richards was delighted to settle in the world's most multicultural city after wandering about Asia and Europe for five years. While updating the Exploring, Shopping, and Places to Stay chapters for this edition, her favorite day started with a morning stroll through Edwards Gardens, followed by an afternoon of devouring the Group of Seven paintings at the McMichael Canadian Art Collection, and ended with drinks and dinner at the Drake Hotel in West Queen West. She has also contributed to past editions of *Fodor's USA, Fodor's Japan,* and *Fodor's Great Britain*.

Amy Rosen is a Toronto-based food and travel writer who has also authored two cookbooks. She pens and illustrates a weekly "Dish" column in the *National Post* newspaper, and is a contributing editor for *enRoute* magazine, for which she ate her way across Canada twice, choosing the best new restaurants in the country. By the time she got to Montreal, she had to buy a new pair of jeans. Amy, a James Beard Award nominee, is currently working on a culinary work of fiction.